REWARD

FOR

SAFE RETURN

CALL

DAVE

403

THANKS

The Selected Papers of Sir Arthur Currie

Diaries, Letters, and Report to the Ministry, 1917-1933

Edited by

Mark Osborne Humphries

LCMSDS Press of Wilfrid Laurier University

0 1 2 3 4 5 6 7 8 9

Printed in Canada

Library and Archives Canada Cataloguing in Publication

Currie, Arthur, Sir, 1875-1933
    The selected papers of Sir Arthur Currie : diaries, letters, and report to the Ministry, 1917-33 / edited by Mark Osborne Humphries.

Includes bibliographical references and index.
ISBN 978-0-9783441-2-2

    1. Currie, Arthur, Sir, 1875-1933--Archives. 2. Canada. Canadian Army. Canadian Corps--History--Sources. 3. Canada. Canadian Army--History--World War, 1914-1918--Sources. 4. Canada--History--1914-1918--Sources. 5. Canada--History--1918-1939--Sources. 6. McGill University--Presidents--Archives. 7. McGill University--History--Sources. I. Humphries, Mark Osborne, 1981- II. Title.

FC556.C87A3 2008   971.061   C2008-902178-9

Printed and bound in Canada
Designer: Matt Symes
Distributed by: Wilfrid Laurier University Press/University of Toronto Press

LCMSDS Press
Wilfrid Laurier University
Waterloo, ON
N2L 3C5
Canada
www.canadianmilitaryhistory.com

Table of Contents

Table of Maps

Note: All maps are reproduced from the *Report of the Overseas Military Forces of Canada, 1918.*

Acknowledgements

This book began as a conversation with Terry Copp. As usual Terry has given freely of his time and resources to see this project through to completion. I am greatly indebted to his friendship and continued support.

I am also greatly indebted to my doctoral advisor, Dr. Jonathan Vance, at the Department of History, University of Western Ontario. Despite his busy schedule Dr. Vance always has time to look over my work and offer insightful comments. One could not ask for a better supervisor.

Countless people have made the Department of History, University of Western Ontario an excellent environment in which to pursue graduate studies in Canadian history. Among those who have impacted me the most in one way or another are Adrian Ciani, Dr. Roger Hall, Dr. Luz Maria Hernández-Sáenz, Richard Holt, Dr. Shelly McKellar, Dr. Francine McKenzie, and Dr. Robert Wardhaugh. There are many others who must remain nameless.

At LCMSDS, Wilfrid Laurier University this book has benefited in one way or another from the assistance of Mike Bechthold, Dr. Geoffrey Hayes, Dr. Marc Kilgour, Dr. John Laband, Dr. Whitney Lackenbauer, Vanessa McMackin, Dr. Roger Sarty, Dr. Andrew Thomson, Jane Whalen and Dr. Jim Wood. Kathryn Rose and Kellen Kurschinski scanned and OCRed numerous letters. Kellen's long hours in front of his laptop are especially appreciated and this book benefited enormously from his time. Sarah Cozzi, my research assistant extraordinaire in Ottawa, copied documents at a moment's notice and was most gracious with her time. John, Tam and Imogen Maker provided a much appreciated home in Ottawa during our research trips. Matt Symes provided the design for the inside of the book, the back cover, and expertly, re-worked my front cover design. His patience while editing the manuscript is greatly appreciated as some days he must surely have wanted to throw in the towel. Judy Humphries, my mother, was an excellent copy editor and her eagle eye for detail was an infinite help in cleaning up the manuscript.

Dr. Tim Cook, Terry Copp, Dr. Andrew Iarocci, John Maker, and Dr. Jonathan Vance all read drafts of the manuscript and provided most valuable feedback. Lianne Leddy, my partner, also read parts of the manuscript, transcribed hand written diaries, and kept me focused on life and the task at hand. In my research I was supported by a Social Sciences and Humanities Research Council Canada Graduate Scholarship, funding from LCMSDS, and research and teaching assistantships from the University of Western Ontario.

Any errors remain my own.

Introduction

This is not a biography of Sir Arthur William Currie nor is it an attempt to chronicle Canada's involvement in the First World War. It is even less a comprehensive military history. Instead, the letters, diaries, and papers collected here provide a window into one of the most tumultuous periods in Canadian history and the life of one of Canada's most important historical figures. Sir Arthur Currie is probably Canada's best-known military commander and certainly the most internationally famous Canadian of the First World War era. In a war that produced more inept than competent generals, Currie stands out as a successful and innovative Commonwealth field commander. His military career has garnered much popular and academic interest.

There are three book length biographies of Sir Arthur Currie. Currie's official biographer, Hugh M. Urquhart, published the lengthiest (although least objective) biography of the Corps Commander in 1950.[1] This *Biography of a Great Canadian* serves the purpose suggested in the title and remains one of the key sources on Currie's life, especially for its long quotes from sources no longer available.[2] A.M.J. Hyatt's *General Sir Arthur Currie: a Military Biography* is the most thorough examination of Sir Arthur Currie the soldier.[3] Hyatt argues that Currie was an extraordinary tactician and that his emphasis on planning, organization, and training made him one of the best corps commanders on the Western Front. He is less interested in Currie the individual. On the other hand, Daniel Dancocks' biography, published around the same time as Hyatt's work,

[1] Hugh M. Urquhart, *Arthur Currie: The Biography of a Great Canadian* (Toronto: J.M. Dent, 1950).
[2] Urquhart's research notes are available at the Archives of the University of McGill.
[3] A.M.J. Hyatt, *General Sir Arthur Currie: A Military Biography* (Toronto: University of Toronto Press, hereafter cited as UTP, 1987). In subsequent references, 'Hyatt' refers to this text unless otherwise noted.

adds much to our knowledge of Currie the man, especially through the author's interviews with Currie's son Garner.[4]

As the commander of the Canadian Corps—Canada's fighting force in the Great War—Currie of course looms large in the standard works on the First World War.[5] Generally, he is portrayed as a brilliant soldier, misunderstood by the rank and file, but respected by his fellow officers. As Desmond Morton and Craig Brown wrote, he epitomised the militia myth, the idea that civilians made better soldiers than stodgy professionals. Portly, putty faced, and awkward, 'even [Currie's] military uniform could not conceal his amateurism.'[6] The reputation of this most famous amateur soldier has benefited immensely from Lloyd George's supposed comment that had the war continued into 1919, the British Prime Minister would have considered replacing Haig with Currie.[7]

There is no doubt that Currie was among the most successful generals of the war, but Sir Arthur was far more than a talented soldier. The mythical Sir Arthur Currie of television documentaries and popular histories is a one-dimensional character, a war hero but little else.[8] The real Sir Arthur Currie was a man of great depth and of enormous contradictions. He was a real estate speculator and embezzler who abhorred gambling within his Corps.[9] He owed his military appointments and business career to political and personal favours, yet he loathed patronage and politics.[10] He was vain and self-promoting, but he

4   Daniel Dancocks, *Sir Arthur Currie: A Biography* (Toronto: Methuen, 1985). In subsequent references, 'Dancocks' refers to this text unless otherwise noted.
5   Some of the standard works on Canada and the First World War include, Tim Cook, *At the Sharp End: Canadians Fighting the Great War, 1914-1916* and *Shock Troops: Canadians Fighting the Great War, 1914-1918* (Toronto: Viking Canada, 2007 and 2008); Tim Cook, *No Place to Run: the Canadian Corps and Gas Warfare in the First World War* (Vancouver: University of British Columbia Press, 1999); A.F. Duguid, *History of the Canadian Forces, 1914-19*, volume 1 (Ottawa: Department of National Defence, 1938); Desmond Morton, *When Your Number's Up: The Canadian Soldier in the First World War* (Toronto: Random House, 1993); Desmond Morton and J.L. Granatstein, *Marching to Armageddon: Canadians and the Great War, 1914-1919* (Toronto: Lester & Orpen Dennys, Ltd., 1989); G.W.L. Nicholson, *The Canadian Expeditionary Force, 1914-1919* (Ottawa: Queen's Printer, 1964; Bill Rawling, *Surviving Trench Warfare: Technology and the Canadian Corps, 1914-1918.* (Toronto: UTP, 1992) Shane Shreiber, *Shock Army of the British Empire: The Canadian Corps in the Last 100 Days of the Great War* (London: Praeger, 1997); John Swettenham, *To Seize the Victory: The Canadian Corps in World War I* (Toronto: Ryerson Press, 1965); Jonathan Vance, *Death So Noble: Memory, Meaning and the First World War* (Vancouver: University of British Columbia Press, hereafter cited as UBC, 1997).
6   R. Craig Brown and Desmond Morton, 'The Embarrassing Apotheosis of a "Great Canadian": Sir Arthur Currie's Personal Crisis in 1917,' *Canadian Historical Review* LX, I (1979): 41.
7   See David Lloyd George, *War Memoirs, Volume II* (London: Odhams Press, 1938), 2016, 2041-2.
8   See, for example, Pierre Berton, *Vimy* (Toronto: McClelland and Stewart, 1986) or Brian McKenna, *The Killing Ground* (CBC, 1988) or more recently Brian McKenna, *The Great War* (CBC, 2007).
9   See, for example, Currie to General Burstall, 14 March 1918, file 1, vol 1, Fonds of Sir Arthur William Currie (hereafter cited as CP), MG30E100, Library and Archives Canada (hereafter cited as LAC).
10   Currie to J.J. Creelman, 30 November 1917, File 1, vol 1, CP, LAC and Currie to John Nelson, 5 February 1919, File 19801226-281, 58A 1 61. 4, Arthur Currie Papers (hereafter cited as ACP), Canadian War Museum (hereafter cited as CWM).

refused to defend himself against baseless public criticism.[11] What makes Currie so fascinating is that he was not a typical soldier.

Born on 5 December 1875 near Strathroy, a small farming community in the flat farming country of southwestern Ontario, at the beginning of his life, Currie had more in common with the privates and corporals of the Canadian Expeditionary Force (CEF) than the generals at General Headquarters (GHQ). His paternal grandparents emigrated from Ireland to Canada in 1838 and took up residence on a 100 acre farm. By the time his parents William Garner Curry[12] and Jane Patterson[13] were married in 1868, the family farm had grown to 300 acres.[14]

Arthur Currie was the third of seven children. He was an intelligent child, skilled at essay writing, debating, and interpreting literature. Sports, however, were not his forte. Awkward and lanky, Arthur was more a bookworm than an athlete. Later in life he commented that his boyhood days were 'different from those of other Canadian lads.'[15] He was an unhealthy child, plagued by 'sick spells' that often kept him at home. At age twelve he earned entrance into Strathroy Collegiate, the local high school, but was kept at home to take special classes because his mother felt that he was too delicate to make the six-mile trek into town. Two years later she relented.

The young Currie lacked direction and purpose. He could be difficult and unruly in the classroom (although deferential to authority), a fighter in the schoolyard, and was known as a prankster among his peers.[16] He was also impulsive, defiant, and self-confident. In debates he was prone to go on too long, refusing to submit to the teacher's time limits or to the arguments of the other students. He was brought up in a deeply religious and devout Methodist household, yet he shunned organized religion.

Currie apparently intended to become a lawyer—or perhaps a doctor—but the death of his father in 1891 forestalled those plans. The issue was money.

---

11 Currie to Sir Edward Kemp, 27 February 1919, Reel C4333, vol 102, Fonds of Sir Robert Laird Borden (hereafter cited as BP), MG26H, LAC and Currie to Lieutenant Colonel Cy Peck, 25 April 1919, File 19801226-284, 58A 1 61. 7, ACP, CWM.

12 Arthur Curry changed the spelling of his name to the less Irish 'Currie' around 1896, although it was consistently misspelled by Hughes and others during the war. See Urquhart, 12.

13 No information is available about Jane Patterson's background.

14 There are few sources on Currie's early life. The sources for the information contained in the following paragraphs (unless otherwise noted) are, Dancocks, Hyatt, and Urquhart.

15 Urquhart, 7. Dancocks claims that Currie said the opposite about his boyhood days but this would seem to be a misreading of the original quote. See Dancocks, 8.

16 Colonel William Beatie [sic] to Arthur Currie, 27 November 1918, file 19801226-277, 58A 1 60. 6, ACP, CWM; Dancocks, 9-10.

As the story goes, Currie instead trained as a teacher, earning a third class certificate. Although he tried to find a job, he failed to secure a position. Without employment, he returned to Strathroy Collegiate to try for an 'honours pass to university.'[17] It is unclear why Currie would try for entrance to university if he could not afford the tuition. Perhaps like many boys his age, Currie was drifting, unsure of his future career and prospects. In 1894, Arthur quit school a month before his final examinations. Apparently a quarrel with one of his teachers precipitated the move. What exactly the quarrel was about is unknown. Like many young men at the turn of the century, Currie decided to book passage westwards, hoping to make his fortune in the railway boom.[18]

Currie arrived in Victoria, British Columbia in the summer of 1894 to stay with his great aunt, Orlando Warner. He found a teaching job in the small community of Sydney where he stayed until 1896 when he managed to secure a better position in Victoria. Like many promising young men of the professional classes, Currie joined the Canadian militia. He was not from a military family (neither of his brothers served in the Boer War or the Great War) and like many people at the time he may have viewed joining the militia as a career move. Although it was a military organization, it was also a club for elites. Currie began his military career as a bombardier with the regiment known as the BC Brigade, Canadian Garrison Artillery (5th Regiment of Artillery).[19]

Currie was apparently a capable teacher, but the classroom did not seem to agree with the farm boy from southwestern Ontario. In the autumn and winter of 1899-1900, a long illness forced him to take a leave of absence from teaching. Throughout his life, Currie suffered from bouts of stomach problems and periodic diarrhea. Given the ambiguous medical terminology of the period, it is impossible to determine the nature of his illnesses. Their timing and the treatments recommended by his doctors suggest that the symptoms may have been induced by stress. In 1900, his doctors recommended a change of profession and Currie left teaching for good to become an insurance salesman.

Currie had yet to find his way. As Urquhart wrote, 'in 1900 Currie had few friends, [and] was the diffident, inexperienced, overgrown boy.'[20] While he may have had few friends, he began to develop a few close, meaningful, lifelong

17   Urquhart, 7.
18   The best general overview of this period in Canadian history remains, Robert Craig Brown and Ramsay Cook, *Canada, 1896-1921: A Nation Transformed* (Toronto: McClelland and Stewart, 1974).
19   On the Canadian Militia in Canada before the Great War, see Desmond Morton, *Ministers and Generals: Politics and the Canadian Militia, 1868-1914* (Toronto: UTP, 1970).
20   Urquhart, 16.

relationships. The first was with J.S.H. Matson, his boss at the insurance firm of Matson & Coles. Matson saw Currie as a younger version of himself and treated him as his protégé. Under his tutelage, the unsuccessful teacher and farm-boy without means would become a prominent Victoria businessman. The second relationship was with his wife, Lucy Sophia Chadworth-Musters whom he married in the summer of 1901. Soon after being married, Currie had already earned enough money as an insurance salesman to assume the rank of captain in the militia. For the first time in his life, he had found success, professionally and personally.

Over the next few years, Currie rose quickly in the militia and in business. In 1904, Matson turned over the insurance agency to Currie who was already making contacts in the local business community as a Freemason and president of the Young Men's Liberal Association. Despite his success, the world of business was not a perfect fit for his personality. Currie was by all accounts a pleasant individual, but he was an introvert by nature. 'Currie was never really at home in his social activities,' wrote Urquhart, 'nor did he care for the social round as such. He had a faculty of getting on with men and had his own circle of acquaintances, all of whom no doubt looked upon him as a friend. Actually, he had few friends. He was companionable but it was only possible to get so far with him. His own particular set was restricted and was a mixed one in respect of interest and companions.'[21] Despite being reserved, Currie continued to meet with personal and financial success.

In 1908. Arthur Currie entered into a real estate partnership with J.A. Power to form the firm of Currie and Power. The profits from the firm helped to support Currie's growing family. In 1902, their first daughter, Marjorie, was born while Garner Currie, a future soldier himself, appeared in 1911. By all accounts Currie was a loving husband and caring father. His personal correspondence has not survived but there is every indication that Lucy and Currie were happily married and that he was devoted to her and his young family. At the same time, his commitment to his regiment grew.

In 1909, Currie was promoted to lieutenant colonel and became commanding officer of the 5th Regiment. At six foot two inches, jowly, and overweight, to the modern eye he does not look like a commanding officer, but was not the only non-athlete to rise to prominence in the prewar militia. Currie took courses of

21 Urquhart, 17.

instruction at the Esquimalt Defences and like every other officer on the west coast, participated in the annual exercises. In August 1913, Currie had his first test as a military commander. Coal miners in Nanaimo had been on strike for almost a year when severe rioting broke out in the city. Against the orders of politicians and staff officers, Currie and the commanding officer of the 88th Regiment sent troops to quell the disturbance. According to Urquhart, Currie's quick thinking allowed the 5th to secure the city without directly engaging the strikers. The next day his soldiers combed neighbouring towns with orders to search homes and businesses for illegal weapons. Although his men did find a sizable cache of arms in a store basement, he had acted without legal authority. Brown and Morton described the events as 'the longest and one of the most controversial examples of "strike duty" in the history of the militia.'[22] The Victoria papers, however, supported Colonel Currie's actions. In either case Currie left the 5th less than a month later. Although his tenure as commanding officer was not officially over until January, in early September he went on leave pending retirement from the active militia at the age of thirty-eight..

While he was in command of the 5th, Currie's wealth and business holdings began to blossom. The real estate boom in British Columbia drove land prices through the roof. Like many land speculators, Currie racked up enormous paper profits, convincing his friends and colleagues to invest their savings in the market. By 1913, however, the boom went bust and the market turned sour. Currie found himself overextended, in possession of a number of expensive properties which he had bought on credit but could no longer sell. He was not alone in his financial trouble. Nationwide economic woes gripped Canada in 1913-14. As Currie's fortunes dipped, so too did those of the friends whom he had convinced to invest in the market. At least one angry former acquaintance would later describe him saying 'the man is crooked as very many people in Victoria know [... he has had a] career of intrigue, underhanded dealing, and actual crime.'[23] While there is no evidence that Currie was involved in any underhanded business dealings before 1914, the economic crisis led him to commit an act that was out of character.

After announcing his retirement from the 5th, Currie was inundated with requests to take command of a new Victoria Highland militia regiment, the 50th. Although he was reluctant to accept the position which required significant contributions from his personal finances, Currie was convinced to accept by

---

22 Brown and Morton, 48.
23 Unsigned letter to Sir Robert Borden, 1 February 1915, cited in Brown and Morton, 53.

Garnet Hughes, the new regiment's major and the son of Canada's Minister of Militia, Sam Hughes.

Sam and Arthur had first met several years earlier when both had belonged to the Dominion Rifle Association. Soon after Currie took over command of the 5th, they came into conflict. In 1912, Sir Sam gave orders for the 5th's band to parade for a local Conservative Party event, but Currie refused to order the regiment out on the grounds that it was against the Militia Act to use the regiment for partisan, political purposes. The elder Hughes was furious and went to Victoria to personally sack the unknown militia colonel who had dared to defy his orders. When they met, Currie stood his ground against the colonel, refusing to give in, daring the Minister to take action against him. When Currie was done making his case, the ever-unpredictable Sir Sam clasped Currie's hand instead of his neck. 'Well, Currie, I came out here to get your scalp,' the Minister exclaimed, 'but you're alright.'[24] He liked Currie's boldness and his willingness to stand on his principles.

Although his finances were steadily depleting, Arthur accepted command of the 50th Regiment, partly because the start-up cost for uniforms, trophies, and regimental silver were guaranteed by a prominent local businessman. For various reasons that were not at all uncommon at the time, Currie had the regiment's funds deposited in his own personal bank account. At the same time he was inching ever closer to bankruptcy. '[Currie's] high spirits and jovial ways seemed to leave him,' wrote a friend, 'He grew up all of a sudden. His attitude toward things changed. He was restless, he could not keep still, and there seemed to be something weighing upon his mind.'[25] He could not unload his land holdings and had no money to pay his creditors. In the summer of 1914, the temptation of the regiment's money in his bank account grew to be too much. At the end of July, Currie used $10,883.34 granted from the department of Militia and Defence to pay his personal obligations.[26] He was a desperate man in a desperate situation. As Brown and Morton argued in 1979, Currie had misappropriated official funds to avoid personal bankruptcy, a criminal offence under both military and civilian law. As for so many others, war offered an escape from personal problems.

When war broke out, Hughes initially offered Arthur command of Military District Eleven (Victoria), but he declined. In the few months that Currie had

---

24 Urquhart, 26.
25 Quoted in Urquhart, 31.
26 Brown and Morton, 51.

been in command of the 50th, he and Garnet had become friends. The younger Hughes wired his father, asking for a more prominent appointment for Currie. Garnet's efforts were successful and Sir Sam offered him command of one of the infantry brigades being mobilised for the CEF, a position which he accepted. As Currie sailed for France he wrote a letter to Matson asking him to hold off the creditors and the law. 'Ask [those in the regiment] to keep quiet and I'll straighten out things shortly,' he wrote to his mentor.[27] Currie did not attempt to pay the debt for three years.[28]

Currie's appointment owed much to the intervention of Garnet and Sir Sam Hughes. He had not served in the Boer War and he was not the most experienced of militia officers. Sir Sam believed in the idea of the amateur soldier though, and in his mind Currie was as capable as any Permanent Force officer. In fact, Hughes disliked what he saw as the sycophantic anglophilia of the Permanent Force officers and preferred part-time soldiers to the professionals. In September he went so far as to send Canada's only Permanent Force infantry battalion, the Royal Canadian Regiment, to Bermuda for garrison duty. In September 1914, Currie took command of the 2nd Canadian Infantry Brigade. The brigade sailed for England, arriving in Plymouth on 14 October. The next few months were spent in training on Salisbury Plain, where the Canadians spent a legendary winter in rain-soaked bell tents, caked with mud. In February, the Canadians were finally sent to France where they went into the line near Neuve Chapelle. The first major British operation of 1915 took place soon after, with the Canadians providing 'demonstrations' on the left flank. The first real test for Currie came to the east, at the now infamous town of Ypres later that spring.

While the size and detail of the documentary records of the CEF preserved in Ottawa is unmatched anywhere else in the Commonwealth, relatively little personal information on Currie survives from this period. As A.M.J. Hyatt noted, his personal diary for 1915-16 is little more than a record of appointments and meetings.[29] Most of his letters from the period have not survived, and those that are available offer little insight into the life of the brigade commander. Most of what we know about Currie from this period comes from later recollections, the observations of fellow officers, and the official records. Judgements about his performance as a brigadier are mixed as he made some controversial decisions.

27 Currie to Matson, 29 September 1914, 'A.W. Currie file,' vol 361, BP, LAC.
28 See Brown and Morton, 53-9.
29 Hyatt, 45.

When the front lines stabilized in the autumn of 1914, only a small salient of Belgian territory remained in British hands. The Ypres Salient became a symbol of British determination to protect neutral Belgium and the focal point of the British sector of the Western Front for the next four years. The British and Germans first fought over the salient late in November 1914 and by the spring of 1915, the lines had changed very little. With the German army secretly sending a number of divisions to the Eastern Front to fight the Russians, a diversion was needed to hide the troop movements. The Ypres Salient was chosen for the attack and to test a new weapon. On 22 April, the German army released experimental chlorine gas from metal cylinders installed in the walls of the trenches. A similar technique had been tried in Russia earlier in the winter, but with little success. At Ypres, the special operation was a resounding success. French colonial troops on the Canadian left bore the brunt of the assault and many of them broke and ran. [30]

Confusion reigned in the Canadian and British lines. Brigadier General Richard Turner, who had be awarded a Victoria Cross in the Boer War for gallantry on the battlefield and was now in command of 3rd Brigade, sent back alarming (some argue erroneous) reports from his headquarters, confusing matters at divisional and corps headquarters. In comparison, Currie appears to have acted calmly and coolly under pressure. He deployed his battalions to tactically important ground and managed to hold off the German advance. Two days later, the Germans unleashed a second cloud of gas, this time against the Canadians. The German assault came close to breaking the Canadian line, opening up gaps between the 2nd and 3rd Brigade. Currie requested British reinforcements, but received inconclusive responses. After instructing the commander of the 8th Battalion, Lieutenant Colonel Louis Lipsett to withdraw if he deemed it necessary, Currie went back to the lines of General Headquarters to personally find and muster the reinforcements needed to plug the gaps. Although these were the actions of an unconventional commander (he probably should never have left his headquarters), they demonstrated that Currie trusted his subordinate commanders and was willing to take personal action to protect the men under his command. The next day the German attacks were renewed but the Canadians again held

---

30 On the German attack see the German official history (hereafter cited as GOH), Reichsarchiv, Der Weltkreig, 1914 bis 1918, Band 8 (Berlin: E.S. Mittler und Sohn, 1931), 35-48. For a translation of this section of the German Official History see Mark Humphries and John Maker, 'The First Use of Poison Gas at Ypres, 1915: A Translation from the German Official History' Canadian Military History 16, 3 (2007): 57-73 and the forthcoming Mark Humphries and John Maker (editors), Germany's Western Front: Translations from the German Official History of the Great War, Volume II (Waterloo: WLU Press, 2009).

their ground, and the British and French forces were able to counter-attack or reinforce the wavering line that the Canadians had held against all odds. With their strategic reserve deployed to Russia, the Germans had insufficient troops to exploit success. The threat to Ypres was ended.[31]

In the months to come, Currie's 2nd Brigade participated in a number of minor but costly offensives at Festubert in May and Givenchy in June. At the same time, the second contingent of Canadian units began to arrive in England. These became the 2nd Canadian Division and in September a Canadian Corps was formed under the command of Lieutenant General Sir Edwin Alderson who had formerly commanded 1st Canadian division. On 13 September, Currie replaced Alderson at 1st Division while Richard Turner was given command of the new division. Currie's 2nd Brigade had consisted of four battalions of approximately 1,000 soldiers each. Now he was in command of the 1st Canadian Division with 18,000 soldiers under his charge, not to mention artillery, engineers, the medical services, and communications troops. Over the following year, Currie proved himself a competent divisional commander. He also had his first serious run-in with Sir Sam Hughes.[32]

After the battle of Neuve Chapelle back in March 1915, Currie had created a minor stir when he submitted a report critical of the performance of the Ross rifle, the Canadian-made sporting arm championed by the Minister of Militia. Now, following his promotion to 1st Canadian Division, he refused to sanction Garnet Hughes for command of 1st Brigade on the grounds that he was too inexperienced. With Sir Sam attempting to run the CEF as his own personal fiefdom, it was a bold stand to take, especially considering that Garnet had won Currie his own position as a brigade commander. Nevertheless, by personally explaining his decision to Garnet, Currie managed to avoid a direct break with either the younger or senior Hughes. He would unsuccessfully try the same tactic in 1917.[33]

In the meantime, Currie's future was being shaped by events in which he did not directly participate. In April 1916, Turner's 2nd Division found itself in a disastrous, small scale action known as the Battle of the St. Eloi Craters. At St. Eloi, Turner and his subordinate commanders misjudged the Canadian

31 The best and most recent account of the Second Battle of Ypres is found in, Andrew Iarocci, *Shoestring Soldiers: The 1st Canadian Division at War, 1914-1915* (Toronto: UTP, 2008). See also, Cook, *At the Sharp End, Volume I,* 109-160; Daniel Dancocks, *Welcome to Flanders Fields: the First Canadian Battle of the Great War, Ypres 1915* (Toronto: McClelland and Stewart, 1988); Duguid; Nicholson, 49-88.
32 See Iarocci; Cook, *At the Sharp End, Volume I,* 161-291; Duguid; Nicholson, 93-129.
33 See, Duguid, Appendix 111; Iarocci; Roger F. Phillips, *the Ross Rifle Story* (Sydney: J.A. Chadwick, 1984).

positions and as a result suffered immense casualties. It was the second time that he had confused the situation at the front, although on both occasions Turner had faced trying and confused circumstances. Although Alderson recommended that Turner and one of his brigadiers be relieved, the Canadian government had other plans. The British Expeditionary Force's Commander in Chief, Sir Douglas Haig, recognised that it would be unwise to create a breach between Canadian and British officers and instead relieved General Alderson, exiling him to England to train Canadian troops there. His place at the Canadian Corps was taken by the exceptionally able Sir Julian Byng. Turner's reputation never really recovered from the debacle. Only the personal intervention of Canadian officials and the goodwill of the Minister of Militia prevented him from being sacked. Although Currie had made mistakes at Ypres, his transgressions appeared mild in comparison. At Second Ypres he had acted, perhaps impetuously, but at least in the interests of his men and his mission. In some circles, Turner came to be seen as unreliable whereas Currie appeared consistently competent.[34]

At Mount Sorrel in June, Currie showed the same initiative and confidence that he displayed at the Nanaimo strike and at Second Ypres. When a German attack opened up a gap in the Canadian lines, he ordered corps troops forward to plug the hole although he technically had no authority to do so. His quick action probably saved the Canadians from a significant reverse. Currie's self-confidence and willingness to gamble might have led him to financial ruin before the war, but in battle these were essential qualities.[35]

Later in the summer, the Canadians were transferred to the Somme front where British troops had been fighting to a stalemate since 1 July. The Somme attacks had been planned for late summer, but were launched prematurely in response to the German offensive at Verdun, which had come close to breaking the back of the French Army. Intended to relieve the pressure on the French, the premature British attacks of 1 July were an unmitigated disaster with some 60,000 casualties on the first day of the battle alone. Despite the terrible bloodletting, the offensive did draw German strength away from the French front and drove a final nail into the German high command's plan for a war of attrition. The alternative would have been to leave the initiative to the Germans, allowing them to choose the time and place of battle. Unlike Great Britain and France, Germany was

---

34 See, Cook, *At the Sharp End, Volume I*, 323-42 and Tim Cook, 'The Blind Leading the Blind: The Battle of the St. Eloi Craters,' *Canadian Military History* 5, 2 (1996): 24-36; Nicholson, 129-46.
35 See Cook, *At the Sharp End, Volume I*, 343-80; Nicholson, 147-53.

fighting a war on almost every square inch of its frontiers. The Somme may have seemed pointless to the 'Tommies' fighting in the trenches, but it forestalled German plans, relieved pressure on Britain's Allies, and helped to bring about the removal of the German Supreme Commander.

When the Canadian Corps arrived on the Somme in September 1916, they had grown to be three divisions in strength.[36] The Somme was not exactly a resounding success. In fighting at Thiepval Ridge on 26 September, Currie's 1st Division failed to keep pace with the neighbouring British Corps and in October his division failed to take an objective known as Regina Trench. Communications had proved unreliable, and the combination of a lack of shells and a determined enemy proved deadly. In two months' fighting the Canadians lost 24,029 men. The Corps eventually took the ground that they were ordered to occupy, but at a hitherto unimagined cost.[37]

Currie was determined to learn from his failures. He compiled a report which concluded that officers needed to spend more time developing an extensive battle plan, that soldiers needed to train specifically for the ground that they would fight on, and that objectives needed to be more than mere coordinates on a map. This began a process of self-reflection and self-evaluation that became Currie's hallmark.[38]

After the Canadian Corps had grown to four divisions in the winter of 1916–1917, Currie visited the French sector of the Western Front to learn from French experiences at Verdun. In a report to Julian Byng, Currie emphasised the importance of extensive artillery support, the close co-ordination of all arms, and the delegation of authority. Like other Commonwealth commanders, he recognised the importance of the platoon as the tactical unit and argued that junior commanders should be given more authority to act on their own initiative. As a divisional commander, his findings had a limited impact, but success at the Battle of Vimy Ridge would highlight their importance.[39]

The Battle of Vimy Ridge of 9–12 April 1917 was the most successful engagement of Currie's career as a divisional commander. On Easter Monday

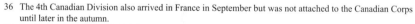

36 The 4th Canadian Division also arrived in France in September but was not attached to the Canadian Corps until later in the autumn.
37 See Cook, *At the Sharp End, Volume 1*, 405-526; Nicholson, 160-200.
38 Hyatt, 58-61; For a recent examination of the British experience, see Robin Prior and Trevor Wilson, *The Somme* (New Haven: Yale University Press, 2005).
39 See 'Old Wine in New Bottles: A Comparison of Canadian and British Preparations for the Battle of Arras,' in *Vimy Ridge: A Canadian Reassessment*, Geoffrey Hayes, Andrew Iarocci and Michael Bechthold, eds. (Waterloo: Wilfrid Laurier University Press, 2007), 65-86.

1917, all four Canadian divisions successfully captured their objectives and held the ridge against subsequent German counter-attacks. The 1st Division had the deepest axis of advance on 9 April and successfully pushed the Germans out of ground that they had held since 1914. Vimy was the Corps' most important battle to date, but it was never as significant to Currie as the later engagements of 1918. For Currie, Vimy was an operational success, an impressive feat, but strategically unimportant. For him, it was the final one hundred days of the war that was the Corps' crowning achievement.[40]

Following minor actions at Arleux and Fresnoy in May 1917, Byng was promoted to command Third Army. For the British, his replacement at the head of the Canadian Corps seemed clearly to be the newly knighted Sir Arthur Currie.[41] Although Sir Sam Hughes had been dismissed as Minister of Militia the previous winter, his shadow still seemed to loom over the Canadians in Europe.[42] For the Government of Sir Robert Borden, the appointment of the Corps Commander was a political decision of immense importance.

Borden believed that it was Canada's destiny to assume a more prominent role in the British Empire. This required political clout and the First World War provided that opportunity. For the Borden Government, the Canadian Corps became Canada's National Army, a symbol of Canadian power and potential. It was hoped that victories on the battlefield would resonate at the Imperial War Cabinet and alter the relationship between Canada and the mother country. It was thus essential that Borden appoint a Corps Commander who could achieve these lofty aims.[43]

Technically, Sir Richard Turner was the more senior Canadian officer and Sir George Perley, the Minister of Canada's Overseas Ministry, had promised him command of the Corps when the time arose. Turner had been hard at work away from the fighting in England, having replaced Alderson the previous autumn. He had preferred to remain in the field and had only accepted the appointment on Perley's promise of a future field command. Turner was also a friend of the elder Hughes and the Hughes camp. Currie's appointment was sure to pose political problems, but Sir Arthur was clearly the superior military commander. The British were also insistent on Currie and would not have accepted Turner,

40 Currie to General A.C. Macdonell, 19 April 1922, File 33, vol 11, CP, LAC.
41 Currie Diary, 6 June 1917, file 191, vol 43, CP, LAC
42 See Desmond Morton, *A Peculiar Kind of Politics: Canada's Overseas Ministry in the First World War* (Toronto: UTP, 1982).
43 See Robert Craig Brown, *Robert Laird Borden: A Biography, Volume II* (Toronto: MacMillan, 1980); Robert Laird Borden, *Robert Laird Borden: His Memoirs* (Toronto: Macmillan, 1938).

whom Haig regarded as 'not the best possible commander of a division.'[44] On 15 June 1917 Currie's appointment was confirmed and he took over command of the Corps.[45]

Currie's tenure as Corps Commander is well documented in the daily diaries and letters reprinted in this collection. As a Corps Commander, his personal flaws served him well on the battlefield. His aloofness and separateness allowed him to make decisions that might have weighed more heavily on other commanders. Just as he had been quick to learn from his peers in business, he was willing to delegate authority and accepted a level of competence in his subordinates that may have proved threatening to others.[46] These traits also cost him many friends along the way.

Soon after being appointed Corps Commander, for example, Garnet Hughes was recommended as his replacement at 1st Canadian Division. Again Currie refused to promote the younger Hughes because he did not believe that he would make a competent field commander. This time the two old friends parted company for good and Sir Sam mounted a personal campaign against the Corps Commander which would culminate in a libel trial a decade later. In August 1918, Major General Louis Lipsett, a close friend, allowed foreign dignitaries to visit his division without first consulting Sir Arthur. Currie sacrificed their friendship over what might have been a minor disagreement between other men.[47] Even Major General David Watson, who personally paid some of Currie's debts in 1917, had a falling out with the Corps Commander in 1919 when he felt that he was not being given due recognition in Currie *Report to the Ministry*. Currie put the interests of the Corps above his own. As Sam Hughes had observed in 1912, Currie stood on his principles.[48]

Currie's letters and diaries from 1917 to 1919 reveal some inconsistencies in the behaviour of the Corps Commander—or at least in our historical memory. As legend has it, Currie tried to prevent the Canadian Corps from going to Haig's battle of Passchendaele in the fall of 1917. He is described as having virtually refused to fight the battle, taking actions that had he been a British commander

44   Gary Sheffield and John Bourne, *Douglas Haig: War Diaries and Letters, 1914-1918* (London: Weidenfield and Nicolson, 2005), 186.

45   Morton, *A Peculiar Kind of Politics*, 119-26.

46   For a vitriolic discussion of the insecurity of generals, see Lloyd George, *War Memoirs, Volume II*.

47   Rumours were circulating that some of the British generals in the Corps—including Lipsett—believed that they had been passed over for promotion in favour of Canadian officers. While Currie initially disbelieved that Lipsett would try to usurp him, the August 1918 incident may have changed his mind. Currie could overreact when he felt threatened.

48   Hyatt, 68-76.

would have resulted in dismissal. While this assertion comes from a post-war letter to a grieving parent, his earlier writings suggest that he was supportive of the campaign and was more concerned about whether he would fight under General Hubert Gough's Fifth Army or Herbert Plumer's Second.[49] Most likely he did not like the idea of sending his soldiers into what was clearly a mess, but he was probably angrier about missing Byng's Battle of Cambrai, the November 1917 tank action for which Currie had been preparing for months.

Currie's most bitter comments about Passchendaele are attributed to a June 1918 conversation with Sir Robert Borden in which he is reported to have said that the Third Battle of Ypres had been a pointless, unmitigated disaster, and an example of incompetent generalship at its worst. The Canadian Prime Minister and David Lloyd George used this information at the Imperial War Cabinet where Borden's version of the story was inserted into the debate over strategy. While Currie may have objected to the idea of Passchendaele, he would later say that he agreed with Haig that it was a battle that needed to be fought. Sir Arthur was always firmly in the Commander-in-Chief's Camp.[50]

In the popular imagination, Currie is often presented as Haig's opposite number: caring, competent, and innovative in comparison to dispassionate, dimwitted, and conventional. Yet Currie appears to have greatly admired Haig and viewed him with respect, affection, and admiration. His reminiscences about the Field Marshal suggest that these views persisted long after the end of the war. Whether historians have set up a false dichotomy or whether this represents merely another of Currie's many contradictions is a question best left up to the reader and future biographers.[51]

The matter of his personal finances is conspicuous in its absence from his letters and diaries, even though the matter came to a head soon after his promotion to the headquarters of the Canadian Corps. In the summer of 1917, Borden was trying to hold the Union Government together and to prepare for a decisive election. The last thing he needed was for the Liberal opposition to get wind of the scandal and expose the embezzling Corps Commander as a thief.[52]

49 The Canadians did not like serving under Gough on the Somme. Haig's Chief of Staff was aware of this fact and supported Currie's request. See Sheffield and Bourne, 333.

50 See Brown, *Borden*, 135-8; Hyatt, 79-81; See also 'Minutes of the 16th Meeting of the Imperial War Cabinet,' 13 June 1918, vols 13-15, Fonds of Sir George Perley, MG27IID12, LAC; see, Brian McKenna, *The Great War* (CBC Television, DVD, 2007).

51 See, for example, the Brian McKenna docudrama cited above.

52 Borden and the cabinet learned of the scandal days after Currie was promoted after Militia Headquarters did some digging into the unpaid bills of the 50th Regiment. Whether Currie would have still received promotion had the revelation come days earlier is a question that can never be answered.

Currie too seems to have independently realized the importance of settling his debts at the same time, perhaps spurred on by threats from Garnet Hughes. In any event, Currie managed to collect the money from Generals David Watson and Victor Odlum and the funds were paid back through official channels at the Department of Militia and Defence. Although he wrote, 'it is impossible for me to tell you now, Forsyth [sic] the efforts I have constantly made to meet the claim but I assure you that for nearly three years the last thing I thought of at night and the first thing in the morning was this'[53] there is no evidence to suggest that this was the case. As Brown and Morton have shown, by the summer of 1917 he had had ample opportunity to repay the money. He had made no effort. The lack of any reference to the matter in his personal papers reminds us that his long, detailed letters should thus be read with the understanding that Currie was not forthcoming about everything.[54]

With all his human flaws, Currie was certainly one of the most successful generals on the Western Front. Under his leadership, the Canadians fought well at Hill 70, Passchendaele, Amiens, the Drocourt-Quéant Line, the Canal du Nord, Cambrai, Valenciennes, and Mons. Throughout the two years he commanded the Corps, Currie was forced to deal with problems and headaches that few other battlefield commanders had to endure. The Canadian Corps was Canada's National Army and politicians from every province and municipality wanted a share of the glory. Currie was forced to attend endless political meetings and entertain a never-ending flow of political guests to his battlefield headquarters while still planning and fighting a war.

Currie was never comfortable with politics, but during the 1917 general election he and his Corps were thrust to the front of the campaign. Currie did his best to navigate the political morass, but he suffered physically because of it. As in 1899–1900, he had bouts of diarrhea and stomach upset with no apparent physical cause. The longest spell lasted almost a month, coming at the height of the 1917 election campaign and before the Passchendaele battle. By the early winter of 1918, he required a rest.[55]

As we see in the second chapter of this work, the 1917 election had a bitter legacy for Currie. Coming from a Conservative, Hughes' personal attacks took on the air of bipartisanship as Liberals jumped on the bandwagon, accusing

53 Currie to Forsythe, 25 June 1917, quoted in Brown and Morton, 58.
54 See, Brown and Morton.
55 Currie would deny that he requested a furlough, but the Department of Militia and Defence seems to have acted as if he had. See Beaverbrook to Currie, 22 January 1918, file 1, vol 1, CP, LAC.

Currie of being responsible for the high casualties at Hill 70 and Passchendaele. Currie never really understood that he was caught in a political shooting match between the Union Government and the Laurier Liberals. He saw the attacks as personal assaults traceable directly to Sam Hughes and his cabal which he believed were further stirring up the Laurier Liberals.[56]

Meanwhile, in the spring of 1918, Currie's leadership was put to the ultimate test. As the German offensives threatened to break the Allied line, the Canadian Corps was temporarily broken up. For a short time Currie found himself without a field command. Despite his dedication to the Entente's cause and the knowledge that the Allied armies were in crisis, Currie protested even the temporary break-up of the Corps. In letters and his personal diary, he angrily railed against British generals and their perceived incompetence. He argued that the Canadian Corps was a National Army that could not and should not be dissolved. With the support of the Canadian Government, the Corps was reassembled in July, just in time to participate in the final victory offensive of the Great War.

Beginning with the Battle of Amiens on 8 August and concluding with the capture of Mons on the morning of 11 November 1918, the Canadian Corps spearheaded the Allied advance during the war's final hundred days. Currie believed that the Canadian Corps was the pre-eminent fighting force on the Western Front and he was not afraid to tell anyone who would listen. Some misinterpreted his unbridled praise of the Canadian Corps as vanity while other contemporaries mistakenly believed that it represented a new sense of Canadian nationalism—not a universally welcome sentiment in Anglo-Canada. While Currie may have felt that the Canadians fought better than the Imperials, he would have been surprised to learn that later generations attributed Canadian sovereignty to his Corps' battlefield deeds. For him the Corps had won victories for the British Empire and remained a vital part of the Greater British Nation.[57]

In the aftermath of victory, Hughes' attacks grew more vitriolic. The rumours about casualties had grown to include the accusation that Currie had needlessly wasted Canadian lives at Cambrai and Mons—that he had wilfully sent men to their deaths to cover himself and his command in glory. As soldiers grumbled, waiting to be sent home in demobilization camps, Currie heard Hughes and his forces at work in the rumours and gripes that every soldier repeats about the

---

56 Currie to Perley, 10 December 1917, File 3, vol 2, CP, LAC. See A.M.J. Hyatt, 'Sir Arthur Currie and Conscription: A Soldier's View,' *Canadian Historical Review* 50, 3 (1969): 285-296.

57 See various letters in chapters 2 and 3.

higher-ups. He began to demand investigations into the source of the rumours and that disciplinary action be taken. It seemed to Currie that Turner and Garnet Hughes were spreading the rumours directly themselves in hospital wards, demobilization camps, and official meetings. There is no evidence to suggest that they were and Turner even tried to assist the Corps commander. Sir Edward Kemp, now the head of the Overseas Ministry, began to worry about Currie. Sir Arthur was panicked, but he was never in danger of losing his grip on reality as he did in fact have a reason to be paranoid. For all he knew, Hughes was on the verge of releasing his most closely guarded secret just at the moment of his greatest personal triumph. Currie had failed several times before at the pinnacle of success so it is understandable that he became consumed by fear.[58]

Instead of direct confrontation, the Corps Commander's weapon of choice was an historical report. In the spring of 1919, he submitted his *Interim Report on the Operations of the Canadian Corps in the Year 1918* to the Minister of the Overseas Military Forces of Canada. This report, reprinted here for the first time since its original release, is a narrative account of the final year of the war. It is laudatory, but is demonstrative of Currie's deep admiration for the men fighting under him. Originally accompanied by hundreds of pages of ancillary documents and reports on the various branches of service, this main narrative of events is Currie's personal response to the criticisms of Sam Hughes and those Canadians who did not support the war effort. As such, it illustrates Currie's naiveté. As his letters indicate, Currie believed that anyone who understood the accomplishments of the Corps would be immediately won over and inoculated against the Hughes allegations. He saw 1918 as the most significant achievement of the Canadian nation and the British war effort. He also seemed to hope that the achievements of the Corps would protect him from revelations about the 1914 theft. With this in mind, Currie's Report to the Ministry is a telling document, a study as much in the psychology of the Corps' commander as it is a historical account of military operations.[59]

Currie never understood why the Borden Government did not support him against Hughes' accusations or why he was allowed to return home in obscurity without an official vote of thanks from the House of Commons. Currie was probably never aware that the Union Cabinet knew the intimate details about his

---

58 See various correspondence between Currie and Kemp, and Kemp and Borden in Reel C4333, vol 102, BP, LAC;

59 The report was originally printed as, Overseas Military Forces of Canada, *Report of the Ministry, Overseas Military Forces of Canada, 1918* (London: Government of Canada, 1919).

misappropriation of funds.[60] Perhaps the Borden Government was wary about further aligning itself with Currie. After all, who knew what other skeletons were in his closet? What is more likely is that it was not politically expedient for the Government to be drawn into a conflict about the conduct of the war effort. The 1917 election had been the most divisive election in Canadian history and it was best to allow sleeping dogs to lie. If the Government challenged Hughes' allegations it would be a matter for debate. Borden was content to allow Currie to bear the brunt of Hughes' wrath and, if one has a generous reading of the prime minister's lack of action, it could be said that he let Currie's report speak for itself.

With his report submitted, Currie faded from the limelight. He briefly served as Inspector General of the Canadian Militia from August 1919 to April 1920 but found the position deeply unsatisfying. Currie had bold plans for the Canadian militia, but found peacetime budgets and political disinterest to be debilitating. Thus, in April 1920 he left the army for good to become Principal of McGill University, a period in his life which deserves far more attention from future biographers than it has previously been given. Currie was a beloved principal and oversaw the expansion and development of the university for thirteen years. Under his stewardship the university expanded its research and teaching programs and became a world-class institution.[61]

In the later years of his life, the war was never far from Currie's mind. As the letters reprinted here suggest, he often thought back to his military days, keeping in touch with former officers and safeguarding the memory of the Corps. Currie believed that the men of the CEF deserved proper historical recognition. That meant the building of memorials, the writing of acceptable histories, and the suppression of 'filthy lies.' As his letters show, Currie took an active interest in shaping the historical memory of the war. This war of reputations came to a head in a 1928 legal battle.

Allegations that Currie was a butcher had dogged the former Corps Commander for ten years. In the summer of 1927, the unsubstantiated rumours were foolishly reprinted as news in the Port Hope *Evening Guide*. In 1919, Hughes had made his accusations in the House of Commons, protected by parliamentary immunity from libel suits. Back then, even if Currie had thought about suing, he knew

60 Because Currie paid back the missing money so quickly after being promoted to the head of the Corps, neither Borden, Kemp, Perley, or Mewburn ever seem to have told them that the Militia Department had discovered the malfeasance about the same time. See, Brown and Morton, 53-63.

61 See Urquhart, 291-349.

that Hughes had an ace in the hole. By 1927, Hughes was dead and Currie sued. The Currie Libel Trial—or Third Battle of Mons as it was dubbed in the press— took place in Coburgh, during the spring of 1928 and quickly became a national circus. As Tim Cook and Jonathan Vance have pointed out, it was the greatest test for the myth of the Canadian Corps. The small town Ontario courthouse witnessed a parade of important officers, almost all of whom supported Currie unequivocally. The former Corps Commander also received dozens of letters in support from former generals overseas and average citizens across Canada, including the father of George Price, the only Canadian actually listed as killed in action on 11 November 1918.[62] In the end, Currie won a tiny cash settlement but he had secured his reputation.[63]

At Cobourg he seems to have finally put the ghost of Sir Sam Hughes to rest. The trial took a heavy toll on Currie and he suffered a relapse of the stomach irritations which had plagued him all his life. But it seemed to be a cathartic experience. Afterwards, he became more reserved, more introspective. He began to question the meaning of the war, its purpose, and what it had accomplished. He saw a resurgent Germany and rising Japan as new threats to world peace. He wondered how Canada could send 620,000 young men to war, only to abandon them in war's aftermath, denying them pensions and leaving many destitute and without treatment for the physical and mental wounds of war.

In the final days of his life, Currie became convinced that the accomplishments of the Corps were meaningless in the broader scheme of things. He never broke faith with the men who had served under him and what they had accomplished as soldiers, but he questioned the war's greater purpose. He saw that they had not won a kinder, gentler society nor had they destroyed militarism for all eternity. It was not the ideals of the war which had proved faulty, only the politicians to whom the fruits of victory had been entrusted. The former Corps Commander died shortly after Armistice Day on 30 November 1933.[64]

Currie's life was one of transformation. The Bombadier in the British Columbia militia had risen to the highest rank in the land. The student who failed to gain

---

62   James Price of Fort William wrote, 'As father of George Lawrence Price, the only Canadian killed on Armistice Day, I wish to convey to you, Sir, my humble hope that you will succeed in bringing to justice those responsible for bringing this case before the public, because all this simply renews old wounds that are better forgotten.' Quoted in Robert J. Sharpe, *The Last Day, the Last Hour: The Currie Libel Trial* (Toronto: The Osgoode Society, 1988), 226.

63   See ibid; See also, Vance, 180-5 and Tim Cook, *Clio's Warriors: Canadians and the Writing of the World Wars* (Vancouver: UBC Press, 2006), 56-62.

64   See the letters in the final chapter of this book.

entrance to university became the Principal of one of the leading universities in North America. The optimism which fed his prewar land speculations and wartime naiveté had turned to pessimism. Personal failure became personal triumph.

Currie's papers present a portrait of a complex individual, constantly changing and evolving. They provide insight not only into the inner workings of the Canadian Corps, but also the evolution of Canadian society and the memory of the Great War. Sir Arthur Currie emerges from his letters and diaries as a flawed personality and a sound battlefield commander. This is his story in his own words.

A Note on Sources and the Text

Currie's papers are predominantly found at Library and Archives Canada, but there are significant collections at the Canadian War Museum and the Archives of McGill University. Currie's letters can also be found in the papers of the important politicians of the First World War era including Sir Robert Borden, Sir Edward Kemp, and Sir George Perley. This book draws mainly on the largest body of documents held at Library and Archives Canada, the Canadian War Museum, and in the Borden Papers.

The original Currie letters are a joy for the historian to read, mainly because they are almost all typewritten. The majority of his diaries (1915-May 1918), on the other hand, are in messy handwriting and include very little punctuation. The remaining diaries (May 1918-August 1919) were typewritten, either at the time or after the fact. The typewritten diaries are far more detailed, contain punctuation, and full sentences and it is thus possible that they were rewritten after the war. It remains for the reader to judge. For the sake of clarity and consistency, the reader should be aware that the following changes were made to the originals.

Some punctuation has been added to the handwritten diaries, but only where the meaning of the original text would not be altered by the addition of a period or comma. Currie also had a tendency to capitalize nouns, but not consistently. Capitalization has been corrected to the standard usage. In this vein, ranks have been standardised and written out in full. The format used for military units has also been corrected for consistency and is as follows: 1st Battalion, 1st Brigade, 1st Division, I Corps, and First Army. Dates have been left as they were in the originals, except where noted in the text. The spelling of all French and Belgian towns has been corrected and the proper accents added. Spelling of ordinary words has also been corrected to the current Canadian usage, unless an original misspelling is meaningful in some way. In such a case 'sic' is inserted inside parentheses. At times Currie's handwriting is illegible and this is also noted in the text.

Some letters and diary entries have been abbreviated in which case '...' appears to denote the omission. There are many more diary entries in the originals that have been omitted altogether. While the editor chose those entries that appear to contain useful information and did not knowingly exclude any material that seemed to be of importance, future scholars will surely disagree. They are invited to consult the originals.

Except for the addition of accents to French and Belgian towns, the text of *Report to the Ministry* has not been changed. The maps contained within it are taken from the originals. The photographs attached to the report have been replaced by a broader selection of pictures that illustrate the text as a whole. Readers are invited to consult the original, which was first printed as Overseas Military Forces of Canada, *Report of the Overseas Military Forces of Canada for the Year 1918*. London: Government of Canada, 1919.

In compiling the explanatory footnotes, the editor consulted many sources. The most useful and often used were the *Dictionary of Canadian Biography*, especially volumes XIII, XIV, and XV by Ramsay Cook. Gary Sheffield and John Bourne's *Douglas Haig: War Diaries and Letters, 1914-1918*, and G.W.L. Nicholson's *Official History of the Canadian Expeditionary Force, 1914-1919* were equally useful. For the sake of space, these sources are not cited in the text, but should be consulted for further information.

Diaries and Correspondence

1917 - 1919

Corps Commander, May–December 1917

The spring of 1917 was a trying time for the Entente powers. Except for the Canadian gains at Vimy Ridge, the Franco–British offensives of April and May were dismal failures. In February, Russia erupted in revolution and in May and June the French armies mutinied. Although the United States entered the war during the spring, there was no sign of American troops in Europe. At the same time, Germany's attention turned back to the East and the war with Russia. The danger of a separate peace between the Russian government and the Germans seemed to grow every day. In the Balkans, in Italy, and in Mesopotamia the Central Powers held the upper hand. Politicians and strategists in London and Paris debated the possibility of pursuing operations on the periphery, but in the end they could not escape the fact that the war would likely be won or lost on the Western Front.

1 Brigate = more than 1 Battalion

In May 1917, Arthur Currie had been at the front for more than two years. He had commanded an infantry brigade during the German gas attack in April 1915 and then the 1st Canadian Division at Mount Sorrel, the Somme, and Vimy. He was the senior officer with a field command in the CEF and had become known as a competent and reliable tactician. In a letter addressed to Harlan Brewster, the Premier of British Columbia, Currie reflected on the events of the previous year and the factors that had made the Canadian Corps successful on the battlefield.[1]

1 Brigate = more Than 1 Battalion

Currie to Harlan Brewster, 31 May 1917[2]

Dear Mr. Brewster,

1   On Currie's experiences before 1917, see Dancocks, 29-98; Hyatt, 15-67; Urquhart, 37-159. On the strategic situation at the beginning of 1917, see the British official history (hereafter cited as BOH), James Edmonds, *History of the Great War: Military Operations: France and Belgium, 1917, Volume I* (London: Macmillan, 1940), 1-86. For the German perspective, see GOH XII, 1-63.
2   File 1, vol 1, CP, LAC. Harlan Carey Brewster (1870-1918) was Liberal Premier of British Columbia (1916-18).

It was very kind indeed of you to spare the time to write to me as you did on April 18th. And I appreciate your thoughtfulness very much. You are good enough to say that those at home often think of those 'somewhere in France,' and I want to assure you that our thoughts as often dwell on our home city and the province we love so well. If we have merited the approval of our countrymen, we are more than repaid.

I cannot in the space of a letter give you any detailed account of the recent fighting, but I know you will be interested when I tell you, that the victory of the Canadian Corps at Vimy Ridge, is universally regarded as the finest feat of arms performed by British troops in the whole war. In the summer of 1915 France had poured out its blood most freely in an endeavour to capture those formidable heights. The area around Souchez, Carency, Neuville St. Vaast, the Labyrinth (I had my quarters here) marks the last resting place of tens of thousands of the gallant soldiers of our Ally. For two years the Germans had worked incessantly to make the place impregnable, and I believe they thought it was.

After we left the Somme, we came into the line at Vimy, and a few of us were told that before we left Vimy was to be ours. We thought of nothing else, trained and planned for this alone.

The old division was given the place of honour on the right of the Corps, and it is our proud boast today that none went further, none captured more prisoners or war materiel none killed more Germans than those who belong to the units which first upheld Canada's honour on the battlefields of Europe.

We penetrated over six miles into the enemy's defences, capturing all our objectives, and what is considered more remarkable still, captured them all on time. The culminating features of our attack were the taking of the fortified Village of Arleux on April 28th. And of Fresnoy on May 3rd. Although troops on both flanks failed to get on in both cases this division took and held everything as ordered. German officers taken at Fresnoy refused to believe the same troops defeated them that morning as had overcome them on April 9th. They considered such a feat impossible. After the taking of the last-named village a British general in very high command sent an officer to tell me that in his opinion the 1st Canadian Division was the wonder of the British Army.

Now let me tell you what factors I ascribe the victory.

First: to the disciplined valour of our troops, and to their confidence in their ability to win.

No one ever shrugs his shoulders now when speaking of the discipline of the Canadians. There is no crime, the men respect themselves and are held in the highest regard by everyone. They have a proud record to maintain, and are determined that that record sanctified by the blood of so many of Canada's best, shall not only be lived up to but shall be enhanced.

Discipline gives men confidence in themselves and in each other. All British troops are brave, thank God for that, and I would be the last to say that Canadians are braver than the others. Such a statement would not be true. I said the men were confident in their ability to win. That confidence was born of good training. The men knew how to shoot straight and how to use their bayonets—there were many bloody bayonets in the streets of Arleux and Fresnoy. They knew how to use the bomb, the rifle grenade and the machine gun, but best of all they knew the most effective combination of these weapons. They had trained for this particular job, they had rehearsed the attack many times, and each and every man knew just exactly where he was going in the attack, and what he was going to do when he got there. Every feature of the German defence was studied, and definite plans made for the overcome of every obstacle, in so far as it is humanly possible to make such plans before an attack. When things do not go as planned, or when new and unexpected features are encountered, the resourcefulness, the self-reliant initiative of the Canadian is most marked. These are men accustomed to solve their own problems every day. Quickly and accurately they size up the situation and find the solution.

The second factor was the leadership of the officers and NCOs. Napoleon used to say 'there are no bad battalions there are only bad officers.' We have an equally wise saying 'The backbone of our army is the Non-Commissioned Officers.' The high casualties amongst the officers and NCOs proves they were true leaders. They had trained their men, and on the day of battle they led them. Let me give you an example or two. One battalion arrived at its objective with every officer a casualty, yet the men completed the capture and carried out the consolidation. In another battalion a company commander was shot through the arm before he had gone 100 yards. His servant helped him forward not back. Before going 200 yards further a shell knocked out the servant and badly wounded the officer in the leg. What did he do? He crawled another 350 yards to where his men were consolidating their objective. With them he stayed encouraging and cheering them on, giving advice and refusing to be carried out until the work was done.

Good God, Brewster, don't you see we simply must win with leaders like this. I thank God many times that it is my privilege to serve with them.

Another factor was the artillery preparation and support. It was perfect, by far the best we have had in the war. I won't attempt to say more because, being an old gunner when I start to write of the work of the artillery I don't know when to stop. And finally our intelligence and our plan was good. It was a glorious victory, and while I have seen no papers from Canada I am sure the people of Canada are very pleased and proud. The price, I think, was small compared to the advantages gained...

Before closing, permit me to congratulate you on the high honour that the people of British Columbia have conferred on you.[3] You have a great responsibility and I have every confidence you are willing to accept that responsibility and discharge it well.

You will not forget I know that you represent the people of British Columbia and not any particular party.

The war will affect the fate of political parties as well as the fate of all other institutions. Those only will survive which stand the test of true morality. I hope that men will never again give a slavish support to any party unless that party observes always the highest ideals.

I have no idea when I shall see the old town again. Whether spared or otherwise it won't be this year anyway. The war is by no means over, and further severe trials are yet to be overcome. We must and shall win. The Lord has not brought about the alliance of the English speaking people in order that they be overthrown. Keep up the good work at home. We'll do our best here.

With best wishes for your good health and your good fortune, and thanking you again for writing, I am, ever yours faithfully,

A.W. Currie

Diary Entry, 3 June 1917[4]

Fine. Much aerial activity these days. First Brigade arrives in Divisional Reserve. Colonel Peck[5] returns to join his battalion. Brings letter McBride[6]

---

3   Brewster won the provincial election in November 1916.
4   All diary entries in this chapter are transcribed from the original, hand written diaries in file 191, vol 43, CP, LAC.
5   Lieutenant Colonel Cy Peck (1871-1956), the Victoria Cross winning commanding officer of the 16th Canadian Infantry Battalion, was also a Member of Parliament from British Columbia.
6   Sir Richard McBride (1870-1917) the Premier of British Columbia (1903-15) and the Province's representative in London until his death in August 1917.

wrote to Perley.[7] Between 10:30 and 10:45 hostile aeroplane drops bombs on our camp wounding, Colonel Ford (seriously in head), Colonel Templeton (slightly in the head), Captain Napier (in forearm), Lieutenant Nathan (died of wounds), Major Corrigan (seriously in leg), Major Randall (broken ribs), Lieutenant Harrington (in leg and testicle), Lieutenant Duguid (2nd Divisional Artillery). Napier's interpreter and eight other ranks one of whom since died—a young chap twenty-one months in trenches brought to headquarters to be orderly. My cap, British warm raincoat destroyed. I was about ten yards away. Piece brushed by hair and was covered with dirt. Buster Browns...destroyed. Drove back to Chateau D'Acq.

Diary Entry, 4 June 1917

Fine. Visit hospitals to see wounded. When I return, wire from Garnet Hughes[8] re KCMG.[9] In afternoon Griesbach[10] calls, also General Byng,[11] who is very kind in his remarks. Many complimentary telegrams and messages received...

Diary Entry, 6 June 1917

Up at 4:00, with O'Connor[12] and Roberts visit outposts. Third Brigade Headquarters at Thelus Cave, 2nd Brigade Headquarters at Neuville St. Vaast. In afternoon called to Corps and informed by Corps Commander that he was going to take command of Third Army and I was to take over Corps.

---

7   Sir George Halsey Perley (1857-1938), a Conservative Member of Parliament from Quebec, Perley served as Canada's Minister of the Overseas Military Forces until October 1917 and was Canada's representative at the Imperial War Cabinet.

8   Major General Garnet Hughes (1880-1937) was the son of Sir Sam Hughes (1853-1921), the influential Minister of Militia (1914-16). Garnet was second in command of Currie's pre-war 50th Regiment (1913-14) where he was a close friend of the future Corps Commander. In part Currie owed his 1914 appointment as a brigadier to the work of the Minister's son. He commanded 1st Brigade (November 1915-February 1917) and later 5th Canadian Division in England, a formation which was broken up before it saw action. On Sir Sam Hughes, see Ronald Haycock, *Sam Hughes: The Public Career of a Controversial Canadian, 1885-1916* (Waterloo: Wilfrid Laurier University Press, 1986).

9   Knight Commander of the Most Distinguished Order of St. Michael and St. George; Currie's knighthood.

10 Major General William A. Griesbach (1878-1945), the former Mayor of Edmonton (1907), a Member of Parliament (1917-21), and a Senator (1921-45), Griesbach commanded 1st Canadian Infantry Brigade (from February 1917). On the commanders of the Canadian divisions and brigades, see Patrick H. Brennan 'Byng's and Currie's Commanders: A Still Untold Story of the Canadian Corps,' *Canadian Military History* 11, 2 (Spring 2002): 5-16.

11 Field Marshall Sir Julian 'Bungo' Byng (1862-1935) was commanding officer of the Canadian Corps (1916-17) and Governor General of Canada (1921-26). On Byng, see Jeffery Williams, *Byng of Vimy, General and Governor General* (London: Leo Cooper, 1983).

12 Probably Henry Willis-O'Connor (born 1886), Currie's Aide-de-Camp. Currie seems to have referred to him as 'Willis' and 'O'Connor.'

Diary Entry, 7 June 1917

Fine very hot. In company with Griesbach I visit Divisional School, also demonstration at 3rd Divisional School. In office all afternoon. Offensive at Messines and Wytschaete begins. Splendid success.

At the end of May, the Corps' Commander, Sir Julian Byng, was promoted to command Third Army. The Borden Government wanted a Canadian to succeed him and the two clear choices were Arthur Currie and Richard Turner.[13]

Sir George Perely to Prime Minister Sir Robert Borden, 9 June 1917[14]

(Secret) Corps Commander temporarily given higher command but may (?) return to us. Matter will be definitely settled within few days. Intend insisting on appointment Canadian. Don't expect serious objection unpopular so doing [sic]. Turner is senior but his work invaluable here don't want make change and he is of course rather out of touch with front after six months absence. Believe Currie who as senior officer at front is now temporarily in command Corps is considered most suitable for Corps by higher command and also by larger half troops although both officers have many strong friends. Think wisest course and one which would cause least friction and difficulty would be make Currie Corps Commander retain Turner here as GOC with certain measure authority over administrative matter at front particularly on lines communication. Endeavour get War Office make them both Lieutenant General and so preserve Turner's seniority. Turner naturally anxious command Corps as he is by temperament fighting soldier but he will acquiesce cheerfully in our decision. Please cable your views.

Perley

---

13   Lieutenant General Sir Richard Ernest William Turner (1871-1961) received a Victoria Cross in the Boer War. During the Great War, Turner commanded 3rd Brigade (September 1914-August 1915) and 2nd Canadian Division (August 1915-November 1916). In December 1916 he was promoted to Chief of the General Staff (Overseas Ministry) and sent to England where he acted as head of Canadian troops in England and military advisor to the Borden Government. Some politicians and officers believed that Turner should have been given command of the Corps in 1917 because he was more senior than Currie and a charismatic leader. However, on the battlefield his performance was uneven.

14   Reel C4355, vol 136, BP, LAC. Sir Robert Laird Borden (1854-1937) was the Conservative Prime Minister of Canada from 1911 to 1920. Borden took an active part in directing Canada's war effort and used the First World War to advocate for a more prominent Canadian position within the British Empire. His unrestrained conduct of the war divided Canada along ethnic-linguistic lines and effectively shut the Conservative Party out of Quebec for decades. See Robert Craig Brown, *Robert Laird Borden: A Biography* (Toronto: Macmillan, 1975-80).

Diary Entry, 10 June 1917

Fine. In afternoon Sims[15] calls. Tells me recommendation re my appointment not yet received in England. Lie [double underlined in original]. Says Garnet's friends boosting him. Apparently wanted to suggest a dicker if he dared. Made my position of not accepting any appointment with strings to it quite clear...

Diary Entry, 14 June 1917

Go to England in morning at request of Sir George Perley. Arrive at 2:00 pm crossing in dense fog. Lillie[16] arrives 5:03. See Perley at 5:30, remain to 7:15. Ethel, Garner and Marjorie[17] all arrive during evening. Dinner in our room at Carlton.

Diary Entry, 15 June 1917

Very hot and sultry. See General Peyton[18] at 9:00 am. Sir George Perley at 10:30 and Turner and Perley at one. It was decided that I take the Corps and my attitude towards the appointment of Garnet Hughes fully explained to them and agreed to by them. Lunch alone and order boots and British warm [raincoat]... After dinner Garnet Hughes calls and we have a three hour wrestle.[19] To bed very tired and exhausted.

Diary Entry, 16 June 1917

Very hot...many people call in morning. See General Turner at Argyll House...[20] Leave at 4:00 pm for France. Arrive at Boulogne at eight. Officer Commanding

15 Lieutenant Colonel Reginald Frank Manley Sims (1878-1951) was a Boer War veteran and an official in the Ministry of the Overseas Military Forces of Canada.
16 Lady Lucy Sophia Chadworth-Musters Currie (1875-1969), Currie's wife, stayed in Brighton, England while her husband commanded the Corps. Lucy and her husband were constantly in touch and Sir Arthur seems to have taken every opportunity to visit her. He usually referred to her as 'Lille' or 'Lill.'
17 Ethel Currie (born 1881) was Arthur Currie's younger sister; Marjorie (1902-1972) and Garner (born 1911) were Currie's children. All three stayed at Brighton with Lucy.
18 Major General Sir William Peyton (1866-1931) was Haig's Military Secretary at General Headquarters.
19 Currie opposed promoting Hughes to command 1st Canadian Division. Currie's motives are not entirely clear, although it is possible that Hughes' poor performance at the Second Battle of Ypres as a young officer was partially to blame. More likely, Currie did not want to sustain Sir Sam Hughes influence within the Corps. It is alleged that Hughes stormed out of the room threatening that one day he would make Currie pay. See Hyatt, 71-6. On the Hughes-Currie rivalry, see Tim Cook, 'The Madman and the Butcher: Sir Sam Hughes, Sir Arthur Currie, and the War of Reputations,' *Canadian Historical Review* 85, 4 (2004): 693-719.
20 Argyll House was headquarters of the Ministry of the Overseas Military Forces of Canada from 1916. On the Overseas Ministry, see Desmond Morton, *A Peculiar Kind of Politics: Canada's Overseas Ministry in the First World War* (Toronto: UTP, 1982).

ship, American officers on board, dinner at Boulogne. Dyer,[21] O'Connor and I arrive at Camblain[22] at midnight...

Combined Diary Entry, 22 June–10 July 1917

On 25 June: Army horse show occurred at which we won a first and nine seconds. While at the show word was received that Germans had fallen back off Hill 65 to north of Souchez river. Sent word... to 4th and 3rd Divisions to press on our front to south of river. This was successful by 10th Brigade. At night 12th Brigade relieved 10th and continued pressure, getting practically all the objectives set down for the 28th. This pressure was kept up and by the 29th we had advanced one and a half miles on a front of two and a half miles. The 12th and 9th Brigades doing the job at small loss!... Many prisoners and machine guns were captured and a great many Germans killed. The 85th Battalion for its first real offensive did splendidly... Early in July or late in June the 2nd Division took over line north of Souchez River from 46th who attacked on morning of July 1st but were driven back the same evening. Fifth Brigade going in just north of river and 6th Brigade on left. On June 27th Duke of Connaught visited area...

Diary Entry, 10 July 1917

Fine. To Army conference where plans are slightly changed. I ask to take Hill 70. This is agreed to and 1st Division is to move at once being replaced by 31st. In afternoon, have conference of divisional commanders and outline plans.

Diary Entry, 12 July 1917

Very hot. Went to Albert via Arras and Bapaume. Passing Somme battlefield, lunch with King at Byng's Headquarters, afterwards knighted in square there. Many officers invested, five knighted... [the] King was very gracious.

In late June and early July 1917, the British Army was preparing to follow up on its successes at Messines with operations that would come to be known as the Third Battle of Ypres. Sir Douglas Haig first intended to break out from the Ypres Salient and advance along the coast, pushing the Germans out of Belgium thus securing the channel ports. The initial objective was Passchendaele Ridge.

---

21 Brigadier General Hugh M. Dyer (1861-1938) was commanding officer of 5th Canadian Infantry Battalion until June 1917 when he was promoted to command the 7th Canadian Infantry Brigade, a post he held until September 1918.

22 Canadian Corps Headquarters.

The Canadians were ordered to support this operation by making a diversionary attack towards Lens, an important city to the north of Vimy Ridge. Haig hoped that this attack would pin down a number of German divisions as the main British effort was made in the Ypres Salient. Currie spent much of July planning for what came to be known as the Battle of Hill 70.[23]

Diary Entry, 23 July 1917

Very hot. At 1:00 am 116th Battalion (Colonel Sam Sharpe) raids east of Avion. Two officers and fifty-two other ranks prisoners. Very successful. Our casualties seventy-four. Had hand fight at railway and drove Boches[24] to ground. Then blew in dugouts. Battalions first effort in forenoon. Commander-in-Chief[25] comes to conference at 2nd Division Headquarters afterwards, visiting Vimy Ridge...

Diary Entry, 2 August 1917

Heavy rains. Call on 4th Brigade, 5th Brigade, 22nd, 24th, 25th, 26th Battalions. Lunch at Army. Decide on further postponement on account of weather. General Watson[26] calls in afternoon. Attend concert and afterwards dine at 1st Division Headquarters. See... 1st Division Band. Many old members of 5th[27] Band. First Division at Bracquemont.

Diary Entry, 3 August 1917

Rained very hard all day. In afternoon General Lipsett[28] called, also called O'Neil and Loomis.[29] Go to Army to discuss large raid on Hill 70. Agree to reduce it. Call at 3rd Division on way home.

---

23 See Hyatt, 76-7.
24 'Boche' was trench slang for 'the Germans.' Currie—and others—also used the spelling 'Bosche.'
25 Field Marshal Sir Douglas Haig (1861-1928) was the controversial Commander-in-Chief of the British Expeditionary Force (1915-19). Haig has been vilified as a butcher by some historians and lauded as a competent commander by others. Currie seems to have admired and respected Haig and his leadership. Among the many books on Haig, see Gary Sheffield and John Bourne, *Douglas Haig: War Diaries and Letters, 1914-1918* (London: Weidenfeld & Nicolson, 2005) and John Terraine, *Douglas Haig: The Educated Soldier* (London: Leo Cooper, 1990). For the most vitriolic attacks see, John Laffin, *British Butchers and Bunglers of World War I* (London: Sutton Publishing, 2003) and Denis Winter, *Haig's Command: A Reassessment* (London: Viking, 1991).
26 Major General Sir David Watson (1869-1922) was commanding officer of 4th Canadian Division and a newspaper man from Quebec City.
27 Currie was commanding officer of the 5th Regiment of Artillery in Victoria, British Columbia (1909-13).
28 Major General Louis James Lipsett (1874-1918) was a British officer who commanded 2nd Brigade (September 1915-June 1916) and 3rd Canadian Division (June 1916-September 1918). Lipsett died on 14 October 1918, the last British general killed during the Great War.
29 Major General Frederick Oscar Wilson Loomis (1870-1937) was commanding officer of 2nd Canadian Infantry Brigade (June 1916-December 1917, March-September 1918) and 3rd Canadian Division (from September 1918).

Diary Entry, 5 August 1917

Weather clearing. In morning attended large church service at Rachecourt regarding anniversary of war. Over 5,000 officers and men present. Presentation of Belgian decorations and March past afterwards. General Peyton to lunch also with Grenfell—the horse master of artillery.

Diary Entry, 11 August 1917

My wife's birthday. Showers heavy at times. Visited 4th Division Headquarters in morning and inspected divisional school. Afterwards witnessing 9th Brigade manoeuvres. Very interesting and instructive. Sprained muscles in right leg in evening and laid up in consequence. Army Commander called. Zero day 15th decided on.

Diary Entry, 14 August 1917

Anniversary of my wedding. Wired to Lill. Macdonell[30] and Burstall[31] called. Eleventh Brigade advanced their posts... Army Commander called...

Combined Diary Entry, 15–18 August 1917

For reports of the battle see other files. It was altogether the hardest battle in which the Corps has participated. There were no fewer than twenty-one counter-attacks delivered, many with very large forces and all with great determination and dash. The attacks were made by 4th, 5th, 2nd, and 3rd Brigades and were completely successful. Not an inch of ground being lost. Four German divisions were accounted for vis-à-vis 7th, 8th [German Infantry Divisions], 11th and 4th Guards Reserve [Infantry Divisions]. Our casualties so far about 5,600 but in my opinion the enemy casualties must be close to 20,000. Our gunners, machine gunners and infantry never had such targets. Forward Observation Officers could not get guns for all their targets. Many of the young officers showed up splendidly and everyone is very pleased. Congratulatory messages were received from Commander-in-Chief, General Plumer,[32] General Byng, Second Army, XIII Corps, XI Corps, 5th Division, 6th Division, General Gordon Lennox and many

---

30 Major General Sir Archibald Cameron Macdonell (1864-1941) commanded 7th Brigade (December 1915-February 1916, May 1916-June 1917) and 1st Canadian Division (June 1917-May 1919).

31 Major General Sir Henry E. Burstall (1870-1945) was General Officer Commanding Canadian Corps, Royal Artillery (September 1915-December 1916) and commanding officer of 2nd Canadian Division (from December 1916).

32 General Sir Herbert Charles Plumer (1857-1932) commanded Second Army (1915-17) and again from March 1918 to the end of the war. See Geoffrey Powell, *Plumer: the Soldier's General* (London: Leo Cooper, 2004).

others. It was a great and wonderful victory. GHQ regard it as one of the finest performances of the war. Weather splendid.

Diary Entry, 19 August 1917

Fine. On Thursday, Friday, and Saturday preceding, Boches big guns shelled Corps Headquarters. Second Division forced to move from Sains-en-Gohelle... Saw all units of 2nd Brigade very cheerful, very tired but very proud. Colonel Adamson,[33] Major Stewart, Captain Papineau,[34] Major MacKenzie in to dinner... Leg is getting better. Tenth Brigade relieves 11th.

Diary Entry, 21 August 1917

Sixth and 10th Brigade attack partially successful. Germans were about to attack us and troops met in no mans land. After withstanding eight counter-attacks, 6th Brigade came out of Cinnabar.[35] Left battalion of 10th did not get on, but others did and very well. Five and one-third German Divisions already located, four of which have been withdrawn from line, their losses extremely heavy. Get telegram congratulation from Commander-in-Chief. Third Division relieve 1st and part of 2nd.

Diary Entry, 23 August 1917

Cloudy. Showers. At 3:00 am, 44th Battalion attacked Green Crassier successfully. Enemy lose heavily in counter-attacks but push us off east of Crassier. Very heavy fighting going on. Visit 4th Division. Lunch with General Ross[36] and with him see all battalions of 5th Brigade. Forty-fourth Battalion pushed off Green Crassier.

The Battle of Hill 70 was Currie's first operation as Corps Commander and he had achieved a victory in his own way. On 7 July First Army assigned the Canadians to capture the city of Lens by direct assault, but Sir Arthur was not happy with the British plan. Although he had been in command barely a month, Currie boldly submitted a new operational outline. Instead of an advance through

33 Lieutenant Colonel Agar Adamson (1865-1929) was commanding officer of the Princess Patricia's Canadian Light Infantry.

34 Major Talbot Mercer Papineau (1883-1917) was grandson of Louis-Joseph Papineau. Panineau was well known in Montreal social and political circles. His correspondence with Henri Bourassa on French Canadian involvement in the Great War was published in Canadian and British newspapers.

35 Cinnabar Trench.

36 Brigadier General John Munro Ross (1877-1959) was commanding officer of 5th Brigade (July 1917-August 1918).

the city, his revised plan called for the capture of Hill 70 which dominated Lens to the north. Currie believed that by capturing this important topographical feature, he would force the Germans to evacuate the city. He also suspected that the enemy would not give up Hill 70 without a fight. He figured that if the hill could be taken, the defenders would destroy themselves trying to retake it.

Currie was right on all accounts. When the assault went in on 15 August, the Canadians successfully took their objectives. Over the next few days the Corps held its ground against numerous German counter-attacks. Subsequent Canadian assaults between 21 and 25 August secured the Corps' gains and brought much of Lens into Canadian hands. More importantly, the Canadians wore out five German divisions in only a few days. But success carried a price. Almost 9,200 Canadians had been killed, captured, or wounded between 15 and 24 August. Nevertheless, from a tactical and strategic point of view, Currie's plan had been a resounding success. It demonstrated that the new Corps Commander knew the value of terrain and the importance of attacks with limited objectives. It also showed that Currie was an innovative commander, willing to think and act independently. These were traits that would become the hallmark of his operations in 1918.[37]

Diary Entry, 26 August 1917

Fine. Sir George Perely arrives, visits Vimy. In afternoon I go to see 1st Division also 1st, 2nd, 3rd and 4th Battalions. Army Commander and I visiting, also Colonel Ross to dinner. Band of 28th play.

Diary Entry, 27 August 1917

Rained very heavily all afternoon and night Commander-in-Chief inspected 1st and 2nd Divisions. Near Maisnil-Bouché he saw the 4th and 5th Brigades, the 6th were at Estrée-Cauchie, the 1st and 2nd Brigades near Mingoval. After lunch he saw the 3rd Brigade at Marle-les-Mines. All looked very well and the Chief was more than pleased and said so. Sir George Perely saw the parades. In the evening, Burstall, Lipsett, Watson, Perely, Dodds...[38]

---

37   See Nicholson, 269-97 and Morton and Granatstein, 160-70. See also BOH 1917 II. For the German side of the battle, see GOH XIII, 65-8.
38   Brigadier General William Okell Holden Dodds (1867-1934) was commander of the 5th Canadian Divisional Artillery (January-May 1917, July 1917-December 1918).

Diary Entry, 1 September 1917

Conference at Army Headquarters. Afterwards motored to Cassel with Radcliffe[39] and O'Connor had lunch with Mitchell of Second Army Headquarters. Then went to... II Corps (Jacobs) Headquarters then back to tea with General Plumer. I went on to Boulogne to dinner.

Diary Entry, 2 September 1917

Crossed to England on leave. Very rough... Met by Captain Rogers and car. Lillie did not receive my wire in time to meet me but came up at 7:30. Stayed at Carlton.

Currie spent the next two weeks on leave in England shopping, visiting his family, and meeting Canadian officials in London before returning to France on 16 September. As soon as Currie got back from England he became ill with diarrhea and stomach problems, symptoms that plagued the Corps Commander throughout his life in times of high stress.[40]

Combined Diary Entry, 18 September–2 October 1917

Had picture painted. Felt ill and for next three weeks; quite ill for first time in ages. Very sick stomach, sleepless nights. Colonel Peters treating me. On the 22nd, 23rd, 24th and 25th had Corps Rifle meeting, a big success in every way. Corps sports on 29th were also great success. Line very quiet, several attempted raids by Boche which were unsuccessful... Conferences were held and all plans confirmed and decided on. Practice over taped courses regularly held. Larger models made out.

Diary Entry, 3 October 1917

Informed that two divisions were to be withdrawn. Might go north.

Moving north meant that the Canadians would be committed to the fighting in Flanders. In July the battle known as Passchendaele began as an operation with definite objectives (Ostend and Zeebrugge), but by the end of September it had become an attritional slugging match. The initial objective of Passchendaele

---

39 General Percy Pollexfen de Blaquiere 'P de B' Radcliffe (1874-1934) was Brigadier General, General Staff Canadian Corps (June 1916-April 1918).
40 The best discussion of Currie's health problems is in Dancocks.

Ridge remained in German hands and any hope of a breakout towards the coast had long ago evaporated. Haig's decision to continue the battle after the failure of his initial plan remains one of his most controversial decisions of the war. While historians debate whether operations should have been called off, in October 1917 the Canadians did not have that luxury.

Currie was ordered to submit a plan for the capture of Passchendaele village on 13 October. Currie's letters suggest that the Corps Commander did not object to the operation itself but that he did refuse to serve under General Hubert Gough's Fifth Army. [41] In Currie's eyes, General Gough had proved incompetent at the Somme and Passchendaele and he preferred that the Canadians serve under Plumer's Second Army instead. As the commander of a dominion corps, responsible to both the Canadian Government and British GHQ, perhaps Currie was given more leeway than other British corps commanders to make demands of his superiors. On the other hand, Haig's diary suggests that the change was made on 5 October at the behest of his Chief of Staff, Launcelot Kiggell, [42] not because of any complaint from General Currie. In any event, the Canadians moved north to Second Army on 18 October and began preparing to capture Passchendaele. [43]

Diary Entry, 4 October 1917

Rained very hard all day. Visited Base to meet General Graham[44] and Colonel Hamilton. Arrived at understanding as to re-enforcements and supernumeraries... General Morrison[45] and General Lindsay[46] accompanied me.

On 5 October Sir George Perley moved from Canada's Overseas Ministry to become the Dominion's High Commissioner to Great Britain. He was replaced by

---

41 General Sir Hubert de la Poer Gough (1870-1963) commanded Fifth Army from 1916 to his 1918 dismissal. See Anthony Farrar-Hockley, *Goughie: The Life of General Sir Hubert Gough* (London: Hart-Davis, 1975).

42 Lieutenant General Sir Launcelot Edward Kiggell (1862-1954) was Haig's Chief of Staff (December 1915-January 1918).

43 See Nicholson, 298-317, Morton and Granatstein, 165-9, and Sheffield and Bourne, 333. On Currie at Passchendaele, see Dancocks, 112-21; Hyatt, 77-89; Urquhart, 172-93. For two recent examinations of the battle, see Robin Prior and Trevor Wilson, *Passchendaele: the Untold Story* (New York: Yale University Press, 2002) and Peter Liddle, *Passchendaele in Perspective: the Third Battle of Ypres* (London: Pen and Sword, 1997). See also BOH 1917 II and for the German perspective, GOH XIII.

44 Major General Edward R.C. Graham (1858-1951) was Deputy Adjutant General Base, 3rd Echelon.

45 Major General Sir Edward W.B. Morrison (1867-1925) was the General Officer Commanding Canadian Corps, Royal Artillery (from December 1916).

46 Major General William Bethune Lindsay (1880-1933) was Chief Engineer of the Canadian Corps (from March 1916).

Sir Edward Kemp[47] *at the head of the Overseas Ministry with Sydney Mewburn*[48] *taking over the portfolio of Minister of Militia and Defence in Ottawa.*

Diary Entry, 7 October 1917

General Watson called. In company with Farmar[49] and Ross went to conference at Second Army Headquarters, where certain information was given as to future probable moves. War correspondents Robertson, Kidman and [illegible] to dinner.

Diary Entry, 9 October 1917

Second Army attack towards Passchendaele going very well. Fifth Corps representative come to take over. Moves re divisions announced at Conference divisional commanders. In evening went to 4th Division concert at Bruay dining with Watson afterwards. Boyd the Brigadier General, General Staff V Corps, comes.

Diary Entry, 10 October 1917

Stormy rain. Fine in Afternoon. Monsieur Roy[50] arrives from Paris. In afternoon show General Fanshawe[51] about. Take him to 1st and 2nd Divisions. Dine at Army in evening. Lipsett, Watson also Farmar there. Radcliffe returned from leave having been recalled.

On 16 October, Currie submitted an intricate plan of attack which called for close cooperation between infantry and artillery. The operation to capture Passchendaele village was divided into three phases to begin on 24 October. Because the plan required extensive support by the artillery and engineers, Currie was forced to delay the assault by several days to ensure that all preparations were completed on time. Although there were objections at GHQ to the postponement, Currie was supported by General Plumer who trusted the Corps Commander's judgement. The date for the initial attack was set for the

47 Sir Albert Edward Kemp (1858-1928) was an Ontario Member of Parliament and the Minister of the Overseas Military Forces of Canada (1917-20).

48 Sydney Chilton Mewburn (1863-1956) was elected in 1917 from Hamilton, Ontario to the House of Commons and served as Minister of Militia and Defence (1917-20).

49 Major General George Jasper Farmar (1872-1958), a veteran of the Nile Expedition and the North African Campaign (1898), Farmar was Deputy Adjutant and Quartermaster General, Canadian Corps (from 1916).

50 Senator Philippe Roy (1868-1948) was Canada's High Commissioner to France (1911-38).

51 Major General Sir Robert Fanshawe (1863-1946) was commanding officer of the 46th Division.

26th with the second and third phases to begin on 30 October and 6 November respectively.[52]

Diary Entry, 18 October 1917

Fine in morning drizzle in afternoon. Went to Ypres and called on divisional commanders. (Russell: New Zealand,[53] Monash: Australian[54]) in morning... Mitchell General Staff Officer (GSO) I and de Maliséy, French liaison at Second Army to lunch... Conference in evening. The battlefield looks bad. No salvaging has been done, and very few of the dead buried, particularly on 3rd Australian Division's front.

Diary Entry, 22 October 1917

Fine. In morning Duke of Connaught inspected 12th and 7th Brigades who looked very well indeed. He lunched with us. Sir Herbert Plumer was also present, also Murray, the Duke's staff officer, in the afternoon. They inspected the 2nd Brigade who Prince Arthur said looked the best of all three. Major General Wright[55] American officer dined in evening. Conference as usual. Fifth Army attacked fair success.

Diary Entry, 23 October 1917

Fair at times but showery and colder. Conference of divisional commanders in morning. At conclusion Commander-in-Chief arrived, went over plans with us. Visited model and remained to lunch also Curly Birch[56] and [illegible] the ANC[57] in afternoon. Maxse[58] came over, also Wright and his aid Captain Kelly. Conference as usual.

Diary Entry, 26 October 1917

Rained during night. Attacked at 5:45. Fourth Division (46th Battalion) got off well and took all objectives. Third Division attacked with 9th Brigade on

52 See Hyatt, 82-83; Nicholson, 318-39; Morton and Granatstein, 165-9.
53 Major General Sir Andrew Hamilton Russell (1868-1960) commander of the New Zealand division for the duration of the war.
54 General Sir John Monash (1865-1931) was commander of the Australian Corps. See Geoffrey Serle, *John Monash: A Biography* (Melbourne: Melbourne University Press, 1982).
55 Probably Major General William M. Wright, an American divisional commander.
56 General Sir James F. Noel Birch (1865-1939) was Haig's Chief Artillery Advisor.
57 Currie probably meant the Australian and New Zealand Army Corps (ANZAC).
58 Lieutenant General Sir Ivor Maxse (1862-1958) was commanding officer of XVIII Corps. On British Corps Command in the Great War, see Andy Simpson, *Directing Operations: British Corps Command on the Western Front, 1914-18* (London: Spellmount Publishers, 2005).

right (43rd & 58th [Battalions]) 8th Brigade (2nd CMR on left) the defences at Bellevue. At first they were checked for some hours and came back, but with a most magnificent rally and reinforced by Foster with the 52nd, they fought all afternoon and finally got their objectives. It was a truly magnificent performance. Many congratulatory messages received...Bombed and shelled. In afternoon visited division commanders at Ypres.

Diary Entry, 29 October 1917

Fine. Visited divisional commanders, Canadian Corps Heavy Artillery in morning. Corps commanders conference at Hoograft in afternoon. General Gough called to ask me to postpone. Refuse to do so and confirmed refusal again at 7:00 pm. Bombing at night...

Diary Entry, 30 October 1917

Fine morning. Good get away for attack. Twelfth Brigade on right (72nd, 78th, 85th Battalions) got their objectives including Crest Farm on time. Third Division on left (5th CMR, 49th Battalion, Pats).[59] Pats did extraordinarily well taking Meetchele, after very heavy fighting. Papineau killed. Forty-ninth fairly well. Heavy casualties, held up at Furst Farm. CMRs very well [and captured] Source Farm [and] Vapour Farm. Imperials on flank failed again as they did on the 26th. This checked our progress on left very, very much. Army Commander and others called during day. Bombed severely and heavily shelled by HV gun[60] at night. Too close to be comfortable. Fighting was very severe and success great.

After the first phase of the attacks, Currie took time to report to the Overseas Ministry.

Currie to Lieutenant General Sir Richard Turner, 30 October 1917[61]

Dear Turner,

...As you know, we are very busy now. We attacked last Friday, and had very hard fighting gaining possession of the Bellevue Spur. This is a position which resisted the assaults of several divisions previously, and it is very gratifying to

---

59 Princess Patricia's Canadian Light Infantry.
60 High Velocity Gun.
61 File 4, vol 2, CP, LAC.

have been able to get it at the first shot. Our troops were held up in the morning and did what Sir Herbert Plumer says has not been done previously in this battle. They fought very hard all afternoon, taking one pillbox after another, and at night were able to report all objectives in our hands. From one row of pillboxes they took eighteen machine guns. It was one of the finest performances which the Canadians have yet done, and drew from the Commander-in-Chief and from several army commanders most congratulatory messages. We advanced again this morning, and present reports indicate all objectives in our hands. Today's fighting is very important, and I look for a very severe struggle. We have already broken up several very determined counter-attacks. As usual the flanks are giving us a little trouble. With best wishes always,

Yours ever,

A.W. Currie

The fighting at Passchendaele had been exhausting and cases of 'shell shock' were common among officers and men.

Currie to Lieutenant General Sir Travers E. Clarke, 1 November 1917[62]

[No salutation],

...We have now been in this area over two weeks, and since our arrival I have had continuously employed all my engineer companies making roads, trails, etc. They have worked practically night and day, for such things were almost non-existent before we came in. The work has been carried on under the most trying conditions, the enemy trying to interfere with our road making to the greatest possible extent. However, the companies have done extraordinarily well. They have suffered heavy losses, and the officers who are left are feeling the strain to a very great degree. We are just about half through with our job, and unless I can furnish some relief to these officers many of them will break down before their work is finished.

We have an understanding with the Canadian authorities in England, whereby we are privileged to exchange a certain number of officers here, who are in need of a rest, with officers in England. I would like to send to England for rest and change, three majors, three captains and eighteen subalterns, replacing them by an equal number of officers from England. I have them there in our 5th Division,

---

62   File 1, vol 1, CP, LAC. Lieutenant General Sir Travers Edward Clarke (1871-1962) was Deputy Adjutant General and Quartermaster General, GHQ, 1st Echelon.

and I hope you will agree with, and help me to carry out my suggestion. If you do, will you please ask for these officers. As you realize, the battle which we are now fighting is a very important one, and I desire to leave nothing undone which can make for its success.

A.W. Currie

Diary Entry, 3 November 1917

Cloudy misty. Corps commanders conference at Ten Elms. Heavy counter-attacks on our position in morning. Repulsed leaving few prisoners in our hands...

Diary Entry, 6 November 1917

Fine in morning later rain. At 6:00 am the 1st and 2nd Division attacked. First Division left, 2nd Division right. Both were eminently successful, taking all their objectives on time. These included Passchendaele, Mosselmarkt. About 500 prisoners taken. Fighting severe. Telegrams came from Haig, Plumer, Horne,[63] Byng. Connaught visited wounded at Casualty Clearing Stations in afternoon.

Diary Entry, 8 November 1917

Fine. Cloudy. Cold... In morning inspected and addressed 8th Brigade. Corps commanders conference here at 3:30. Situation reviewed and plans for next operation approved. Sir Herbert Plumer announced that he was handing over Second Army to Sir Henry Rawlinson[64] preparatory to going to Italy...

Diary Entry, 9 November 1918 *1917 Mistake?*

Fine cloudy, cold. Sir Herbert Plumer called to say good-bye. Was very much and visibly moved. Visited 1st and 2nd Divisions at Ypres. Ketchen[65] and Griesbach to dinner.

---

63 General Sir Henry Sinclair Horne (1861-1929) was commanding officer of First Army from 1916 to the end of the war. See Don Farr, *The Silent General: Horne of First Army* (London: Helion and Company, 2007).

64 General Sir Henry Seymour Rawlinson (1864-1925) was commanding officer of Fourth Army in the Hundred Days Campaign of 1918. He spent much of 1917 planning the aborted landings on the Belgian coast. See Robin Prior and Trevor Wilson, *Command on the Western Front: The Military Career of Sir Henry Rawlinson, 1914-1918* (London: Leo Cooper, 2004).

65 Major General Huntly Douglas Brodie Ketchen (1872-1959) was a Conservative Member of the Legislative Assembly of Manitoba. Ketchen commanded 6th Brigade (June 1915-April 1918).

1917 *(handwritten)* *mistake?* *(handwritten annotation)*

Diary Entry, 10 November 1918

Attack at 6:05 by 2nd Brigade with 3rd Imperial Brigade on left. We got all our objectives. So did they but they did not mop up Vocation Farm and they retired in very bad and pronounced disorder, amounting to a panic. They came back to their original line. We held fast—making a defensive flank but leaving ourselves in a very bad salient; the hostile artillery was the most severe and violent we ever experienced. The weather was very bad all day. The Army Commander called.

Second Brigade's attack was the final British attack of the Battle of Passchendaele. The Canadians had secured Passchendaele village and much of the ridge at a cost of 15,654 casualties. It was a heavy price to pay, but more than 240,000 British soldiers had been lost in the Ypres Salient since the beginning of the battle, many of them trying for the same objectives at home. Currie would be criticised for the high casualties, but whether the ground gained was worth the cost was not a question that the Corps Commander was in a position to answer (although, as his letters show, he believed that it was worth the price). Strategic decisions were made by Sir Douglas Haig and the British Government with Ottawa setting the limits of Canadian involvement in the war effort. Avoiding the fight at Passchendaele would have required the intervention of Ottawa, something that was impossible given the Borden government's stance on the war. Unfortunately for Currie, as the Corps' commanding officer he was an easy target for such criticism.[66]

Diary Entry, 11 November 1917

Fine. Visited 1st and 2nd Divisions at Ypres. Passing through a bombing barrage. General Jacob and Army Commander called. Headquarters bombed at night.

Currie's responsibilities extended far beyond the battlefield. As the commander of what was essentially Canada's national army, many prominent Canadians had an inherent interest in the Corps. This made it a political entity, something with which Currie was uncomfortable. Sir Arthur took the time to answer dozens of letters from politicians, businessmen, and newspaper editors throughout the

---

66 Nicholson, 323-6.

war, but never really understood politics and tended to believe that people's goodwill would generally prevail.

Currie to Sir William Hearst, 14 November 1917[67]

Dear Mr. Hearst,

Permit me on behalf of all ranks of the Canadian Corps to thank you for your kind letter of the 19th September. To know that our efforts are appreciated in Canada, and that those at home are proud of the record of the Corps, is an inspiration to us.

As the press will have informed you, we have been very seriously engaged lately. We were brought to this part of the battlefield for a special purpose. It was absolutely necessary to gain certain ground, and in order to make sure of it the Commander-in-Chief sent for the Canadians. We have successfully accomplished the task assigned to us. We made four attacks, all of which were eminently successful and tonight Passchendaele, the goal for which so many hard-fought battles have taken place, is within our lines, despite the most stupendous efforts on the part of the Germans to resist our advance and to recover it after its loss.

The year 1917 has been a glorious year for the Canadian Corps. We have taken every objective from the enemy we started for and have not had a single reverse. Vimy, Arleux, Fresnoy, Avion, Hill 70 and Passchendaele all signify hard fought battles and notable victories. I know that no other Corps has had the same unbroken series of successes. All this testifies to the discipline, training, leadership and fine fighting qualities of the Canadians. Words cannot express the pride one feels in being associated with such splendid soldiers. The only regret one has, and it is a very sincere one, is that one has lost so many gallant comrades, men whom a young country like Canada, or in fact any country, could ill afford to lose.

Thanking you for all your good wishes, which I most cordially reciprocate,

I am ever yours faithfully,

A.W. Currie

---

67 File 2, vol 1, CP, LAC. Sir William Howard Hearst (1864-1941) was the Conservative Premier of Ontario (1914-19).

Diary Entry, 20 November 1917

Drizzle. Webber[68] GSO I 2nd Division leaves for GHQ to take charge of anti aircraft gun work. Third Army launch their big tank attack. Four-hundred-and-fifty tanks go in without artillery preparation with subsidiary attacks [illegible] along whole army front. Very successful. Cavalry have moved forward and gone through.

Diary Entry, 21 November 1917

Raining. Radcliffe, O'Connor and I leave for Paris lunching at Amiens. Arrive Paris 4:45 stay at Meurice, tea there. Give interviews to French Press. Roy calls and we all dine at La Rue. Afterwards to Theatre Michel.

Diary Entry, 22 November 1917

Fine. In morning prepare my speech for afternoon, lunch at Cafe de Paris. Opening of war pictures at 2:30. Radcliffe, Morrison and O'Connor with me. Roy receives me with officers from French Army, British Ambassador, etc.

Currie spent the next few days in Paris, attending official functions. On 23 November he was presented with the Croix de Guerre and returned to Corps Headquarters three days later. As the guns of Passchendaele fell silent, the Canadian federal election took centre stage. The previous July the Union Government had passed the Military Service Act (conscription) despite significant opposition from various sectors of Canadian society, most notably among French Canadians and farmers. The 1917 election was a virtual referendum on conscription and the Union Government's war policy. To ensure victory, Prime Minister Robert Borden enfranchised women with close relatives serving in the military and took the vote away from 'enemy aliens.' He also distributed the votes of soldiers serving overseas in a creative way. Currie supported conscription but detested politics. He was wary of becoming associated with the Borden government's questionable electoral tactics, but as Canada's most important soldier it was impossible for him to remain apolitical in an election fought over

---

68   Brigadier General Norman W. Webber (1881-1950) would return to the Canadian Corps to become Brigadier General, General Staff (April 1918-October 1918).

military policy. He believed that his own future as Corps Commander was tied to the outcome of the election and the adoption of conscription.[69]

Currie to Lieutenant Colonel John J. Creelman, 30 November 1917[70]

My dear Creelman,

I acknowledge the receipt of your letter of the 20th October, and beg to say that I find no fault whatever with your having published the letter I gave to you on leaving the 1st Division last winter. From the editorial to which you refer, and from what I have read in other newspapers, I gather that the political campaign is being conducted on the same low level as previous ones. It is too bad that the public men of Canada cannot refer to their opponents in even courteous terms. I am glad to hear you say that in your opinion the opponents of the Military Service Act will not have an opportunity of upsetting it. I feel that any interference with its provisions, or any delay in its operation will mean the death of this corps. I feel that months have already been wasted, and even if the men who are being called up now are got into training at once we shall need them very badly before they will be fit to send. If they don't come at all within three months I feel that this corps may still consist of four divisions, but probably only nine battalions each; in six months, it would probably consist of only two divisions, and in a year from now not more than one. It would suffer not only by reason of its losses in numbers but in the loss of morale of those remaining. The men who are here now are committed until peace is declared. If no others are sent to help them they can look forward to nothing else but to be killed or permanently maimed. Many of our men have already been wounded three or four times. Yet the exigencies of the service deemed that they be again sent to the firing line.

The death struggle is approaching, and if Canada neglects to put forth her full strength in that struggle such an action can be considered not only a desertion of the men in the trenches, but a desertion of the Empire as well. The Empire is fighting for its life, and must see this thing through. If we do no play our part, we cannot hold up our heads in honour at its conclusion, no matter what that conclusion is. Furthermore, I believe the withholding of men at the present time might have a great influence on the situation in Australia and South Africa. I

69 On the conscription election, see J.L. Granatstein and J.M. Hitsman, *Broken Promises: A History of Conscription in Canada* (Toronto: Oxford University Press, 1977). On French Canada in the Great War, see Gérard Filteau, *Le Québec, le Canada et la guerre 1914-1918* (Montreal: L'aurore, 1977). For an analysis of Currie's response to conscription, see Hyatt, 90-97 and Hyatt, 'Arthur Currie and Conscription.'
70 File 1, vol 1, CP, LAC. Lieutenant Colonel John Jennings Creelman (1882-1949) was the former commanding officer of 2nd Artillery Brigade and a prominent Montreal businessman.

believe the fate of the Empire is at stake, and I cannot believe that the people of Canada for one minute understand the true situation. I know that they have been deceived. They have been constantly told that Canada has raised 450,000 men; they assume that these men are capable of taking their places in the firing line; they have all studied arithmetic, and when they add the number who are serving in France to the number who have become casualties, and subtract that total from this 450,000, they naturally conclude that there must still be a couple hundred thousand available for service. What they have not been told is that out of that 450,000 probably 100,000 were no use. If they add to that 100,000 the number who disappear through sickness and what we call the normal wastage, they will find that there are at the present time very, very few available for reinforcements.

You know I have always done my best to keep politics out of the corps, and I shall continue to do so. It must have surprised you when you read the remarks of the Honourable Frank Oliver[71] who, I believe, accused me of owing my decorations and my promotions to the Borden Government. You know how little they had to do with my decorations, and I do not think that anybody could say that they put themselves out any to secure for me my present appointment. I cannot take any action to influence the present election, but if I thought the situation in Canada was serious enough to possibly prejudice the successful operation of the Military Service Act I would be disposed to tell the people of Canada how serious the situation is, even if by so doing I had to give up my present position.

I hope you will pardon me for having written such a lengthy letter, which you will understand is a purely personal one. I thank you for your congratulations re the Passchendaele battle. I can tell you briefly what the situation was when we were called upon to undertake that task. Others had repeatedly failed to take the ridge, and it was imperative that it should be taken or much of the previous fighting would count for naught. In order to make sure of success, the Commander-in-Chief called on the Canadian Corps, and I am proud to say the Corps delivered the goods. The obstacles that had to be overcome in the way of defences of the Boche and bad communications on our part were simply staggering. The fellows have never worked so hard or fought with such grim determination. This has been a wonderful year for the Corps. It has fought

71   Frank Oliver (1853-1933) was owner of the Edmonton *Bulletin* and a Liberal Member of Parliament from Alberta (1896-1921).

continuously and has never once failed, a record I am assured which is enjoyed by no other similar formation.

Thanking you for all your good wishes, which I most cordially reciprocate, I am,

Yours ever,

A.W. Currie

Currie to Dudley Oliver, 30 November 1917[72]

Dear Mr. Oliver,

I am greatly concerned over reports which come to me indicating that the return to power in Canada of the Union Government is by no means certain. I am not much interested in governments, but I am deeply interested in the state of the Military Service Act. I believe that if its operation is interfered with, or even delayed, that such a thing would be a catastrophe. It would mean the death of the Canadian Corps. You probably know as well as I do just what reinforcements we have available in England, and you must also know that they will be all used up in a very short time. If other men are not forthcoming, it means that the Canadian Corps as a fighting unit will practically disappear. It will also mean that Canada will not only have deserted the men here but will practically have deserted the Empire as well. The death struggle is fast approaching; the Empire must see it through; and if we do not play our part to the end it will mean almost that we do not care to remain a part of that Empire.

You know how I have always tried to keep politics out of the Corps, and how I have refrained from taking any part in or giving any opinion in matters controversial, yet I am as interested in this for the sake of the Corps that I would do anything I possibly could to see that its strength and fighting efficiency was maintained. I am considering the advisability of sending a message to Canada. If I did send such a message, it would mean that I might practically have to submit my resignation at the same time. Much as I would dislike to do this, I would have no hesitation in so acting if the situation demanded it. Over here we learn that circumstances often demand the sacrifice of the individual.

None of my correspondents in Canada tell me that the fate of the Government is uncertain. The only information suggesting that such a thing is likely comes to me from Sims and from Sir George Perley. Whether these men are unduly

72   File 3, vol 2, CP, LAC. Dudley W. Oliver (born 1874) was manager of the Bank of Montreal's London offices during the Great War.

nervous or not I do not know. I know that you must be in receipt of considered opinion, and I am writing to ask if you will be good enough to give me the benefit of the information in your possession, or can you, through the means at your disposal, get an unbiased opinion. My action will be largely governed by what you are able to tell me. I apologise for troubling you in this manner but believe you will not mind.

With best wishes always, ever yours faithfully,

A.W. Currie

Diary Entry, 1 December 1917

Fine. Inspected Neuville St. Vaast camps in morning, office in afternoon. Boche make large and successful attack in Cambrai area on 30th taking many guns and claiming some 4,000 prisoners. They overran two divisional headquarters (the 12th: Scott,[73] and 55th: Jeudwine[74]). Bad day.

Dudley Oliver to Currie, 3 December 1917[75]

My dear Sir Arthur:

On receipt of your letter this morning I at once called on Mr. Hector McInnes, who is representing the Premier of Canada over here in connection with the elections and is his most confidential man and the man who is best informed on all Canadian affairs in London at the present time.

I need hardly tell you that your letter caused me a great deal of anxiety and worry as surely you must know that without you in your position at the front the Canadian Corps would, in my opinion, deteriorate and lose its present standing which is the highest in France. And for this reason I wished to assure myself that there was no possibility of your doing this but feeling that I was not in a position to alone take the responsibility of advising you, I had Mr. McInnes interview Lord Beaverbrook.

I need not tell you that both of these men will treat your letter as strictly confidential, but evidently Lord Beaverbrook was as much upset as I was and I understand over the telephone that he has already telegraphed you to this effect.

I have no idea as to what message you intended sending to Canada, but at the present time your duty to Canada is certainly where you are, and if the troops

73   Major General Sir Arthur B. Scott (1862-1944) was commanding officer of the 12th Division (from 1915).
74   Lieutenant General Sir Hugh S. Jeudwine (1862-1942) was commanding officer of 55th Division (from 1916).
75   File 3, vol 2, CP, LAC.

will only support the Union, as I feel sure they will, I do not think there is a chance that they will not be returned to power. This morning the feeling before I saw Mr. McInnes was that some of the pessimistic views which you heard expressed are largely indulged in as a means to stimulate interest and I find that the best opinions incline to the belief that in the last analysis, Canada will vote the right way. Sentiment is turning more and more in our favour, principally because of the methods adopted by the Opposition. For instance, farmers in Ontario who might otherwise be influenced by the $2.25 wheat are expected now on the Election Day to come to the conclusion that it is a question of French domination for all time or no French domination unless the Union Government is elected.

Voting here seems to be going very well and will be a landslide if one may judge from what one sees and hears and the total vote in Great Britain and Europe will be from a quarter to one third of the total vote, say one third of what the vote would have been under the former franchise, that is without mothers, widows, wives and sisters, or a quarter under the present franchise. Laurier[76] will carry all Quebec with the exception of some four to six seats, but he must get sixty to seventy seats elsewhere in Canada, which good opinion says he cannot do...

With my very kindest regards, yours most sincerely,

Dudley Oliver

Currie to Dudley Oliver, c. 7 December 1917 (undated)[77]

Dear Mr. Oliver,

I wish to thank you sincerely for your letters of the past week. Your advice has been a great help to me and I am quite sure it is eminently sound. One can readily see how one's every action is misinterpreted by politicians these days. I cannot understand how a man like Sir Wilfrid Laurier could descend to such false and dishonourable conduct, and could wilfully lie in the hope of getting some advantage for his party. It is very annoying to me to be mixed up in this party strife. The Government seem bound to associate me with them, and that

---

76   Sir Wilfrid Laurier (1841-1919) was the Liberal Prime Minister from 1896 to 1911 and leader of the opposition during the Great War. Laurier supported the war effort but did not support Borden's Military Service Act and refused to join the Union Government in 1917. See O.D. Skelton, *Life and Letters of Sir Wilfrid Laurier* (Toronto: Oxford University Press, 1921).

77   File 3, vol 2, CP, LAC.

being the case the Opposition are bound to knock me every chance they get. You know that I do not wish to be associated with anything political...

Yours faithfully,

A.W. Currie

Diary Entry, 8 December 1917

Fine, With Watson saw engineers and machine gun company of 4th Division in morning. Lunched with him and saw 12th Brigade at training in afternoon. Informed by General [illegible] that Belgian King had conferred on me *Grand Officier de l'ordre de la Couronne* with Belgian *Croix de Guerre*. Harold Daly[78] arrived in afternoon. He and Cy Peck to dinner. Peck told me Argyll House was wondering how I was really going to vote.

During the election, mud was viciously thrown by both the Liberals and the Unionists. The Liberals accused Borden of tricking the Quebec electorate in the 1911 election when he had painted Laurier as the militarist and imperialist. Now, they said, Borden was the one conscripting citizens for Imperial wars. On the other side, the Unionists questioned the patriotism of the Liberal politicians arguing that they had abandoned the war effort and the Empire by failing to join the Union Government. Sir Arthur Currie was caught in the crossfire between the two sides. Because he was overseas fighting a war, he had little hope of defending himself against these baseless accusations.[79]

Currie to Sir George Perley, 10 December 1917[80]

Dear Sir George,

Today I received a telegram from Canada addressed to 'General Sir Arthur Currie, or to the Acting Commander of the Canadian Corps.' This telegram was signed by Stewart Lyon[81] and many other editors of Canadian newspapers. The address indicates to me that in the minds of these gentlemen there was a doubt as to whether I was in command of the Corps, this doubt having arisen

78   Lieutenant Colonel Harold Mayne Daly (1880-1969) was a British Columbia lawyer and Boer War Veteran. Daly was a staff officer during the Great War and became an important figure in the Conservative Party after the war.

79   On the divisive election, see Morton and Granatstein, 170-89; Robert Craig Brown and Ramsay Cook, Canada, *1896-1921: A Nation Transformed* (Toronto: McClelland and Stewart, 1976). An interesting (albeit sensationalist) account of the election from one of Currie's most vocal detractors is, W.T.R. Preston, *My Generation of Politics and Politicians* (Toronto: D.A. Rose Publishing Company, 1927).

80   File 3, vol 2, CP, LAC.

81   Thomas Stewart Lyon (1866-1946), the managing editor of *the Globe*.

from statements which I understand Sir Wilfrid Laurier and others of his party made in Canada to the effect that I had been removed from the command of the Corps owing to the inefficiency and the excessive number of casualties at Passchendaele. In my letter to you yesterday, I asked that some denial be made of this report by a person occupying an official position, and I suggested that either you make it in the capacity of High Commissioner for Canada, or that the Secretary of State for the Colonies deny it in a cable to the Governor General of Canada. There is no use its being denied by McInnes,[82] because he is the representative of Sir Robert Borden in England, and the people of Canada would consider that they had as much right to believe Laurier as to believe him.

I would ask you to do this in justice to myself. You know how I have striven to keep clear of politics, but both sides seem determined to mix me up in it. I do not consider that it is fair that in the propaganda issued by the Government my name should appear so prominently. When it does, the Opposition of course consider it good political tactics to throw mud, and some mud always sticks when thrown. To have gone through what anyone who has been here for three years has had to go through, and to have given the very best that is in one to the service of your country, would almost justify one in hoping that your own countrymen would not refer to you as a murderer. It seems hard to understand that as a result of the success of the Canadians at Passchendaele, where they achieved what others had tried so hard to do and had failed, the French Government should award me the *Croix de Guerre* and the Belgian Government the decoration of the *Grand Officer de l'Ordre de la Couronne* with the Belgian *Croix de Guerre* as well, and in face of all that, that your own countrymen should do their best to knife you in the back.

I think also that you have the means at your disposal not only to officially deny the statement that I have been removed from the command of the Corps, but to do something to point out how unjustified is the accusation which is being made. I have played the game with everyone from start to finish and have a right to expect that it will be played with me. Occupying the position I do, I must trust to others to see that I am not wrongly accused.

Yours faithfully,

A.W. Currie

---

82   Probably Hector McInnes.

On 17 December 1917, the Union Government was returned to power which secured the fate of the Military Service Act. Currie's Corps was thus assured the reinforcements that it required, but Sir Arthur's name had become inextricably associated with the Borden government.

Diary Entry, 21 December 1917

Fine. Left at 8:00 am for Boulogne on leave, arrived in Brighton at 10:30 pm and very much surprised [the family, they are] all at home, sat up very late. Had a long talk with Kiggell on the way over.

Except for a trip into London to make social calls and shop on Christmas Eve, Currie spent the next few days quietly in Brighton taking long walks in the afternoons.

Diary Entry, 25 December 1917 (written as 24th in diary)

Christmas Day. Fine. All very happy. Spend day quietly, go for walk in afternoon. Willis spends day with us.

Diary Entry, 27 December 1917 (written as 26th in diary)

Fine. Go to London by slow train. Oliver lunches with us. Many calls. See Kemp in afternoon...dine with Harvey Daly. See Garnet Hughes

Diary Entry, 28 December 1917 (written as 27th in diary)

Sit for picture. Lunch with Kemp and Turner. Go with latter to Argyll House. Have tea with Mrs. Chas Maclaren Mrs Bill Herridge. Dine alone with Lill.

Corps Commander, 1918

Nineteen-eighteen did not begin with promises of victory. In January, Allied fortunes were at their lowest point during the war. The Passchendaele offensive dealt a blow to the German Army but also sapped the strength of the British forces. The French Army, parts of which mutinied in the spring of 1917, was still considered unreliable. The Americans entered the war the previous spring but had yet to appear on the Western Front in significant numbers. Most significantly for the Entente, on 18 December 1917 Germany concluded an armistice with the new Bolshevik government in Russia which freed up dozens of divisions for offensive action on the Western Front. At the same time the war in Italy stagnated allowing the Germans to transfer several divisions to the West. The enemy's losses at Passchendaele were thus offset by gains from other sectors of the front while British numbers could not be so easily replaced. Manpower shortages forced the BEF to reduce the number of battalions in a division from twelve to nine, increasing the proportion of artillery and machine guns to infantry, but effectively cutting the rifle strength of a British corps by about one quarter.

The Canadian manpower situation was better. In December, the Borden government won the federal election, thus securing an untapped source of replacements. When the War Office ordered the Canadian Corps to reorganize its divisions along the lines of the new nine-battalion division, Currie and Borden were able to refuse, arguing that a less efficient fighting formation would be the result. Conscription and the break-up of the 5th Canadian Division in England allowed Canada to maintain the strength of the Canadian Corps and even increase the establishment of each battalion by 100 men. In 1918 the Canadian Corps became the largest Commonwealth corps on the Western Front with a strength almost double that of its British counterparts. Whether it was prudent

for Canada to maintain such a robust presence on the Western Front when the British were lowering their own numbers is a matter for debate.[1]

Diary Entry, 2 January 1918[2]

Very fine. Brothers comes in morning. Take family to show in afternoon. In evening have fun with the kiddies. Last night with them. God bless them.

Diary Entry, 3 January 1918

Leave Brighton by motor for London, give Major Jack nearly two hours at studio. Lunch with Kemp at Ritz. Others present Sir William Robertson, Walter Long,[3] Perley, Gow,[4] Turner...dine with Lillie, set out with Harold Daly.

Currie returned to France on 4 January.

Diary Entry, 9 January 1918

Fine but cold. Lecture at Corps School, lunch with Tuxford.[5] Snows very heavily all afternoon. Odlum's[6] raid successful. Two machine guns captured.

Diary Entry, 11 January 1918

Visited Hayter[7] and 10th Brigade Headquarters. Raining. General Turner comes in afternoon to discuss proposed changes in organization. Odlum calls in evening.

Diary Entry, 18 January 1918

Raining. Sir Edward Kemp arrives at 5:00 pm to discuss question of re-organization. Some French officers arrive as well and dine with us.

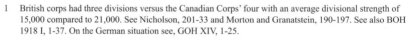

1   British corps had three divisions versus the Canadian Corps' four with an average divisional strength of 15,000 compared to 21,000. See Nicholson, 201-33 and Morton and Granatstein, 190-197. See also BOH 1918 I, 1-37. On the German situation, see GOH XIV, 1-25.
2   Diary entries from January-May 1918 are transcribed from the original, hand written diaries in file 191, vol 43, CP, LAC.
3   Sir Walter Long (1854-1924) was the British Colonial Secretary under Lloyd George (1916-19).
4   Colonel Walter Gow (born 1872) was the Deputy Minister of the Overseas Military Forces of Canada.
5   Brigadier General George Stuart Tuxford (1870-1943) was commanding officer of 3rd Brigade (from March 1916).
6   Brigadier General Victor Wentworth Odlum (1880-1971) was commanding officer of 11th Brigade (from July 1916).
7   General Ross John Hayter (born 1875) was commanding officer of 10th Brigade (December 1917-October 1918), and Brigadier General, General Staff, Canadian Corps (from October 1918).

Diary Entry, 19 January 1918

Kemp goes to 4th Division, to 3rd Division lunches with Army Commander. Many brigadiers etc. 1st and 2nd Divisions here to meet him. We have a long interview again in afternoon. He leaves with Sims about 5:30 pm for Boulogne. Some French officers dine with us again. Concert after dinner, during day they were shown maps, plans, etc. of Vimy Ridge and battle was explained then going over ground with general staff

Diary Entry, 20 January 1918

Fine though dull in office in morning and most of afternoon. Army Commander calls and has tea. Go to church in evening to hear De Pencier.[8]

Diary Entry, 21 January 1918

Dull some rain. Attend funeral of General Sheppard head Flying Corps of First Army who was killed on Saturday. It is thought he fainted and so lost control of his machine. Tenth Battalion[9] furnished firing party. Second Division relieves 4th. French officers visit schools and machine gun depots. Their last evening is very jolly evening. Go to new theatre opened at Camblain l'Abbé by YMCA.

The bitter December election had lasting effects for Currie. Rumours began to circulate that he was unfit, that his health had failed, or that he was on the verge of being removed from command. Some of the gossip probably originated with Sam Hughes and his friends, but the federal election had politicised Currie and the Canadian Corps and left him with many enemies, known and unknown. The Corps Commander was unused to public criticism and he had a difficult time understanding the allegations. Perhaps he misread his role as an eminent Canadian representing the country abroad and the bitterness in Canada as the country was tearing itself asunder during the election. Rumours about health problems were especially troubling to Currie as he did suffer occasional bouts of debilitating diarrhea and nausea in times of high stress. Perhaps there was more truth in the rumours than the gossips in England and Canada knew.[10]

8   Bishop Adam de Pencier was the Bishop of New Westminster, British Columbia.
9   May also be 16th Battalion as the original is unclear.
10 See Dancocks, 123-5; Hyatt, 96-7. See Cook, 'The Madman and the Butcher,' 703-4 and Hyatt, 'Arthur Currie and Conscription.'

Currie to Charles Swayne, 23 January 1918[11]

Dear Charlie,

How good of you to write to me. Your letter must have arrived at Corps Headquarters a day or so after I went on leave about Christmas time. I think I left here on December 21st, and spent the next two weeks with my family who are now living down at Brighton. It was the first Christmas and New Years that I have had with them in five years, and to say that we enjoyed it very much is to put it very mildly. While I was away on leave, I intended to have a good leave and so gave instructions that none of my mail was to be forwarded to me. I tried to forget the war for the fortnight, yet such a thing was of course impossible. When I got back about the 5th of January there was so much to do that it is only now that I find the time to say to you how very much I appreciate your kindness in remembering me. I remember as well the days when we used to walk through the reserve together, or else take the same tram into town, or home again at night.

I thank you very much, Charlie, for the kind words in which you have referred to my services in this war. Any success that has come to me has been won for me by the wonderful soldiers I have been privileged to command. I cannot begin to express to you the regard in which the Canadians are held in the Allied armies. They are looked upon as being the most efficient Corps on the whole Western Front. There are many factors which contribute to that efficiency. In the first place, our men are full of resource and when a difficulty or situation confronts which has not been provided for, they are not the kind to stand around and do nothing simply because they have 'no instructions.' It is always well in such circumstances to do something, and the natural common sense, which is such a pronounced Canadian characteristic, usually tells one the best thing to do nine times out of ten. Then our chaps are peculiarly quick to learn, and they are not casual. This is a job which must be done, and the more we learn about killing Germans the sooner peace will be declared and the sooner we can get back to Canada, therefore, we study our job thoroughly, and in the execution of our plans nothing is left to chance. Our fellows are also full of grit, determination, and initiative. Where there is a will, there is a way, and with us difficulties are made only to be overcome. I can give so many instances to show where the initiative of the Canadians has helped greatly. For instance, good roads are essential to

---

11   File 4, vol 2, CP, LAC; Charles Robert Swayne (1880-1943) was editor of the Victoria *Colonist* (1917-43).

victory, and with heavy traffic and bad weather many of the roads in this country become quagmires. We thought that plank roads, somewhat after the lines of the old corduroy roads of Ontario, would serve a useful purpose. We suggested it and were pooh-poohed at first, yet finally we were given permission to go ahead. Then there were no planks available, and none could be brought up. We next suggested that we be given a saw-mill, and permission to cut down trees in the forest near where we were preparing to fight. In due time we got this saw-mill, set it up, and made our own planks and our own roads. These roads proved such a boom that they are now generally in use up and down the whole front. Our men are well disciplined. To me, discipline is simply the self-control which makes you do the right thing at all times. We are given a conscience which tells us what is right, and what is wrong, and at our schools and in our training camps we are taught the right way of doing military things. If we have the self-control to do that right thing always, we are well disciplined, and in the Canadian Corps I am proud to say the standard of discipline set and maintained is high. That our men are gallant and determined fighters has been proved on many hard-fought fields of battle. Furthermore, a strong feeling of confidence in each other permeates the Corps. The officers have confidence in the men, and the men have confidence in the officers. If a man is set above his fellows in that he is given non-commissioned or commissioned rank, he must deliver the goods or give way to somebody who can. It makes no difference who or what he is, or who or what he has been; if he is the right man in the right place, he will be promoted rewarded, if not, he loses his job. The result is that every man in the Corps knows that he stands on his own two feet. And so I say that confidence in each other is an outstanding feature, and without confidence you cannot win many battles. Then the morale is very high. This is owing chiefly to the record of victories won. Our Corps has been uniformly very successful. The men have tasted victory, and nothing but victory will satisfy them. Do you know that there are units in this Corps who have served now for nearly three years in France, and who in all that time have never lost a single inch of ground, have never failed to take and consolidate every objective assigned to them?...

The year 1917 was a truly wonderful year for the Corps, and now let me tell you something which you will scarcely believe, our casualties were less last year than the year before in these units which were in the field throughout both years. You will remember one of our divisions only took the field in the middle of 1916. In the spring of 1917, we carried out a great many very successful raids;

then came Vimy; later on in the same month Arleux; in May we had the battles of Fresnoy and the Generating Station; in June we had Avion; during July we had a lot of fighting in the outskirts of Lens; and in August fought one of the most successful fights in our history—the battle of Hill 70. Things were quieter in September, and in October we moved back to the old Ypres Salient, there to engage in one of the hardest, and one of the most successful fights of the war, the culmination of which was the taking of Passchendaele. In this connection you will pardon me for mentioning a personal thing which happened today. Lieutenant General Orth, representing the Belgian King, came to Corps Headquarters today and invested me with the *Grand Officier del Ordre de la Couronne*, and the Belgian *Croix de Guerre* as well. I received this distinction solely on account of the magnificent work of the Canadians at Passchendaele. I may also say that the French, after that battle, awarded me the French *Croix de Guerre*. I know that some try to convey the impression that the battle of Passchendaele was too costly. It is true that our casualties were heavy, but before we fought our first battle on the 26th October I gave the higher authorities an estimate of what our casualties would be, and I was within two hundred of the right figure. We fought there four battles, and in each were eminently successful, winning the highest praise from the Commander-in-Chief and many others. It is impossible for me to tell you all the story of that fight; and besides many excellent accounts of it have appeared in the press. In connection with it, I do not know which branch of the service is entitled to the most praise. The infantry who stormed the hostile trenches and beat off the counter-attacks, the artillery who prepared the way for the infantry and who supported the attacks, the engineers and pioneers who made the roads which enabled the guns to be brought forward, thus made victory possible, the medical services who have always done so well, but who excelled all past performance in these battles, the supply people who never failed once in getting forward rations, engineer materiel and munitions of all kinds, all gave evidence of the highest soldierly qualities and the determination to win. We left there in November, and have been in the line ever since. Ever since its formation nearly two and a half years ago the Canadian Corps has never been out of the line, only when moving from one place to another.

In December it was our turn to receive news of the great victory in Canada, and nothing that we have ever performed in France has more inspired the people of Canada than their message to us on December 17th.[12] We know that the people of Canada are determined to back this Corps with all the strength at their disposal, and we here are more than ever determined to prove ourselves worthy of the confidence and trust imposed in us. While a soldier in the field has no time to indulge in matters political, yet all were most keenly interested in the result of the election. There were some who tried to stampede us into believing that the opponents of the Military Service Act would win. They told us that Canada was enjoying such prosperity that their thoughts were all on material gain rather than on sacrifice, yet those of us who have for more than three years now seen men sacrifice everything, even life itself, for what they believed to be right, could not believe that the fathers and mothers, the sisters and brothers, the wives of such heroes could do nothing else than support the living and keep faith with the dead. As I say, we are prouder than ever of being Canadians, prouder than ever of our Home Land, more determined then ever to guard her honour, and more ready to die in her defence.

Before closing, Charlie, I want for a moment or two to refer to personal matters. Towards the end of the election campaign there appeared in many of the papers in Canada a report that I had asked for leave; that owing to the strenuous life I had been living my health had given out and that I was about to return to Canada on furlough. I believe that some darkly hinted that I had been relieved of my command. Let me say to you that there never was the slightest foundation for either of these reports, and I have every evidence that they were put out by agencies hostile to me. I have never applied for furlough because I did not need it, as my health was never better than at the present time; my relations with the higher command have never been more cordial, and I have never had more evidence that my services were satisfactory. In due time these reports were denied, yet in many instances the unpublished denial still repeated that I had intended going on furlough but that I was remaining at the personal request of the Commander-in-Chief. This again was entirely false. You can see that even in the denial it was suggested that my health had given out. You know that before a man is retired it is often intimated that his health has failed. This report was put out by those who are jealous of my position, who would like to have it themselves or get it for their friends. My strength with the Corps is my weakness with many. The Corps know that I am not a politician and they have confidence

12   The date of the federal election.

that every man will be fairly and squarely dealt with. This attitude does not suit everyone, yet I know that it is one the people of Canada will most cordially approve of. To me the only thing that matters is the efficiency of the Canadian Corps of which the people of Canada are so proud, and which they have lately given such positive evidence to stand behind. As far as I am able I shall never allow any influence to interfere with the efficiency of the Corps, and I shall do only what I think is right on all occasions no matter who or what is affected by that determination. There are many things in connection with the Corps of which the people of Canada are ignorant, and must remain ignorant until we all get home again. I seldom see the Canadian papers and perhaps you can tell me what the people of Canada believe is the condition of my health. I know that they do not want their sons commanded by a man who is not able to give all his time and attention to his work, and if the impression can be created that my health is going it might possibly pave the way for the ambitions of others to be realized. Let me once more give you the solemn assurance that there is no truth, and never has been any truth, in the report that my health was indifferent or that I was not getting on well with the higher command.

And now I feel that I have wearied you with a long and tiresome letter. Please hand it over to dear old Sam to be read. Some time I hope to write him a long letter. I hope everything is going well with him, that his health remains good, and that good fortune will always be with him. Please remember me to all who you think would be interested, and with best wishes always.

I am, dear Charlie, ever yours a faithfully,

A.W. Currie

Currie to Harlan Brewster, 27 January, 1918[13]

My dear Mr. Brewster,

The Canadian mail received this morning brought me your letter of December 27th, and I desire at once to thank you for your, cordial good wishes for the coming year. These I must heartily reciprocate, and with you pray that the coming year will witness the return of peace. I would like to offer my congratulations to you on the manly stand you took in the recent elections. I am quite prepared to believe that those who opposed the Union Government were in many cases actuated by honest motives, yet I feel that to have done anything which would

13   File 1, vol 1, CP, LAC.

mean interference with the immediate operation of the Military Service Act would be a calamity. I know that many people in Canada did not understand the urgent need of reinforcements, and possibly they were not to blame for their ignorance because in many published statements they were told the number of men who had been enlisted and were not told the number of enlistments which were of no use to us, yet 'all's well that ends well,' and we here have every confidence that the new government will do everything possible to keep Canada's fighting forces in the field at full fighting strength. The message received from Canada on December 17th was an inspiration to us all. It made us more than ever proud of our Home Land, and more than ever determined to act so as to always merit the approval of our countrymen there.

I suppose it is impossible to have it otherwise, but many false impressions gain ground in Canada. I know the people think that last year the casualties were very high. That is true, yet it is also true that the casualties in 1917 were less than those in 1916, although in 1917 there were a great many battles fought; in fact, it was almost one continuous battle. When I say the casualties were less last year than the year before I am referring to the 1st, 2nd, and 3rd Divisions, and not to the 4th Division, because the latter was here only six months in 1916, and so cannot be included in the comparison. Very wrong statements have been made in Canada about the casualties here. For instance, the Honourable Frank Oliver is reported to have said that the casualties at Hill 70 were the most severe yet sustained. Such a statement is absolutely false. Again, it has been stated that the casualties at Passchendaele were as great as those at the Somme. That statement is also very false. I shall not attempt to describe to you the conditions under which the last battle was fought because so much has already appeared concerning it in the Canadian press, but I will say this, that never have we fought under worse conditions. It was at the very end of the season when bad weather had set in, when roads, trails and other communications were at their worst, and when there was much evidence of that tired feeling which comes after great hardships have been endured. We went to Passchendaele because it was absolutely necessary for it to be taken. All other troops in the British Army, with the exception of the Canadians, had tried, and to make absolutely certain of success we were brought there. No finer feat of arms has ever been performed in this or any other war. No one regrets casualties more than I do. I regret them more than people in Canada because the latter have no idea, and can have no idea, of the conditions under which battles are fought or victories won. Criticism, a public man like you has long since found out, is oft times very cruel. No army can win battles without confidence in itself and in its leaders, and the fact that the Canadians have been so uniformly successful testifies in the highest possible manner not only to their fine fighting qualities but to the confidence which exists between all ranks. I know and the men know that I shall never ask them to attack until every possible preparation has been made, every possible reconnaissance carried out, every possible detail arranged for, and every plan minutely scrutinized and approved, and I also know that when Canadians attack under these conditions success must come, and will come.

I note that you say that you have read with some interest of my application for furlough, and you were good enough to say that you were disappointed that I was not able to get away. I would like to say, Mr. Brewster, that at no time have I ever applied for furlough, nor thought of applying for furlough. I am not staying because the Commander-in-Chief asked me, because there was no reason for his asking me to stay. To anyone who has been constantly at the front for three years the strain is bound to be severe, yet I am glad to tell you that my health was never better than it is at the present time, nor was I ever more anxious to stay and see the thing through. I feel that I have learned a great deal in the last three years about beating the Boche. The knowledge I have can be put to the best use right here, and here I am determined to remain as long as I am able to. As an old friend, I may tell you that there are some who would like to have the position in which I now am, and I am quite certain that they are the ones who initiated this propaganda; they are the ones who have tried to create the impression in the public mind of Canada that my health was gone, and that a change would be desirable. I would also like to say that my relations with the higher command were never more cordial than they are now. I suppose one should not worry about false reports of this character, yet one does not like to think that not only are one's friends, but the public generally in Canada, misinformed, and that those who are guilty of sending forth false reports are doing so from purely selfish and unpatriotic motives.

...Please remember me most kindly to any of my friends whom you run across, and with best wishes always,

I am ever yours faithfully,

A.W. Currie

Currie to Lord Beaverbrook, 27 January 1918[14]

Dear Lord Beaverbrook,

I acknowledge the receipt of your letter of the 22nd instant, and am glad to have your assurance that the statement regarding my proposed furlough did not originate with the *Canadian Daily Record*. It is hard to understand, though, how such a statement could originate in Ottawa, as the news must first have been sent to them from this side of the Atlantic. I know that in the Canadian press at that time a great many statements appeared about my health giving way, about my application for furlough, about my being relieved of the command of the Canadian Corps, etc. These were in due time denied, yet in many instances the denial was as bad as the original statement for it indicated that while I was not going on leave my health was still indifferent. I know that these reports were very persistent, and I have the firm belief that it was propaganda on somebody's part. I am very glad to be able to tell you that my health was never better than at the present time. I eat well, sleep well, think clearly, and am as happy as it is possible for anybody to be in similar circumstances. If those who would like to see me removed from the command of the Canadian Corps hope that such a thing will be brought about in the near future on account of my health, I am afraid they are likely to be disappointed.

Returning again to the item which appeared in the *Canadian Daily Record*, I probably expressed myself rather badly to Hughes. What I did say was this, that the *Canadian Daily Record* was sufficiently *au fait* with the facts to know that I had not applied for furlough, and that the Commander-in-Chief had not asked me to remain, so that even if such a cable were sent out from Canada there was no need of republishing it here, particularly when it conveyed an entirely false impression. In conclusion let me say that I know full well that your constant desire is to assist Canadians in every way that lies in your power, and that in the past you have on many occasions given evidence of your wish and ability to so act. I thank you very much for the assurance of your firm belief in the efficiency of your fellow Canadians.

With cordial good wishes,

I am ever yours faithfully,

---

14 File 1, vol 1, CP, LAC; Sir William Maxwell Aitken (1879-1964) was a newspaper baron and the head of the Canadian War Records office for much of the war. He was also involved in the intrigues which brought down the Asquith government. Currie believed that Beaverbrook was similarly involved in the intrigues against him. See Tim Cook, 'Documenting War and Forging Reputations: Sir Max Aitken and the Canadian War Records Office in the First World War,' *War in History* 10, 2 (2003): 157-87.

A.W. Currie

PS—As I have mentioned the word 'propaganda' in the above letter I want to make it clear to you that I have never associated the *Canadian Daily Record* with the initiation or dissemination of this propaganda.

Diary Entry, 29 January 1918

Very fine. In company with Morrison and O'Connor went to Boulogne to hospital to attend funeral of Lieutenant Colonel John McCrae,[15] author of 'In Flanders Fields.' Large attendance. On way home called at Number 7 General to see Lou Patterson found her looking better but still much in need of rest ...

Diary Entry, 5 February 1918

With Farmar and Lindsay go to England calling at Erin to see Commander-in-Chief and discuss with him proposed changes. Lunch at Boulogne, arrive London 9:30 go to Brighton arriving there 12:30 am. Found all well.

Diary Entry, 6 February 1918

Leave Brighton for London at 8:00 am. Conference with Kemp at 11:00. Gow and Turner to lunch, leave at 4:00 pm. Tea and dinner at Carlton. Lillie goes to theatre with O'Connor. I go to bed.

Diary Entry, 7 February 1918

Fine. Busy all morning preparing memorandum re new organization and engineer services for Kemp. Dudley Oliver very kind to send stenographer and machine to Carlton. See Kemp, Gow and Turner at 3:00. Get back to hotel at 7:00. Oliver and [illegible] drive with us.

Currie to Sir Edward Kemp, 7 February 1918[16]

Sir,

With reference to the question as to whether the Canadian Corps should be reorganized, into divisions consisting of nine battalions each, I am strongly against the proposal. My reasons are as follows:

---

15 Lieutenant Colonel John McCrae (1872-1918) was a Canadian doctor, Boer War veteran, and author of *In Flanders Fields*.
16 Reel C4330, vol 98, BP, LAC.

A. The Commander-in-Chief in France at an interview on Tuesday, February 5th informed me that he knew of no reason making the reorganization in any way necessary or desirable at the present time. It is true that Imperial divisions are now in process of reorganization on these lines, but the conditions entailing this change, do not in any way apply to the Canadian Corps. The main factor necessitating the change is the question of manpower. In view of the shortage of recruits, it is necessary either to reduce the number of Imperial divisions in the field, or to reduce their establishment. For reasons which do not affect the question under consideration, it was decided to reduce the establishment of Imperial infantry brigades by one battalion in each brigade, and with the personnel thus set free, to bring the remaining three battalions up to their full establishment. It is, however, open to question whether this step would have been taken had not the means been at hand to bring up infantry brigades to the number of battalions (four) which has been found by experience to be the most desirable composition of a brigade. It is understood that the battalion disbanded in each brigade is to be replaced in time by an American battalion, thus serving the double object of restoring the four battalion organization which has stood the test of experience and by close association with trained units and staffs, of training American troops in the conditions obtaining in France more quickly and effectively than would otherwise be possible. The Commander-in-Chief gave me to understand that he considered that no necessity existed to attach American battalions to Canadian formations, for many reasons I strongly deprecate such attachment, and to reduce the number of battalions in a brigade would be to invite it.

B. The manpower question does not, at present, affect the Canadian Corps. Drafts are in sight which should be sufficient to maintain it for a reasonable period.

C. The Canadian Corps has proved itself to be an effective and smoothly working fighting machine. To alter its constitution would be to run a very great risk of reducing the striking value of the force, with no compensating advantages. The suggested reorganization would not entail, as in the case of Imperial formations, the disbandment of one battalion, in each brigade, but a re-shuffling of existing battalions in order to reduce existing brigades to three battalions each and to form new brigades. The four battalions composing existing Canadian infantry brigades have served together under many conditions and have fought side by side in many successful battles. Strong feelings of *esprit de corps* and comradeship have been engendered by this common building up of high traditions. It is hard to over-rate the value of these feelings, which must be to some extent sacrificed if the suggested reorganization takes place. I regard this as a very strong reason why a change should not be made.

E. [sic] The main object in view, both of the War Office and of Canada, is to put the greatest possible number of men in the fighting line at the least expenditure of manpower and money. This object may be gained more economically than by accepting the present suggestion. At present there are in France forty-eight Canadian infantry battalions, organized into four divisions of twelve battalions each. The suggested reorganization into six divisions of nine battalions each (total fifty-four battalions) would, therefore, as far as infantry is concerned, entail the despatch to France of six additional battalions, giving a total addition in round figures of 6,000 men. The number of men per battalion on command, on regimental and extra regimental employ, and, therefore, not available for the fighting line, coupled with the number whom we are ordered to leave out of a battle—those ordered to be left out are largely officers, senior NCOs and specialists, who in case the battalion suffered severe losses would form a nucleus around which it would be rebuilt—may be taken at 400, thus leaving 600 men in each battalion or 3,600 men in the six new battalions available to go over the top. In order to increase the hitting power of the Canadian Corps by this 3,600 men, the suggested organization would involve the creation of six new brigade staffs, two new divisional staffs and one corps staff. This I submit is increasing out of all proportion, the overhead charges, and marks the suggestion as un-businesslike.

In place of the suggestion, I recommend the addition of 100 men surplus to the establishment of each Canadian infantry battalion. This would increase the fighting strength of the Corps by 1,200 more men than the new organization gives, without the increase in staffs, employed men mentioned above, battalion headquarters and transport. It is essential that the 100 men per battalion should be part of the battalion, and should be in no way regarded as reinforcements under the control of the Deputy Adjutant General, Base. Experience has shown that the machinery of existing battalions is capable of dealing with this increase, and I know of no difficulties of supply or administration which cannot be easily overcome. Furthermore, the tactical unit is now the platoon. Unless platoons are fully up to strength, this organization, which comprises a small number of men trained in each of several different functions must suffer in efficiency.

At present, rather than carry out an attack with four weak platoons, companies are frequently reorganized temporarily into three strong platoons, thus losing the proved advantage of the 'square' organization (four platoons to a company, four companies to a battalion, four battalions to a brigade). The necessity for this makeshift and undesirable reorganization of companies, will be obviated by the addition of the 100 men per battalion I ask for, and we can go into a fight with what we believe, and what experience has proved to be the strongest possible fighting organization.

F. The time may come when Canada may find it difficult to produce the reinforcements necessary to maintain the Corps at the establishment, increased either by the addition of six battalions or by the addition of 100 men per battalion as I suggest. I submit that in this case it would be far easier to reduce battalions to normal establishments (i.e. less the 100 additional men) than to reduce the number of battalions or the normal establishment of a battalion. The bad effect on efficiency of the latter alternative has been sufficiently proved.

G. To consider the question of staffs—with the resources in men at present at the disposal of Canada, the reorganization proposed would allow the formation of six divisions. This number is somewhat excessive to be handled as one corps, and it would probably be necessary to organize into two corps, with the corollary of a force headquarters to command and administer them.

Including the 5th Canadian Division, the following staffs of larger formations now exist:

> One Corps Staff
>
> Five Divisional Staffs

The new organization would require the following:

> One Canadian Force Staff
>
> Two Corps Staffs
>
> Five Divisional Staffs

or an increase of three staffs of larger formations. It is pointed out that in the case of Imperial divisions no increase of staffs is necessary. This would necessitate an expansion of thirty-three per cent of existing staffs.

Canadian staff officers are of an excellent class, and have been trained on an effective system in the best of all possible schools—practical experience in the field.

At the same time their experience has been of limited duration and many of them are very young, and I am convinced that to carry out this sudden large

expansion would be to water down to an extent which must impair the efficiency of staff work, with inevitable reaction on the fighting troops and corresponding diminuation [sic] of the present very high value of the Canadian Corps.

H. The provision of personnel for specialist services necessary to complete the new formations entailed by the suggested reorganization, machine gun services, signal services, and engineers, presents great difficulties and could not be made at short notice.

I. I consider it desirable that the Corps be strengthened and made more nearly self-supporting in the matter of heavy artillery, but this can be effected by the addition of heavy batteries, without in any way altering the existing formations...

In the foregoing arguments I have endeavoured to show that the small addition proposed by me will make a far more efficient fighting force, and will produce more actual fighting men, at much smaller cost, than would be the case if reorganization were carried out by the Canadian Corps on the lines adopted in the case of Imperial divisions.

In conclusion I can only say that I have the firmest convictions that there is no good business reason, neither is there any good military reason why the proposed reorganization should be carried out in the Canadian Corps.

A.W. Currie

Diary Entry, 9 February 1918

Fine. Spent morning interviewing people. General Hille, Sir Clifford Sifton,[17] Sir Campbell Stuart;[18] Oliver gives luncheon party. Sir Chas Parsons,[19] Odlum, Willis, Lillie, Mrs. Oliver, myself and [illegible]. After lunch we motor to Brighton, find all well.

Diary Entry, 10 February 1918

Fine. Go to church with Marjorie and Garner in morning. In afternoon for drive with Lillie and children. Clark comes at 4:00 stays to 10:00.

17 Sir Clifford Sifton (1861-1929) was the former Minister of Immigration in the Laurier Government and spent much of the war in Great Britain where he worked behind the scenes to bring western Liberals into the Union Government. See D.J. Hall, *Clifford Sifton* (Vancouver: UBC Press, 1981).

18 Lieutenant Colonel Sir Campbell Stuart (1885-1972) was born in Montreal, Stuart was the Military Attaché in the British Embassy in the United States (1917-18) and was director of the *London Times* during the interwar period.

19 Possibly Sir Charles Algernon Parsons (1854-1931), the inventor of the steam turbine and naval engineer.

On 11 February Currie returned to France.

Diary Entry, 14 February 1918

Misty in morning. Army Commander presented Belgian decorations... In evening we had a dinner at officers club of all those who came out with the 1st Canadian Division three years ago as officers and who are now in it. There were about 110 present and we had a splendid time. I was almost overcome by the warmth of my reception. Speeches were made by Watson, Lipsett, Burstall, Macdonell, Morrison, Radcliffe, Farmar, Prince Arthur, Dudley Oliver and myself. It was a very enjoyable and successful reunion.

Diary Entry, 19 February 1918

Very fine... In afternoon the monument erected to the memory of the gunners at Le Tilleuls was unveiled by me. Many officers of Canadian and Imperial artillery. Generals Horne and Byng present. Lipsett calls at Corps Headquarters. Early this morning the 6th Brigade (27th Battalion) successfully raid hostile trenches in Avion capturing six prisoners, we had two men slightly wounded.

[handwritten annotation: Very NB: Why is the 6th Brigade also called the 27th Battalion?]

Currie to the Lord Bishop of Fredericton, 21 February 1918[20]

My dear Lord Bishop,

...We are all very busy here now getting prepared for the coming German offensive, not doubting our ability to defeat him no matter when he comes. As a result of my visit to England I was able to obtain the sanction of the minister to certain proposals which, I am sure, will make us a strong fighting organization and a greater hitting force than ever. The Canadian Corps was never more conscious of its power nor confident of its ability to worthily uphold Canada's honour than it is today. In our struggle here it is a great comfort and inspiration to know that the people of Canada are whole heartedly supporting us and praying for us. I am very glad indeed that I have been privileged to meet you, and hope to see you again in Canada.

Ever yours faithfully,

A.W. Currie

---

20 File 1, vol 1, CP, LAC.

Diary Entry, 23 February 1918

Fine. Commander-in-Chief inspects our defences. Meet him at Thelus with Army Commander. Have Prince Axel and officers of Danish navy to lunch. At 3:00 pm, Commander-in-Chief comes to Corps Headquarters and meets officers. Expresses himself as greatly pleased ...

At the beginning of March, Currie spent much of his time inspecting units, receiving visitors, and meeting with his officers. Everyone was expecting the German Spring Offensive to begin at any time, but it was unclear where the blow would fall. All the Corps Commander could do was wait and prepare for the coming offensive. As he describes in his Report to the Ministry, the Canadian Corps spent most of its time laying wire, building strong defensive positions, and creating secure communication networks. These were nervous days for Currie and the BEF.[21]

Diary Entry, 10 March 1918

Very fine. In morning inspected machine gun units at Auchel. In afternoon with many others, witness shooting by field guns against dummy tanks at Vimy Ridge. Rode over with Brothers.

Diary Entry, 11 March 1918

Very fine. In morning addressed YMCA representatives and visit headquarters 1st Division. In afternoon rode to Verdrel to inspect Motor Machine Gun Brigade. Found it bad... It is thought the coming German offensive will begin in a few days. Most likely places on this army front: Bois Grenier, Neuve Chapelle, Hill 70; on other fronts: Arras, Cambrai.

Currie to Sir Edward Kemp, 13 March 1918[22]

Dear Sir Edward,

...While writing to you, let me tell you that last night we carried out two successful raids against the enemy. Each raiding party brought back a prisoner, identifying a distinct regiment in each case. They killed a great many Germans, blew up many dug-outs with mobile charges, destroyed several trench mortar and

---

21 See Morton and Granatstein, 177-8. On British preparations, see BOH 1918 I, 38-134. On German planning for the Spring Offensive, see GOH XIV, 50-92.
22 File 2, vol 1, CP, LAC.

machine gun emplacements, and captured a machine gun. Our own casualties were very light, only one being severely wounded.

In these days when everyone is on tip-toe expecting the German offensive to begin, it is most important to get prisoners and thereby keep in touch with what your enemy is doing and planning. The weather has been abnormally fine, and it certainly looks as if, as the French say, '*Le bon dieu est Boche.*' When one compares the weather we are having now with the weather we had last March when we were preparing for our offensive, one cannot help feeling that the Boche is having a little the best of it. Everyone is working very hard. The day is never less than seventeen hours, and there are seven days in each week.

A.W. Currie

Diary Entry, 21 March 1918

Fine, went to England at request of Minister regarding organization. Arrived 4:00 pm. Lill arrived at 6:00 pm. Kemp and Oliver to tea and dinner. Ordered to return to France.

At 4:40 am on 21 March the German offensives finally began. The blows came between the Sensée and Oise Rivers. The first day of the Kaiser's battle saw the Germans advance three miles and in some places the British broke and ran. A German breakthrough seemed possible if not probable. Although the Canadians, stationed near Vimy Ridge, escaped the attack, Canadian Cavalry and the Motor Machine Gun Brigade saw action as Currie describes in his Report to the Ministry. When the offensive began, the Corps Commander was still on leave in England.[23]

Diary Entry, 22 March 1918

Very fine. Conference at Kemp's office at 10:00. Left at 10:50, caught train at 11:20. Crossed in torpedo boat destroyer, arrived Calais 5:45 and Camblain l'Abbé at 8:00 pm. Kiddies came up in morning. [Yesterday the] German offensive began. They penetrated our battle zones and continued progress on Friday. Battle on fifty mile front. Second Division in army reserve

---

23 The most recent work on the German Spring Offensives is David T. Zabecki, *The German 1918 Offensives: A Case Study in the Operational Level of War* (London: Taylor and Francis, 2005). See also the classic Martin Middlebrook, *The Kaiser's Battle: 21 March 1918: the First Day of the German Spring Offensive* (Toronto: Penguin, 1995). On the Canadians, see Nicholson, 362-77 and Morton and Granatstein, 177-8. See also BOH 1918 I, 161-544 and GOH XIV, 105-269.

As the German blows continued to fall, GHQ informed Currie that his divisions would be extracted and placed in reserve under various British commands. On 23 March, 1st and 2nd Divisions went to the Strategic Reserve and First Army respectively. On the 26th, 3rd and 4th Divisions were ordered to Henry Horne's First Army. Without any of his divisions, Currie was temporarily without a field command. The Corps Commander understood the gravity of the situation, but he protested the breakup of the Canadian Corps. The Overseas Ministry too demanded that Haig restore the Canadian divisions to Currie's control. While Currie's insistence that the Canadian Corps only fight as a unit demonstrates his commitment to Canadian nationalism and the men under his command, his argument was militarily questionable. The British Army came remarkably close to defeat in the spring of 1918 and as Haig noted in his diary, the Canadians— the strongest formation on the Western Front—had yet to be committed to the most important battle of the war. Horne thought Currie was suffering from a swollen head, but Sir Arthur had the backing of the Canadian government. By mid April three of Currie's four divisions were back under his command.[24]

Diary Entry, 23 March 1918

Fine. Battle continues. Germans advancing...Second [Division] ordered to rendezvous near Arras. First will now be in reserve, 3rd and 4th in line.

Diary Entry, 24 March 1918

Very fine. Reports from battle front are better. Third Army has done very well. Fifth Army secure. Saw all divisions.

Currie to Sir Edward Kemp, 24 March 1918[25]

Dear Sir Edward,

I have your telegram in which you tell me that the Prime Minister would be glad to have, through you, information daily concerning the part taken by the Corps. I shall endeavour to do this as well as possible. So far the Corps has not been actively engaged. Certain readjustment of troops has taken place in order to place ourselves in the best possible position for meeting the attack, which is bound to come. I expected them to attack this morning, as there was every indication yesterday that they would. Our line has been slightly extended

---

24   See Nicholson, 378-86. See Sheffield and Bourne, 405. See also, Morton, 161-5.
25   File 2, vol 1, CP, LAC.

owing to troops being withdrawn to fill gaps elsewhere. I can give you no more information concerning the general battle than what appears in the press. I believe the Boche has assembled every available man and gun of his army on this front. I believe he hopes to separate the British from the French Army, and then to defeat the former. We are probably in the midst of the biggest crisis in the war.

Our success or otherwise depends entirely on how well we fight. As far as the Canadian Corps is concerned I promise you that it will inflict far more casualties than it receives. There is nothing more that I can tell you now.

Yours faithfully,

A.W. Currie

Diary Entry, 25 March 1918

Saw all divisions. Very fine weather. Saw machine gunner from 1st Motor Brigade. Heard from him how well our men had done, also of the confusion among men. Nurses and staff of hospital running away. Everything very windy down there, gale increasing the further back you went. Third Army holding. First and 2nd Divisions of ours out. Second working on right: bombing at night.

Diary Entry, 26 March 1918

Very fine. Saw all divisions. Army conference in afternoon. Second Division ordered south by march route. Burstall calls on way. Heavy bombing at night, high velocity guns shooting up everything in back areas.

Diary Entry, 27 March 1918

Colder but fine. Went to [illegible] Corps. First Division move by bus at night. Both 2nd and 1st reporting to X Corps. Discharged over 2,000 drums of gas. About a week ago discharged 5,000 drums, the biggest ever on the British front with very excellent results. Issue a special order.

Currie is often portrayed as a commander unable to connect with his troops on a personal level. He may have lacked charisma but he certainly tried to motivate his men. Unfortunately his efforts often fell flat with those serving at the front. High diction may have lifted the spirits at home, but it was little comfort to the men in the field.

Special Order by Lieutenant General Sir Arthur Currie, 27 March 1918[26]

In an endeavour to reach an immediate decision the enemy has gathered all his forces and struck a mighty blow at the British Army. Overwhelmed by sheer weight of numbers, the British divisions in the line between the Scarpe and the Oise have fallen back fighting hard, steady and undismayed.

Measures have been taken successfully to meet this German onslaught. The French have gathered a powerful army, commanded by a most able and trusted leader and this army is now moving swiftly to our help. Fresh British divisions are being thrown in. The Canadians are soon to be engaged. Our Motor Machine Gun Brigade has already played a most gallant part and once again covered itself with glory.

Looking back with pride on the unbroken record of your glorious achievements, asking you to realize that today the fate of the British Empire hangs in the balance, I place my trust in the Canadian Corps, knowing that where Canadians are engaged there can be no giving way.

Under the orders of our devoted officers in the coming battle you will advance or fall where you stand facing the enemy.

To those who will fall I say, 'You will not die but step into immortality. Your mothers will not lament your fate but will be proud to have borne such sons. Your hand will be revered forever and ever by your grateful country and God will take you unto Himself.'

Canadians, in this fateful hour, I command you and I trust you to fight as you have ever fought with all your strength, with all your determination, with all your tranquil courage. On many a hard fought field of battle you have overcome this enemy. With God's help you shall achieve victory once more.

As Currie issued his special order to the troops departing his command, he also penned a letter to Haig's Chief of Staff requesting that the Corps be reunited as soon as possible.[27]

---

26   Reel C4330, vol 98, BP, LAC.
27   See Nicholson, 379-82.

Currie to General Sir H.A. Lawrence, 27 March 1918[28]

My dear Lawrence,

I know that the Army Commander has represented to the Commander-in-Chief that, in the great battle now proceeding, the units of the Canadian Corps are most anxious to fight side by side, and I am sure the people of Canada wish it also.

While I do not wish for a moment to make a single suggestion that would embarrass the Chief in the slightest degree, I cannot help but point out that the best will be got out of the Corps if it fights as a unit, and now of all times we want to get the best out of everybody and every organization.

The Corps is in high spirits and will fight the Hun to Berlin or to the sea, yet if a division is thrown in here and another there, it hasn't a chance to do its best.

From the very nature and constitution of the organization it is impossible for the same liaison to exist in a British Corps as exists in the Canadian Corps. My staff and myself cannot do as well with a British Corps in this battle as we can with the Canadian Corps nor can any other corps staff do as well with the Canadian divisions as my own.

I know that necessity knows no law and that the Chief will do what he thinks best, yet for the sake of the victory we must win, get us together as soon as you can.

Ever yours faithfully,

A.W. Currie

Diary Entry, 28 March 1918

Cloudy and cold. Line holding in the south. Boche now attacking both sides of Scarpe. Third Division went under XIII Corps yesterday. Fourth Division being relieved by I Corps. We are now hurrying battalions to right of XIII Corps. High velocity gun has been shelling Ecoivres all morning. Fifteenth Division which has been moved away in buses has been stopped and is being brought back.

Diary Entry, 30 March 1918

Mixed weather. Rain, wind, cold. Take over XIII Corps' front. We now have from Souchez River to Pont de Jour. Went to First Army to see the King.

---

28 Ibid. General Sir Herbert Alexander Lawrence (1861-1943) replaced Kiggell in February 1918 as Haig's Chief of Staff.

Also called on XVII Corps. Rained very heavily all afternoon. Rawlinson has succeeded Gough who was relieved...

Diary Entry, 31 March 1918

Fine. Cloudy at times. Saw Lipsett in morning. Remained in during afternoon—Radcliffe going out to XVII and VI Corps. Every indication of an attack tomorrow. Great deal of movement in back country of enemy. XVII Corps Artillery a little windy. Seems to me both XVII and VI Corps a little windy at times. We are holding a ten mile front with two divisions. Altogether too much but owing to lack of men in British Army it cannot be helped. I am told we have 430,000 men in Mesopotamia, what a splendid place for a reserve. This is all owing to England's blasted commercialism. The situation seems better tonight.

On 6 April Brigadier General Norman William Webber arrived to replace Radcliffe as Brigadier General, General Staff, Canadian Corps. Changes were also taking place at the highest levels of command. During the March battles, the British needed French assistance as they never had before. This finally forced Douglas Haig to accept a unified system of command whereby General Foch[29] became Supreme Commander of the Entente forces at the end of March. A week and a half later, on 9 April, the second phase of the German offensive began between Armentières and La Bassée. Again the Canadian Corps missed the brunt of the assault.[30]

Diary Entry, 9 April 1918

Anniversary of Vimy. Visit 3rd, 4th, and 1st Divisions. Very heavy harassing fire on all our back country particularly at Mont St. Eloi, Ecoivres and Acq. Boche attacks Portuguese who as expected bolt. British division on flank also give, particularly 40th. He penetrates to Festubert, le Touret, Lacouture, Estaires, Bac-St-Maur and Sailly taking over 100 guns. He raids our 2nd Brigade capturing one gun and six other ranks. He is immediately counter-attacked, the gun and men are rescued and seven prisoners captured.

---

29   General Ferdinand Foch (1851-1929), Supreme Commander of the Allied Forces (1918).
30   On the Doullens Conference, see BOH 1918 I, 538-544. On the Second phase of the German Spring Offensive see BOH 1918 II and GOH XIV, 260-310.

Diary Entry, 10 April 1918

Both yesterday and today very foggy. Boche assault and capture Messines in morning which is retaken in afternoon. Division at Armentières ordered to withdraw to line of Lys. Harassing fire continues in back areas. Eleventh Brigade raid enemy capturing ten prisoners. Situation does not look good tonight. Divisions are not fighting well and it seems to me the time has arrived for a big decision to be taken. I think we should keep in touch with the French retiring behind the Somme. We are ordered to take over more line, three divisions to hold 28,000 yards of front from north of Hill 70 to the Scarpe. I am not satisfied with artillery distribution and have made representations accordingly. For instance, we took over 6,000 yards from XVII Corps leaving them 4,000 yards. We took over two heavy brigades leaving them five heavy brigades.

Diary Entry, 11 April 1918

Cloudy and misty. Night passed quietly. We begin to relieve 46th Division on Hill 70 front. The Germans continue their offensive with much success. We claim we evacuated Armentières successfully, the Germans claim they took 3,000 prisoners. Many British troops are not fighting well. This is what I expected and what I often claimed during 1917 would be the case. Many of them will not fight and do not fight. The Portuguese ran away. This was also to be expected. I was told by the Army today of their overpowering the guard of the bicycles of the Cyclist Battalion and stealing the wheels. I also was told of a Royal Naval Air Service [squadron] burning many of their machines before the Germans got within miles. I believe that many of the stories of our successful fights with German planes behind the lines to be pure bull.

Diary Entry, 12 April 1918

Saw the Army Commander[31] in the morning looking very pale and very worried. Sent Lieutenant Colonel Bell and Major Wilson with a staff captain off to organize two railway battalions into a brigade. In afternoon inspected and thanked the Motor Machine Gun Brigade for their service in the south. Organized four new machine gun companies (128 guns) one for each division. Also organized the Canadian Corps Reinforcement Centre, corps engineers etc.

31   Sir Henry Horne.

into two brigades. MacPhail in charge of one and Hughes in charge of another. Bombing at night. Very fine weather.

Diary Entry, 14 April 1918

Cloudy. Cold... Army Commander called in afternoon, resented any reflections on fighting ability of British Divisions. They do not want the truth they want camouflage and they're getting it. Oh God how they are getting it and how the British people are getting it in all the balderdash being published in the press. Yesterday I suggested to him that I could spare him some eight-inch and some 9.2.[32] Today he proposes to take some six-inch and some sixty pounders, the very things we need most. On this front of 28,000 yards I have:

Forty-eight	Sixty-pounders
130	Six-inch guns
Thirty	Eight-inch guns
Thirty-six	9.2
Eight	Six-inch guns
TOTAL:	252 heavies

Diary Entry, 15 April 1918

Cold and dreary. Visited Hayter, Loomis and Tuxford in the morning. In office in afternoon. French Commandant of Arras called to see me in afternoon re looting in Arras. There is a determined attempt to blame the Canadians for all the looting there.[33]

Currie to Sir William Hearst, 15 April 1918[34]

My dear Sir William,

It was with feelings of the greatest satisfaction that I received your letter of the 22nd February and the unanimous resolution of the Legislative Assembly of Ontario, the full text of which has been promulgated to the Corps. It was a happy coincidence that such an expression of convictions and fixed determination of the people of Ontario should have reached us almost at the moment when the enemy was launching another, and the greatest of his efforts, so aptly described in your resolution as 'unscrupulous and brutal attempts at domination.'

32 Eight-inch and 9.2 inch guns.
33 This is described in Charles Harrison, *Generals Die in Bed* (London: Noel Douglas, 1930). Currie describes his reaction to Harrison's work in the final section of this book.
34 File 2, vol 2, CP, LAC.

If anything more had been wanting to reveal the purpose for which Germany plunged the world into the horrors of war, and the methods by which that purpose is achieved, the ruthless participation of a disarmed Russia, and the relentless spoliation of the helpless East, serve to make it ever more abundantly clear; and the knowledge of what his triumph would mean to civilization and humanity should steel every arm, and stouten every heart to endure till final victory is assured.

The struggle is now reaching its most critical stage. Blinded by the glare of conquest, drunk with the lust of blood, the enemy has determined to crush the Allies or perish in the attempt. Regardless of human life, and caring nothing for the suffering and misery involved he is hurling dense masses of troops against the British front. With heroic fortitude the onslaught has been met and the line remains unbroken but the days to come will undoubtedly demand the fullest measure of sacrifice not only from the troops in the field, but from all the people at home, and in order to achieve victory the full weight of the Empire, both in men and resources, must be thrown in. It is therefore a source of the greatest encouragement and satisfaction to us all to know that the people at home are fully alive to the situation, and resolved to do their full part towards attaining the great result.

Will you please convey to the members of the Legislative Assembly and to the people of Ontario the grateful thanks of all ranks for the warm expressions of appreciation contained in your message, for the trust you place in the Canadian Corps, and for the promise of continued loyal support. Contemplating the past with just pride and hearts filled with gratitude to God who has crowned our efforts with victory, let us all resolve to face the future with calm confidence and unwavering faith, each one determined to do his utmost for Christianity and Civilization, and to preserve righteousness and freedom for stricken mankind.

Ever yours faithfully

A.W. Currie

Diary Entry, 17 April 1918

[Clipping missing] The above was cut from the *Times* of 17th April. I wonder if Balfour[35] appreciates the unutterable disgust with which this is read by all who know the truth. Hypocrisy oh how it has the English people enslaved! We don't

---

35 Sir Arthur James Balfour (1848-1930) was a former British Prime Minister (1902-05) and Foreign Secretary under Lloyd George.

want the truth, camouflage is preferred. Yesterday the 2nd Imperial Division left their trenches. Our 2nd Division took them back and then handed over to the Imperials

Diary Entry, 24 April 1918

Cool and cloudy. In morning visited all battalions and 2nd Brigade. Lunched with Macdonell. In afternoon, Lipsett, Hill[36] called. Germans renew their attack on junction [of] British and French. Heavy fighting but our line remains almost intact.

Diary Entry, 28 April 1918

Anniversary of Arleux. Cloudy but warm, to church in morning. Corps commanders conference at Rachecourt. We are ordered to get ready to go out of line and make an attack.

Diary Entry, 3 May 1918

Fine and warm. Anniversary of Fresnoy... GHQ ask for Motor Brigade again. Although they fought for eighteen days in Fifth Army and suffered fifteen per cent casualties, no officers recommended for decorations have been so rewarded. It is a damned shame. I hear that Army reports that Canadians are very stout fighters, good on the defensive and also on limited objective offensives though they shake their head at what we might do in open warfare owing to the absence of regular officers. They forget that our leaders have seen more war in the last three years than the British Army did in its previous 100 years.

Diary Entry, 4 May 1918

Fine. Visit 1st Canadian also 4th in forenoon. Army Commander calls in afternoon. Sir Edward Kemp arrives about five accompanied by Sims. His private secretary, also Colonel Ross and Kemp's nephew to dinner.

Diary Entry, 5 May 1918

Heavy rain at night. Second Brigade relieved by 15th Division last night. Attack expected this morning but did not materialize. Kemp left about 10:30. Went for ride in afternoon. Heavy thunderstorm...

---

36   Brigadier General Frederick William Hill was the former Mayor of Niagara Falls, Ontario and the commanding officer of 9th Brigade (January 1916-May 1918).

[handwritten: Marin Lov 14ᵗʰ/15 @ 3:05 pm]

Diary Entry, 6 May 1918

Fine though cloudy. See 2nd Brigade on march to Liencourt. In afternoon demonstration of moving heavy ordinance by light railway.

[handwritten: or 00:05   GMT]

Diary Entry, 7 May 1918

Close at Camblain l'Abbé, turning over to XVIII Corps and to XVII Corps, go to see Burstall at Basseux and on to see Rennie. Lunch with Griesbach and on to Pernes. Curley Birch and General Heath[37] call.

Currie did not consistently keep a daily diary between 8 May and 16 August 1918. Instead he wrote several cumulative entries. It is unclear when these entries were written, but unlike his earlier diary entries the surviving copies are typewritten, in paragraph form.

Combined Diary Entry, 7–25 May 1918[38]

From the 7th to the 25th May Canadian Corps Headquarters was at Pernes. Billeted in the doctor's house. [After a period] of a few days the weather was fine and warm. The 2nd Division are still with VI British Corps in the [Third Army area]. Other three divisions, and the 74th British Division [which is attached] to the Corps, are engaged in open warfare training...Manoeuvres and tactical schemes are being carried out [and the] units of the Corps have been inspected including field ambulances [and the] Canadian Light Horse, etc.

During this period several war correspondents visited the Corps for about four days (Mr. Mackenzie, Mr. Blacklock)

Another visitor to the Corps was the Bishop of London, Ontario, who is to spend about two weeks here. During his stay he is the guest of 'A' Mess. Canadian hospitals at Etaples and Doullens bombed; many nursing sisters, doctors, attendants, and patients killed and wounded.

Diary Entry, 26 May 1918

On the 26th May the Corps moved to Bryas (three kilometres from St. Pol). Beautiful chateau, well back from the main road, vast grounds, and a lovely garden. The 4th Canadian Division moved to Pernes. Much night bombing going on. Boche night bombing plane brought down in flames, falling near Pernes.

---

37   Major General Sir Gerard Moore Heath (1863-1929) was the Engineer-in-Chief at GHQ (from 1917).
38   Subsequent diary entries are taken from typewritten transcripts in file 194, vol 43, CP, LAC.

Training in open warfare still being carried out by all branches of the Corps. Much attention is being paid to musketry.

By the end of May the German attacks had created a significant bulge in the Entente line. On 27 May the third phase of the German spring offensives began as the German armies advanced on the Chemin de Dames eventually covering some thirty miles and reaching the River Marne. The attack was locally successful but the German High Command failed to draw in French and British reserves from Flanders as had been hoped. At the end of June the Canadian Corps was still unbloodied and awaited a visit from Prime Minister Robert Borden. Currie was anxious that the Prime Minister spend more time with the soldiers of the Canadian Corps than with the politicians and dignitaries in England and at GHQ.[39]

Currie to Robert Borden, 28 June 1918[40]

Dear Sir Robert,

We have been informed from the War Office of the Canadian Representative that your visit to France has been arranged somewhat as follows:

Saturday June 29th, arrive at Paris Plage, where the night will be spent. Sunday, June 30th: lunch with the Commander-in-Chief, have tea with Sir Julian Byng, and arrive at Canadian Headquarters about 7:00 pm. Monday with the Canadian Corps, party to be split up and sent to various places. Tuesday, spend the afternoon with the Corps.

May I be permitted to make the following observations regarding these arrangements. In the first place, do you realize that when you arrive in France you are only two hours away from Corps headquarters, and that it is proposed for you that you spend twenty-four hours visiting the Canadian Representative's headquarters at Paris Plage and the headquarters of two British generals, whereas thirty-six hours is considered sufficient for you to spend with 105,000 Canadians who have fought and suffered, and many of whom will die before you have an opportunity of seeing them again. I feel quite certain, Sir Robert, that while the Corps is prepared to realize the urgency of the engagements of yourself and party it will be very much disappointed that out of the weeks, and probably months, you will spend on this side of the water it is to have the honour of your company

39   See BOH 1918 III and GOH XIV, 311-90.
40   Reel 4328, vol 93, BP, LAC.

for a mere thirty-six hours. It may be that before you return to Canada you will find it convenient to come and see us again, when you will take sufficient time to learn the true feeling of Canada's fighting forces. I have not yet been informed whether it is the intention of Mr. Rowell, Mr. Calder, and Mr. Meighen to leave as on Tuesday at noon, but I sincerely trust such is not their intention and that they may stay with us some time longer.

The second observation I have to make is this: that I do not propose to pay any attention to any arrangements made by others as to what you are to do while you are in the Corps' area. If we are to have you and your party for only such a very short space of time surely it can be left to us to suggest what you shall do while you are here. I hope that you will have a pleasant crossing and that we may have the privilege and honour of welcoming you at Corps Headquarters at the earliest possible moment.

Yours faithfully,

A.W. Currie

Combined Diary Entry, 1–30 June 1918

During the month of June the Corps remained at Bryas. The weather with the exception of the last week was extremely fine and quite warm. The 1st Canadian Division are at Villers Châtel; the 3rd Division are at Norrent-Fontes; the 4th are at Sachin-le-Buich; the 74th Division are at Le Cauroy. St. Pol, Pernes, and other back area towns have been frequently shelled.

Went to England on the 5th on leave. With the exception of about five days in London, remained in Brighton. Met Sir Robert Borden and his party of cabinet ministers. Attended Sir George Perley's dinner in honour of the Prime Minister. Conferences with the Overseas Minister, the Prime Minister etc. Returned from leave on 19th June. On the 25th, 3rd Canadian Division relieved 2nd Canadian Division in the Third Army area, the latter returning to the Corps.

In the meantime the 4th Division sports meeting was held at Pernes on the 16th June; the 1st Divisional sports at Tinques on the 17th June; Corps troops sports at Pernes on the 19th; on the 23rd June the 3rd Division held their sports at Linghem, which I witnessed; the same day the 2nd Division held their sports at Basseux.

The visitors to the Corps during the month were: General Logie,[41] General Cruickshanks, and Major Sullivan who remained about four days. The prairie premiers, the Hon. Messrs. Martin, Norris and Stewart,[42] who remained for three days. All saw quite a lot of the Corps and were very much impressed. On the 29th Hon. Messrs Rowell[43] and Calder arrived;[44] and on the 30th Sir Robert Borden, Hon Arthur Meighen,[45] Mr. Christie and Mr. Blacklock arrived. On the night of the 30th dinner at Corps for Sir Robert Borden at which the divisional and certain brigade commanders were present. Brass and kiltie bands provided music.

Diary Entry, 1 July 1918

On Dominion Day, July 1st the Corps sports were held Tinques. It was a day that will long be remembered by those present. The programme was varied and the events of a high order not a single hitch occurring from the first event at 10:00 am to the concluding number, a concert party by one of the divisional troupes. Lunch at one o'clock at which over 100 guests were present including representatives of all the Allies. The guest of honour was the Duke of Connaught [illegible]

Combined Diary Entry, 2–14 July 1918

On the 2nd July the Prime Minister and his party visited and addressed several brigades of the Corps. The Prime Minister, Mr. Christie and Mr. Blacklock left for Paris on the morning of the 3rd to open a Canadian hospital, Messrs Calder, Rowell and Meighen remaining for another day or two.

Corps Headquarters remained at Bryas until the 15th July, during which time the weather was exceptionally fine enabling much valuable training to be carried

---

41 Major General William Alexander Logie (1866-1933) was District Officer Commanding Military District Two (Toronto).

42 William Melville Martin (1876-1970) was the Liberal Premier of Saskatchewan (1916-22); Tobias Crawford Norris (1861-1936) was the Liberal Premier of Manitoba (1915-22); Charles Stewart (1868-1946) was the Liberal Premier of Alberta (1917-21).

43 Newton Wesley Rowell (1867-1941) was the former leader of the Liberal Party in Ontario. Rowell was elected to the House of Commons in the 1917 election as a Unionist candidate. He later argued the Persons Case before the Supreme Court of Canada and the Privy Council and co-chaired the Rowell-Sirois Commission on Dominion-Provincial Relations (1937-40). See Margaret Prang, *N.W. Rowell: Ontario Nationalist* (Toronto: UTP, 1975).

44 James Alexander Calder (1868-1956) was a Liberal Saskatchewan politician elected as a Unionist candidate to the House of Commons in 1917, he held various cabinet positions including Immigration and Colonization and the Department of Agriculture. He died in office as a Conservative senator.

45 Arthur Meighen (1874-1960) was an important minister in the Union Cabinet who succeeded Borden as Prime Minister (1920-21). He was again Prime Minister for a brief period in the summer of 1926. See Roger Graham, *Arthur Meighen: A Biography* (Toronto: Irwin Clarke, 1960-65).

out. On the 14th July General Mewburn, the Minister of Militia in Canada, General Wilson,[46] Colonel Ballantyne (Minister of Marine)[47] Colonel Osborne[48] and Major Creighton arrived at Corps Headquarters.

Diary Entry, 15 July 1918

On the 15th July the Corps moved to Duisans. The chateau, while not as large as the one at Bryas, is very nice, and has a beautiful garden. The Corps has now relieved XVII British Corps, and the 2nd and 4th Divisions are in the line. A strenuous policy is being adopted and the Boche is being continually worried by raids and active patrolling. Successful raids in which prisoners and machine guns were captured were carried out by the 10th Brigade, the 54th and 102nd Battalions. General Mewburn and his party are getting around quite a lot and are very much impressed by what they see.

On 15 July the German Army began its final offensive of the war. Striking in the direction of Paris, dozens of divisions hammered the French and American forces in what came to be known as the Second Battle of the Marne. Although some enemy divisions managed to get across the river, on the 18th two French armies mounted a counter-attack, forestalling further German gains. By 20 July, the German advance had to be suspended indefinitely. Reeling from influenza, malnutrition, and the casualties of the spring, the German Army was a shadowy reflection of the force which had first reached the outskirts of Paris in 1914.

Between the beginning of March and the end of July 1918, the Canadian Corps reported casualties of 2,135 killed and 8,254 wounded. These are remarkable figures given that the Canadians avoided the bulk of the German offensives. Artillery barrages, raids, and the 'wastage' of trench warfare took their toll even if the Canadians were not directly in the line of the advancing German infantry. That the Canadians were the most intact formation on the Western Front in July

---

46   Major General Erastus William Wilson was the District Officer Commanding Military District Four (Montreal).

47   Charles Colquhoun Ballantyne (1867-1950) was a Conservative from Quebec elected as a Union Member of Parliament in 1917, Ballantyne served as Minister of Marine and Fisheries and Minister of the Naval Service (1917-21).

48   Colonel Henry Campbell Osborne (1874-1949) was the Secretary-General of the Canadian Arm of the Imperial War Graves Commission.

1918—that they remained 'unused' in Haig's words—gives some indication of the intensity of the spring fighting.[49]

Diary Entry, 19 July 1918

On the 19th of July a party of twenty-six newspaper proprietors from Canada visited the Corps and remained about three days. They were shown over the light railways, Vimy Ridge, and saw quite a lot of the Corps. The weather has been very sultry and there have been some bad thunderstorms. The 72nd Battalion carried out a successful raid with only slight casualties to themselves. Gas has been successfully projected.

Diary Entry, 30 July-7 August 1918

From the 30th July to the 7th August Corps Headquarters was at Molliens–Vidame. During this time the troops were on the move into the new area. The headquarters accommodation is poor and very much scattered. The weather has been rainy. On the 7th August Corps Headquarters moved to Dury. The chateau is very nice and is surrounded by very nice grounds. The weather has faired up.

After the cessation of the German offensives, the Entente prepared to strike a counterblow. General Rawlinson of Fourth Army had been preparing a limited operation to retake the ground lost in the spring around Amiens, including the vital railway link with Paris. Foch liked the plan and committed French as well as British and Australian troops to the operation. The Canadian Corps, so successful in previous operations and largely intact despite the fighting of the spring, was a natural choice to spearhead operations alongside the Australians. On 8 August the Entente forces launched a methodical attack that quickly grew into one of the most successful operations of the war, far surpassing the gains initially envisioned for a limited operation. The German Army was not as strong as Rawlinson expected and as the assaulting troops went in, the German line was breached and the Kaiser's army fell back. Amiens was a tactical and strategic victory. The German official history named the battle 'the Catastrophe of 8 August,' the beginning of the end for the German Army. By the 20th, the Canadians had advanced fourteen miles on a wide front at the price of 11,822 casualties.

---

49 On casualties see Major Cathcart's figures, RG 24, vol 1844, file GAQ 11-11E, LAC. See BOH 1918 III, 217-322 and GOH XIV, 390-505.

Currie was immensely proud of the victory at Amiens and the performance of the Canadian soldiers under his command. After the bulk of the fighting ended, he penned one of his 'special orders.' He also wrote to officials in the Overseas Ministry and friends back home with the good news that had been so long in coming. Although Currie did not resume keeping a daily diary until 15 August 1918, the preparations and fighting are described in detail in his Report to the Ministry.[50]

Special Order by Lieutenant-General Sir Arthur Currie, 13 August 1918[51]

The first stage of this Battle of Amiens and one of the most successful operations conducted by the Allied armies since the war began is now a matter of history.

The Canadian Corps has every right to feel more than proud of the part it played. To move the Corps from the Arras front and in less than a week launch into in battle so many miles distant was in itself a splendid performance. Yet the splendour of that performance pales into insignificance when compared with what has been accomplished since zero hour on August 8th.

On that date the Canadian Corps—to which was attached the 3rd Cavalry Division, the 4th Tank Brigade, the 5th Squadron RAF—attacked on a front of 7,500 yards. After a penetration of 25,000 yards the line tonight rests on a 10,000 yard frontage. Sixteen German divisions have been identified, of which four have been completely routed. Nearly 150 guns have been captured, while over one thousand machine guns have fallen into our hands. Ten thousand prisoners have passed through our cages and casualty clearing stations, a number greatly in excess of our total casualties. Twenty-five towns and villages have been rescued from the clutch of the invaders, and the danger of dividing the French and British Army has been dissipated.

---

50 On Currie at Amiens, see Dancocks, 149-56; Hyatt, 113-7; Urquhart, 230-9. Three are numerous sources on the battle itself and the fighting during the Hundred Days Campaign. See, for example, Daniel Dancocks, *Spearhead to Victory: Canada and the Great War* (Edmonton: Hertig Publishers, 1987), J.P. Harris and Nail Barr, *Amiens to the Armistice: the BEF in the Hundred Days Campaign, 8 August-11 November 1918* (London: Brassey's, 1999), Shane Schreiber, *Shock Army of the British Empire* (Westport: Praeger, 1997), and Tim Travers, *How the War was Won: Command and Technology on the Western Front, 1917-18* (London: Routledge, 1992). See also BOH 1918 IV, 7-162. On the German army, see Reicharchiv, *Schlachten des Weltkriegs, Band 36: Die Katastrophe des 8 August* (Oldenburg: Stalling Verlag, 1930) and GOH XIV, 549-67.

51 Reel C4334, vol 104, BP, LAC.

Canada has always placed the most implicit confidence in her Army. How nobly has that confidence been justified: and with what pride has the story of your gallant success been read in the home land! This magnificent victory has been won because your training was good, your discipline was good, your leadership was good. Given these three, success must always come.

From the depths of a very full heart, I wish to thank all staffs and services—the Infantry, the artillery, the cavalry, the engineers, the machine gunners, the Independent Force, consisting of the Motor Machine Gun Brigades and the cyclists, the tank battalions, the RAF, the Medical Services, the Army Service Corps, the Ordnance Corps, the Veterinary Services, the Chaplain Services, for their splendid support and co-operation, and to congratulate you all on the wonderful success achieved. Let us remember our gallant dead whose spirit shall ever be with us, inspiring us to nobler effort, and when the call again comes, be it soon or otherwise, I know the same measure of success will be yours.

A.W. Currie

Currie to Sir Edward Kemp, 15 August 1918[52]

Dear Sir Edward,

Two days ago I wrote to you a letter with reference to our operations. Since that time no advance has been made nor have we attempted any other than clearing up the situation around the village of Parvillers. I may say that it was intended that we should go on, but on a thorough examination of what confronted us I decided that to attempt an advance at the present time would cost enormous casualties, and so I advised against making any further advance now.

We find ourselves up against the old Boche defences, as they existed previous to the Somme battle of 1916. The system immediately opposite us was the one from which he retired voluntarily, and so the old trenches are there as they were in 1916. They are good trenches with plenty of deep dugout accommodation, machine gun emplacements, and wire. In an attack on such trenches we cannot count on the element of surprise which helped us so much in the battle of the 8th, and to attempt to force a passage in the face of this uncut wire would be altogether too costly an operation. I saw the Army Commander and presented these facts to him, following it up by a letter in which I stated what I thought should be done. I am glad to say that GHQ have approved my recommendation, and so the danger for spoiling what has been a wonderfully successful operation is past. We are going to do everything possible to make the Boche believe that we are going to continue our attack, and possibly we will, but not before we get ready. This information is strictly confidential and solely for your own use.

Yours faithfully,

A.W. Currie

Currie to Brigadier General F.W. Hill, 15 August 1918[53]

My dear Hill,

Thank you very much for your letter of the 10th. I know just how hungry you are for details of the fight, but I am afraid I have not the time to give you very much news. I admit that up to the present the London press, for some reason best known to themselves, have said very little about the part the Canadians played in this battle.

I am enclosing, herewith, a Special Order which I have issued, which details very briefly the measure of success we achieved.[54] I am glad to be able to tell you that your old brigade has done particularly well. They were given what looked to me to be the hardest nut of all to crack. They got a very bad start, owing to the fact that before the operation we held a very narrow strip across the River Luce, and in this narrow strip the brigade had to assemble. It was a very ticklish thing to do, and required perfect control and discipline in order not to disclose their presence to the enemy. They began the assault against a hill which loomed up like the Rock of Gibraltar. They had very hard fighting but took their objective on time, one battalion alone capturing thirty-eight machine guns.

What worried me more than the actual operation itself was getting the troops and guns into position without arousing any suspicion on the part of the Boche. All movement for many miles behind our lines had to be carried out at night, yet the whole Corps had to be assembled on a comparatively narrow front. The move also was so hurried, and the necessity of secrecy so urgent, that many things which are normally done in preparation for an attack had to be left undone, that is, we had to trust our training for a great deal. I knew that if we arrived at a zero hour without sustaining a heavy gassing or heavy artillery fire that all would be well, and so it turned out.

---

53 Ibid.
54 See above, 13 August 1918.

We now find ourselves up against the old German defences as they existed before the battle of the Somme, and the part immediately in front of us is that part which he evacuated. This means that the old lines are still there with plenty of machine gun emplacements, deep dug-outs, pill boxes and wire. We need now an entirely different kind of operation. Four years of war has taught us that troops cannot cross uncut barbed wire without suffering enormous casualties, and I am not going to have a good operation spoiled by over-zealousness. You will from time to time be seeing many of our wounded, and from them will get the story in greater detail.

I know what you say regarding the lack of interest your predecessor[55] showed in the work at Witley. For many months past officers from there had told me that he was taking absolutely no interest whatever in his work. I presume that when he finally learned that the 5th Division was to be broken up he decided to look for something else. We are told that the salary he received in his present appointment is a particularly large one, and from the reports one reads in the press concerning the dividends, etc. of the company, one can well believe that it is within their ability to pay high salaries. It appears to be about the worst case of profiteering I have ever heard of. Garnet has been an exceedingly lucky officer, beginning the war as a major with practically no experience whatever in military matters and, after spending eighteen months in France he found himself a Major General with a CB, a CMG, and a DSO, and now apparently fixed in a position from which he derives a very large income.

I believe that there is a great work for you to do there. What you do there is reflected in what happened here, and you will be entitled to share in whatever measure of success can be achieved in the field. I sincerely hope that the authorities really do something to compensate you for the sacrifice you are making for the good of the cause, and I shall repeatedly urge upon them the justice of making it good to you. There is a great deal more I would like to write about, but you can well understand, Hill, how busy one is.

With best wishes always, ever yours faithfully,

A.W. Currie

---

55 Garnet Hughes.

Diary Entry, 18 August 1918

Weather still continued warm. General Rawlinson phoned about 9:30 to say that Lord Derby[56] and Premier Clemenceau[57] were visiting the Corps Area today; that he had phoned to General Lipsett asking him to have the 7th Brigade on parade. The latter came in to see me regarding the above-mentioned visit, when I explained to him the discourtesy which was being paid to me. I told him that he and his staff and the 7th Brigade were entitled to every honour which could be given them by a visit from Lord Derby and Clemenceau, but that I did not think it right for anyone other than myself to order any unit of the Corps to parade. About 12:30, Haseltine, Aide-de-Camp to the Commander-in-Chief, phoned to me stating the Premier Clemenceau would be west of Domart at two o'clock, and asking me if I could be present. I answered that I was otherwise engaged, and spent the afternoon with the 1st Division, 4th Division, 11th and 12th Brigades. General Rawlinson came in to see me later and told me how well pleased he was with the appearance on parade of the 7th Brigade. I replied that I was glad he was pleased, but I took occasion to remind him that in my opinion he had no right to order the parade direct. He readily agreed with this contention, and said he was sorry. I also told him that I thought it was discourteous to me for Lord Derby and Premier Clemenceau to see on parade any units of the Corps without first calling at Corps Headquarters. General Lipsett came in later in the evening, and seemed to be somewhat concerned over what action I was going to take with reference to the incident.[58]

Diary Entry, 19 August 1918

Situation normal. The 1st Division and the 4th succeeded in straightening out their line in front of La Chavette and Fransart, making a good jumping off line for future operations against the Fresnoy–Hattencourt–Punchy line. We received intimation that the Corps was to be relieved at once by the French and to move north.

56 Edward George Villiers Stanley, the 17th Earl of Derby (1865-1948) was Secretary of State for War (1916-18) and the British Ambassador to Paris (1918-20).

57 George Benjamin Clemenceau (1841-1929) was Prime Minister of France (1906-09, 1917-20) and an architect of the Treaty of Versailles.

58 This incident may have precipitated Lipsett's transfer to 4th British division three weeks later. Ironically, Currie acted in a similar manner at the beginning of November following the liberation of Valenciennes.

Diary Entry, 21 August 1918

Weather still continued very hot. In morning went to gun park at Longeau, where our captured guns now number 187. Visited units of the 6th Brigade and 4th Brigade entraining at Longeau and Boves. General Webber went to the Third and First Army to find probable destination of 2nd and 3rd Divisions.

After the Battle of Amiens, the Entente began an all out assault on the German Army. The race was on to achieve victory before the onset of winter suspended offensive operations and gave the enemy time to recover. The Germans had advanced deep into French territory but in places had abandoned the well-constructed defensive positions they had built up over the previous three years. The Entente intended to break the enemy's back before the Germans had a chance to regroup on the old defensive system known as the Hindenburg Line.[59] *On 20 August the French Third Army struck the first blow, advancing five miles in two days. Over the following week British and French armies began to land alternating hits on the enemy.*

At the end of August the Canadian Corps was assigned to First Army and given the difficult task of breaking the Drocourt–Quéant Switch (known as a the DQ Line), one of the strongest positions on the Western Front and the key to the security of the Hindenburg Line. After breaking through the enemy's defences, the Corps was to advance towards the Canal du Nord, outflanking the Hindenburg Line and forcing a German retreat. Unlike previous battles, Currie had very little time for planning. At Vimy Ridge in 1917, the Canadian Corps had three months to prepare for the attack. At Hill 70 and Passchendaele he was afforded several weeks. In the autumn of 1918, Currie often only had days to develop a plan, coordinate the infantry, engineers, cavalry, tanks, air forces, and artillery, and prepare the men for open warfare. The German Army was also far from defeated and was staging an orderly withdrawal, desperately trying to stabilise the front along a new defensive line.[60]

Diary Entry, 22 August 1918

Closed Headquarters at Dury. Called on General Monash, Australian Corps Headquarters at Glisy, General Toulagre French Corps Commander at Hangest.

---

59 A German defensive system constructed in depth during the winter of 1917.
60 See Nicholson, 386-424; Morton and Granatstein, 218-22; Schreiber is the best monograph on the final Hundred Days Campaign. See also BOH 1918 IV, 163-383 and GOH XIV, 568-87.

Lunched with Army Commander. Called on General Byng at Frohen-le-Grand and came on to our Corps Headquarters at Hautecloque, near St. Pol. General Byng was good enough to say that he considered the operation of the Canadian Corps in the Battle of Amiens to be the finest operation of the war. Upon reaching Hautecloque, received an order from the First Army to be prepared to advance east of Arras on or after the 25th instant. I called Generals Burstall and Lipsett into conference this evening and gave objectives and boundaries. Second Division Headquarters at Etrun, 3rd Division La Cauroy.

Diary Entry, 23 August 1918

Last night 2nd Division took over the line from Neuville Vitasse north to Tilloy. Cyclist Battalion and other odds and ends hold line from here to the Scarpe. We took over from the XVII Corps at 12:00 noon, opening headquarters at Noyelle-Vion. I called on the Army Commander on the way up... Sir Edward Kemp arrived about 3:00 pm and left Saturday 24th, immediately after breakfast. He proposed to visit the Amiens battlefield, returning to Montreuil at night.

Diary Entry, 24 August 1918

The Commander-in-Chief called at 3:30 and explained the future task of the Canadian Corps which was to attack due east, keeping our left flank on the River Scarpe and after breaking the Quéant–Drocourt line we were to turn south and come in behind the Hindenburg Line. We were not though to begin our advance until the Third Army had captured Henin Hill. The Army Commander was present at the time. During the day, the 6th Brigade at Neuville Vitasse advanced their line some 500 yards or more, capturing an officer and twenty-five other ranks. It was decided the attack would not take place on the 25th.

Diary Entry, 25 August 1918

It was learned this morning that the report from the Third Army that they had already captured Henin Hill was incorrect, and the 52nd Division, its left division and the one immediately on our right, seemed to be very sticky. After a further conference with the Commander-in-Chief it was decided to proceed with the attack of the Corps tomorrow the 26th, the XVII Corps being ordered to conform to our movements and to pass around the north of Henin Hill, attacking it from that flank and from the rear. I went to the 2nd and 3rd Divisions and thoroughly explained the probable future actions of the Corps... I decided to attack at three o'clock instead of the usual dawn hour, hoping in this way to surprise the enemy. The preceding nights had been very bright moonlight and as the forecast was good it was considered justifiable to advance the hour.

Diary Entry, 26 August 1918

The night was overcast with clouds and it was none too bright at zero hour. However the attack started on time and so far (9:30 am) has gone very well indeed. The 3rd Division attacking with the 8th Brigade have already taken Orange Hill and Monchy and are continuing eastwards. The 2nd Division, with the 4th Brigade in advance, have captured Chapel Hill and their troops are in the vicinity of Guemappe. The 6th Brigade, following close on their right flank, are to clean up the pocket at Neuville Vitasse and Wancourt. The 5th Brigade are moving forward and have been ordered to capture Wancourt Tower. The 7th Brigade are following in close support of the 8th Brigade, and the Independent Force,[61] under General Brutinel,[62] are endeavouring to exploit down the Cambrai road. I received word this morning that Major F.A. Robertson (Fanny) was wounded yesterday and lost a leg. He had already lost an eye on the Somme. In the afternoon visited headquarters 51st Division, 2nd and 3rd Canadian Divisions, thoroughly explaining to divisional commanders future plans. The Commander-in-Chief and General Horne called at Corps Headquarters and outlined what the future policy would be. Late reports showed that the 6th Brigade had captured Wancourt Tower on the Wancourt Ridge, but that the 3rd Division were not quite as far advanced as it was reported at one time. They were counter-attacked late in the afternoon from Jig-saw Wood. So far we over-ran the 214th [German] Division and identified the 35th and 39th [German Divisions].

Diary Entry, 27 August 1918

Considerable rain during the night. The 3rd Division, principally the 9th Brigade, pressed on capturing Bois du Sart and Bois du Vert but were checked and driven back from Boiry. Attacking late in the morning the 2nd Division completed the capture of Wancourt Ridge by the 6th Brigade, the 5th Brigade passing through and capturing Chérisy. The 4th Brigade continued its advance along the Arras–Cambrai road and late in the afternoon captured Vis-en-Artois.

---

61   The Canadian Motor Machine Gun Brigade.
62   General Raymond Brutinel (1872-1964) commanded the first mechanized force in the British Expeditionary Force, the Canadian Motor Machine Gun Brigade.

This has made a very fine advance for the 4th Brigade, being about 10,000 yards in two days. The Commander-in-Chief and the Army Commander again called with reference to future plans. The 4th British Division is now at our disposal. During the day the 51st Division, now in the Canadian Corps, reported the capture of Greenland Hill, but in the afternoon they were counter-attacked and the line tonight is on the west of the hill.

Diary Entry, 28 August 1918

Considerable rain daring the night. The 3rd Division reported the capture of Pelves by the 7th Brigade... The 3rd Division made very satisfactory progress today, the 7th Brigade capturing Jigsaw Wood thereby cleaning op a very troublesome corner. The 9th Brigade captured Boiry-Notre-Dame and Artillery Hill to the north of it. This was a very important operation. The 8th Brigade pressed on between that and the Cambrai–Arras road, captured 70 Ridge, Remy Ridge and Haucourt, thus breaking the Fresnes–Rouvroy Line north of the Arras–Cambrai road. The 2nd Division at 12:30 attacked the Fresnes–Rouvroy System south of the road and succeeded in getting most of the front line, but they never cleared up the support line. I saw General Burstall in the afternoon, who was somewhat disappointed at their progress. I asked him to make sure by sending up his reserve battalions that the line he then held would be turned over to General Macdonell at night. The 2nd Division were very heavily counter-attacked at nine o'clock by a fresh division and forced back practically to the line from which they jumped off in the morning. This will interfere seriously with the future events as the 1st Division must take the Fresnes–Rouvroy Line before getting a jumping off line against the Quéant–Drocourt System. On returning to Corps Headquarters, I notified the Army that we would not be able to proceed with the attack on the latter system before August 31st at the earliest. During the night the 3rd Division were relieved by the 4th British Division, and the 2nd Division by the 1st Division. I also, to better protect our flank between Plouvain and Hamblain which I regard as our most sensitive point, created a machine gun force under General Brutinel. He practically relieved the 7th Brigade, and his special mission is to guard against counter-attacks from the direction of Hamblain. The losses were quite heavy today.

Diary Entry, 29 August 1918

The weather has turned quite fine again. This morning at 6:30 the 51st Division again attacked and captured Greenland Hill, but they have not got along as far as is necessary. I believe fresh troops should be put in there in order to force the Germans back completely to the Fresnes–Rouvroy Line north of the Scarpe. Only by this means can we make use of the Fampoux valley for heavy artillery. The counter-battery artillery situation is not satisfactory. Too many of our guns are still behind the Vimy Ridge, and I believe success will be more certain were we to attack on the front between the Scarpe and Lens, putting our right flank on Biache-St-Vaast and our left on Sallaumines Hill. This would enable us to get all the guns which are now behind Vimy Ridge well down on the plain to the east of it. Being there they could engage the guns north of the Scarpe which now take on our advance in enfilade. This is very necessary because our only road, the Arras–Cambrai road is practically under field gun fire. It is very important that it should be cleared of this menace. I regard the fighting in which we are about to engage as the most serious we have taken on for many months, and at the Quéant–Drocourt line I look for very severe fighting indeed. We are now trying to break the hinge of the German position, and if we are successful great and important results might reasonably follow. If we could let the cavalry through on this northern flank, it is conceivable that all his troops between Bapaume and Péronne and on the Somme might be rounded up. For this reason the Boche will fight us very hard. Further south I believe he is fighting simply a rearguard action having his mind fully made up to retire to the Hindenburg Line.

In the afternoon, the Army Commander held a conference here to decide on the action of the cavalry. Personally, I do not think they will be of any great advantage to us. During the day, Brutinel's Brigade, consisting of the cyclists, his own Motor Machine Gun Brigade, and part of a battalion of machine gunners, improved the line very much on our northern sector, advancing it nearly one thousand yards on a fifteen 1,500 yard frontage. This was about the first time the cyclists have been actually engaged. They took a number of machine guns and about twenty prisoners. The 4th British Division improved their line considerably, advancing it roughly about 1,500 yards. The division on our right advanced and claim to have taken Hendecourt and Riencourt, but our people do not consider that they have cleaned up the situation of Hendecourt at all.

Diary Entry, 30 August 1918

After a fairly quiet night, the 1st Brigade pushed around, the south of our boundary and attacked the Fresnes–Rouvroy Line on the flank. The attack has proceeded very well and they are now in possession of Upton Wood, the Fresnes–Rouvroy Line as far north as the Vis-en-Artois Switch which they also hold. I held a conference at General Macdonell's headquarters east of Neuville Vitasse and outlined the plan for future operations. Believing the Quéant–Drocourt line to be the back-bone of his resistance we have decided to put all our strength against it, not to attack it until we are ready, and then to go all out. The 2nd and 3rd Divisions have moved further back and are fast recovering. I saw some of the units today, who looked a little tired but otherwise very well.

Diary Entry, 31 August 1918

Weather somewhat unsatisfactory. Heavy, cold rain fell in the early morning. The 2nd Brigade captured the balance of Olive and Ostrich Trenches joining up with the 4th British Division at the Cambrai road. They took sixteen machine guns out of Ocean Work, and killed or wounded the entire garrison. The Third Army are not advancing at the time of our next attack. Although GHQ have issued orders to them to keep close touch with us on their left, the Third Army have issued orders that their advance is to take place after we break the Quéant–Drocourt line. I took this up with Sir Charles Fergusson,[63] who pointed out that the reason he was not advancing was on account of having no tanks. I agreed that he would find it very difficult. He promised to have a division in close touch with our right division, and in case we broke through it was to follow closely on the heels of our division turning the line from its rear. Late this afternoon General Matheson[64] of the 4th Division came to see me and informed me that the 4th Division would be unable to carry out the attack owing to the physical condition of the men and to their lack of numbers. This has forced me to change the plans, and I have now arranged to put in another brigade of the 4th Canadian Division, thus shortening up Matheson's front. This will interfere with the exploitation we expected to be able to do. A regiment (10th Hussars) of the cavalry have been placed at my disposal and I have attached them to Brutinel's force, which will operate down the Arras–Cambrai road. An additional brigade of heavy artillery

---

63 General Sir Charles Ferguson (1865-1951), commander of XVII Corps, Military Govenor of Cologne (1918-20), and Governor General of New Zealand (1924-30).
64 Major General Sir Torquil Matheson (1871-1963) was commanding officer of 4th (British) Division.

has arrived, but I shall still be short one heavy brigade which I expected, it not being able to arrive at the time GHQ said it would be here. I find also that the VIII Corps are particularly sticky in moving their heavy artillery east of the Vimy Ridge.

Diary Entry, 1 September 1918

The day gives promise of good weather. In the morning I saw the XVII Corps, and induced them to change their plans somewhat. The way they had it arranged was that some two hours after zero their attack was to begin. This exposed our flank to such an extent as to prejudice the success of our operation. It is now arranged that a brigade follows immediately behind our right brigade and on crossing the Quéant–Drocourt line turns south. When we pass through the line, the 63rd Division is to follow on our right and exploit towards Inchy. I saw General Macdonell, General Watson, and General Matheson. The Army Commander called during the afternoon. Early this morning the 15th Battalion attacked the Crows Nest, executing a very fine manoeuvre in order to get in its rear. They captured something like six officers and 200 other ranks, including the battalion commander and his adjutant. About noon the Germans counter-attacked our positions near the junction of the 1st and 4th Divisions, and temporarily drove our men out. They were immediately counter-attacked by the 5th and 72nd Battalions, who captured 100 prisoners. Everything looks promising for the success of tomorrow's operation providing we can get a good start at zero hour.

Diary Entry, 2 September 1918

This morning at five o'clock, the Quéant–Drocourt Switch was assaulted on a frontage of 7,000 yards; the 1st Division on the right, 3,000 yards; the 4th Division in the centre 2,500 yards; and the 3rd British Division on the left 1,500 yards. All our first objective, which included this trench system, was captured on time. The 4th British Division have made but little ground since; the 4th Canadian Division have made some, while the 1st Division have pushed on and taken the Buissy Switch, Villers-Cagnicourt, Cagnicourt, and gone on quite a mile beyond this latter place. Their performance since coming into the line, August 29th, has been quite remarkable. We have taken today quite some prisoners. I looked to get a great many guns, but the slow progress of the attack on the north has given the enemy a chance to get many of his guns away. The morale results of this victory will be great, while the military results must be considered as splendid. During the night (Sunday–Monday) the 5th Battalion, who were counter-attacked yesterday, were again counter-attacked by, what prisoners say, [was] six battalions. The 5th were driven in, but counter-attacking themselves with their reserve company they restored their line and captured over 100 prisoners, enabling them to kick off with the rest in the morning. I regard this as an unusually fine performance and quite up to the best things done by this battalion which, since coming to France, has never lost an inch of ground to the enemy, nor ever failed to take its objective.

Diary Entry, 3 September 1918

I moved the Corps advance headquarters to the 1st Divisional Headquarters east of Neuville Vitasse, and there held a conference at 9:00 am with the divisional commanders of the 1st and 4th Imperial Divisions and the 1st and 4th Canadian Divisions, giving them instructions to patrol energetically, following up such patrols with sufficient strength to gain the high ground overlooking the crossings of the canal. During the night the 4th Imperial Division captured Etaing taking about eighty prisoners. The 4th Canadian Division were unable to get on, but the 1st Canadian Division practically obtained their final objective. I regard the performance of this division since it took over the line on August 29th as one of the finest performances in all the war. They have fought practically continuously, have assaulted and captured the two trench systems, namely the Fresnes–Rouvroy Line and the Quéant–Drocourt line, and have altogether penetrated nearly five miles. In all yesterday we captured nearly 7,000 prisoners, making over 11,000 since beginning operations here, and over 21,000 since August 8th. As a result of our victory yesterday, the hinge of the German system has been broken and the Third Army enabled to advance, which they are doing today all along their line. It is a question whether our victory of yesterday or of August 8th is the greatest, but I am inclined to think yesterday's was. The Commander-in-Chief, the Chief of the General Staff, and others called to personally express their appreciation. Today we find that the Boche is practically retiring across the Canal du Nord.

*The Canadians had succeeded in pushing the Germans off the Drocourt–
Quéant Line in a difficult fight but the advance cost the Corps 5,622 casualties
in only two days of fighting. The next goal was the unfinished Canal du Nord,*

even more of a formidable obstacle. Currie had reservations about attacking across the canal.[65]

Diary Entry, 4 September 1918

Yesterday we completed the driving of the Boche to the east of the Canal du Nord, releasing quite a number of French civilians in the little village of Ecourt. One of them on meeting General Morrison this morning kissed him most affectionately... It is my opinion that a frontal attack on the German positions east of the canal would be unwise for the following reasons:

1. The canal itself is a serious obstacle,
2. The marshes on the eastern side make difficult going,
3. It is strongly defended by machine guns from the trench system running parallel to the canal,
4. The high ground to the east gives a perfect command of the approaches,
5. The more we advance to the eastward the more violent becomes the enfilade fire.

From all sides come reports of most bitter fighting in the Quéant–Drocourt line. The German dead must be far in excess of ours. In one part of the field an officer counted forty-six Canadian dead and over 400 Boches.

Diary Entry, 9 September 1918

Weather still unsettled. Spent the day with the 4th Division, particularly with General MacBrien[66] and General Hayter. In the afternoon received a letter from the Military Secretary stating that the Commander-in-Chief had given instructions for General Lipsett to take command of the 4th British Division in succession to General Matheson who is going to the Guards Division.

Diary Entry, 10 September 1918

Informed General Lipsett of the above and notified the army that he would be prepared to take over the 4th Division on the 18th, and that I proposed to recommend General Loomis as his successor. General Lipsett expressed a

---

65 See Morton and Granatstein, 222. See also BOH 1918 V, 1-123.
66 Major General Sir James Howden MacBrien (1878-1938) was the commander of the 12th Canadian Infantry Brigade (from December 1916), Chief of the General Staff (1919-27), and Commissioner of the Royal Canadian Mounted Police (1931-38) .

preference to remain with the Canadians. The Army Commander called with reference to future operations.

Diary Entry, 16 September 1918

Another very fine day. In the morning I held a Conference of divisional commanders and outlined future operations. General Embury[67] to lunch. In the afternoon I inspected the 11th Canadian Infantry Brigade near Chapel Hill and presented Honours and Awards to them. Colonel Ross, the head of the Military Postal Services in Canada called. A large Gotha[68] was brought down last night.

Diary Entry, 18 September 1918

At 9:30 am held a conference of divisional commanders to further discuss future operations. 11:30 am General Dawnay[69] and Sir John Fowler,[70] who is head of the Signal Services in France, called with reference to proposed increase of Establishment, and they remained to lunch. At three in the afternoon the Brigadier General, General Staff and myself attended a conference at Ecoivres. Major Blair came to Corps Headquarters to show me the new Huot automatic rifle[71] which I think is a very good weapon. It uses the Ross rifle as a framework.

Diary Entry, 23 September 1918

In the morning visited the 1st Brigade near Hendecourt, the 1st Engineer Brigade of the 2nd Division and the heavy artillery. Considerable fighting has taken place these days along the canal, the enemy being quite determined to retain a footing on our side. This suits our plans very well as, if he does retain his footing, he will not bring down his barrage on the canal itself, which is our first obstacle to cross and might prove very troublesome.

Diary Entry, 24 September 1918

We held our final conference at 9:30 this morning, being attended by all divisional commanders including General Winter[72] of the 11th Division. The

---

67 Brigadier General John Fletcher Leopold Embury (1875-1944) was commanding officer of the 2nd Canadian Infantry Brigade (January-March 1918) and from June 1918, the Officer-in-Charge at Canadian Section, GHQ.
68 A twin engine German bomber capable of carrying over one thousand pounds of explosives.
69 Major General Guy Dawnay (1878-1952) was Major General, General Staff, GHQ (1918-19).
70 Sir John Sharman Fowler (1864-1939) was Director of Army Signals for the BEF during the First World War.
71 The Huot Automatic Rifle was a Canadian weapon based on the abandoned Ross rifle. The war ended before it was adopted for use by the Canadian Corps.
72 Brigadier General Ormond d'Epee Winter.

final plans were approved and everyone appeared confident. General Byng called during the afternoon to discuss matters concerning the boundary.

Diary Entry, 25 September 1918

Spent the morning visiting all battalions of the 2nd Brigade and the 3rd Battalion of engineers which suffered so severely as the result of hostile bombing yesterday. Two bombs fell at Warlus and caught a battery just coming from the gas testing house. There were over sixty casualties and over forty deaths. The fuse of the bomb was found and appears to have British markings. This would indicate that possibly a bomb from one of our own machines[73] got loose and fell. The company was filled up immediately the officer commanding being allowed to pick his man from the Reinforcement Centre...

Diary Entry, 26 September 1918

The weather continues fine and gives every promise of being good for the battle which is scheduled to begin at 5:20 am. All troops are busy moving to their assembly positions. There is too much transport on the roads, but the chief offenders are the troops of the XVII Corps. Last night the 85th Battalion suffered about seventy-five casualties from bombing at the station in Arras. Had the train got away on time all would have been well but the train service was interrupted owing to the fact that a battalion of the 11th Division was not on time. This battalion was late owing to the pernicious habit of French trains blocking the roads. Today the French and Americans launched their big attack around both sides of the Argonne Forest. Twenty American divisions and fifty French divisions are taking part.

Diary Entry, 27 September 1918

The attack began at 5:30, the morning being slightly overcast and I was afraid it was a little dark. However the attack has progressed according to schedule time. Troops and guns and tanks have succeeded in crossing the canal. The Boche artillery reply was not as heavy as expected, testifying to the efficiency of our counter-battery work. He continues to shell Inchy very heavily as was to be expected, this being a place which several main roads pass through. I was told this morning that the big attack by the Americans and French was going

73 Airplanes.

very well, the intention being to push it much stronger today. Gouraud,[74] who is in command of the French rather felt his way yesterday, being afraid that the Germans might play the same trick on him as he did on them east of Rheims. Tomorrow an attack is to be put in by the French and the Belgians, with the King of the Belgians in command. On Sunday the Fourth Army are to make their big effort to smash the Hindenburg Line. Reports also indicate that interior-troubles may appear in Germany within the next week... The fighting was quite severe in spots, while it took a long time to mop up Sains-lez-Marquion and Marquion. We captured a German battery completely horsed. Among the prisoners was a Count who commanded a cavalry brigade. He was very much annoyed because someone, whom he said looked like a Jap, took from him his buttons, his shoulder straps, his Iron Cross, his ring, his money, and made him carry a stretcher about six kilometres. He was given lunch at Corps Headquarters, where he paid a great tribute to the attack as carried out this morning, and stated further that in the German Army everyone agreed that the Canadian troops were most to be feared in all the Allied armies. During the afternoon the Commander-in-Chief, the Chief of the General Staff, the Army Commander, General Godley,[75] and a number of others called. Today's success jeopardizes the hold of the enemy on the Quéant–Drocourt System north of the Scarpe, and he may be expected to fall back to Douai. We have overcome the obstacle of the canal and in a few days should take Cambrai, which is a great distributing centre for this area. The fall of Cambrai might easily mean the fall of Douai.

With the Canadians across the canal, Currie ordered the advance to continue towards the city of Cambrai. Although armistice rumours began to circulate, the Germans still hoped to hold off the advancing British long enough to establish a new line of defence along the Rhine. The Rhine provided a natural defensive position on Germany's frontiers and the High Command hoped that by shortening the line, the tired German divisions could regroup. It was thus imperative that the Entente forces keep up the pressure on the retreating enemy.[76]

---

74 General Henri Gouraud (1867-1946) commanded French Fourth Army.
75 General Sir Alexander Godley (1867-1957) was commanding officer of XXII Corps (1917 to the end of the war).
76 See Nicholson, 425-27 and Morton and Granatstein, 228-33. See also GOH XIV, 639-74 and BOH 1918 V, 124-211.

Diary Entry, 29 September 1918

The day opened clear and fine but chilly. The attack was resumed, the 3rd Division took the Marcoing Line down to the canal, also in the XVII Corps area, and continued their advance finally capturing St. Olle, which is on the Arras–Cambrai road and a suburb of Cambrai. The 4th Division got nearly as far as the railroad. The 1st Division were again unable to make much ground. I visited all divisional headquarters. Yesterday Colonel Gow called especially to ask what divisional commanders or brigadiers, if any, could be spared to take appointment in Canada. The big attack by the Fourth Army made by the Americans and Australians was not the success expected. They went in on a very narrow front with a very great many tanks. One of the American divisions did well, but the other forgot to mop up and suffered the usual penalty, the Germans coming out of their dug-outs and shooting them in the back. When the Australians advanced in order to go through the Americans they were held up and since then have been mopping up Germans and Americans.

Diary Entry, 30 September 1918

Weather was cloudy and cold. The attack was continued by the 3rd and 4th Divisions. The 3rd Division penetrated into Neuville St. Remy, advanced to the junction of the Arras–Cambrai road and the Bapaume–Cambrai road, and finally got a post right on the canal bank just outside of Cambrai. They also took Tilloy. The 4th Division attack went well at first, but they were heavily counter-attacked and driven back to the railroad though they retained possession of Sancourt. I visited all divisional headquarters and held a conference at the 4th Division, where arrangements were made for an attack on the whole front tomorrow morning. In the afternoon I visited the hospital. Colonel Gardiner of the 38th Battalion died this morning. General MacBrien who was wounded on Saturday was evacuated. The PPCLI lost their Colonel, Charlie Stewart.

Diary Entry, 1 October 1918

The attack began at five o'clock and, as has been the case each day forestalled a German attack which was to be made at 5:30. The 3rd Division gained ground to the extent of 1,500–2,000 yards, the 4th Division advancing 2,500 yards, which positions were held. The 1st Division's attack started off very well and at the beginning they were highly successful taking Blecourt, Bantigny and Cuvillers and getting some men into Abancourt. They were immediately counter-attacked. These counter-attacks were the most violent in character, heavily driven home and made in large numbers, with the consequence that little ground was gained. Today we met nine German divisions and must have inflicted very heavy casualties on the Boche. The artillery never fired as much ammunition as today and many of the targets were fired on over open sights. It is estimated that one thousand prisoners were taken, which brings our total for these operations to over 6,500. We have met in this battle thirteen German divisions, making a total of forty-seven since August 8th, and have captured 150 guns, making a total of 450 since the same date. The Germans have fought as here very, very hard, and when it is considered that this is one of their most important strategic flanks the reason for the violence of their counter-attacks can be appreciated. When it is considered that each day our attack forestalled a German attack, it is quite possible and I believe probable that they intended to retake Bourlon Wood and may possibly continue the attempt. We have suffered very heavy casualties, particularly in officers, and some of our battalions have none... The forty-seven divisions fought by the Canadian Corps since August 8th is twenty-five per cent of the German Army, so that we have more than pulled our weight.

Diary Entry, 2 October 1918

...I have been told that the progress of the Belgian–French attack in the north has been greatly retarded owing to the confusion existing in the Belgian Army, the staff work of which has been very bad. The same thing applies to the big attack of the American Army. They are so hopelessly confused that it will take some time to disentangle the units. Their supply arrangements have broken down completely.

Diary Entry, 5 October 1918

The weather continued fine but fairly cold. In the morning I visited the 2nd, 3rd and 4th Divisions with reference to future operations. In the afternoon went to the 10th Brigade Headquarters. During today the enemy began to retire on all the fronts north of Verdun to the right of our IV Corps. Rumours are still very prevalent about the confusion occurring to the north owing to the bad staff work of the Belgian Army, and the same thing may be said to apply to the American Army. It seems that both have a great deal yet to learn about the handling of troops in battle.

Diary Entry, 7 October 1918

Last night patrols of the 11th Division practically evacuated the position they were holding between the left flank of the 11th Division and the canal at Aubencheul, thus rendering it unnecessary to carry out the operations planned for tomorrow morning. This shortens our front a good deal besides making it more secure. I visited the 11th Divisional Headquarters, also those of the 2nd, 4th, and 3rd and the headquarters of the 9th Brigade. Lieutenant Colonel Armitage[77] of GHQ and Major Thompson, Aide-de-Camp to Sir Douglas Haig, were here for lunch. The latter informed me that it was the intention of His Majesty to send the Prince of Wales to the Canadian Corps for a month's attachment. He is to be accompanied by Major Thompson and Lord Claude Hamilton.[78] The Army Commander also called with reference to operations of tomorrow ...

Diary Entry, 8 October 1918

...Final plans for the attack tomorrow were completed and the attack ordered for 1:30. I am somewhat anxious about this attack, because the first orders received stated that we were not to try to cross the canal until the Third Army had secured Awoingt. This they have not yet succeeded in doing and unless we go tonight before they reach Awoingt we shall not be able to go until tomorrow night.

Diary Entry, 9 October 1918

The attack began at 1:30 and has proved a brilliant success. By eight o'clock this morning troops of the 3rd Division had passed through Cambrai north, south, east and west. They met with very little opposition but did take some sixty-five or so prisoners, many of whom I believe were left behind by the Germans to start fires, as new fires have been breaking out in different parts of the city all day. A day or so ago received instructions from the Army that our parties nominated to look for booby traps were to report to Third Army officials who evidently were determined to get all the credit for the capture of Cambrai. In that they were forestalled and it is a fitting climax to all the hard fighting of the Corps in this section that to us has fallen the honour of being the first troops to enter and pass through the city. Of this there is no doubt and in future should never be any question... The unusual hour of one-thirty was evidently a great surprise and

77 General Sir Charles C. Armitage (1881-1973) was GSO I and liaison officer at GHQ in 1917-18.
78 Lord Claud Nigel Hamilton (1889-1975).

an effective one as well. The troops advanced under a barrage travelling at the rate of 100 yards in two minutes. They met with little opposition except at the bridgeheads. For less than 200 casualties they have successfully overcome the obstacle of the canal and have captured 400 prisoners. An engineer officer, Mike [sic] Mitchell[79] by name, performed a very gallant act at one of the crossings inasmuch as alone he dashed across the bridge and shot a number of Germans who were preparing to blow it up and as a consequence saved two bridges from destruction... This morning General Webber drove into Cambrai and brought me some roses back from a garden there. This beautiful city has been wilfully set on fire by the Boche. We are doing our best to confine the damage but much destruction has already been wrought.

By 10 October the Canadians had captured the city of Cambrai with the German army in retreat beyond. Casualties had been heavy. In September alone the Canadians reported 4,368 killed and 13,985 wounded. By the end of October the two month total was 6,124 killed and 20,770 wounded. The Corps was exhausted but kept up the pursuit, now advancing north of the Scarpe towards the Belgian city of Mons. By the end of the battle of Cambrai, the state of the German Army had deteriorated. Although the enemy was still resisting the advance, the pace of their retreat had quickened. With each passing day it became less likely that the Germans could form a new line of defence.[80]

Diary Entry, 11 October 1918

The 49th Division relieved the right brigade of the 2nd Division last night, and in conjunction with the latter continued the advance this morning. At first they started very well but shortly afterwards were counter-attacked heavily in which the enemy used tanks. These were engaged by the artillery and driven back. The 49th Division, however, did not make much progress. The 6th Brigade continued the attack and captured Iwuy and are well beyond it tonight. The 2nd Division are being relieved tonight by the 51st Division, who with the 49th will constitute the XXII Corps, to whom we turned over at five o'clock and took over the front now held by the 1st Canadian Division, the 56th Division and the 11th Division. Today the enemy were driven from the Quéant–Drocourt line north of the Sensée River and our 1st Canadian Division has advanced several miles

79   Coulson Norman Mitchell (1889-1978) won the VC for actions on 8/9 October 1918.
80   On casualties see Cathcart; On German plans to establish a new line of defence see, GOH XIV, 660-674.

on that front. Since going into the line they have captured nearly 200 prisoners and have altogether done very well indeed. The Prince of Wales, Lord Claude Hamilton, his equerry, and Major Thompson... called. They are being attached to the Canadian Corps and will arrive on Monday next.

Diary Entry, 13 October 1918

The 56th Division crossed the Sensée River at Aubigny-au-Bac, where they captured two officers and 199 prisoners. They were counter-attacked during the day and forced hack to the river. I visited their headquarters and also the 11th Division. The reply of the German Government to President Wilson's reply to their first note has created a great deal of talk, and speculation is rife as to what the upshot will be. My opinion I expressed in my telegram in reply to one from Sir George Foster[81] [the] Acting Prime Minister. General Embury was here to lunch. General Davis and General Winter dined with as tonight. General Brutinel received the sad intimation of the death of his eldest son and is leaving for Paris immediately.

Diary Entry, 14 October 1918

Nothing happened on our front today. Enemy has not retired. An attack was launched by the Second Army, the French and the Belgians, and has progressed very well. Roulers has been captured and some 8,000 prisoners taken. This increases very much our threat to Lille. General Lipsett was killed today near Saulsoir. I understand he was out in front of our advanced posts some few hundred yards, making a personal reconnaissance. This seems such an unnecessary passing and has cost the county the life of a very valuable and experienced officer. The Prince of Wales accompanied by Major Thompson, arrived today to spend a month with us.

Diary Entry, 15 October 1918

The weather has become cold and wet. There is no change on our front but the Second Army and the Belgians have made considerable progress and are offering a very serious check to Lille from the north. President Wilson replies to the

---

81 Sir George Eulas Foster (1847-1931) was a Conservative Member of Parliament from New Brunswick (1882-1900) and Ontario (1904-21) and a Senator (1921-31). Foster served as Minister of Finance and Minister of Trade and Commerce. See W. Stewart Wallace (ed.), *Memoirs of the Right Honourable Sir George Foster* (Toronto: MacMillan, 1933).

German note in an effective though rather long-winded way. General Lipsett was buried this afternoon in the military cemetery at Quéant. There was a very large attendance and an impressive address delivered by Major Kilpatrick, Chaplain of the 42nd Battalion. The firing party and the hand came from his old battalion, the 8th. General Prower arrives to take up the work of GSO (S) Training. The appointments of Alex Ross[82] and Bob Clark[83] are confirmed as brigadiers.

Diary Entry, 17 October 1918

...News from all fronts remains particularly good. Our troops have taken Lille. It is also unofficially reported that Turcoing and Roubaix have also fallen and the three cavalry divisions have entered Bruges. The Navy have taken Ostend. Further gossip is that the Kaiser has been deposed and that the German Government is willing to accept any peace terms offered. Such news is always too good to be true, yet it is well within the range of probability.

Diary Entry, 20 October 1918

This morning I went by way of Marquion, Oisy le Verger, Aubencheul to the headquarters of the 1st Canadian Division at Lewarde and to the Chateau at Massy, and decided on the former as Corps Headquarters. I then tried to get to the 1st Brigade Headquarters, but after trying half a dozen roads could not reach it owing to craters having been blown in all the roads. I then went out to Hornaing and found the 3rd Field Ambulance with whom I lunched. A few of our wounded came in from Wallers about a mile in front, where the battle was still going on. Resistance has stiffened all along the front today though we are tonight within five miles of Valenciennes. The 10th Brigade on the right, next to them the 11th, the 3rd and the 1st. We have released in the different towns more than 40,000 civilians and it is a most inspiring sight to go through these towns and witness the joy of the inhabitants. All the houses are decorated with French flags and people seem overjoyed to greet the British soldiers. In many cases last night they dug up wine they had buried for years to share it with the troops. Many of the men had a bed to sleep on again but whether alone or not I cannot say. There are about 25,000 civilians in Denain. Colonel Peck was the first British soldier to arrive in Hornaing, where he was set upon by the inhabitants, who hung garlands

82   Brigadier General Alexander Ross (1880-1973) was commanding officer of 6th Brigade (from October 1918).
83   Brigadier General R.P. Clark, the commanding officer of 2nd Brigade from October 1918.

about him and pinned flowers on almost every part of his coat. Nearly every woman in the town, I am told, kissed him. Considerable progress has been made all along the line, but the fact remains that the enemy is making a very orderly and practically unmolested retirement. Our trouble is that the troops are very tired and that the getting forward of supplies is becoming very difficult owing to the distance away of rail heads. Our higher authorities do not seem well enough organized to push their rail heads forward fast enough. We are moving Corps Headquarters in the morning to Lewarde.

Diary Entry, 22 October 1918

I spent most of the day in the office going through recommendations for honours and awards. The Army wired to know if General Webber could be spared to take up the position of Director of Demobilization in England. I have therefore asked for the immediate recall of General Alex Ross to take the 10th Brigade,[84] and I shall bring General Hayter in to act as Brigadier General, General Staff.

Diary Entry, 23 October 1918

In the morning I went to the XXII Corps at Escaudoeuvres, bringing with me as far as Cambrai Lieutenants Mitchell and Mackenzie. We went by way of Aubigny-au-Bac and returned by Ramillies, Eswars, Paillencourt. Lunched with the 4th Division at Auberchicourt. Our men were never so well placed for billets since they came to France. Everyone is in a house, and the majority have beds. The people are more than kind to them. Many of the units have voluntarily given up fifteen per cent of their rations to the inhabitants, who have made it up by gifts of vegetables.

Since the Battle of Cambrai, the Germans had been retreating rapidly, putting up only mild resistance. At the end of the month, however, the German Army congregated at Valenciennes and Mont Houy, intent to make a stand where the terrain favoured the defender. On 26 October Currie was called to First Army Headquarters where he and the commander of XXII Corps were given the task of capturing the two positions. The assault was scheduled for the 28th. Despite the impending operation, on the evening of the 26th Currie found the time to

---

84   Currie probably meant Brigadier General John Munro Ross. See Nicholson, 542.

reflect on the Corps' victories of the previous month in a letter to a newspaper man back home.[85]

Currie to Harold Daly, 26 October 1918[86]

Dear Harold,

...I am glad to hear you speak so kindly of the Corps. It is very gratifying to us all to be told that the people of Canada are satisfied with what it has accomplished. Naturally I am prejudiced, but I believe it is hard to estimate the exact value of the results of our attacks. You, no doubt, have seen a copy of my recent order, in which I set forth what the Corps had accomplished since August 8th. It is a truly marvellous story, and the half has not yet been told.

We were the spearhead of the attack at Amiens, and in the battle of Arras and the battle of Cambrai, formed the flank to the big attack of the Third and Fourth Armies. I venture to say now that this flank attack by the Canadian Corps will form one of the most interesting subjects for future study by military students. A flank attack is always a hard attack, and in this case our flank was exposed for twenty-five miles. The Germans fought us exceedingly hard all the way, for whenever the Canadian Corps goes into battle he seems to throw a far higher proportion of men and ammunition at us than he does at any other part of the front. He assumes that if he stops the Canadian Corps, everything else stops. This is a point that should be remembered by the people of Canada when they think of the casualties the Corps has to sustain, but yet, in view of all we have accomplished, I do not think anyone has any right to complain of the casualties.

You probably have not heard very much of the Corps since the battle of Cambrai, but because you have not you must not assume that we have been out of the line and resting. I said that in our advance on Cambrai, we had our left flank exposed for twenty-five miles. After being relieved in front of Cambrai, we went to the western edge of that flank and began to roll it up, and tonight we are half way through the city of Valenciennes, much further east than we were when we left the Cambrai front. In this operation we have released more than fifty thousand French civilians, and you can imagine their joy at that release. We have now left far behind the area of trenches, shell holes, dugouts, and barbed wire, and I hope never to see them again. The country we are now in is a very clean one with good roads, nice villages and towns. Every man has a good billet, and

---

85 See Nicholson, 448-60 and Morton and Granatstein, 228-33.
86 File 1, vol 1, CP, LAC.

most of them are in beds. The populace are exceedingly kind, and to be able to release them has been an inspiration to all our men. They are hearing from these people's own lips what it means to be under German rule.

I am glad to see that the temper of Canada is to fight this war out to a finish, and that peace when it does come must be a peace that will last for many, many years. We do not want to have to do this thing all over again in another fifteen or twenty years. If that is to be the case, German military power must now be irretrievably crushed. This is the end we must obtain if we have the will and the guts to see it through. To me the present situation is one fraught with much danger. I hope that when we make peace there exists in Germany a form of government which possesses some stability. We do not want to make peace with a lot of Bolshevists, and there is a danger of Bolshevism becoming rampant in Germany. Furthermore, if Bolshevism does appear there, it may easily spread to France and England, and we might go from the frying pan into the fire.

Reverting to the Corps again, despite all of our losses we are in fair shape. There are enough men in England to replace all casualties and many thousands more, but they did not arrive in England to be well enough trained when they were wanted. Furthermore, we have felt the need of officers very much. The authorities in England did not appreciate our wants in that regard as they should have. In other services, such as the signallers and machine gunners, we find that we have to do as much training in France as they do in England. I do not wish to quarrel with the authorities there but the manner in which training has been carried out has never been satisfactory. Though I do see by the speeches made at the big dinner they held on the anniversary of the arrival of the First Contingent in England, it was plain that the credit for the Corps' victories belonged chiefly to the work done in England.

I am afraid the old gang is still doing business. I notice that the Canadian authorities apparently hired a few writers to report that dinner. Hall Cain seems to be of those chosen. In an article which he writes, he makes the 1st Canadian Division march down the Strand past Westminster on their way to Salisbury. In his description of the battles fought, an outsider would conclude that the victories won by the Canadian Forces in France were won altogether by the Second and Fourth Divisions. Why Canada will waste the people's money in paying fiction writers to write the history of the part it played in this war is more than I can see. The absolute rot put out by the Canadian War Records is astounding.

When the Prime Minister was here last summer, I protested against this book known as 'Canada in Flanders' being styled as the official story of the Canadian Expeditionary Force, but apparently all to no avail. I stated my reasons very clearly in a letter to Sir Edward Kemp, a copy of which letter I sent to the Prime Minister. All that was done with my latter was to hand it over to Lord Beaverbrook, who wrote me saying that in finding fault as I did I was casting aspersions on one of the most noted Canadian writers, namely, Charles G.D. Roberts,[87] who, as you know, is another writer of poetry and fiction. I cannot help whether I cast aspersions on Roberts or not, but I do say that Volume III of 'Canada in Flanders' bears no more resemblance to the true story of the period it depicts than a mutton stew does to the sheep itself. I am afraid, though, that it is still too much to hope that things in England will ever be run satisfactorily.

With all good wishes, and hoping that before another October comes around that I may see you again in Ottawa, I am ever yours faithfully,

A.W. Currie

Diary Entry, 27 October 1918

Today I attended a most interesting ceremony. A week ago the city of Denain had been captured by our 4th Division, and the people held in the cathedral of that city today a thanksgiving service, conducted by the priest and associate clergymen. The Prince of Wales attended, as well as all the officers of the Corps staff, all the officers of the 4th Division staff, and many others. We were received at the entrance of the church by the clergy, and young girls presented bouquets of flowers. Within the church a high mass was celebrated, and the priest gave a most eloquent address. On coming out of the church we were each presented with a souvenir flag. During the ceremony I am told most of the women in the congregation were in tears. After leaving the church the 10th Canadian Infantry Brigade marched past, the Prince taking the salute. The saluting point was at the statue which had been erected to a famous French General, but the statue itself, which was of bronze, had been removed by the Germans. I lunched with the 4th Division, and afterwards attended a conference at Army Headquarters to discuss future operations. An outline was agreed upon, and I immediately went to inform General Watson, whose troops were involved. I also visited the heavy artillery and told them.

---

87 Sir Charles George Douglas Roberts (1860-1943) a Canadian poet and writer known as 'the father of Canadian literature.'

Diary Entry, 28 October 1918

I suffered today from a slight attack of diarrhea and remained in the office all day. General Webber left to take up the appointment of Director General of Demobilization in England and General Ross Hayter came to Corps Headquarters as his relief. General Jimmy Ross arrived from England to take command of the 10th Brigade. The XXII Corps attacked Mont Houy and, after being successful in the morning, were kicked off by counter-attack in the afternoon. As the possession of this was supposed to be in their hands before we were relieved, and as they expressed their inability to recapture it, a change was necessary in the plans. It was arranged by the Army that we relieve 1st Division on the night of the 29th/30th.

Diary Entry, 29 October 1918

...Plans were completed which involved our attacking on Friday morning. It is reported today that Austria-Hungary has thrown in her hand and that Turkey has expressed her willingness to do likewise, though the announcement of the latter has been withheld. The German's are dropping leaflets telling our men that they do not wish to fight any more and asking that we call it off.

Diary Entry, 30 October 1918

In the morning visited the 4th Division at Denain and the 3rd Division at Wallers, at the former completing arrangements for the attack to take place on November 1st. In the afternoon motored to Villers Châtel. A year ago today we fought the battles of Crest Farm and Mosselmarkt.

Diary Entry, 31 October 1918

Spent most of the day in the office in connection with honours and awards. Went over to see General Macdonell in the afternoon with reference to certain changes on his staff. Today at noon an armistice took place between Turkey and ourselves, while later this evening Austria agreed to an armistice on very favourable terms to us.

Diary Entry, 1 November 1918

In conjunction with the XXII Corps of the First Army, and the left of the Third Army we attacked at 5:15 and the news so far is that we have taken all our objectives with quite a number of prisoners. I am told that the ground is simply littered with German dead. I know that it was not the intention of our fellows to take many German prisoners as, since they have lived amongst and talked to the French people here, they have become more bitter than ever against the Boche. The attack this morning was carried out by the 10th Brigade, and represented an advance of 3,500 yards on a 2,200 yards frontage. The XXII Corps have twice failed to take Mont Houy and a few days ago we extended our southern boundary to include this place.

Currie to Sir Edward Kemp, 1 November 1918[88]

My dear Sir Edward,

I am very glad indeed to hear from you, and to learn that you are back again at your post in London. As you can well imagine, your going to Canada gave rise to all sorts of rumours that you were going to remain there. Like myself, your health was supposed to have failed. The best I can wish you is that you feel as well as I do this morning.

Since August 8th the Corps, as you know, has been continuously engaged. The full story of its operations is well known to you. With you, I regret the number of casualties, but I do not consider that anyone can regard them as excessive when the extent and severity of the operations are considered. You cannot meet and defeat in battle one-quarter of the German Army without suffering casualties. Furthermore, there is one thing that Canadians must always understand and that is this: as soon as the Germans realize that the Canadian Corps is engaged in the battle, they hurl divisions and ammunition at it in much greater proportion than they do at any other section of the front.

In the severe fighting just north of Cambrai, on a five mile front, they opposed us with thirteen divisions reinforced by thirteen independent machine gun units, whereas on a ten mile front south of Cambrai only six German divisions were engaged. One does not wish to publicly say so, but it would almost appear that the Germans concluded that if they could stop the Canadian Corps they could stop the others.

This morning we attacked again to the south of Valenciennes, and have taken all our objectives. This attack was on a 2,200 yard front, and the penetration already extends to 3,500 yards. We have taken quite a number of prisoners, and

---

88   File 2, vol 1, CP, LAC.

they tell me the ground is simple piled with German dead. We put on a very heavy concentration of artillery and seem to have caught them in the middle of a relief, and furthermore, since our men have released the French civilians in the areas they have traversed, and have talked with these civilians concerning their treatment by the Germans, their feelings towards the enemy have become much more bitter so that this morning I can well imagine there were not quite as many prisoners taken as usual. Only Watson's people were engaged, and of them so far only Ross's lot. As the result of these operations I hope that the city of Valenciennes will be in our possession tonight.

I hope you soon keep your promise to come across and spend some time with us.

Ever yours faithfully,

A.W. Currie

Diary Entry, 2 November 1918

The operation yesterday was one of the most successful the Corps has yet performed. There were not more than 1,400 bayonets in the attack yet the prisoners taken were nearly 1,800 and the number of dead actually counted on the ground over 800. Seven guns were also taken besides a great many machine guns and trench mortars. Our casualties were not 450 of whom less than 100 were killed. Yesterday the 38th Battalion crossed the canal south of Valenciennes, and the 72nd north; both worked their way through the city and entirely cleared the Boche by 7:30 this morning. The 11th Brigade passed through the 10th Brigade, cleared Marly early in the morning, and tonight our line is quite a mile east of Valenciennes. The 49th Division on our right were very sticky all through the operation. The 3rd Division also got a post across the canal.

Diary Entry, 4 November 1918

The Third and Fourth British Armies together with the First French Army attacked today on a wide front meeting with much success, capturing 15,000 prisoners and over 200 guns. Indications last night suggested the possibility of a counter-attack on our front, and this morning we laid down a counter-preparation with the result that the enemy retired and our troops advanced a further 2,000 yards, passing through the town of Onnaing on the north. Corps Headquarters moved to Denain today, the 4th Division having moved to Valenciennes. I saw all brigades concerned in the operation, namely the 11th on the right, the 12th in the centre, and the 8th on the north. The weather was very fine.

Diary Entry, 5 November 1918

All troops advanced this morning. The 11th Brigade took Rombies and secured a bridge-head across the Aunelle River. The 12th Brigade took Quarouble, and the 8th Brigade Vicq. On Sunday the civilian authorities at Valenciennes expressed a desire to thank the Canadian Corps for the part they have played in the deliverance of Valenciennes. They asked for a ceremony on Wednesday morning, which was arranged, but on this becoming known to the Army authorities they cancelled our arrangements and said that the Army would make the show an Army one. They said that the XXII Corps should be included, and that the Army Commander should be the person to receive the address and the flag. They issued orders asking us to parade four companies, each of a strength of 150, the XXII Corps to do likewise and our troops to take a position on the right of the line and march past first. The action of the Army is unaccountable and is resented by the Corps, especially when they changed their order on Wednesday putting the XXII Corps on the right of the line and our troops last. Colonel Gibson, Colonel Morrison and General Thacker[89] from Argyll House arrived to discuss matters in connection with demobilization .

Diary Entry, 6 November 1918

...I held a meeting at Corps Headquarters with representatives from the Minister, and had present all divisional commanders with their principal administrative officers, besides the principal officers of the Corps staff. We came to very satisfactory conclusions regarding demobilization and received an assurance that the chief wish of the Corps to be returned by units to Canada would receive the favourable consideration of the government. General Russell of the New Zealand Division had lunch, bringing with him Lieutenant Dick Gordon to take up his duties as Aide-de-Camp with me.

By the beginning of November, it was clear that the Allies had defeated the German Army on the battlefield. Yet it was still possible that the Entente advance would stall at the Rhine if the Germans were allowed to establish a new line

---

89   Major General Percival Edward Thacker (born 1873) was Adjutant General at the Overseas Ministry.

of defence. General Foch thus ordered the BEF to keep up the pressure on the retreating army until an armistice was signed. For the Canadians this meant pushing onward towards Mons. While the war in the field was coming to an end, the question of demobilization created new problems.

Currie to Sir Edward Kemp, 6 November 1918[90]

Dear Sir Edward,

I have today held a meeting at Canadian Corps Headquarters which was attended by Brigadier General P.E. Thacker, Colonel F. Morrison, and Lieutenant Colonel Gibson, all from Argyll House, as well as by the principle officers of Corps Headquarters and divisional commanders, accompanied by their chief administration officers. The object of the meeting was to discuss certain questions in connection with demobilization.

The following were the points discussed:

1. The method of organization of Canadians in France for dispatch to Canada. It is unnecessary for me, unless you especially desire it, to recapitulate the factors which have forced me to the conclusion that the only satisfactory way to return troops to Canada is by complete units and not by drafts. The organization for doing so is already in existence, whereas if the units are re-grouped in any other manner, the organization necessary to deal with their return would have to be improvised and as no improvised organization works smoothly or efficiently. The officers in charge of units have had large experience in moving troops, in looking after records etc., and it seems to me they are the ones who can do the work most efficiently. Furthermore, if they are returned to Canada by units you maintain the discipline, which is a very important factor. If you do not, I would not care to answer for the discipline. I am sure I am speaking for the Corps when I say it is their unanimous wish to be returned by units and not by drafts.

2. Some order for their return will have to be decided upon, and the meeting today was unanimous that the units should return in the order of their arrival in France, namely, the 1st Canadian Division first, followed by the 2nd, 3rd and 4th in succession.

3. It is understood that dispersal areas will be organized in Canada. The opinion of the meeting was that any man whose home is not near the locality selected for the dispersal of his unit should have the option of declaring whether

---

90 File 2, vol 1, CP, LAC. On demobilization, see Desmond Morton and Glenn Wright, *Winning the Second Battle: Canadian Veterans and the Return to Civilian Life, 1915-1930* (Toronto: UTP, 1987).

he will accompany his unit to its place of demobilization, or whether he will be sent as soon as possible to the place of dispersal nearest to his home.

4. As regards units not forming part of a division, it will be necessary to select places of demobilization in Canada. These are mostly small units, and for the voyage back to Canada they should be fitted in to complete the loads of ships which are not fully filled by the larger units.

5. The question was raised as to whether it would be preferable to crowd men into ships to such an extent that they had to sleep by reliefs. We are of the opinion that, even at the expense of taking twenty per cent longer to return all Canadians to Canada, men should not be crowded unduly.

6. As regards men taking their discharge in England, I am informed that the orders at present against this are very rigorous. I realize the main disadvantages of discharging men in England, and am of the opinion that all should be notified that no such applications for discharge will be entertained. It is of course realized that it would probably be unjust not to deal with some cases in another way.

7. As regards men serving terms of imprisonment, and men under suspended sentence, I am of opinion that all suspended sentences should be remitted on leaving France or England for Canada. I am also in favour of the remission of un-expired portions of sentences which have been passed for purely military crimes but I think no announcement of the intentions of dealing with such cases should be disclosed before peace is declared. The remission of un-expired portions of sentences will no doubt have to be discussed with the Imperial authorities when they are considering the question of the proclamation of an amnesty of any kind. Should sentences be remitted, I do not think men should be allowed to return to Canada with their units, who feel keenly any disgrace brought upon them by the crimes of these men.

8. We discussed another point, namely, the possibility of concentration by complete divisions in suitable centres in Canada. For instance, it would be a splendid thing if the 1st Division or the 2nd Division, or the 3rd or the 4th, could be concentrated say at Quebec or Montreal, and there reviewed by the Governor General and the Prime Minister before proceeding to their dispersal areas. Such a thing may, of course, not be possible but the holdings of such a parade on the historic Plains of Abraham would be a fitting close to the part a division has played in this great struggle.

I sincerely trust that this recommendation to return the Canadian troops to Canada by units will be adopted by our Government. Doing it in any other manner will cause grave dissatisfaction and a heart-burning [sic], and as I said in the beginning we have in existence now the necessary organization to deal with this question.

Yours faithfully,

A.W. Currie

Diary Entry, 7 November 1918

...The ceremony at Valenciennes took place and was a very frosty affair; no Canadians attended except the troops on parade and myself, who was ordered to go by the Army Commander. It was not my intention to attend, and I would not have been there had I not received the order. General Hayter accompanied me in order to see his old brigade march past... Today the emissaries from the German Government passed through the French lines under a flag of truce to ask from General Foch the terms of armistice. The crews of the German fleet have mutinied at Kiel, killing their officers and seizing the ships. It begins to look as if the end is coming fast.

Diary Entry, 8 November 1918

Our troops have again made good progress advancing an average depth of 5,000 yards, being tonight within six miles of Mons. They have also crossed the Condé–Mons Canal in several places. The delegates sent from Germany to get from General Foch the conditions of the Armistice met him today, when it was found that they were not clothed with plenipotentiary powers. They were given until Monday at 11:00 am to submit Germany's answer. General Embury and Colonel Gow had lunch with us, the latter intending to spend some time with the Corps.

On 9 November the Canadians prepared to take Mons, a symbolic city where the British fired their first shots of the war in August 1914. Four years before, the BEF was in retreat, fighting a desperate rearguard action in an attempt to avoid encirclement. Now, by a twist of fate, First Army and the Canadian Corps stood at the gates of Mons as the Armistice was being negotiated at Compiègne. On 8 November the Army Commander, Henry Horne, wrote to his wife, 'I hope we get to Mons as it would be a great satisfaction to me to take [the city], as

I commanded the rear guard of the I Corps when we lost it four years ago last August.' While Currie too was aware of the historical importance of the city, he did not want to sacrifice lives needlessly just as the fighting was coming to an end.[91]

Diary Entry, 9 November 1918

The weather continued very fine, and our troops made excellent progress, reaching the line about a mile or so west of Mons. I saw both the divisions involved, and in my visit could not help but be struck by the difference in the treatment accorded by the Germans to Belgium and that accorded to the French. In France, all the mines had been destroyed, while just over the line, in Belgium, they were all working. I have no doubt but what the Bosch intended was to keep Belgium, provided he won the war, and therefore thought it good policy to appease the citizens of that country.

Diary Entry, 10 November 1918

Both divisions continued to make progress, and passing through Jemappes, early reached the canal on the outskirts of Mons, where they encountered heavy machine gun fire. I gave instructions that if the town could be captured without many casualties, the pressure should be continued. Today, while three German prisoners were being brought into our cages through Jemappes, they were set upon by some women of that town and killed. The women first struck them over the head with their wooden shoes, and afterwards used hatchets. Today, President Poincaré[92] visited Valenciennes and was received by a guard of honour from the 72nd Battalion. In his address to the assembled populace, he referred in most congratulatory terms to the Canadians. The Corps Headquarters moved today to Valenciennes. M. Roy, Canadian Commissioner at Paris, arrived at Corps Headquarters last night.

Currie wanted to limit Casualties, but Horne wanted the city taken. 'At Mons the Boche is defending the canal and the [area] to the north of it,' wrote Horne to his wife the day before the Armistice was signed, 'I am pushing the troops to get on round the south...I feel pretty sure that it will be carried tomorrow.'

---

91 See Horne to his wife, 8 November 1918, Papers of General Lord Horne of Stirkoke (hereafter cited as HP), Archives of the Imperial War Museum, London (hereafter cited as IWM). See also, Nicholson, 461-85 and Morton and Granatstein, 233-6.

92 Raymond Poincaré (1860-1934) was President of France (1913-20).

Currie never explicitly ordered his troops to capture the city. Instead, they were asked to capture a line of hills beyond Mons, an objective that Foch and GHQ had established more than a month earlier. To reach the objective, the Corps would have to pass through Mons itself making the liberation of the city a fortunate, but incidental by-product of a larger operation.[93]

Diary Entry, 11 November 1918

Shortly after midnight the 42nd Battalion found a weak spot at the station, west of Mons, and entered the city. Some fighting took place through the streets, where I saw dead bodies later in the day. The German machine gunners defending the position were all volunteers, and remained at their posts until they were either killed or captured. At 4:30 in the morning the 3rd Division was able to report the complete capture of the town. The 2nd Division had, in the meantime, secured the high ground to the south east and had passed through the southern outskirts of the city in reaching that position, About 7:50 in the morning a wire came from the Army informing us that the Armistice was to come into effect at 11:00 am, when hostilities would cease. At ten o'clock this morning I inspected the 1st Brigade and afterwards addressed them. Hurrying back to Valenciennes I came on to Mons, and in the afternoon made a formal entry. Generals Morrison, Loomis, Ormond[94] and a number of staff officers accompanied me. A squadron of the 5th Lancers[95] formed the escort. Each member of the squadron wore the Mons Medal, and they were commanded by an officer, now lieutenant, but who was a trooper at the First Battle of Mons.[96] The people were most enthusiastic in their reception, and on reaching the square one was met by the civic dignitaries. The Deputy Burgomaster made an address of welcome, to which I replied. There were a large number of troops on parade, representing all units in the 3rd Division. After giving three cheers for the Belgian King and Queen and the people these troops, headed by the 5th Lancers, marched past to the tune of the Belgian national anthem. The thousands of people in the square sang it, and it was a most inspiring situation. After the troops had marched past, we entered the municipal

93   See Horne to his wife, 10 November 1918, HP, IWM; Foch's orders to the BEF to advance to Mons are dated 10 October 1918 and found in WO 158/72, The National Archives (hereafter cited as TNA), Kew. Haig's orders to Horne and Horne's orders to Currie are in WO 158/192, TNA.
94   Brigadier General Daniel Mowat Ormond (born 1885) was the commanding officer of 9th Brigade (May 1918 to the end of the war).
95   The 5th Lancers were one of the last units to evacuate Mons in August, 1914.
96   The First Battle of Mons took place on 23 August 1914 and was Britain's first engagement of the war. At Mons the BEF was forced to retreat from the city, fighting a rearguard action.

chamber and signed the book. The last signature in that book was that of the King of the Belgians, written in the year 1914, before the war. Refreshments were served, and later in the evening I returned to Valenciennes; but I left our troops and the people of Mons celebrating in a most joyous fashion.

Currie was notified of the Armistice while taking a bath at his headquarters. News of the peace gradually trickled down to the divisions, brigades, and battalions of the Canadian Corps. At 8:00 am, the last attack on the Western Front was launched by the 28th Battalion from northwest Saskatchewan which advanced southeast of Mons and pushed through the Boise de Havre towards the canal which ran through the city. Despite notification of the Armistice at 9:00 am, the assault continued. The battalion's war diarist recorded, 'With splendid dash and overcoming somewhat increased resistance the battalion dashed forward and by 11:00 hours had reached [its objective].' Ten minutes before the Armistice, Private George Price was killed by a single German machine gun bullet in the outskirts of Mons. He was the only Canadian killed on 11 November and, as legend has it, was the last Commonwealth soldier to die on the Western Front. Although the attack took place after the Armistice had been signed, it was carried forward at the behest of the commander of the 28th Battalion, not General Currie. The Corps Commander made no attempt to cover himself or the Canadian headquarters staff in glory as Sir Sam Hughes would later allege.

Canada played an important role in the final drive of the war, but had paid a heavy price. During the first eleven days of November alone, 437 Canadians were killed, and 1,275 wounded. Since the beginning of August the Corps had suffered enormous casualties: 11,259 killed and 36,906 wounded, more than twenty-five per cent of all Canadian battle casualties during the Great War. The Armistice ended the fighting and the casualties, but not the war itself. Over the next few weeks the Canadian Corps advanced to the Rhine to take up positions in Germany until a permanent peace treaty was concluded at a later date. While it was clear that the enemy had been defeated, fears remained that the Armistice was merely a delaying tactic. The occupation of the Rhineland was intended to secure the final peace settlement by making it impossible for Germany to resume the war from an advantageous position.[97]

Diary Entry, 15 November 1918

Roy left for Paris this morning, and Gow for Brussels and other centres of interest. I left at 4:20 for Boulogne, for two or three days' leave. We arrived there at about eight o'clock, thus making a most splendid run. The boat left at 10:30; Willis not being able to catch the same, as the second motor did not arrive. I arrived in London at about three o'clock, went immediately to the Carlton Hotel, and Lily met me shortly afterwards. We had tea there, Dudley Oliver joining us. I also saw young Macdowall, who had just returned from being a prisoner of war since April, 1915. We went to 'Hello, America' at *The Palace* that night. The people in London have simply been going mad in their celebrations. The streets were well lit up and densely packed; all sorts of mad dancing and other capers going on.

Diary Entry, 14 November 1918

At noon I went to see Sir Edward Kemp at his Hotel, the Ritz, where he has been lying ill practically since his return from Canada. I remained with him until about one o'clock. Willis lunched with us at the Carlton, and we spent the afternoon shopping. After tea we left for Brighton, arriving there about eight o'clock. We found everybody well.

Diary Entry, 17 November 1918

I sent the car last night to bring up Ethel and the kiddies, and they arrived about half past ten. Ada Gordon and Lou Patterson also called, the latter much upset by certain rumours she has heard. It seems that some of the senior officers in England spend most of their time visiting hospitals and condoling with the wounded; intimating to the latter that the casualties in the Canadian Corps have been altogether too high. This, in my opinion, is about the cheapest and meanest form of criticism that a small person could conceive. General Tuxford, Colonel Brothers and others called, while Jim Slicker spent most of the afternoon with us. We dined in our room, after which I went to see Sir Robert Borden, who arrived this afternoon at about 5:00 pm, accompanied by Sir George Foster, A.L.

---

97 See 'Narrative of Operations Undertaken by 28th Cdn. Inf. Battalion SE of Mons, 8-11 November 1918,' File 426, part II, vol 4936, series IIID3, RG 9, LAC. On casualties, see Cathcart.

Sifton,[98] and a large staff. General Embury and Major Tom Gibson were present. We went fairly into the question of demobilization, and I laid before them as succinctly as I could the attitude of the Corps. We had a late session, and I had to walk back to the Carlton.

Diary Entry, 18 November 1918

We left Charing Cross at 11:35 for France. Generals Plumer, Rawlinson, Budworth[99] and many others were on the train. We arrived at Boulogne at about five o'clock, but it took us until about 2:00 the next morning to reach Mons, the delay being largely owing to fog. I found that the Prince of Wales had left the Corps last Friday, and that the 1st Division had moved forward to begin the march. I decided to put the two old divisions in the lead, leaving the 3rd and 4th concentrated in the Mons area.

Diary Entry, 22 November 1918

Accompanied by General Farmar and Willis, I went to Brussels to see the King of the Belgians make his formal entry into his capital. We were fortunate in getting seats in the Foreign Office, overlooking the Square where the King stood and watched the troops marching past. First came a detachment of Americans, then the French, then the British, and finally a very large detachment of Belgians of all arms. The three first mentioned had only infantry and artillery on parade. I thought the Americans looked the worst, their artillery being very bad. Our troops looked very well, but not as uniformly dressed as one would have liked to see. All units suffered from the fact that the band did not turn out and play the unit by...

Diary Entry, 23 November 1918

In the morning I held a meeting at Corps Headquarters, of the divisional commanders and brigadiers. I was anxious to get their views on two matters— first as to the truth or otherwise of the rumours concerning a certain spirit of unrest amongst the troops; and secondly, as to demobilization. I was much re-assured by what they were able to say regarding the first-mentioned; and from

---

98 Arthur Lewis Sifton (1858-1921) was Clifford Sifton's brother and Premier of Alberta (1910-17). Arthur Sifton joined the Union Government in 1917 and was part of the Canadian delegation to the Paris Peace Conference.

99 Major General Charles Edward Dutton Budworth (1869-1921) was Major General, Royal Artillery (1916-18).

the opinions they expressed regarding demobilization, I was convinced that I had placed the matter before the Prime Minister in a light reflecting the feeling in the Corps. Regarding the spirit of unrest, there is no doubt that some of those who have joined as a result of the Military Service Act have not acquired the proper *esprit de corps*. In the afternoon I wrote a long letter to Sir Edward Kemp regarding demobilization, and also completed a Special Order to the troops with reference to our entry into Germany.

Diary Entry, 26 November 1918

Also spent today in the office, and was able to clear up much outstanding correspondence. Tonight General Rennie arrived at Corps Headquarters for a brief visit. I also received an urgent telegram from the Minister, asking me to furnish for the benefit of Sir Robert Borden, certain information regarding the late operations of the Corps. It seems that a certain section of the American press has adopted the attitude of belittling the importance of the operations of the Canadians. After dinner I wrote a long letter to the Prime Minister, and had maps prepared. I also determined upon sending Generals Morrison and Brutinel to London to give further information to the Prime Minister.

Currie to Sir Robert Borden, 26 November 1918[100]

Dear Sir Robert,

From the Canadian Section at GHQ I learn that you are anxious to have in your possession as soon as possible certain facts relative to the part taken by the Canadian Corps since August 8th, last.

It has been intimated to me that a certain section of the American press is seeking to belittle the work of the Canadians, intimating that what we call the 'Imperial' troops have done the bulk of the fighting. If this is the case, it may be Boche propaganda, but I am inclined to think that the English press are the people to blame, for it is a fact that their reports on the operations since August 8th have in very few cases been fair or just to the Canadians.

If you were able to look up the diary of events of the month of August as published in the 'Times' of September 2nd or 3rd you will see that the word 'Canadian' is used on only two occasions; one giving us credit for taking the village of Haucourt, which we did not take, and the other giving us credit for

100 File 1, vol 1, CP, LAC.

taking Bois Notre Dame. The operations at Amiens are credited to British troops and the word 'Canadian' is not used. They say that Monchy was taken by the English. In fact in one of the paragraphs where the word 'Canadian' is used, they give the credit to British troops for the capture of places which the Canadians took; and the fact they have used in the same paragraph the words 'British' and 'Canadian' shows an intention, or at least a willingness to differentiate between the two words. As they give evidence of a willingness to differentiate sometimes, it has struck me that it would be fair to differentiate always. We are British, certainly, and proud to be called such, but a certain section of the English press are evidently determined on a policy to ignore the word 'Canadian.'

You probably were in London yourself when the Amiens operations were on, and noted that the first reports of these operations, used the word 'British,' exclusively. In fact, in many instances the press have gone further than merely using the word 'British' when we thought they should have used the word 'Canadian.'

I remember they gave credit to the Naval Division for taking Baralle and Buissy; places which were taken by the Canadians, and by the Canadians alone. But examples of this injustice are almost too numerous to mention.

Mr. Livesay,[101] our correspondent, has, on many occasions represented our views at Censor Headquarters, only to be asking what objections the Canadians had to the use of the word 'British.'

I believe the papers have the policy I speak of, and I believe they received their instructions from the highest military authorities.

No doubt, the American papers have taken their news in many instances, from these English papers, and no one can blame them for coming to a wrong conclusion. Our own papers in Canada republished the English articles, and themselves fell into the error, with the result, that the Canadian people do not even now realize the full extent of the operations in which the Corps has taken part, and for that reason, some of them may think the casualties have been unduly heavy. If they read the *Times* diary and see by it that the Canadians took only two miserable little villages in the month of August, and if they know, as they do, that the casualties for August ran into the thousands, no one can blame them for thinking that the casualties were unduly heavy. I often complained of this

101 J.F. Livesay (1875-1944), journalist and author of *Canada's Hundred Days: With the Canadian Corps from Amiens to Mons* (Toronto: Thomas Allen, 1919).

state of affairs, and although we had a Canadian at the head of the Ministry of Information, the fault was not remedied.

You will understand, Sir Robert, how difficult it might be for me in the space of a letter to satisfactorily outline the magnitude of our operations.

Let me first point out that in the German offensive of this year, the only part of the British front avoided by him was that part held by the Canadian Corps and a very small section of trenches on our left. Furthermore, the only part of the British front which was not driven in was the Canadian front.

In the dispatch of the Commander-in-Chief with reference to the German attacks in the spring, you will note that he says that he had made provisions to withdraw the Canadian Corps from the line in order to deliver a counter-attack.

Sir Douglas Haig himself, told me that in the dark days of last spring, the one comforting thought that they had was that he still had the Canadian Corps intact, and that he could never regard himself as beaten until that Corps was put into battle.

I told you last summer what the temper of the Corps was. You heard me publicly state that the Canadian Corps was going to die for I knew the serious nature of the battles in which it would have to be engaged. I stated that the Corps would never be asked to take a position which it would not take, and that the enemy would never be able to drive it from a position, except over the dead bodies of every man in the Corps. What I said has come true.

After a wonderfully successful and secret move in the beginning of August, the Corps was concentrated opposite Amiens, and was placed in the very centre of the attack. The Australians were on our left, while, on the left of them, a very minor operation in comparison to the others, was to be carried out by some Imperial troops. On our right were the French; and we were the spearhead.

In the first day of the battle we made a deeper penetration than had ever been made in this war, either by British, French of German troops, on the Western Front.

I may tell you that when the Battle of Amiens was conceived, our ultimate objective was set at what is known as the 'old Amiens defence line.' We reached that objective the first day, 14,000 yards from where we started in the morning. The battle was continued for some days after, and I believe the success of that battle gave the first grounds for hoping that a big measure of success might be obtained this year. In my opinion, the Canadian and Australian success at Amiens did a very great deal to raise not only the morale of the British Army, but the morale of the British nation. You know yourself, all of the people in England were very much concerned, and many of them were despondent. I know that the army wondered whether they could stop the Boshe from reaching the channel ports, or whether we could prevent a division between the French and the British Armies.

We have feverishly dug hundreds and hundreds of miles of trenches between our lines and the sea, and all thoughts were thoughts of defences. Yet, after the success of Amiens, the whole army looked again to the Rhine.

After five day's fighting at Amiens we came up against old trenches that existed before the Somme battle of 1916, and I wrote to the Army, suggesting that as we had achieved more than our objective, that as the Amiens–Paris railway had been freed, and the danger of the division of the French and British armies dissipated, that instead of fighting through the old wire, old trenches, machine gun emplacements, etc., of the Somme defences, I suggested that the Corps might be withdrawn from the line, put into the Third Army, and used to deliver a blow in the direction of Bapaume. It was a thought I had when we were on the Arras front, shortly after your visit to us. Well, it was arranged for us to come out of the line, but before we did the Third Army launched their offensive, and were going on very well.

Yet, the British Army was confronted with this fact: that the Hinderburg Line was in front of them, and that no success could have far-reaching results unless that Hindenburg System was broken. Who, I ask you, first broke it? Who were chosen for the task? The answer is: the Canadian Corps.

The last of our troops did not get out of the line at Amiens until August 25th. Others, a few days earlier had been hurried up by rail, and immediately went into the line East of Arras. I gave over the command at Amiens on Thursday, the 22nd, and as soon as I arrived in the North, I received an order to make an attack the next Sunday morning. As the Corps has always had a prejudice against attacking on Sunday, I proposed that we attack on Monday, the 26th, and this we did. The battle which began on that day, was continued each day until the 3rd of September, or nine days in all.

On September 2nd we broke the Drocourt–Quéant Switch, and on the 3rd, drove the enemy across the Canal Du Nord. In those nine days we drove the Boshe from six trench systems, each one stronger than the other. In these operations, I had with me the 4th British Division, and right gallantly did they fight; but I repeat, that the first troops to break the Hindenburg System were the Canadian troops, and they broke that system as its most vital point.

I can tell you here, too, that immediately on our south was the XVII Corps, who were told not to allow their troops to take the Drocourt-Quéant line until the Canadians had broken it. I personally went over to the XVII Corps Commander, Sir Charles Ferguson, and protested against this one-sided arrangement, with the result that he put a brigade in behind my right attacking brigade, and they followed behind our troops until they crossed the Drocourt-Quéant System, when they turned south. They had nothing to do with the breaking of the system; it was broken by the Canadian Corps and the 4th British Division, and they alone. The result was, that the troops of the Third Army which had been held up for some days, marched along the road in fours through villages where they had been checked.

After these two successful battles, namely, Amiens and Arras the Chief of the General Staff came to me and intimated that the Commander-in-Chief was particularly well pleased with the conduct of the Canadians, and that he hoped it would not be necessary to employ us in any further big operations during the year. I suppose, at that time, it seemed too much to hope that the Boshe could be finally beaten this fall.

However, other successes were taking place along the front, and our hopes for final victory were considerably raised. It was then decided to ask us to fight again, and the operations which were to result in the capture of Cambrai were planned.

For us they resulted in five days of the bitterest fighting we have ever experienced. We had an exceedingly hard task to do. First, to cross the Canal Du Nord, which was about sixty feet wide and twenty feet deep. Besides this, the bridges had all been blown. On the Boshe side, there was a large stretch of swamp, or marsh; and also on that side there were great fields of wire.

We were limited by the nature of the ground and the obstacles to crossing on a front of 3,000 yards, and we put four divisions across on that 3,000 yards on September 27th. Immediately we crossed the canal, we were on a front of 9,000 yards, performing one of the most difficult and one of the most successful operations of the war.

General Sir Henry Horne, the Army Commander, was most generous in his praise. General Sir Julian Byng, Commander of the Third Army, came to me before the operations and said that he would watch with great interest the result, because he regarded it as a most difficult and intricate manoeuvre. It was entirely successful, and over 200 field and heavy guns were captured by us that day.

The work of our engineers in bridging the canal immediately after the infantry had crossed was of such a character as to win the special praise of the Commander-in-Chief, and the press commented most favourably on it. Let me tell you that those bridges were begun, not only under shellfire, but under machine gunfire, and yet nothing could deter the work of our men. That day we captured Bourlon Wood, the key to Cambrai, and the observation post of the whole country.

We began the battle on September 27th, and continued it on the 28th, 29th, 30th and October 1st. Our attack on each of these five days forestalled a German attack, as documents and prisoners' statements verify.

As long as the enemy retained any power of manoeuvre between the Cambrai–Doullens road and the Sensée River, he fought us for all he was worth, using against us thirteen divisions and thirteen independent machine gun units. The latter are GHQ units, and are only employed when the situation becomes very serious. It was attack and counter-attack every day of the five days. On the 1st of October, he counter-attacked us with the remnants of six divisions and two fresh divisions. These attacks were repelled and ground gained.

The guns with the Canadian Corps fired that day 7,000 tons of ammunition. Our gunners say they never had such good shooting; our sixty-pounders, even, were firing over the open sights.

There was a lull in the fighting then for a few days, but at half-past one, on the morning of October 8th, we attacked again, across the Canal de L'Escaut, and passed to the east of Cambrai. Our troops were the first to enter Cambrai, and they went through it north, south, east and west, before any others took it.

Cambrai, as you know, was one of the largest distributing centres of the Boshe army on the Western Front, and the importance attached to it by the enemy is testified by the severity of the fighting.

Between August 8th and this date, October 2nd, the Canadian Corps had met and defeated forty-seven German divisions, or one-quarter of the German Army on the Western front. It was as if we said to the American Army, to the French Army, to the Belgian Army and to the rest of the British Army, 'You look after three-quarters of the German Army and we will take care of the rest.'

I do not wish to make comparisons, but what I am going to say is for yourself alone, and I would ask you to not repeat it, yet it is true. In the Cambrai operation, on our front of five and a half miles, the enemy used thirteen divisions, on a front of ten miles to the south of us he used six divisions. That shows you the importance he attached to stopping the Canadian Corps. He acts as if he thought that if he succeeded in stopping us, he stopped everything.

We turned over about the 11th to the XXII Corps. We were then between five and six miles east of Cambrai, having fought all the way from Arras, a distance of twenty-five miles, and as no attack was made by the troops to the north of us, you can see that our flank was exposed for that distance, with the result that we suffered enfilade fire from the north all the way. Other troops in the battle suffered only from frontal fire.

I venture to assert, Sir Robert, that the battles of Arras and Cambrai as fought by the Canadian Corps, will receive from military students in the future, a very great deal of attention. As we advanced to the east, the XXII Corps kept following our northern flank, so that, while we were facing east, they were facing north.

About October 11th we exchanged places with them, and so high was the morale of our troops, that despite all their fighting, the very first night they went into the line, they raided the enemy's trenches, capturing an officer and some twenty odd men. They raided again the next night with equal success, and then came to the conclusion that the enemy's resistance was weakening; so they applied more pressure and he began to give. They increased the pressure and drove him back. They rolled up his line on a front of 14,000 yards, drove him east until we forced him across the Canal de L'Escaut at Valenciennes. From the position we took over on October 11th to Valenciennes is a distance of twenty-four miles. By doing this we had passed by the XXII Corps still operating to the east of Cambrai, and were leading them by three miles. We were also miles ahead of the people to the north of us.

We now found ourselves on an island: the River Sensée on the south, the Canal Du Nord on the west, the River Scarpe on the north, and the Canal de L'Escaut on the east. As all the bridges had been blown, further great opportunities had been afforded our engineers, and again they won the special commendation of the Army Commander and the Commander-in-Chief.

For some days there was no severe fighting where we had now reached, but a few days before November 1st we were asked to take over, and did take over another 2,500 yards of front to the south. I may say, this placed in our territory, a position known as Mont Houy, which had twice been captured by British troops, and twice lost. We included it in our attack on November 1st, took it, and kept it. The first part of our attack on that day included an advance of 3,500 yards on a

2,200 yard front. In that operation we captured 1,800 prisoners, buried over 800 Boshes afterwards on the field, and sustained less than 400 casualties ourselves, of whom only eighty were killed; thus causing over 2,600 permanent casualties to the enemy with only eighty permanent casualties to ourselves.

Later in the day on November 1st, we forced our entry into Valenciennes, thereby capturing a very large and important railway centre. We continued the pressure, and fighting on about the same frontage, pressed on both sides of the Valenciennes–Mons road, to Mons. The distance between the two cities is twenty miles which we covered in eight days, fighting all the way. So keen were the men to finish the job that they begged to remain in the line when the time for their relief came; in fact, some battalions would not leave the line; they wanted to be in at the finish. We could have taken Mons on Sunday, November 10th but it would have cost too much to do so.

I appreciated the national pride our country would have if we finished the war with the old battlefield in our possession, and though we were anxious to take it, we did not care to suffer many casualties in doing so. We felt our way all Sunday, and shortly after midnight troops from the 42nd Battalion found an opening. They entered the city, fought through the streets where I saw dead bodies there the next day, and surrounded the enemy machine gunners holding the south. These machine gunners fought to the very last.

By 4:30 in the morning we had cleared the city, and when the Armistice came into effect at eleven o'clock in the morning, we were five miles to the east of Mons.

The Corps had fought continuously from the 8th of August to the 11th of November, and to my mind, there is no doubt, that no force of similar size played anything like so great a part in bringing the proud enemy to his knees...

I do not know how the number of guns we took or the prisoners we took compare with those of other armies, but in the operations which took place between August 8th and October 1st I think I am right in saying that the Canadian Corps took more than one-third of the guns and at least one-quarter of the prisoners.

I hope the information I have given you here is along the lines you require, but as I said before, it is very difficult to say very much in the space of a letter.

I am preparing a very complete report, but as it will be a document of great historical value, it will take some time to get it in proper shape...

A.W. Currie

Diary Entry, 27 November 1918

I left at nine o'clock for Mons in order to meet the King of the Belgians. It was a command, and so one had to go. We first met him at 10:30 in the Parliament Buildings of the Province of Hainault. The King was especially complimentary to the Canadians. He received an address there, and there were presented to him a great many people. We then crossed over to the municipal buildings, in front of which a guard of the 3rd Division, commanded by Lieutenant Colonel Hamilton Galt, was drawn up. The King arrived shortly afterwards, and received a splendid welcome from the people.' In the building the mayor read a very fine address, to which the King responded most eloquently, again referring to the Canadians in a most kindly way, calling them the 'irresistible Canadians.' The Mayor of Mons seems to be a very fine character. In August, 1914, he was forced to march, at the head of the Germans, into Mons. He has been very ill lately, and this was the first ceremony for some time in which he was able to take part. Some of us then went to the private residence of the Governor of Hainault, where we had a luncheon. I have never attended a formal lunch served as this was. We did not sit down at a table, but waiters brought in trays, bearing plates each of which held a roll, a bit of meat and a knife and fork. We helped ourselves to these plates and sat down at different tables in the room. Another course of meat was served in similar fashion, followed by a sweet. I sat at table with General Campbell of the 51st Division, and the second son of the King. After lunch the King again sent for me and talked to me for the rest of the time spent there. He seems a kindly and courteous gentleman, speaks English slowly but with no hesitation, and is altogether of an earnest disposition. There was a service in the cathedral, for which I did not wait ...

Diary Entry, 28 November 1918

...In the evening I wrote a letter to Marjorie, giving in some detail, the impressions one gathered, sending her at the same time books and postcards purchased on the ground. The troops today had a very long and tiring march. It rained most of the day, and the roads were very muddy and congested. They are hurrying us along, it being desired to cross the frontier on Sunday. I am told the reasons for this hurried march are political rather than military.

Supply trains are very late, as up to date supplies have been brought up in lorries from Valenciennes, which is some ninety miles away.

Diary Entry, 1 December 1918

We closed Corps Headquarters at Huy and moved to Vielsam, where we arrived in the afternoon. On the way there I passed through Liege, where the Belgians made such a gallant stand at the beginning of the war. I noticed some of the old forts which had been badly smashed. Called at Spa, headquarters of Second Army, where a conference was held, resulting in our march being held up for two days; the reason for this being the decidedly unsatisfactory nature of the supply situation. Trains are arriving several days late, and the result has been simply chaos. I have never experienced in France such evidence of mismanagement. We lunched with the Army Commander. At Vielsam we are quartered in an old chateau, the property of an Italian baron. Here, the Crown Prince rested for a night on his way to Holland. After his departure it was occupied by German private soldiers, and we found it in an exceedingly dirty state, the floors being covered with straw. It took some time to get the place at all comfortable.

Diary Entry, 2 December 1918

This is Marjorie's birthday. I sent her a telegram two days ago. Spent the morning in the office, but at half past one, attended a reception at the Hotel de Ville, given by the Mayor and Aldermen of the town to Canadian Corps Headquarters. We rode down, and were met in the town by the village band. The people were none too enthusiastic, as this town is practically on the frontier and has many German sympathizers as residents. The Mayor made an address of welcome in French, to which I responded in English. We had the usual white wine, and the band played 'God Save the King.' Immediately afterward I held a conference of divisional commanders and brigadiers to discuss instructions, etc., re our march through Germany.

Diary Entry, 4 December 1918

The weather, which has been misty and rainy for some days, continues the same. In the morning I rode to the frontier, and there crossed with General Macdonell, at the head of his main body. A small cavalry escort preceded us. I saw the 3rd and 1st Battalions go by. There was a moving picture man in attendance. After this, I rode on and saw General Burstall at St. Vith and had lunch with him—my first meal in Germany. Returning to Corps Headquarters, I spent the rest of the afternoon in the office...

Diary Entry, 5 December 1918

This is my birthday, and a very fine day it is. General Embury left for Montreuil early this morning, and General Elliot[102] also went back. I sent with him Major Pat Goldie to show him the battlefields. The Army Commander called during the morning, and in the afternoon I rode out and saw the 10th Battalion on the march. The supply situation is getting a little better, but not much. In the evening the mess gave me a dinner at Corps Headquarters, General Morrison making a speech. All the mess were present. Also General R.P. Clark, together with two officers from Prince Arthur's Regiment, the Scots Greys.

Diary Entry, 6 December 1918

In the morning I rode out to the boundary to see the 2nd Brigade cross, the 5th Battalion going by to the tune of 'When We Wind Up the "Watch" on the Rhine.' They and the 7th Battalion looked very well, but I was not pleased with the 10th. I then rode over to see the 4th Brigade group on the march. The weather continues fine.

Currie to Sir Robert Borden, 7 December 1918[103]

Dear Sir Robert,

While writing to you I would like to tell you how we are getting along in our march to the Rhine.

I am tonight at Schleiden, which is about thirty miles from the Rhine, and the head of our columns will reach there in a couple of days.

We have had some difficulties over the supply question, but I think they are mastered now. The trouble was the delay in making the physical connection between the French railway system and the German, across the devastated area.

Our troops are marching splendidly, and have averaged about thirty miles a day, with so few men falling out as to be not worth mentioning. In many units not a single man has fallen out in all the march. The troops look well and happy and are in the best of health.

The German populace are receiving us with reserve, which is exactly the attitude we want them to adopt, though there is evidence in some quarters of a

---

102 Major General H.M. Elliot was Master of the Ordinance (from April 1916).
103 Reel C4334, vol 104, BP, LAC.

disposition to fraternize. They are anxious to carry out any instructions we give them.

Tonight I am occupying the house of Graf von Spee, a cousin of the late admiral. He received us most graciously and the place is very comfortable.

We have had some bad weather with rain and fog, but on the whole it has been better than what one would expect at this time of the year.

With best wishes to yourself and colleagues I am,

A.W. Currie

As the Canadians approached the Rhine, the battles may have been over, but the war of reputations had just begun. In Ottawa Sir Sam Hughes began to openly accuse Currie of wasting Canadian lives at the Battle of Cambrai. More damningly, he alleged that in the final hours of the war Currie had ordered a senseless attack on Mons after he already knew the Armistice had been signed. Whether motivated by jealousy, senility, or a genuine sense of purpose, Hughes' accusations were a personal attack on Canada's victorious general at the very moment of his triumph.[104]

Currie to Alistair Fraser 7 December 1918[105]

My dear Alistair,

...Speaking from a purely selfish standpoint, Alistair, I wish you could have finished the struggle here. There were many times during those strenuous five months when I would have had your comfort; glad to have taken counsel with you, while there were many occasions on which you would have been the greatest possible help to me. I never knew how much I would miss you until you had gone. However, you did the right thing by going...

When you left, we were at Bryas, with plans for going into the line. We carried out that relief, and moved our headquarters to Dusians, where the XVII Corps Headquarters were. As usual, we immediately began to make things lively for the Bosche. We put on quite a number of raids, with the result that he put in opposite our front two more divisions, at the same time concentrating two other divisions in reserve. He also shelled Duisans almost every night, at the same time, bombing the vicinity frequently.

---

104 The best account of the Hughes-Currie battles of 1918-19 is Cook, 'The Madman and the Butcher.'
105 File 1, vol 1, CP, LAC. Probably Alistair Fraser (born 1883), a lawyer from Nova Scotia.

Towards the third week in July I was told about the operations at Amiens, and, to increase the camouflage in our own corps, ordered all divisions to prepare plans for an attack on Monchy. These plans stood us in good stead. In the meantime, Webber and I, the only ones at Corps Headquarters who knew what was going on, were busy on plans for the Amiens show.

It is interesting now to recall what Sir Robert Borden told me a few weeks ago in London, namely, that as a result of an appreciation of the situation on all the British fronts, the War Council had decided before he left for Canada last summer that the only major operation to be put on by the British Army this year would be our attack at Amiens; all the Allies agreeing to conserve their efforts for the big attack next year.

When you left us, Alistair, you know how much everyone was concerned and how many were almost despondent.

The object of the Amiens battle was to free the Paris–Amiens railway, and to dissipate the danger of dividing the French and British. Well, we made a great point of secrecy and while its too long to tell you of the measures adopted, I may say that we were able to strike the Boche on August 8th without his having the faintest idea that we were in the same area. In fact, he thought that we were in Flanders, preparing an attack on Kemmel, and a great many of the British Army thought the same thing, for we had sent two battalions to Flanders as camouflage.

As far as the British Army is concerned, the Amiens battle was put on by the Canadian Corps, the Australian Corps, while the III British Corps had a very minor part to play. The French were also attacking on the right, with ourselves dead in the centre, acting as the spearhead.

The final objective of that attack was the old Amiens defence line; but so great was our success that we reached it the first day. We kept on, Alastair, for five days at the end of which we had penetrated 24,000 yards on a 10,000 yard front; had captured more prisoners than we had casualties, and taken over 200 guns.

We then came up against the old Somme battlefield, from which the Boche had not been driven in 1916, but from which he had retired. You could see that his wire was still intact; also his trenches, dugouts, machine gun emplacements and gun emplacements.

To show whether I am a murderer or not, Alistair, I may say that I then wrote to the Army Commander an official letter, in which I expressed the opinion that it would not be wise to press the offensive any further, and I advised that the

Canadian Corps be withdrawn from the line, be sent to the Third Army, and that it hit in, driving towards Bapaume. This, you will recall, was carried out as far as the Third Army were concerned. I am not claiming that I suggested the attack, but I do know that it was not contemplated when we attacked Amiens first.

The Third Army struck in and met with considerable success, though they were always confronted by the fact that, sooner or later, they would come up against the Hinderburg Line. As they approached the outpost position of that line they were checked and practically stopped. Who, I ask you, were selected to break that line? The answer is: the Canadian Corps; for as swiftly, silently and secretly as we moved to Amiens, so we moved back to Arras, and attempted to breach at the strongest, yet most vital part of the Hindenburg System, the Quéant–Drocourt line.

After eight days of terrific fighting, beginning on August 26th and closing on September 3rd, we had driven through six systems of trenches and forced the enemy back across the Canal du Nord, while the Third Army to the south of us, who had been held up for days were permitted by our success to advance in focus along the road.

We had thus, in less than a month, fought two wonderful battles and gained two magnificent victories.

On my way up from Amiens, Sir Julian Byng told me that that greatest success in the war up to that time had been our Corps' successes at Amiens, while many people think, and high French and British officers think, that our smashing of the Quéant–Drocourt line was the turning point in the campaign.

It was then that I first thought that the Boche machine was crumbling, for on September 2nd, the day after we broke the line, we found ourselves on a 7,000 yard front, opposed by nine German divisions. This indicated confusion, and a feverish, yet vital determination to stop our progress.

After those two battles the Chief of the General Staff came to me and told me that so pleased was the Commander-in-Chief with our success that he did not intend to use us any more during the year, other than for holding the line. But, becoming convinced that further successes were possible, Foch conceived those four great hammer-strokes at the end of September...

You know the two great distributing centres of the Germans on the British front, namely, Cambrai and St. Quentin. Cambrai is guarded by Bourlon Wood, one of the strongest possible natural positions, and to us was assigned the mission of taking Bourlon Wood. To do that, we had to cross the Canal du Nord.

On September 27th we crossed four divisions on a 3,000 yard front, fanning out at the end of the day to a front of 9,000 yards; capturing 205 guns. We were forced to perform this manoeuvre owing to the swamps on the east side of the Canal du Nord.

Sir Julian Byng came to me before the operation and asked me if I were sure that we could do it, for, he said, we were attempting the most difficult manoeuvre that had yet been attempted in the war. I have told you with what success we met...

On October 1st we attacked on our whole front, but the Boche counter-attacked with eight divisions, of whom two were absolutely fresh. We repelled all these counter-attacks and gained ground. Our artillery that day fired 7,000 tons of ammunition. There was a pause then for a week, and on the morning of the 9th, we took Cambrai, and the next day were six miles beyond it. From that day the war was over.

Between August 8th and October 2nd the Canadian Corps met and decisively defeated forty-seven German divisions. On August 8th the Boche had only 184 divisions, twenty-five per cent of which is forty-six. So you will see, we left it to the American Army, the French Army, the British Army and the Belgian Army to fight three-quarters of the German Army, while we took care of the balance.

Do you now even begin to see the magnificent work accomplished by the Canadian Corps? No force of its size has done anything like as much to bring this war to a close. Had we not fought him as hard and as successfully as we did, it is well within the range of possibility that tonight the line might have been west of Cambrai, with another winter staring us in the face, and a big battle to be fought in the spring.

I ask you in all fairness, was it worth our while to fight this hard and be in the position we are tonight, namely, within a few miles of the Rhine.

And this brings me to the matter of casualties, concerning which you have heard so much criticism. You know what the Corps did up to the time you left; how it held the only part of the British line which did not even bend this spring. I have told you what it accomplished after you left. Yet, the War Office have published a statement which proves that the casualties amongst the Canadian Corps this year are less, in proportion to our strength, than any other part of the British Army.

Shortly after you left, my indigestion disappeared entirely, and thus, I was able to put into these operations every ounce of strength I possessed, and I can truthfully say that for three months I averaged at least seventeen hours a day.

The trouble is, Alistair, that the people of Canada have as yet a very faint idea of what this Corps has accomplished, and some there are, apparently, who desire that the truth shall never be told, and what is told, is oftentimes very much distorted.

This brings me to what you have said is in the mind of a former Minister of Militia.[106] However much one would dislike his slinging of mud, I cannot see how I can stop him. The man is a liar, is at times insane, and apparently is a cur of the worst type.

I put in four years at the front, and am one of the very few who have never been away. In those four years I have never commanded a force which has never failed to carry out the mission assigned to it. I am proud of that record.

To say that the casualties have been excessive is an easy thing to say; but I can imagine nothing meaner, more ungrateful and untrue.

Had that man had his way, the Corps would still be armed with the Ross rifle, which caused more unnecessary casualties by far than any other factor I know of. Had he his way, or had his friends their way, the several appointments in the Corps would not have been held by the best men, but by his friends. Merit would not have counted, but what would have placed them there would have been their willingness to lick his boots.

Apparently he chooses to utter his foul lies where he has the protection of the walls of Parliament. Only a coward would behave as such. I have never intended to go into politics, but if he does what he says he will do, I will not rest until I have (to use his own words) 'skinned the skunk.' I have faced too many dangers and pitfalls in the last four years to be afraid of him.

I am now, as always, without pull. If my record in this war can be tarnished by such as he, then I don't much care.

I thank you for the warning you have given me. I said I would not do anything, but there are one or two things in my mind. I think, when the time comes, I can find a champion. I know you will do what you can, and I thank you for what you have already done.

106 On Currie's inaction, see Cook, 'The Madman and the Butcher,' 709-10.

I know that the gang has been busy. An officer in England of as a high rank as myself has been spending most of his time at hospitals and convalescent camps, condoling with the wounded men and telling them that the casualties in the Corps have been altogether too high, and were unnecessary in many cases.[107] A short time ago I wrote to Kemp about this, and I also wrote to Rowell. You can take this letter if you care to, and show it to those whom you mention are behind me...

Give my love to your mother, of whom I have often thought, and with love yourself, I am dear Alistair,

Yours ever,

A.W. Currie

PS (December 8th)

I started this letter last night, and since then have thought of this.

The attack which you say is to be made upon me can be divided into two phases:

First, the one which can affect my military reputation, and which is to deal largely with casualties.

The second is the purely personal attack.

It might be wise to nullify his criticism in the first; and that could be done in this way. When the House meets, the Acting Prime Minister would probably address the house before our friend. Doubtless, he (the Acting Prime Minister) would make some reference to peace, and the part played by Canada's Army in the bringing about this result. If ever a man had an opportunity of becoming eloquent, to be sympathetically heard, and to impress the people; that would be an opportunity. He could describe what the Corps has done, and I would furnish him the material. In his speech he could make a reference to the inevitable casualties, and could prove beyond the shadow of a doubt and in the most convincing manner, that instead of being larger, they were in reality small when compared with the magnitude of the efforts. In fact, I have a letter in my possession from General Rawlinson, under whom we fought at Amiens, saying that the casualties in the Canadian Corps might well have been from two to three times larger than they actually were. This would take the wind out of our opponent's sails and would leave nothing but the purely personal attack.

107 Currie is referring to Sir Richard Turner whom he believed was responsible for the dissemination of rumours in England along with Garnet Hughes and Lord Beaverbrook.

If the House of Commons chooses to listen to such an attack, that is not my affair.

Would Sir Thomas White or General Mewburn act as I have suggested?

I might just add one other thing. In the session of the House in the spring of 1916, this same gentleman made a statement that John Currie had been blamed for what I had done. I did not know that he had done so until a Toronto paper reached here, and was shown to me by General Alderson. The gentleman who made the statement was then in England, where I wrote him. I have a letter in my possession now, in which it withdrew what he stated, while at the same time he said he would wire to Sir Robert Borden, asking that the statement he made in the House be corrected. That was done, I believe.

Diary Entry. 8 December 1918

The 2nd Division continued their march today, and despite all difficulties of supply, arrived on the line set for this date some weeks ago. The 1st Division are a day's march behind. The cavalry are on the Rhine. I was unable to leave the office because General Burstall came in the morning, remaining for lunch, General Griesbach also came to lunch and I had a long talk with him afterwards. General Radcliffe and General Bill Thwaites came about tea time and are spending the night with us.

Diary Entry, 10 December 1918

Left Schleiden in the morning and first visited the 1st Canadian Division at Euskirchen, where I saw Colonel Cooper who is in charge of the 1st Divisional Wing at the Canadian Corps Reinforcement Centre. He told me of some trouble they were having there with the draftees, and I decided to press that all men now at the Canadian Corps Reinforcement Centre be sent to their divisions as soon as possible. I went on and had lunch with General Burstall at Rheinbach, from there to Duisdorf, which is about two and a half miles from Bonn, and the Headquarters of the cavalry brigade. The others of the staff had gone on a hunt but were not fortunate enough to get a boar, though I believe they did get a couple of foxes and a hare. General MacBrien arrived in the evening to discuss with me the establishment of a division before going to England as one of the *post-bellum* committee dealing with this matter.

Diary Entry, 11 December 1918

Leaving Schleiden at 8:30 we arrived at Bonn shortly before 10:30, coming at once to Corps Headquarters which is situated in the Palais Schaumburg, the home of the Kaiser's youngest sister. Her husband died a couple of years ago. I am occupying the suite reserved for the Kaiser and naturally find it the most comfortable place I have yet been in during the war. I have a large office, a larger bed-room, dressing-room and bath room. I find that the pictures on the wall are mostly of English scenes or portraits of our Royal Family. The books in the cases are English books, all of our well-known authors being represented. At the request of Her Royal Highness I called on her tonight at six o'clock. She is a cousin of Prince Arthur, who had seen her earlier in the day, and on whom she was particularly anxious to impress the fact that her brother did not wish the war. She repeated that he had often told her that he was never in favour of London being bombed, and that he had done his best to prevent the submarine warfare. I notice that all the German Royal Family are particularly anxious these days to tell the world that they were always very much opposed to the war. The Crown Prince is daily giving interviews to this effect and Prince Rupprecht of Bavaria is also doing the same. Her Royal Highness told me that she was very glad we had come, as she was afraid of what the German soldiers would do. She had feared for the safety of the Royal Family. She said that a couple of weeks ago returned soldiers had occupied her house, putting straw on the floor and living here for some days; that they had taken her motor car and gone around and released all criminals from the prisons. While she did not say she regretted the war, she said it had gone on entirely too long and that the end came as a great shock to the whole German people. Apparently they had not looked for defeat. She said that at one time she was intensely proud of her country, while now she detested it. She was anxious for the privilege of telephoning, telegraphing, writing letters to her brother, allowing her cook and butler to circulate after hours, and to ride herself. I told her that these were things with which only the Military Governor could deal, and was very careful to give her no encouragement that restrictions would be relaxed for some time. She spoke English extraordinarily well, as does the house maid who showed me to my apartments this morning, and the Lady in Waiting whom I have not yet met. I lunched today at a hotel and the meal consisted of soup, entree, boiled tongue, pudding and coffee. There seemed to be no difficulty in getting any sort of drink, and I have seen in London more evidence of a shortage of food than here...

Diary Entry, 12 December 1918

After a very comfortable night in His Majesty's bed, I arose this morning feeling quite Prussian in character. Accompanied by many of the officers of the headquarters staff, I rode to the bridge over the Rhine, crossing it just before ten. Taking up a position at the far end, I reviewed the 1st Cavalry Brigade as they passed by...

On 13 December the Canadians crossed the Rhine at Cologne and Bonn.

Diary Entry, 13 December 1918

After a night which promised fine, one awoke to find it raining very heavily with no prospect of letting up all day. Escorted by one troop of CLH, aid accompanied by the officers of the Corps Headquarters, I took up my position on the eastern end of the bridge over the Rhine to witness the march past of the 2nd Division, who commenced to cross promptly at 9:30... The march past was completed at three o'clock and had continued without interruption. After this I went to the west hank of the Rhine and inspected three batteries of six inch howitzers, in position there. I was particularly pleased with the appearance, bearing and discipline of all concerned. The German populace, who seemed quite interested, must have been much impressed. It was a stirring and impressive sight, inspiring to a degree, and must live long in the memory of all who saw it or took part...

Diary Entry, 14 December 1918

Very fine day and a pity we did not have this weather yesterday. At ten o'clock I went to Cologne to attend a conference of the Army Commander when many matters relative to the occupied territory were discussed. I am quite convinced that the Military Governor gives no more promise of being able to carry out his function well, now that he has been installed, than those of us who knew him before expected...

Diary Entry, 15 December 1918

Another mild day, reminding one very much of the climate of Victoria. I remained at headquarters all day. General Percy called during the morning, while Colonel Walker of Calgary lunched with us. I have not seen him since March 1913, when we travelled together on the train from Toronto to Calgary.

He is seventy-two years of age, but has been in England in connection with the Forestry Corps for the last two and a half years.

Currie to General Webber, 26 December 1918[108]

My dear Webber,

Thank you very much indeed for your kind note on the 18th, and for your good wishes to the Corps. As you know, the 1st and 2nd Divisions are holding half the Rhine bridgehead. Corps Headquarters is at Bonn, a really delightful city and where we are most comfortably installed.

'A' Mess is in the Palais Schaumburg, the home of the Kaiser's youngest sister who still lives here and with whom, I am afraid, the ADCs are beginning to fraternize. She is, as you know, Prince Arthur's cousin, and greeted him with a kiss. My apartments are those reserved exclusively for the Kaiser's use. We thought it only appropriate that we should come here and fly the Union Jack from the roof of a German Royal Palace.

The march up here was a very long end trying one; the men averaged nearly twenty miles a day; and the supply question gave us at all times the greatest concern. Despite those difficulties we got through on time, and in keeping with the best traditions of the Corps kept level with the schedule.

The 3rd and 4th Divisions are back not far from Brussels. Today the former is being transferred to the Fifth Army preliminary to demobilization in February. I tried to arrange that they should come up here and relieve the 1st and 2nd but, owing to transportation difficulties that was found impracticable. I hope that the 1st Division may follow the 3rd in March, the 2nd in April, and the 4th in May so that there is a possibility of us all being home early in the summer.

In case you have heard, or may hear, about any trouble in one of our brigades, let me tell you that last week I went to the 3rd Division, in order to investigate for myself something that happened in the 7th Brigade. There was really not a great deal in it, though we are all very much hurt that it should have happened. It seems that one day a considerable body of men, principally from the machine gun battalion and the 49th Battalion, held meetings, paraded the streets, and declared that they would not wear packs, etc. There was no rioting, no drunkenness, no fighting, and no destruction of property. Everything is normal now, and those who so misbehaved are most bitterly ashamed of themselves.

---

108 File 19801226-278, 58A 1 61.1, Sir Arthur Currie Papers (hereafter ACP), Canadian War Museum (CWM).

You probably will recall steps we were forced to take during the summer to deal with that same machine gun battalion, and will remember my inspection of it at Mar-les-Mines, after which we put in a new second-in-command, and later in the fall sent Moorehouse to England, and brought out Balfour. You will also remember my taking up with the late divisional commander the question of his always requiring so many lorries to carry the packs.

Our demobilization plans have not yet been definitely decided upon, and I wish to goodness they were, for I have as yet been unable to announce anything of a definite character to the troops.

Most cordially reciprocating your good wishes, and with best wishes always, I am, dear Webber, ever yours faithfully,

A.W. Currie

Corps Commander, January–August 1919

New Years Day, 1919 found the Canadians stationed on the Rhine. For Currie, it was his sixth Christmas away from Canada. Although the fighting ended in November, the New Year brought fresh challenges. Morale dipped as unrest among the tired soldiers grew and the second and third waves of the 1918–19 influenza pandemic spread amongst the men. Back home, strikes, coal shortages, fears of Bolshevik uprisings, and uncertainty about the process of demobilization threatened to destabilize the Dominion. The war effort, which had kept the Union Government together for more than a year, was no longer the rallying cry that it had been in 1917. Over the course of the year, the thin veneer of bipartisanship holding the Union Government together slowly began to peel away. As problems with demobilization and returned soldiers mounted, it became less and less crucial for the Borden Government to defend the Corps Commander. The personal attacks of Sir Sam Hughes and Liberal politicians vexed Sir Arthur. For him the war had been a great triumph—personally and for the Canadian Corps. Currie did not understand how anyone in Canada could see matters differently, unless it was as a result of inaccurate information spread by his jealous enemies. He thus believed that it was the Government's duty to set straight the accomplishments and record of the Canadian Corps. Currie's decision not to directly address the accusations would haunt him for the next decade.

As Corps Commander, Currie was faced with a number of pressing issues at the beginning of 1919. In January, the final Canadian demobilization scheme had yet to be approved by the War Office. The reorganization of the Canadian Militia was also becoming an increasingly significant concern. Would the numbered battalions be perpetuated by militia units in Canada? Would Canada remain on a semi-permanent war footing, opting for a larger Permanent Force than in the decades before the war? Discipline was also beginning to deteriorate in the Canadian Corps, a new problem for Currie who prided himself on the Corps' professionalism.

Diary Entry, 1 January 1919[1]

From now until January 1st, 1919, I have neglected keeping this diary. In that time, the weather generally has been very good, reminding one so much of the climate of Victoria and Vancouver. There have been only a few days of rain. We have had a great many visitors, principally from our own divisions in the rear and a few from Canada. Prince Albert and Major Gregg spent three days with us during the last week of the year, promising to return about January 7th, when I believe 'B' Mess propose holding a small dance. We expect the Prince of Wales also on that date... The trip to Koblenz was a very pretty one, being along the banks of the Rhine all the way. Ruined castles, and those of more modern constructions are passed at frequent intervals, while on the east bank, one sees many vineyards, from whose grapes the famous Rhine wines are made. Koblenz is at the junction of the Moselle with the Rhine; at the very point of juncture there is a large equestrian statue of William I. Lunching with General Hines,[2] I met General Bullard,[3] who commands the American Second Army. We have found no trouble whatever from the German citizens in our part of the occupied area. There has been a little trouble amongst our own troops, but hardly worth mentioning. Some officers have so far forgotten their position as to drink too much. Now and then we hear of a German who has had his eye blacked, but the only serious thing has been the holding up and robbing of some German citizens. We have found the gang engaged in this work and they will be tried for the offence. The principal ring leader was an ex-officer of the Scots Guards, now a Sergeant Major with us, and a man who holds the MC, DCM, and MM.[4] We have of course, a certain number of bad men with us; furthermore, the troops feel that the Germans are not being made to feel strongly enough that we came here as a conquering army. In fact, there are more restrictions placed on the conduct of our own troops than on the Germans. There has been some trouble in Cologne, which has been very much exaggerated by the Military Governor, Sir Charles Fergusson. When we came here, we all said that sooner or later, he would find

---

1   Diary entries are taken from typewritten transcripts in file 194, vol 43, CP, LAC.
2   General John Leonard Hines (1868-1968), commanding officer of 4th Division (AEF) and Chief of the General Staff, US Army (1924-26).
3   General Robert Lee Bullard (1861-1947), commanding officer of Second Army (AEF).
4   Medals: Military Cross; Distinguished Conduct Medal; Military Medal.

some reason, good or bad, for putting Cologne out of bounds to the Canadians. Owing to lying reports from his Assistant Provost Marshall he has done so, in a telegram, so worded as to be regarded by us as a deliberate insult. Certain correspondence on this subject is now taking place. We are making no defences of any sort, though, we have a scheme of defence, ready and understood... Christmas and New Year's passed off very quietly, though our turkeys did not arrive until late. I am leaving for the Canadian Section, GHQ tomorrow morning (3rd January) and from there, will go to England to further discuss with the Overseas Minister, matters pertaining to demobilization. On the way, I am to go to Namur to receive from the head of the American Mission, an American decoration, they having given me their Distinguished Service Medal. I have also received in the New Year's Honours List, the GCMG[5] and only wish I could share it with every man in the Corps, to show I am indebted for this distinction. Before Christmas, Marjorie was operated on for throat trouble, but I am glad to hear, has fully recovered. On December 16th the Commander-in-Chief visited the Corps area, seeing some troops of all brigades on his way through. He remained some three hours with us, and promised to return later on. He went to England on the 20th and, I am glad to know, received a splendid reception: all army commanders accompanied him.

Currie to Sydney Mewburn, 1st January 1919[6]

My dear Mewburn,

Thank you very much for your letter of the 29th November. Let me first tell you how the Corps is at present situated.

After the signing of the Armistice, the first intimation that we received as to our future movements was to the effect that the whole Corps would move to the Rhine, and I made arrangements for the 1st and 2nd Divisions to lead, my intention being that, as they would be the first to be demobilized, by moving them first they would cross the Rhine in that order. After a time there, they could be shipped by train to the Base to get ready for demobilization, their places being taken at the Rhine by the 3rd and 4th Divisions.

Shortly after the first intimation, we were told that only two divisions of Canadians were to go and I allowed the 1st and 2nd to proceed, my intention being that, after they spent a short period holding the bridgehead, I would

---

5   The Most Distinguished Order of Saint Michael and Saint George.
6   File 19801226-280, 58A 1 61.3, ACP, CWM.

endeavour to get them to the Base or somewhere near there, and replace them at the bridgehead by the 3rd and 4th Divisions, thus giving all divisions an opportunity of seeing something of Germany...

Since [the march to the Rhine] everything has been normal. Of course, there has been the odd fight, when somebody blacks a German's eye or does something equally trivial. I think the behaviour of the troops has been splendid. This morning the Army Commander confided to me that the Canadians were especially picked to form such a large proportion of the forces holding the bridge-head, because of their superior discipline. I am not going to try to make you believe that all our troops are Sunday-school lads. We have the foolish officer, who so far forgets himself as to get drunk, but these are very, very few indeed. We have, too, the bad character, who meets the lone German in the dark and relieves him of his watch, but these cases are also negligible, and hardly worth mentioning. I am only telling you of it to lay the full situation before you.

Furthermore, there is no doubt that our men feel keenly that the Germans have not been made to suffer, and are now not being made to suffer sufficiently, for all the crimes they have committed. The area we occupy is a splendidly rich area, with signs of wealth and prosperity on every hand. The people look to be well fed and prosperous, and when our troops see this and compare this place and the people who live here with the devastated areas of France and Belgium, and the people of France whom we relieved, they feel more bitter than ever against the Boche. This makes them somewhat restless, in fact there are placed upon them by higher authority more restrictions then are placed on the Boche themselves.

On top of all this, there in an intense desire to get back to Canada. I know the pressure that is being brought to bear on you to see that this is carried out. Our people in England have been pressing the War Office, who have agreed to release two Canadian divisions for demobilization, the first of which is to sail for Canada in February. As it was impossible, owing to transportation difficulties, namely, supply of cars, etc, to get the 1st Division beck in time to sail for home first, it became necessary for me to nominate either the 3rd or the 4th and, because it was raised first, I nominated the 3rd. A few days ago it began its march westward to a point from which it will he shipped by rail, as cars become available, to the Base. By the time it is ready to embark, we hope to be able to follow it by the 1st, then by the 2nd, and finally by the 4th. We know now that it will be impossible to arrange for either the 3rd or the 4th to come to the Rhine...

We are finding it difficult to get the demobilization machinery in smooth running order, owing to the fact that Corps Headquarters is so far sway from our Canadian Section at GHQ, and from London. I am leaving here the day after tomorrow to go to Montreuil to see Embury, and afterwards to London to see Sir Edward Kemp. Had we been able to get the Corps concentrated near the Base, for even a few weeks, we could have carried out the scheme of demobilization much mere satisfactorily then we are able to do now. You know how anxious the Corps was to return to Canada by units. You can have no idea how strong the rank and file, as well as the officers, felt concerning it, and I could have wished that it had been possible to send the complete units back to Canada without any transferring of personnel here...

Regarding the future of the Canadian Militia, I feel that I cannot too strongly urge that some policy be laid down. I had a long talk with Elliot, when he was here, about it and I know he talked with others. Naturally those of us here have often discussed it yet it would be hard to give you in concentrated form the opinion of the Corps. Almost every man has a different opinion, but there are some things on which they are generally agreed. In the first place, all desire to see the Militia removed from the realm of politics. It is not meant by that that any change should take place in the Militia Department itself or in the responsibility of the Government in the matter, but it is felt that those who are responsible for whatever Militia system we have, should be guided by only what is thought to be for the good of the service, and should be not influenced by whether a thing is politically expedient or not. For instance, no government should ever be defeated on its Militia policy. I do not know just how things are in Canada now, but when I left it was difficult for a man to get a position, even as caretaker of a drill ball, unless he belonged to, or would vote for the party in power. I know all parties preach a lot about doing away with all patronage. We all hope that such is really the case.

I am all with you in your desire to link up the units constituting the Overseas Force with the old units in Canada. We must work together to see that this is done, for it would be to our lasting disgrace if we were to allow a system which would not perpetuate the traditions so hardly won in the field. Then again, I think our old ideas regarding the Permanent Force were sound, namely, that they should be largely an instructional force. There are many who want to see a great increase in the Permanent Force of Canada. While some increase may be necessary, I am not one of those in favour of the large Permanent Force. Whether we might in all units have permanent adjutants, permanent sergeant majors, etc. is a matter for consideration.

Personally, I think we must extend the cadet system, and I have certain strong views regarding universal service, which I believe you share. We ought also to have staff colleges, more or less supplementary to the staff college in England, and we ought to make it easier for officers to take these courses without too great financial loss. There ought also to be a more frequent interchange between officers of the British Empire. I shall write you again on this subject, and will be indeed glad to hear your views on the main principles which should govern our organization. There is no doubt that a great many officers and men in the Corps are anxious to know what our future policy is to be. There are many excellent men who would, I believe, continue in our Militia service if they knew exactly what the future might make possible for them. If these men get back into civil life, we may find it hard to get them to return to the Militia service; and what we do want to avoid is for our permanent Militia service to become the home of the man of rather indifferent ability who likes the easy but respectable job.

I note what is your policy regarding appointments and everyone here is most grateful for your stand in that regard. While many of them will be glad to take up these appointments when they arrive in Canada, they do not wish to leave their commands here before it is necessary. You will, of course, appreciate their feelings towards the units in which they are serving. Again I feel that some of them look forward to a few months rest after they return to Canada, for few, I believe, really realize the great strain under which they were labouring. All of us have become considerably older.

Regarding your kind remarks. I assure you, Mewburn, that they are most welcome and much appreciated, but I do not want your job, old man, at any cost. You are doing mighty well where you are, and I hope will long remain our Minister of Militia. I have no desire or intention to enter political life. I dislike politics as I dislike the devil, and the manner in which I have had to fight some political soldiers, or soldier politicians, has not generated any longing to be what the world calls a politician.

When making up your mind as to the positions to offer some of our generals, do not overlook Loomis. I do not know what his intentions for the future are, as I have not discussed them with him. Mark my words: Loomis is one of the most brilliant of all Canadian soldiers. I regard him as a peculiarly outstanding man, who at times is not understood. He is sound, able, efficient, upright, honourable and loyal, a really fine character. Burstall. I know, looks forward to remaining a number of years yet in the service. He has had a very long service, and should in a few years be able to retire with a decent pension. Macdonell has also had a long service, and would do well in any position in your gift. I do not know what Watson's wishes are, and I would not like to discuss these matters with them unless at your request.

I have met here on officer of Ludendorff's staff.[7] He was a banker for many years in London before the war, and I think, in 1913 was the guest in Canada of one of our prominent railway magnates there. He says that he considers that Germany's downfall began when she started the submarine wars. He states that had it begun with 200 submarines instead of fourteen that there might have been some hopes of winning. He also states that the German Higher Command realized that they were bound to be defeated during 1918 on land, when the Canadians broke the Hindenburg System between August 26th and September 2nd. He is also quite positive in his statements that no troops were anything like as much feared or respected by the Germans as the Canadians.

I am having a map prepared showing our advances during the fighting since August 8th. It tells its own story. I am also having that story written up in quite full detail, as the story and record of that last one hundred days fighting is one of which we are all very proud. In it, you and your organization are entitled to a great share.

Now, I feel that I have wearied you with all this long letter. I would write oftener, Mewburn, only there is so much to tell that I find it difficult to bring myself to begin a letter, and, as you know, I never made a practice during the war of writing letters to official people in Canada.

With many thanks for the constant and sturdy support you have always given Canada's troops in the field, and cordially reciprocating your good wishes,

I am, ever yours faithfully,

A.W. Currie

Diary Entry, 7 January 1919

Fine weather. The day was spent in preparing memoranda setting forth the views of the Corps on demobilization. I also attended the opening of the gallery of photos. Lord Beaverbrook presided and Sir Edward Kemp declared the

---

7   Erich von Ludendorff (1865-1937) co-commander of the *Oberst Heeresleitung* (Supreme Command) from August 1916 with Paul von Hindenburg (1847-1934).

exhibition opened. Sir Robert Borden and myself also spoke. I met a great many people whom I knew and many others came and introduced themselves to me...

Diary Entry, 9 January 1919

I breakfasted with Sir Robert Borden this morning, and spent the balance of the morning fulfilling engagements at the hotel. In the afternoon we went to the Royal Academy to see the exhibition of paintings. Had tea at the Carlton and accompanied Cy Peck to Dewars where I saw an exhibition of famous pictures and old furniture. In the evening Sir Edward Kemp gave a dinner at the Military Club to the ministers visiting London and the heads of departments. Many speeches were made.

Diary Entry, 14 January 1919

Spent the morning fulfilling engagements. Also called on the Minister during the afternoon, particularly with reference to what General Rennie told me of his conversation with General Turner. In the evening went to a dinner given by the officers of the Pay and Record Department. Lord Shaughnessy,[8] Sir George Foster and myself spoke.

Diary Entry, 16 January 1919

Called on General Brutinel at Headin, where he occupied the old Press Chateau. He is engaged in writing the narrative of the operations of the Corps during the last hundred days of the war. Had lunch with General Brutinel and in the afternoon motored to Tournai, meeting at dinner General Loomis, General Draper,[9] and Captain McGregor, VC, 2nd CMRs.

On 17 January, General Embury informed Currie that the War Office disapproved of the Canadian demobilization plans. Sir Arthur was determined that the Canadians would return home according to the scheme which fit the Corps' needs best, not a plan designed to calm political tensions in England. The British scheme, which demobilised individual soldiers according to their employability, was designed to ease the transformation of the British war-economy back to peacetime. British officials feared that a different Canadian

---

8   Thomas George Shaughnessy (1853-1923), American born railway tycoon who found his fortune in Canada as president of the Canadian Pacific railway (1899-1918).
9   Brigadier General Dennis C. Draper (born 1875), commanding officer of 8th Brigade (from May 1918).

scheme would breed resentment and disaffection among Imperial soldiers. However, the Imperial solution was not practical for Canada and Currie was determined to see that his scheme was implemented.

Diary Entry, 18 January 1919

Weather still continues vary fine. Not hearing satisfactory news from General Embury I motored to Lille and telephoned to him from there, using the office of Colonel Jack Churchill[10] for that purpose. Here I committed an amusing *faux-pas* with reference to his brother, the Minister of War. I returned to Tournai for the night.

Diary Entry, 22 January 1919

I called on the Minister about eleven o'clock. We had a conference immediately and found that the matter on which I had come was no further advanced. The Minister's officers were taking further steps during the afternoon. We dined alone in the evening, Colonel Magee joining us in the Palm room.

Diary Entry, 29 January 1919

Spent all day at headquarters dealing with honours, correspondence, etc. I learned today the disquieting news of a strike on the railways running out of Calais. Altogether, I found the situation, as far as the British Army is concerned, most unsatisfactory. Their scheme of demobilization, scrapped so many times, has proved very unsatisfactory inasmuch as the army is now practically immobile. I am more than ever convinced that the scheme for demobilization which we have consistently advocated is the only correct solution of the problem, and I would not be a bit surprised if, in a few months time, the only troops in France organized properly will be those remaining of the Canadian Corps. I found that, after an uneventful period on the Rhine, the Corps completed its move back to the Liege–Namur area on the 26th. Headquarters of the 4th Division are at La Hulpe, and these I must visit as soon as I can.

Diary Entry, 4 February 1919

Left at nine o'clock this morning for Liege, where I saw a review of troops of the 1st Canadian Division. The salute was taken by Lieutenant General Jacques,

---

10 John Strange-Spencer Churchill (1880-1947), Winston Churchill's brother.

a Belgian corps commander with headquarters at Liege. The arrangements were very well made and everything passed off without a hitch. The streets were crowded with people, all of whom were very enthusiastic and accorded a most splendid reception to the units. I was very proud of the old division and have never seen a smarter turn out. After the review, a reception was held at the Hotel de Ville and later a luncheon was given by the Burgomaster. I did not attend either of these ceremonies. General Rawlinson called during the afternoon, and later on General Burstall came in.

As Currie and his officers prepared the Report to the Ministry, some of the generals under his command grew worried that they would not be given their due. With the battles over, everyone wanted a share of the glory. If Currie was unused to dealing with politicians and political mudslinging, he was equally unprepared to massage the egos of the generals under his command. Sir Arthur saw his Report to the Ministry as an objective, historical document which would set the record straight for the Canadian people, thus torpedoing any criticisms. Naively, he did not understand that the report was also a political document. Currie was deeply hurt when Major-General David Watson asked to proof the report before it was submitted to the Overseas Ministry. Apparently he believed that the 4th Division might not be given its proper share of the glory.

Currie to Major General David Watson, 4 February 1919[11]

Dear General Watson,

I have your [letter] dated 30th January 1919 in which you ask that, before I give my approval to the narrative of the last hundred days fighting, now being prepared by the Corps staff under my supervision, it be first submitted to you. You state that you consider it essential, in order that this narrative be correct, that this procedure be adopted in so far as your division is concerned.

I have no objection whatever to your seeing this narrative, in fact I would like you to see it. I would like you and your staff to interest themselves in it, because I am very anxious that it should not only be complete but accurate, but to intimate that, under the arrangements now pertaining, justice would not be done to your division, is to insinuate something which I don't like.

11   File 19801226-281, 58A 1 61.4, ACP, CWM.

The staff officer whom you were good enough to send is there not only for the purpose of helping in the compilation of this document, but he is there as your representative to see that the narrative, as far as it relates to the operations of the 4th Division, is complete and accurate. If you haven't confidence in his ability to do that, then I suggest that you recall him and send another staff officer. If he has reported to you that there is a danger that justice will not be done to the operations of the 4th Division, then I would like to know about it, but to suggest that a corps commander should submit a narrative, compiled under his supervision, to his divisional commanders before sending it forward is to make a somewhat unusual request. I venture to say that in the 4th Division it is not the practice of the divisional commander, before forwarding any narrative which may be compiled under his supervision, to send the proofs of that narrative to his brigade commanders. If you expect your brigade commanders to have confidence in your ability to do justice to the operations of their brigades, I think I am justified in asking you to have confidence in my ability to do justice to the operations of the 4th Division.

I am sorry you did not mention this matter to me when I was there yesterday, for it may be that I am taking your letter in the wrong spirit but, frankly, the tone of it hurts.

Yours faithfully,

A.W. Currie

At the beginning of February, Canadian demobilization plans were given final approval by the War Office. Currie was aware that demobilization was also becoming the all consuming political issue back home. On 5 February, the Corps Commander explained his support for the Canadian demobilization scheme in a letter to the editor of the Vancouver World.

Currie to John Nelson, 5 February 1919[12]

My dear Nelson,

...We are now anxiously looking forward to the time when we can get home. Our 3rd Division is arriving in England on its way to Canada, the others will follow in the order 1st, 2nd, and 4th, a certain proportion of Corps troops going with each division. If present arrangements hold good, we ought all to be out of

12 Ibid, ACP, CWM. John Nelson (1873-1936), owner and editor of the Vancouver *World* (1915-1921).

France by the first of May and all to be in Canada early in June. The limiting factor is Canada's ability to move the troops from Halifax and St. John. We are told to make our arrangements not to send more than 30,000 a month up to April 1st when in that month 40,000 can be handled, and 45,000 the month after.

I have fought very hard for the principle of demobilising the Corps by units. There were many reasons which influenced me, all of which I think will arise to a reasonable mind. First, I regard demobilization as a military operation, not as an economic problem. As long as we remain part of an army of occupation we must remain thoroughly organized from a military point of view, and you cannot do that if you withdraw for purposes of demobilization, men simply because they have been here longest, or because they have been married, or because they are farmers, miners, etc. If you do, your whole military organisation would crumble, and I have had enough experience in war to know that organisation counts for a very great deal.

Furthermore, I wanted the people of Canada to see these men as units. I wanted the city of Vancouver to welcome the 7th Battalion as a battalion, and so with the 29th and the 72nd. I want the days that they arrive there to be red-letter days in Vancouver's history. The men deserve it, and the people want to welcome them, but great and all as Vancouver is you can't do it if this week so many butchers turn up, and next week so many miners, and the next week so many labourers, and so on. Furthermore, in order to get the men to their own door-steps happy, contented, and under some form of discipline, which is necessary, you must let them go back under the organizations which trained them, fought them, looked after them in the field, on the march, in battle, and in billets. Napoleon said that the discipline of an army meant everything, and that it could be destroyed in four days. As usual he was right.

That part of your letter dealing with the political situation and the outlook for the future is interesting. I do not know, Nelson, what I shall do when I return to Canada. I thank God that I am alive, and that the first thought that comes to one's mind is to devote the rest of one's life towards bettering the condition of all those who served in France, their wives, families or any other dependants. I believe that the survivors have not been permitted to survive for nothing.

I do not want to enter what is known as the political game. I do not like it, for I do not like the motives which influence men in shaping their political activities. I shall never again be the slave of any political party. I will do only what I think is right and no motive will make me not act otherwise. Such a principle does not pertain in modern politics. Playing the game in military service has a different meaning to playing the game in politics. I can well understand how disgusted the people are with the old system of running things, for the people at heart are sound and can always be trusted. Whether I shall remain in the military life of Canada or any other country, I do not know, for nothing definite has ever been said to me yet. I know that the world is in a turmoil. In fact, I have often wondered whether we have yet accomplished the mission we have set out to do. We were going to rid the world of militarism, of hypocrisy, we were going to make it a better place to live in, and I do not think we can yet say that we have accomplished that much. The whole world is in a turmoil, and the whole world is armed, and the outlook is not satisfactory, I do not intend to make any rash promises, to form any rash alliances. I think the best thing for me to do is to wait until I can get back to Canada, and to become more familiar with Canadian thought, Canadian sentiment, Canadian conditions socially, morally, politically, and otherwise. However, I have so many things to attend to in connection with this demobilization that one has little time to give these matters.

With all good wishes to you personally, and asking you to remember me kindly to any of my Vancouver friends,

I am, ever faithfully yours,

A.W. Currie

Diary Entry, 7 February 1919

Last night was a very cold night, one of the coldest we have had in France or Belgium. General Griesbach and his Aide de Camp Lieutenant O'Connor had lunch with us on the way to Brussels where Griesbach goes on his way to Paris in order to see Sir Robert Borden before leaving for Canada. I discussed with him certain suggestions which we both thought should govern the future military policy there. Griesbach has always been such a splendid soldier and good fellow that one hates to see him go, but the old Corps is gradually breaking up...

As Canadian generals were beginning to leave the Corps, Currie's British superiors reflected on the Corps Commander and the role he played in the final operations of the war. It is unclear what motivated Sir Henry Horne to produce a confidential report on Sir Arthur Currie's conduct, but it is likely that it was commissioned by the Overseas Ministry.

Confidential Report by General Sir Henry Horne on Lieutenant General Sir Arthur Currie, 7 February 1919[13]

Lieutenant General Sir Arthur Currie has continued his successful command of the Canadian Corps throughout the operations of 1918, displaying his many great qualities as a leader, commander, and organizer. His thoroughness and attention to detail have ensured good plans of operations which his energy and determination have carried through. He has brought the discipline and training of the Corps to a high level. He has inspired and created an *esprit* and morale throughout all ranks which is second to none. His perseverance and tact have overcome and smoothed away many difficulties connected with the organization of the Corps and the Canadian Forces. He has at all times afforded me as the Army Commander loyal support and energetic co-operation. I have felt perfect confidence that any task I called upon General Currie to perform would be carried through to my satisfaction. My confidence has been justified.

Diary Entry, 9 February 1919

Weather is clear and cold. Last night I received a letter from Sir Robert Borden asking me to Paris as soon as convenient and I have wired that I would go next Thursday. I have also wired to Lady Currie to come over then.[14]

As Currie prepared to depart for Paris to attend the Peace Conference, he reflected on the war's meaning for Canada. Currie had been one of the Corps' most vocal boosters since assuming command in June 1917. Although he consistently argued that Canadians were superior soldiers, often criticizing British officers and politicians, he did not seem to equate the Corps' success on the battlefield with any new sense of Canadian identity. Like most English speaking Canadians in the first decades of the 20th Century, Currie understood Canada to be part of a greater British Nation. Like many imperial nationalists, he believed that the British Empire was Canada's natural gateway to the world, not a yoke weighing down the Dominion. When Currie compared Canadian successes to British failures, he still spoke of them as successes for the British Nation. Canadian soldiers were superior, but in the same way that a Scottish

---

13   File 19801226-281, 58A 1 61.4, ACP, CWM.
14   On the Paris Peace Conference see Margaret Macmillan, *Paris, 1919: Six Months that Changed the World* (New York: Random House, 2001).

regiment might be better than an English unit. For Currie, 'Canada' and 'Britain'
were indivisible.[15]

Currie to M.H. Dobie, 9 February 1919[16]

My dear Dobie,

...[I] note what you say regarding my receiving something more tangible than a vote of thanks. Of course, I have heard something of this from others, and am quite prepared to believe that opposition to it would develop. From the time I first became associated with Canada's Overseas Forces I have met with opposition, and found it almost as difficult a task fighting political soldiers as I have fighting Germans.

If anybody takes any objection to what I have said in recent messages I cannot help it, but I have said nothing but the truth. The Canadian Corps is the hardest hitting force in the world, and the best in the Empire, and if you were here you would be the first to say so. I am quite prepared to believe that the people of Canada do not yet know the part that Canadian soldiers have played in bringing this war to a conclusion.

I am not writing to you, Dobie, to have my letter published, or even shown to anyone. I do not write for publication, and when I write to my friends it is for them alone but I am prepared to state publicly everything I am going to tell you and it cannot be denied. There are many things that have happened in this war of which British people are not proud, but in those things the Canadians are not concerned. What I refer to will be told you many times in the future.

On the 1st of August there were on the whole Western front 184 German divisions. In the battles from August 8th to October 3rd, between which dates all the really hard fighting was done, the Canadian Corps met and defeated forty-seven of those divisions so decisively that fifteen have never since been heard of. Forty-seven divisions is just over twenty-five per cent, of the total German divisions so that you see that while the Canadians were defeating twenty-five per cent of the total German forces, it left to the American Army, the French Army, the Belgian Army, and to the rest of the British Army the task of looking after

---

15 On conceptions of Canadian nationalism and Empire at the time of the Great War, see Carl Berger, *The Sense of Power: Studies in the Ideas of Canadian Imperialism* (Toronto: UTP, 1970). For a contemporary account of the Anglo-Canadian sense of national identity from a British perspective, see Richard Jebb, *Studies in Colonial Nationalism* (London: E. Arnold, 1905).

16 Ibid. M.H. Dobie of the Victoria Chemical Company..

the other three-quarters. Am I not justified in saying that these four Canadian divisions are the hardest hitting force in the world?

I want to tell you also, Dobie, that the Canadians were only used in what Foch calls decisive battles, that is, battles in which, if victories were won great results might follow. Who, I ask you, formed the spearhead of the battle at Amiens, a battle fought, as far as the British Army was concerned, principally by Canadians and Australians. This battle, outside the material results, did more to raise the morale of the British Army and the British Nation than anything else. The Canadians were the spearhead of that attack, though for days the fact that they were in it was withheld from the public, and the victory was accorded to British troops. It is true we are British troops, and proud to be known as such, but there are times when Canadian soldiers cannot understand why they are sometimes called Canadians, and at others British. If a crime is committed we are certainly Canadians; if a victory is won we are often called British.

Following the Amiens battle came the breaking of the Hinderburg Line, something which had to be done before final victory could be hoped far; and who broke that line? The Canadian Corps did it in the battle which began on August 26th and closed on September 2nd. Do you knew when Ludendorff admitted—and of this I have positive proof—that he had lost the war on land? It was when the Canadians broke the Quéant–Drocourt line, and our authority for that in a statement of Captain Finkel, who served throughout the war as a member of Ludendorff's staff..

Now let me tell you another thing. You have read Sir Douglas Haig's despatch. He tells you that from the 1st August the British Army met and defeated ninety-nine German divisions. Let me tell you that there are more than fifty divisions in the British Army. Of those ninety-nine divisions, forty-seven were met and defeated by the Canadian Corps. You are a mathematician, Dobie, and I leave it to you if I am not right in saying that the Canadians were the hardest hitting force in the world. Why do the French call us 'Foch's Pets'? Simply because Foch put us always where he had to count on victory.

I could go bask to Passchendaele if I liked. It is a fact that cannot he denied that Australians tried for Passchendaele and failed. So did the New Zealanders, and so did the British. Did the Canadians fail? No. Let me tell you another thing, Dobie. Not a single Canadian gun has been captured by the enemy in this war. Can any other nation say as much? For over two years, Canadian troops have never failed to take an objective, nor have they lost an inch of ground once consolidated. Can any other troops say as much? Do you realize, Dobie, that I have battalions in the old 1st Division that in four years of war have never failed to take an objective, and have never been driven from an inch of ground by the enemy. Can even the Guards say as much?

In your letter you say that there are many of our people, born in the old country, to whom my messages seem offensive. How can the truth be offensive to anyone? If Canada is the home of these people, I think they should take a pride in what the soldiers of Canada have done, and not try to belittle their achievements. You say that officers who have served under me in France do not hesitate to say that I praise my own troops too much. No officer who has ever served under me knows as much about this war and what has happened on all its fronts as I do, because I have never missed a day. You say that my friends hold it would be better policy on my part, and would show better taste, if I were more moderate in my praise of the Canadian Army. The time has gone by, Dobie, when I am going to map out my conduct along the lines of what would be political.

I should think the world was tired of hypocrisy, but some people seem to be particularly thin skinned when it comes to what is good taste. The curse of the British Empire is that some people are always considering what is good or what is bad form. They care not for what is honest, just, or true. They are quite willing to be hypocrites if they exhibit good form.

You will agree that I have not written very much to Canada, and have never sent a message off my own bat as it were. I have only replied to telegrams that have been sent me, and from time to time have issued Special Orders, of which I am not ashamed. As I said earlier in this letter, it is for yourself alone, but this I do want you to know, Dobie, that I am not going to be dishonest with myself or unfair to the troops I have had the honour to command simply in order to please some people!

With all good wishes, and thanking you again for your letter,

I am ever yours faithfully,

A.W. Currie

Diary Entry, 12 February 1919

General Loomis arrived at this headquarters last night and we discussed with him and General Embury certain matters regarding demobilization. He proceeded to Tournai later in the day, General Embury and Colonel Folger going to Brussels regarding horses, while Colonel Ralston[17] and myself left for Paris. We lunched at Poix and arrived in Paris about five o'clock, going at once to the Majestic Hotel, the headquarters of the British delegation at the Peace Conference. We obtained rooms there and dined there. After dinner I had a long and most interesting chat with Sir Douglas Haig, and about 10:30 went with Colonel Ralston to Sir Robert Borden's room where we chatted until midnight.

Diary Entry, 13 February 1919

The cold weather has broken and rain is falling. At eleven o'clock I went to the La Perouse Hotel, where the Canadian delegation have offices and there met Sir Robert Borden, Sir George Foster, and Messrs Sifton and Doherty.[18] I outlined to them how demobilization was proceeding, and we discussed withdrawal of the Canadian troops from Russia.[19] Lunched at the Majestic, and after a walk spent the afternoon with Mr. Dafoe,[20] the editor of the *Winnipeg Free Press*. I received word first that my wife had missed the boat and would not arrive until tomorrow. Later on I received a telegram saying that she was in Folkestone but would not arrive in Paris until tomorrow night...

Diary Entry, 14 February 1919

...In the afternoon I attended the preliminary session[21] of the Peace Conference and heard President Wilson read the proposed constitution of the League of Nations, after which he delivered a very fine speech in support of the idea. Other speakers were Sir Robert Cecil,[22] and the Honourable Mr. Barnes[23] for the British, Signor Orlando,[24] for the Italians, a member of the French Cabinet, whose name I have forgotten, and also the principal representative of the Japanese delegation. It was a most interesting occasion and I was glad of the privilege of attending.

17 Lieutenant Colonel James Layton Ralston (1881-1948) of the 85th Battalion and Minister of National Defence (1926-30, 1940-44).
18 Charles Joseph Doherty (1855-1931), Minister of Justice and Attorney General (1911-21) and a member of the Canadian delegation to the Paris Peace Conference in 1919.
19 Canada sent an expeditionary force to Siberia and a contingent of troops to Northern Russia in the autumn of 1918 to shore up the Russian Monarchy against the Bolshevik Forces..
20 John W. Dafoe (1866-1944), appointed as editor of the *Winnipeg Free Press* by its owner Clifford Sifton in 1901, Dafoe held the post until his death in 1944.
21 This was actually a plenary session of the conference at which Wilson presented the draft covenant of the League of Nations. See MacMillan, 95-97.
22 Lord Edgar Algernon Robert Cecil (1864-1958), Minister of Blockade (1916-18) and British Representative to the Paris Peace Conference in Charge of Negotiations for the League of Nations.
23 George Nicoll Barnes (1859-1940), Labour Party Leader (1910-11), Minister of Pensions under Lloyd George (1916-17), and League of Nations Commission leader at the Paris Peace Conference.
24 Vittorio Emanuele Orlando (1860-1952), Prime Minister of Italy (1917-1919).

The session took place, in the famous Clock Room of the French Foreign Office, and the proceedings were presided over by M. Clemenceau. President Wilson[25] left Paris later in the afternoon on his return to the United States. I returned to the Majestic Hotel about 6:30, and just as I was leaving there for the station I found that my wife had arrived at the Ritz, where she had been since early morning. Going there I found her quite ill and suffering from grippe.[26]

Diary Entry, 15 February 1919

My wife was so ill that she could not leave her bed, suffering intense pain in her side and generally throughout her body. I remained in the hotel all day. General Brutinel arrived from Hesdin...After dinner we discussed the preliminary report on the operations. Later on I sent for a doctor, and Dr. Blay responded.

Diary Entry, 17 February 1919

Lady Currie being no better, I got the nurse, Miss Lord, who had accompanied her from Boulogne. Her condition remained about the same. I went to the offices of Sir Robert Borden in the morning. Sir William Orpen[27] came at 2:30 and commenced a painting of myself. I remained in the hotel all afternoon.

Diary Entry, 18 February 1919

A little change in my wife's condition. I was out for a short time in the morning, and General Radcliffe came to lunch with me. Orpen came again in the afternoon and General Gough had tea with me. Invitations arrived for Princess Patricia's wedding, for the party at St. James's Palace, and for a reception at the British Embassy in honour of the Prince of Wales.

Diary Entry, 20 February 1919

[Dr. McCullough and Dr. Lewis] came to breakfast with me, and there met Dr. Blay. They again agreed on the diagnosis as intercostal neuralgia. The fever has more or less left and condition is less critical. I took them to lunch at the Café Paris returning to the Hotel where I spent the rest of the day.

---

25 Woodrow Wilson (1856-1924), President of the United States (1913-21), author of the Fourteen Points, and architect of the League of Nations.
26 Influenza.
27 Sir William Orpen (1878-1931), Irish portrait painter and official British war artist.

As Lucy recovered from complications of influenza, the rumours surrounding Currie were reaching their peak. Bored soldiers gossiped and in the winter of 1919 the Canadians were sick and tired of waiting to go home. Many of them had been overseas for years and with no war to fight, they had little to do except complain. Typically, many soldiers blamed their fate on the higher-ups. Currie did not understand that most of the rumours were simply idle talk. Instead, Currie saw Hughes, Turner, and their minions working everywhere to destroy his reputation and diminish the accomplishments of the Corps. While Currie's paranoia was based in fact (after all, Hughes was mounting a vicious campaign), his belief in a wide ranging conspiracy and his insistence that Canadian officials investigate the source of the rumours only added fuel to the fire.

Currie to Sir Edward Kemp, 27 February 1919[28]

Dear Sir Edward,

You will remember I spoke to you some time ago about certain rumours which were flying around England concerning myself. I find that the position is still being spread and I think if an effort were made the source might be found.

The rumours I refer to are those about my being a murderer of Canadian troops, about my being bombed, and shot at, and booed, and God knows what else. All these things are most malicious lies. I am not in England to defend myself, nor to take any action to correct these impressions.

I repeat that I think these slanders are being encouraged. It seems to me that I have a right to ask for some protection. I have not even heard of the officers in command of several camps being asked to take any action to locate the evil influence or to remove the wrong impression.

Your faithfully,

A.W. Currie

Sir Edward Kemp to Sir Robert Borden, 5 March 1919[29]

Dear Sir Robert Borden,

...I take it that the mention you make of the prevalence of rumours of an exaggerated character may refer to some rumours of a personal character in reference to General Currie. Therefore I think perhaps it is desirable, as he may have spoken to you about this, that I should attach hereto copy of a letter written

28   Reel C4333, vol 102, BP, LAC.
29   Reel C4333, vol 102, BP, LAC.

to me by General Currie,[30] and my reply to the same. I did not say in my reply all that I intend to say to General Currie when he comes here.

You will see by General Currie's letter that he makes reference to rumours regarding himself originating in England. This is not at all correct. I have made enquiries from many different sources and the rumours really come in my opinion from other ranks who come over here from France, but the discussion regarding the matters to which General Currie refers takes place in France as well as in England.

There is a lot of idle gossip similar in character to the kind of things the soldiers talk about in Canada, as well as over here. General Currie must not try to convince himself that there is anyone here after him with a view of destroying the good reputation which he has built up for himself in military matters, but on the other hand he must take the ordinary means of contradicting these rumours at the proper time, and I am under the impression that the best way to do it is in the way I suggested to him in my letter. But to start out to hold investigations in the camps here and possibly in France in regard to such matters, in my opinion, would only have a tendency to exaggerate their importance.

Of course those of us who have been in public life for considerable periods understand how to handle this sort of thing better than General Currie.

I remain yours faithfully,

A.E. Kemp

Kemp was less worried about finding the source of the rumours than he was about exaggerating their importance by conducting public inquiries and investigations. Unbeknownst to Currie or Kemp, gasoline was being poured on the fire in Ottawa. On 4 March, Sir Sam Hughes rose in the House of Commons and made his long awaited public attack against Currie. Under the protection of Parliament, Hughes accused the Corps Commander of needlessly wasting Canadian lives. 'Were I in authority,' boomed the former Minister of Militia, 'the officer who, four hours before the Armistice was signed, although he had been notified beforehand that the Armistice was to begin at eleven o'clock, ordered the attack on Mons thus needlessly sacrificing the lives of Canadian soldiers, would be tried summarily by court martial and punished so far as the law would allow. There is no glory to be gained, and you cannot find one Canadian soldier

30   See Currie's letter of 27 February 1919.

returning from France who will not curse the name of the officer who ordered the
attack on Mons. '[31] *It was his most vitriolic assault yet.*

Meanwhile, in England speeches in the House of Commons and rumours in
the camps were the least of the Overseas Ministry's worries. On the night of 4/5
March 1919, frustrations with demobilization boiled over and Canadian troops
stationed at Kinmel Camp in Rhyl, Wales rioted. Five Canadian soldiers were
killed in fighting which saw members of the CEF turn rifles and bayonets on
each other.[32]

Diary Entry, 6 March 1919

General Brutinel came in the morning and we went over the final draft of
his report. We lunched at the hotel, went for a drive in the afternoon, and in
the evening took Willis to dinner and to the Opera Comique where we saw 'La
Tosca.'

Diary Entry, 8 March 1919

We were out in the morning. Had lunch with M. and Mde. Roy. In the afternoon
Lady Currie shopped, while I called on General Pershing.[33] In the evening Sir
Robert Borden gave a large dinner party at the Hotel Majestic. After dinner we
went downstairs to a dance, where we remained until midnight.

Diary Entry, 9 March 1919

We left Paris about ten o'clock in the morning...We came up through Roye,
Amiens, where we had tea at the famous Godberg Restaurant, Albert, Bapaume,
Arras, deviating a little to see Neuville Vitasse. From Arras, we went up the
Lens–Arras road over Vimy Ridge, coming back through Neuville St. Vaast, Mt.
St. Eloi to Camblain L'Abbé, where we had dinner at the officer's club, meeting
there Major Sydney Booth, who is in charge, and Major Jack, the artist. After
dinner we motored on, and I called in to see General Brutinel at Headin. From
there we went to Montreuil, and called at the Canadian Section [GHQ] who gave
us a very fine supper, which was much appreciated. We arrived at Boulogne
about midnight, and spend the night at the Folkestone Hotel.

31 House of Commons Debates, 4 March 1919, 207.
32 On the Kinmel Camp riots see Desmond Morton, '"Kicking and Complaining": Demobilization Riots in the
    Canadian Expeditionary Force, 1918-19,' *Canadian Historical Review* 61, 3 (1980): 334-360.
33 General of the Armies John Joseph Pershing (1860-1948), commanded the American Expeditionary Force
    (1917-19). See Frank E. Vandiver, *Black Jack: The Life and Times of John J. Pershing* (London: Texas A&M
    University Press, 1977).

Diary Entry, 10 March 1919

We left Boulogne at 10:30, having no difficulty over the passports which had not been vised [sic] at any time during my wife's stay in France. We arrived in London without incident shortly after three o'clock and went to the Carlton Hotel. I went up to see the Minister and was with him, Colonel Gibson[34] and General Embury until nearly eight o'clock. I had come across to England, not only to see Lady Currie home but at the request of Sir Robert Borden, to enquire into the cause of the Canadian riots at Rhyl. According to the Paris papers we had concluded that the whole 3rd Canadian Division had rioted. It was a great relief to find out at the Minister's office that no 3rd Canadian Division troops were involved but that the trouble makers were men of the Forestry Corps and railway troops. The reports were very grossly and shamefully exaggerated, disclosing an attitude on the part of the English papers which, to say the least, is very much to be regretted, and will cause bitter feeling. There is no doubt that the men at Rhyl were very much disappointed inasmuch as they had been told of sailing dates which on several occasions had been postponed, for our military authorities in England were not able to live up to their programme for February.

Diary Entry, 11 March 1919

I sent for General Loomis who came in from Bramshott this morning and had breakfast with me. I then attended a meeting at the Minister's office at eleven o'clock but at which I was disappointed not to find General Turner present, for it had been intended to take up certain personal matters with him. I thought I detected in his report on the Rhyl disturbances an inclination to ascribe the cause of the trouble to the demobilization of the Corps by units, something which had nothing whatever to do with the case as no Corps troops were involved, and only a very, very few had gone to Canada at this date. At this meeting we prepared an answer to be sent to Ottawa in reply to a request from General Mewburn that I furnish a special report on the Mons operation. This I declined to do, pointing out that as the Canadian Corps was still an integral part of the British Army these reports would have to be obtained through the regular channels, but I pointed out that our war diaries and summaries of operations were very complete and were already on file in the Record Office. I was also shown a telegram setting forth a

---

34 Colonel Thomas Gibson (born 1875), Assistant Deputy Minister, Overseas Ministry.

number of very silly questions that had been asked in the House as to the number of proclamations I issued to the troops during the elections of 1917, and also the number sent to Canada...

Diary Entry, 14 March 1919

In the morning General Loomis came in, and I learned from him that Colonel Johnson of the 2nd CMR had left for Canada with a very wrong impression concerning myself. This was conveyed to him at Argyll House, who told him that his request to have the 2nd CMR's again become a British Columbia unit was vetoed by the Minister on my recommendation. This statement was a lie, but was in harmony with a great many other statements of Argyll House where I am concerned. He also told me of the Bolshevistic tendencies of the Rev. W. Barton, Chaplin of one of the Camps there...We left Folkestone at 3:30 English time and arrived at Boulogne 6:30 French time. I went immediately to the Canadian Section, where I spent the night...

Diary Entry, 18 March 1919

Colonel Panet[35] left for England, where I sent him in order that he might visit all the units of the Corps troops awaiting sailing to Canada. In the afternoon I went to Brussels to the Royal Palace and had tea with the King and Queen. Mde. Edvina sang. There were about twenty-five people present. General Morrison returned in the evening from showing a party of Americans over the Vimy Ridge and explaining to them the battle.

Diary Entry, 23 March 1919

Although it snowed hard last night, the day was very fine indeed. Sir Robert Borden and I called on the French Commandant at Lille, after which we went via Menin to Ypres. I took Borden and Foster; Sifton went with Macdonell, and Dougherty with Hayter. From Ypres we went through St. Julien, Poelcapelle, Westroosebeke, Passchendaele, Zonnebeke and Potijze, and back again to Ypres. We went out by the Lille gate, visiting the railway dugouts and the Canadian Cemetery there, then went on past Shrapnel Corner, Kemmel, and Neuve Eglise to my old headquarters at Petit Pont Farm, where we found that the old couple had returned to their ruined home. They were overjoyed to see us again; Sir Robert

---

35   Lieutenant Colonel Arthur Hubert Panet (1877-1944)

and I going in and having coffee, while Sir George Foster took a nap in the car. We then went up by Hyde Park Corner, around Hill 63, through Ploegstraat, Nieppe, Estaires, Lestrem, Locon, Bethune, Noeux-les-Mines, Gouy Servins to Camblain L'Abbé, where we arrived about seven o'clock. The others turned up shortly afterwards, while General Burstall was there before us. After dinner, Major Jack, the artist, sang. We all turned in early.

By the end of the month, Hughes' allegations were still unchallenged in the House. With Borden and much of the cabinet overseas and preoccupied with the Peace Conference, no one in Ottawa had risen to defend Currie. It was a fight that the Union Government did not want to join. As long as it remained a personal dispute between two individuals, the Government could avoid a debate on Canadian casualties and other questions about its conduct of the war. Currie did not understand the Government's reluctance to defend his name and the reputation of the Corps he loved. He continued to believe it was his superiors' responsibility to respond in public to any criticism of him, as a servant of the Government.

Currie to Robert F. Green, 30 March 1919[36]

My dear Bob,

...let me say that it would be impossible for me to accept the Lieutenant Governorship of British Columbia. I realize the great kindness to me of those who have made the suggestion, but you know, Bob, that I have not sufficient income to justify me in trying to follow in the footsteps of the Honourable C.W. Patterson [sic][37] or Sir Frank Barnard.[38] Were I a wealthy man, I would like it very much as it would give me an opportunity of obtaining that rest which I am beginning to realize I need very much.

As long as the fighting was on and as long as the responsibilities regarding demobilization continue, one of course will keep up, but when the time comes for the doffing of khaki I know one will feel the relaxation very much. It would also afford one the time to write one's experiences in this war, and also enlarged

36 File 19801226-282, 58A 1 61.5, ACP, CWM. Robert Francis Green (1861-1946), a Member of the Legislative Assembly of British Columbia (1898-1907), Member of Parliament (1912-21), and senator (1921-46).
37 Thomas William Paterson (1851-1921), Member of the Legislative Assembly of British Columbia (1903-07) and Lieutenant Governor of British Columbia (1909-14).
38 Sir Francis Stillman Barnard (1856-1936), Businessman, Member of Parliament (1888-1902), Lieutenant Governor of British Columbia (1914-19).

reports of the action of the Corps, which I know full well are all too little known to the people of Canada.

Do you know that I have had letters from people in Victoria, saying that they thought it would be just as well for me not to say that the Canadian Corps was the hardest hitting force of its size in the Allied armies? This discloses to me that there are some people who do not believe such a statement; some who still think that, because a thing is Canadian, it cannot be quite as good as if it were stamped 'Made in England.' I never said a truer word in my life than when I said that the Canadian Corps was the greatest fighting force in these armies. There is no Corps in any army that has had the universally successful record this Corps has had, and despite all people say about casualties it will be found that these were not excessive in view of the results obtained, and, if the British figures are to be believed, were less in proportion to the numbers engaged of the British, Australian, and Canadian Expeditionary Forces in France.

Just now it appears that there are some who do not want to hear the truth about what the Corps did. They prefer to spend their time in uttering most malicious and vicious lies about matters concerning which they know very, very little. I am surprised that the House of Commons sat and listened to what it recently heard. Sam Hughes says I ordered the attack on Mons four hours before the Armistice was to come into effect, or at seven o'clock on the morning of November 11th. As a matter of fact I knew at five o'clock in the morning that Mons had been captured by us during the night. The casualties were very small indeed. But his most amazing statement is the one where he says I deliberately slaughtered the Canadians in order that the 5th Division would have to be broken up to supply the necessary reinforcements. As his son commanded the 5th Division, a division created solely that his son might be made a Major General, discloses to everyone the reason for Sir Sam's animosity.

I did not think any constituency in Canada would be content to have as its member a man who would do such a cowardly, mean and vicious thing, yet apparently that is what one must look for in politics, and that is why I never hope to enter public life. Yet I am not going to say that I never will. I am not such a fool as to believe that I can control the soldiers' vote, but such is my feeling for what these men did that I would do anything to further their interests, even if the actions thus forced upon me were very much against my inclination...

A.W. Currie

Diary Entry, 31 March 1919

The day was fine. In the morning Sir Douglas Haig came and had breakfast. He was accompanied by General Curly Birch, General Clive the Intelligence Officer and Major Heseltine, his Aide de Camp. Divisional commanders and brigadiers now in France were present. He left to catch his train at 9:45, and was very kind in his remarks about the Canadians before leaving. I then went to Aubelais, where I saw the 18th and 19th Battalions leaving for England. I lunched with General Tremblay[39] and in the afternoon visited the headquarters of all battalions of the 5th Brigade.

On 2 April Currie received an urgent wire asking that he and General Burstall report to London immediately.

Diary Entry, 2 April 1919

General Burstall joined me at Boulogne and we crossed on the morning boat, arriving in London a little after three. We went immediately to the Minister's office and found that he desired principally to discuss with us the constitution of a General Court Martial to try the Rhyl cases. I selected a court. We got back to the Carlton about six o'clock, where my wife was and where we spent the evening.

Diary Entry, 3 April 1919

I went to the Minister's office at eleven o'clock and in company with General Turner we discussed many matters, principally with reference to the relationship between Argyll House and the Corps. I lunched in the hotel and in the evening left for Brighton, arriving there a little after eight o'clock.

Diary Entry, 5 April 1919

We left Brighton at about ten o'clock and motored to London. I went to the Naval and Military Club to attend a luncheon given by Sir Edward Kemp. There were present besides Sir Edward, General Turner, Sir Robert Borden, Major Bristol, Mr. Lefroy of *Canada*, Mr. Campion of the Associated Press, Mr. Lacey Amy, Mr. Fred James, two other reporters who had been officers in the Corps, and myself. After luncheon Sir Edward Kemp made a statement, the

---

39   Major General Thomas Louis Tremblay (1886-1951), the commanding officer of the 22nd Battalion (1916-18), and 5th Brigade (from August 1918).

publication of which he authorized. He was followed by Sir Robert Borden, who also gave out a statement. I was asked if I had anything to say, and the only thing I authorized was that demobilization was our principal concern now, and that I thought everyone connected with it was doing the very best possible to get the men home in as short a time, and as happy and contented as possible. With reference to any criticisms regarding myself, I said that I did not consider it the time nor the place to answer them, but that they all could be answered. General Turner gave out a statement which was much longer. I did not care very much for the idea of this luncheon...

Currie spent the next few weeks inspecting the departing troops and meeting dignitaries in London.

Diary Entry, 14 April 1919

In the morning I went to Halpe to meet the different commanding officers of the 4th Division, in order to discuss with them the matter of battle clasps, and also to get their opinion as to the advisability of Canadians joining in the parade in London of overseas troops. The majority favoured our participation, a conclusion with which I, personally, do not agree, as I cannot consider it right for Canadians to march through the streets of London with black troops and Chinese no matter if the latter are British subjects...

Cy Peck, the former commanding officer of the 16th Battalion and Member of Parliament from British Columbia, was the only member of the House to challenge Hughes' allegations and defend the reputation of the Corps Commander.

Currie to Lieutenant Colonel Cy Peck, 25 April 1919[40]

My dear Colonel,

...With you, I have felt a disappointment that no member of the Government took issue with Sir Sam Hughes. I am looking forward to such action being taken by the Prime Minister on his return. I am still a servant of this Government, and naturally look to them for protection. I am not going to demand any Courts of Enquiry, but I would welcome any Court of Enquiry if this Government desired to have one.

40   File 19801226-284, 58A 1 61.7, ACP, CWM.

I am going to have prepared a statement of the casualties from the beginning of 1916. I think it will he most interesting, and that it will prove most conclusively that in the last hundred days of the war our casualties were small, not only in proportion to the results obtained, but in proportion to the other battles concerning which no criticism his been made...

I have read your speech, Peck, with great pleasure, and I sincerely congratulate you on the manner in which you first impressed your personality on the House of Commons. I quite agree with you that it is not advisable to keep up the washing of dirty linen a moment longer than is necessary, but I am sincerely grateful that you have expressed your intention of camping on Sam's trail. To have acted as he has done proves that he is not a manly fighter. I am now looking up certain correspondence with reference to the John A. Currie incident.[41] It is not the first time that Sam has intimated in the House of Commons that I was the Currie that should be blamed for things attributed to the other man. At that time I wrote to him a letter, and received one in reply thereto, in which he acknowledged that he had been misinformed and in which he assured me that he had wired to Sir Robert Borden asking Sir Robert to inform the House that he—Sir Sam—had not been justified in the insinuations made. I shall send you a copy of my letter to him and his reply to me.

I am now in England, and will not return again to France. I came across to attend the dinner of the officers of the 2nd Division, and as all troops of the Corps will be out of France in a few days I thought I might as well remain here. I shall remain in England until all the troops of the Corps have left for Canada, and than I shall hurry home as quickly as possible.

The old battalion expects to sail in a day or so, although we are being subjected to a considerable interruption in shipping owing to the strikes at Liverpool and Southampton. I know just how glad you will be to see the battalion, and how glad they will be to see you, for I do not believe any of my commanding officers enjoy the love of their men to the extent that you do.

With all good wishes and renewed thanks for your confidence and support,
I am yours ever,
A.W. Currie

41   At the Second Battle of Ypres, Brigadier General John A. Currie

Diary Entry, 29 April 1919

Lady Currie came to town with me. We lunched together, and in the afternoon saw a performance known as 'The Heart of Humanity.' As a film production it is very good indeed, but as a representation of Canada's war effort I do not like it...

Diary Entry, 3 May 1919

We all came up from Brighton early in morning. I said good-bye to the Minister, and in the afternoon the parade of dominion troops took place through London. The weather was particularly fine, and everything passed off extremely well. We got away to the minute and arrived at Buckingham Palace just as the King took up his position at the saluting base. I saw the Canadians go past, having left the parade to stand beside his Majesty. I thought they were simply splendid, and I was very proud. When the last of them had passed, I hurried down the Mall and caught up with the head of the column at Trafalgar Square. I saw them again as they entered Hyde Park and was impressed by the good march discipline shown. People were most enthusiastic all the way. This note is written many days after the event, and from all sources since the march I have heard it given as the universal opinion that the Canadians were the best turned out, the best-drilled troops, and marched the best. We all returned to Brighton in the evening.

On 11 May 1919, Currie took his family to France for a tour of the old battlefields.

Diary Entry, 11 May 1919

Left Brighton about 6:30 and motored to Folkestone, having the whole family with me. Without any delay we got on board and the boat left about eleven o'clock. We had a pleasant run across, the sun shining brightly and the sea being perfectly smooth. Colonel Bovey met us at the boat and we all went to Wimereux for lunch. We left immediately afterwards for Cassel where we arrived about four o'clock in a perfect down-pour of rain. We stayed at the Hotel Sauvage. After tea the weather cleared and we motored through Hazebrouck, Merris, Calistre, Bailleul, St. Jean Capelle, Locre, Hoograft, and back again to Cassel. At Hoograft we saw the old sisters, who returned there in January. They were all overjoyed to see us and we spent a pleasant hour with them.

Diary Entry, 12 May 1919

We got away from Cassel about 8:30, motored to Steenvoorde, past Ten Elma, through Vlamertigne to Ypres. We had a good walk around the town, and then motored out past St. Jean, Vilchy, St. Julien, Westroobeke, Passchendaele, Zonnebeke, and Potije, back to Ypres where we had lunch in a church army hut. We left immediately after lunch, down past the Lille gate, Bedford House, through St. Eloi, Voormizeele, Vieratraat, past Kemmel, through Neuve Eglise, to my old headquarters at Petit Pont Farm, where we called. From there we went down past Hill 63, Ploegstaeert, Nieppe, Armentières, where my first headquarters were and which I recognized; through Neuve Chapelle to La Bassée. From there we passed through Beavry, and down across the Notre Dame Ridge to Camblain L'Abbé where we spent the night very comfortably at the Saskatoon Club.

Combined Diary Entry, 13–14 May 1919

We got away about ten o'clock, went through Carency up to the King's OP on Vimy Ridge; back through Souchez, Lievin, and Lens where we spent a little time; on to Douai, where we had lunch. From Douai we followed our advance of the last month through Denain, Valenciennes and on to Mons where we had tea. After that we motored to Brussels, where we spent the night, putting up at the Hotel Astoria. In the morning we took a good drive around Brussels, then down to the field of Waterloo, where we spent an hour or so. From Waterloo we came through Nivelle to Mons, Valenciennes and on to Cambrai, down the Cambrai–Bapaume road to Fontaine-Notre-Dame, where we turned north, passing through Bourlon village and crossing the canal at Moeuvres. Came on up to the old Corps Headquarters near Quéant, where they insisted on going down into one of the dugouts. We then came out the Arras–Cambrai road, following it down to Arras. We went north along the Arras–Lens road to Latileul and Thelus, then back through Neuville St. Vaast and Mount St. Eloy, to Camblain L'Abbé, where we spent the night.

Diary Entry, 15 May 1919

We got away about ten in the morning went down the Arras–Bapaume road to Courcelette, where we had lunch at the Labour Group Headquarters. After lunch we went on to Albert, turned south through Bray, reaching the Amiens battlefield at Rosières, came right up through Caix, Tailleaux, to Demiun, crossed over to

Villers Brettoneux, and on to Amiens where we had tea. Came back to Wimereux through Abbeville and Montreuil.

Diary Entry, 16 May 1919

We were unable to get the morning boat because they refused to load on it the motor car. We spent the day visiting hospitals, the du Nord Hotel, and the old town of Boulogne, where we visited amongst other places the old barracks and the dungeons underneath. We also spent considerable time in the very beautiful cathedral. We left Boulogne about five o'clock, and got across to Folkestone about seven. Had dinner at the Pavilion Hotel and got away about nine o'clock. We came via Hastings, Eastbourne and Seaford to Brighton, arriving there about one o'clock. There was considerable delay at Seaford where we stopped to get oil and petrol. Everyone was exceedingly tired and glad that the trip was over.

Although Sir Arthur was occasionally called upon to attend meetings in London, after returning from France he was able to relax for the first time in nearly four and a half years.

Diary Entry, 17 May 1919

Made an early start for town. I attended a Council Meeting in the morning and in the afternoon we went to Sir Julian Byng's at Thorpe leaving London at five o'clock and arriving there at seven. Sir Julian lives in an old-fashioned, commodious and comfortable house about seven miles from Harwich.

Diary Entry, 18 May 1919

Sir Julian and I walked to church, while the others motored. After lunch we went out into the garden and grubbed an old stump.

Diary Entry, 28 May 1919

I have not been feeling very well for nearly a month, and think it is the effect of the relaxation...

Diary Entry, 27 June 1919

Friday Ethel and my wife came up with me in the morning. In the afternoon we attended a garden party at Buckingham Palace, the first of its kind to be held. There was an enormous crowd present, and I met many army officers and others whom I knew. The King and Queen separately moved about amongst the people on the grounds and from time to time chatted with some. A few people were presented, Lady Currie and my sister being of that number. I had some five minutes or so chat with His Majesty, chiefly concerning reports of disturbances by Canadians in England. Sir Douglas Haig was there and seemed to be holding a little reception of his own most of the time. We returned to Brighton in the evening. Garner came up to town with me and spent a very happy afternoon with Minnis at the Zoo.

Diary Entry, 1 July 1919

We came to town in the morning. Sir Campbell Stuart lunched with me at the Carlton and I spent the afternoon at the office, not going to the Perley reception. In the evening I attended a Canadian dinner at the Connaught rooms. This was presided over by Sir George Perley, and a very large gathering assembled. After the usual toasts to the King and the Royal Family, Lieutenant Colonel Amery,[42] in an eloquent but somewhat long speech, proposed the toast to Canada, to which Mr. Sifton and Mr. Doherty replied. Mr. Sifton is a very rapid speaker; in fact he goes so fast that his sentences become somewhat involved. He spoke very well, though. Mr. Doherty speaks much more slowly, in fact he errs on the other side. He is a pleasant speaker, tells, a good story, and there was much good meat in what he said. Colonel Hamar Greenwood[43] proposed the toast to the Overseas Military Forces of Canada. He is a pleasant speaker. General Turner and I replied.

Diary Entry, 10 July 1919

We came to town in the morning and I saw the Minister, who informed me that he brought a message from General Mewburn saying that I could have the position of Inspector General in Canada. He was unable to tell me what the functions of this office were, and what the salary attached to it was. He asked me if he might wire to Mewburn to say that I would take it. I told him 'No,' but that he could write to Mewburn saying that I would discuss it with him when I arrived there...

On 13 July, Currie and Lucy returned to Paris for the victory parade.

---

42 Leopold Amery (1873-1955), First Lord of the Admiralty (1922-24) and Colonial Secretary (1924-29).
43 Sir Hamar Greenwood (1870-1948), a Canadian born British Member of Parliament (1906-1920). He was the last Chief Secretary for Ireland (1920-22).

Diary Entry, 14 July 1919

We left the hotel at 6:30 and drove to the assembly point. The parade started at 8:30 and was one of the most splendid sights it has been my good fortune to see. The march was about seven miles long and the route was packed with cheering people all the way. I never hope to see such splendid enthusiasm. It was a proud day for all the Allies, and must have been doubly so to the French populace. The troops taking part in the procession were the first to pass under the Arch of Triumph since the Germans marched down the Champs Elysees in 1871.[44] My wife had a good seat in the Hotel Astoria. Willie rode with me in the procession. I got back to the hotel about noon, and in the afternoon we went to Versailles going all over the beautiful gardens there. In the evening we dined at the Presidency with all the Allied generals. It was a brilliant and splendid function.

Currie left France for the last time as Corps Commander on 16 July 1919.

Diary Entry, 19 July 1919

This is the day the peace celebrations were held throughout the Empire and must forever be a red-letter day to all British subjects. It was celebrated by a march of representatives of all the Allied troops through London. They marched in alphabetical order, the Americans under General Pershing leading. Marshal Foch headed the French troops, while the British were led by Field Marshal Haig who was accompanied by his staff and generals. General Turner and I rode with the Canadians in the procession, who looked very well despite the extremely short notice they had, for until Friday afternoon it had been decided not to participate, a decision in which I had not been consulted and with which I did not agree. Although invited by the War Office to ride with Sir Douglas Haig I had decided not to go unless Canadian troops were on parade. Pressure was brought to bear on Argyll House, who had made the decision. The pressure came from Buckingham Palace and the Premier. Everybody agrees that it was a splendid procession, though rather tiring for those who participated. I got back to the Hotel about four o'clock where we remained until the evening. Ethel, Marjorie, and Garner went to the fire-works in Hyde Park while Lady Carrie

---

44   After the Franco-Prussian War.

and I dined at the Ritz with General and Lady Radcliffe...After dinner there was dancing and altogether we had a very gay and pleasant evening.

Currie to Brigadier General F.O.W. Loomis, 12 July 1919[45]

My dear Loomis,

...I appreciate very much your taking the time to outline to me at such length your appreciation of the situation in Canada. One gathers that the strike situation is somewhat better and one hopes that it is not merely the lull before a further storm.

It is certainly most pleasing to us all to know that the returned soldier, throughout Canada, has acted in a most honourable way towards law and order. One did not expect anything else, although we all know that in every large body of men there are always some looking for trouble. I believe the desire of a great majority of our fellows, when they get home, is to get back to work as soon as possible. They all realize that after the enormous waste of four years of war, it is necessary for everyone to work, and work hard, in order to recover what we have lost. The people who do the most talking are those who do the least work. It is a happy augury for the future that the returned soldier will not tolerate Bolshevism in any form. I read an item in the press the other day that the Government were going to pursue Bolshevism to the bitter end and I hope that they are sincere in their efforts.

I am going to sail from here on August 21st on the *Metagaman*. I have always been busy since coming from France and I suppose if I waited here for another six months there would always be some correspondence turning up requiring an answer.

I was not sorry to be detained here until the Overseas Minister got back, but the news he brought was not of a very satisfactory or satisfying character and I have decided to go to Canada as soon as possible.

Your letter states that you believe the Government are sincere and desirous of doing everything possible for returned soldiers, both senior and junior. The news brought by the Minister would not lead me to take so optimistic a view. I shall look forward to discussing this matter with you further when I see you.

Regarding your KCB,[46] the only official notification you will receive will be the London Gazette and Willie will send you a couple of copies of it as

45   File 6, vol 3, CP, LAC.
46   Knight Commander of the Order of Bath.

soon as published. I do not consider it necessary for you to make any formal acknowledgement. Possibly it might be arranged for the Prince of Wales to confer on you the honour of Knighthood, during his stay in Canada. I will take that up with him. If not possible, arrangements will be made for the Governor General to perform the ceremony.

I have your letter about Colonel Cole, and I am afraid that he is doomed to disappointment. He was awarded the DSO[47] for services in France but the decoration he now seeks would be one for his long service in the Canadian Militia and should properly come through the Militia Department and the Government at Ottawa, but owing to the resolution which has passed the House of Commons, I feel sure that the Government will not make such a recommendation. All honours are now stopped, except those specified in their resolution, unless it be to those who had been recommended for a decoration before the terms of the resolution were made known to the King. There is nothing that I can do to help Colonel Cole get what he is seeking.[48]

When I get to Montreal, Loomis, I intend to stay for only a few days. Naturally you will sympathize with me in my desire to get up to Western Ontario to see my mother. I must go to Ottawa and learn definitely what their intentions are and then I must get out to the coast as soon as I can.

Regarding the offered Inspector-Generalship, that is something I will not accept.

I thank you for your kind invitation for my wife and myself to spend a day or so with you, if your house is ready, but please do not count on that. I am afraid people would be making an office out of your home and that would be inconvenient and annoying.

I look forward with keen pleasure to seeing you again. Please remember me kindly to any old friends.

With all good wishes ever yours faithfully,

A.W. Currie

Diary Entry, 28 July 1919

Garner and his mother came up with me in the morning. General Brutinel came to say goodbye and at eleven o'clock I attended a meeting of the Council,

---

47 Distinguished Service Order.
48 In 1919 the House of Commons passed a resolution which ended the practice of bestowing British honours on Canadian Citizens

lunching afterwards at the officers' club. We left town shortly before three o'clock and went to Tirbright to see Marjorie and the Musters, and then on to Brighton, where we arrived about eight. At three o'clock in the afternoon at Paris the peace conditions were signed. There was much rejoicing and celebration throughout the country, and we were sorry we had left London so early.

Diary Entry, 5 August 1919

Harold and I went to London in one car, while the rest of the family and Forsyth came up in the Rolls, which had a lot of bad luck on the way owing to too much weight. In the morning I called to see Radcliffe, Lord Lytton,[49] and Sir Douglas Haig. The week previous I had called on many old friends at the War Office and had said goodbye... I lunched with General Byng at the Carlton. There I said goodbye to Lord Birkenhead[50] and Winston Churchill...[51]

Diary Entry, 7 August 1919

We got away about 10:45 in the morning and motored first to Wilford, where my wife's father is buried. Then we went to Colwich village, where we saw the rector, who agreed to show us through the old church where my wife's grandfather at one time officiated. We lunched at Colwich Hall, which is now a public house, after which the rector joined us and we went through the old church; a very interesting place it was...

Diary Entry, 9 August 1919

We left the hotel shortly after breakfast and went to the boat, going on board before noon. Fred Richardson had come from London to see as off. We have very comfortable quarters on the *Carolina*, with my wife and I in one large stateroom, Ethel and the two children in another, with a sitting room in between. The day was quite warm and in the afternoon I got away some mail. The boat pulled out of the dock early in the evening and, I think, left about midnight.

---

49 Lord Victor Alexander George Robert Bulwer-Lytton (1876-1947).
50 Frederick Edwin Smith (1872-1930), a close personal friend of Winston Churchill, he held various positions in the Asquith government.
51 Winston Leonard Spencer Churchill (1874-1965), soldier, politician, and Prime Minister (1940-45, 1951-55). Churchill held various posts during the war including First Lord of the Admiralty (1911-15) and Minister of Munitions (1917-19).

Diary Entry, 10 August 1919

The weather is very fine and warm. We expect to arrive in Halifax next Saturday. There are about 400 first class passengers on board, about 400 repatriated men and officers who have served in the Imperial Army, nearly 400 of our own officers and wives and dependants, and a great many other ranks...

Diary Entry, 13 August 1919

The weather has moderated and is now fine, pleasant and cool. I have been bothered very much with indigestion for a week and am feeling much better this morning. Garner is enjoying the trip immensely and before we sailed wagered me ten shillings that he would not be ill, and also wagered me ten shillings that I would be ill.

Diary Entry, 15 August 1919

A very fine and pleasant day. I tried the plan of not eating anything all day, and found it worked very well.

Diary Entry, 16 August 1919

The weather is squally and rainy this morning. The Captain informs me that it will be after midnight tonight when we reach Halifax.

Visit of General Sir Sam Hughes to the Front, August 1916. Left to Right: Sir Sam Hughes, Major General Garnet Hughes, and Brigadier General St. Pierre Hughes (PA 698).

Sir Robert Borden (lifting his cap) visits the Western Front in March 1917. Major General Sir Archibald Macdonell is standing behind him (PA 879).

Lieutenant General Sir Julian Byng, commanding officer of the Canadian Corps, 1916-1917 (PA 1356).

Brigadier General Victor Odlum, October 1917 (PA 2117).

Lieutenant General Richard Turner (PA 8006).

Major General David Watson (PA 2115).

Mud and barbed wire through which the Canadians advanced during the Battle of Passchendaele, November 1917 (PA 2165).

Portrait of Lieutenant General Sir Arthur Currie after assuming command of the Corps in June 1917 (PA 1370).

Interim Report on the Operations of the

Canadian Corps during the Year 1918

First Period, January 1–March 21

Disposition

After the Battle of Passchendaele the Canadian Corps returned to the Vimy sector and settled down to the routine of trench warfare—the front held on January 1 extended from Acheville to Loos (both inclusive), a total length of approximately 13,000 yards. In order to allow the divisions to absorb more quickly the fresh drafts newly received and to make rapid headway with the training of the officers and NCOs, it was my intention to hold the Corps front during the winter with two divisions in the line and to keep two divisions resting and training in reserve. The pressure of circumstances and the large amount of defensive work to be done caused me to deviate from the original intention, and the normal dispositions adopted throughout the winter were as follows:

> *In the line:*
> Two divisions on a two-brigade front, and one division
> on a one-brigade front.
> *In reserve:*
> Training and resting, one division.

In this way the four Canadian divisions had each approximately one month out of the line and in addition they had the opportunity of doing a certain amount of training by brigades when in the line...

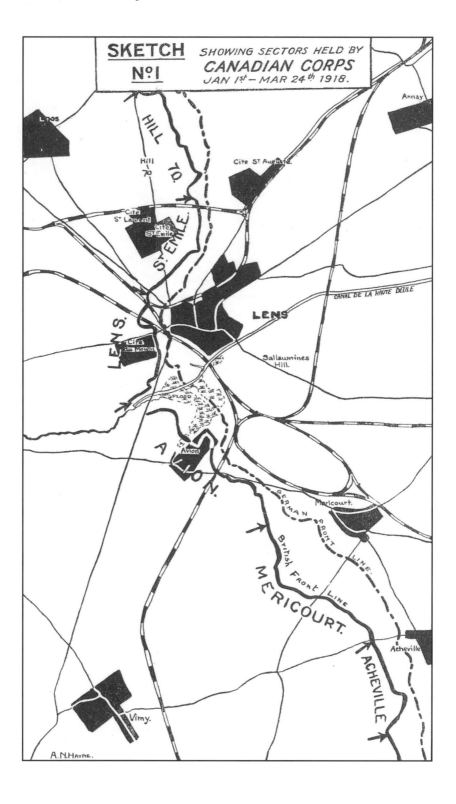

Organization

With the disappearance of the Russian front it was easily foreseen that the Germans would be able to turn the bulk of their forces against the Allies on the Western Front, and that their resources in men and materiel would be such that our power of resistance would be severely tried. In order to prepare for the coming test, and with the lessons of previous fighting fresh in my mind, it was resolved that every effort should be made to bring the Corps to the highest possible fighting efficiency. This I undertook to do in consultation with the divisional commanders and the heads of the various arms, services, and branches, by eliminating, as far as was in my power, everything which was not conducive to efficiency in administration, training, or fighting.

Lessons from previous fighting had shown that certain branches of the service should be strengthened and reorganized. The engineers and machine guns in particular were not able to accomplish their tasks in battle without drawing heavily on the infantry for additional personnel—the more severe the battle, the more severe were the losses suffered by the infantry, and at the same time the more men required by the engineers and machine guns. This diversion of the fighting strength of the infantry to meet the needs of the engineers and of the machine guns, and the interference for the same reason with the training or resting of infantry battalions when out of the line was most unsatisfactory. I submitted, therefore, proposals which were designed to give sufficient personnel to these services, and which would stop the drain on the infantry.

At this time the British Army was undergoing far-reaching alterations in its organization. The situation as regards manpower appeared to be such that, in order to maintain in the field the same number of divisions, it was necessary to reorganize the infantry brigades from a four-battalion basis to a three-battalion basis. Other changes of less importance were also taking place. Although the situation of the Canadians regarding reinforcements appeared to be satisfactory so long as the number of divisions in the field was not increased, a proposal was made to adopt an organization similar to the British, that is, to reduce the number of battalions in the Canadian infantry brigades from four to three. Concurrently with this change, it was proposed to increase the number of Canadian divisions in the field from four to six. I did not think that this proposal was warranted by our experience in the field, and I was quite certain that, owing to the severity of the losses suffered in modern battles, the manpower of Canada was not sufficient to meet the increased exposure to casualties consequent on the increased number of Canadian divisions in the field. I represented very strongly my views to the Minister, Overseas Military Forces of Canada, and, on further consideration, it was decided to drop this project, and to accept instead my counter-proposal, vis-à-vis, to increase the establishment of the Canadian infantry battalion by 100 all ranks, to proceed with the reorganization of the engineers and machine gun services, and to grant the various amendments suggested to establishments of other arms and branches. I am glad to be able to say that my proposals regarding the reorganization of engineer services, machine guns, etc., as well as the increase in strength of the infantry battalions, received the favourable consideration and support of the Commander-in-Chief.

Defences

It will be recalled that the ground held by the Canadian Corps throughout this period had been captured by the Canadians in the Battle of Vimy and subsequent actions, and held by them practically since its capture, except for a short interval during the Battle of Passchendaele. The area had been considerably improved during this time, and a very complete system of trench railways, roads, and water supply were in operation. Very comprehensive defences had been planned and partially executed. Behind Vimy Ridge 'lay the northern collieries of France and certain tactical features which cover our lateral communication. Here...little or no ground could be given up...' (See Sketch Number 2). A comparatively shallow advance beyond the Vimy Ridge would have stopped the operation of the collieries, paralysing the production of war materiel in France, as well as inflicting very severe hardship on the already sorely tried population. In conjunction with the shortage of shipping which practically forbade an increase in the importation of coal from England, the loss of the northern collieries might have definitely crippled France. On the other hand, a deep penetration at that point, by bringing the Amiens–Bethune railway and main road under fire, would have placed the British Army in a critical position, by threatening to cut it in two and by depriving it of vital lateral communication.

The tactical and strategical results to be gained by a moderate success at that point were so far-reaching in effect that, notwithstanding the natural difficulties confronting an attack on that sector, it was fully expected that the German offensive would be directed against this, the central part of the British front. The French knew well the value of the ground here. To recapture it in 1915 they had engaged in the most savage fighting of the war and sacrificed the flower of their

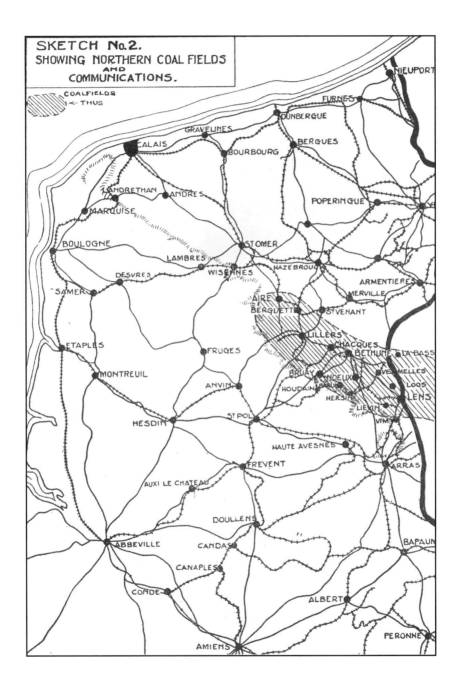

SKETCH No. 2.
SHOWING NORTHERN COAL FIELDS
AND
COMMUNICATIONS.

regular army. Although the British front had later been extended to the south, and Vimy Ridge had become the centre sector of the British Army, the French always manifested the deepest interest in this sector, and it was often visited by their generals and other officers of high rank.

With the prospect of a German offensive now confronting us, I ordered that the defences should be revised, to take advantage of the lessons recently learned and to embody the latest methods. Moreover, instructions had been issued by the First Army defining the policy of defence to be adopted and the methods to be followed. The completion of the revised corps defences and the execution of the new army programme resulted in the organization of a very deep defended area, consisting of successive defensive systems, roughly parallel to the general line of the front and linked together by switch lines sited to protect both flanks. Each defensive system was designed to protect definite topographical features, the loss of any one of which would considerably handicap the defence by uncovering our artillery.

As planned, the main framework of the defence in depth was based upon machine gun positions, protected by belts of wire entanglements so placed, in relation to the field of fire of the machine guns, that they were enfiladed over their entire length. The whole area was compartmented in such a way that the loss of ground at any one point could be localised and would not cause a forced retirement from adjoining areas. Machine gun emplacements of the Champagne type were constructed, and dugout accommodation for the machine gun detachments was provided in the deep tunnels of these emplacements. This framework was completed as rapidly as possible by trenches and by defended localities organized for all-round defence. A great many dugouts were made to accommodate the garrisons of these localities, and for dressing stations and battle headquarters. Advantage was taken of the possibility of utilising the subways tunnelled in 1916–17 for the attack on Vimy Ridge, and in addition steps were taken to create an obstacle on the southern flank of Vimy Ridge by the construction of dams to enable the valley of the Scarpe to be flooded as required. Trial inundations were made to ensure the smooth working of these arrangements.

A great deal of care was given to the distribution of the artillery in relation to the policy of defence. Three systems of battery positions were built so as to distribute the guns in depth and sited so as to cover the ground to the northeast, east, and south, in case the flanks of the Corps should be turned. These batteries were protected with barbed wire entanglements and machine gun positions against a sudden penetration of the enemy, and they were designed to become the natural rallying points of our infantry in this eventuality.

Successive lines of retirement were also prepared, battery positions were selected, organized, and marked, cross-country tracks were opened up, and observation posts, echeloned in depth, were located and wired in. On Vimy Ridge alone, seventy-two new battery positions were built and stacked with ammunition: these positions could be used either for the distribution of the Corps artillery in depth, or as positions which reinforcing artillery could immediately take up in the event of a heavy attack. The greatest energy, enthusiasm, and skill was employed in the prosecution of the work by all concerned, and I am greatly indebted to Major General 'P de B' Radcliffe, then Brigadier General, General Staff, for his untiring and devoted efforts.

The weather being much finer during the months of January, February, and March than is generally the case, very good progress was made, and the following defensive works were completed in rear of the main front line defensive system:

> 250 miles of trench
> 300 miles of barbed wire entanglements
> 200 tunnelled machine gun emplacements

In addition to the above, existing trench systems, dugouts, gun positions, and machine gun emplacements were strengthened and repaired. Each trench system was plentifully marked with signboards and many open machine gun positions were sited and marked. Machine gun positions, defended localities, and certain portions of trenches were stored with several days' supply of ammunition, food, and water for the use of the garrisons.

The importance attached by the French to the Vimy Ridge sector was further emphasised by the visit of General Roques, formerly Minister of War, and at that moment attached to the Cabinet of the Minister of War. Having thoroughly inspected the defences of the Canadian Corps, he expressed himself as satisfied that every effort had been made to secure the Vimy Ridge against any surprise attack.

Activity

The front held remained comparatively quiet during January and, except for minor patrolling encounters and occasional shoots, nothing beyond the usual activity ever prevailing on a front held by this corps occurred. In the months of February and March little or no work was being done by the enemy on his actual defences, but roads and disused trench railways were being repaired. In the rear areas his ammunition and engineer supply dumps were increasing in number and in size, while fresh battery positions were appearing almost daily. Furthermore, hostile aircraft and anti-aircraft guns were very active in preventing reconnaissance by our aeroplanes.

Early in March it was considered that the enemy's front opposite us was ready for offensive operations. No concentration of troops had been observed, but the numerous towns and villages in close proximity to the front provided extensive accommodation and made it possible for him to conceal such concentrations. Conditions so favourable to the Germans required relentless vigilance on the part of the Corps Intelligence Organization, as we were dependent on the efficiency of this branch of the service for timely warning against surprise attacks. In addition to the preparations above mentioned, the enemy assumed early in February a very aggressive attitude, raiding our lines very frequently, using for the purpose specially trained storm troops. His destructive shoots and intense gas shelling were also of frequent occurrence. I decided to quell this activity, and numerous counter-raids, retaliation shoots, and gas projections, especially in the Lens sector, soon had the desired effect. Prisoners captured in our raids stated that all their divisions had been brought up to strength and were undergoing hard training in the tactics of semi-open warfare. They stated, or left it to be understood, that the forthcoming German attacks were based on a very deep initial penetration and the rapid exploitation of success. No indications were given as to the points at which attacks would be launched, but they stated that every one of their sectors was prepared and practically ready. It was also definitely established that the enemy reserve divisions were kept near railways, ready to be moved quickly to the parts of the front selected for the coming drive.

Second Period, March 21-May 7

Battle of Amiens

In the early morning of March 21 the enemy launched a violent attack on the fronts of the Fifth and Third British Armies. It was soon evident that the opening stages of the battle were going in favour of the Germans, and that, notwithstanding the strenuous resistance offered, our defences were being overrun, more particularly the southern portion of the British line on the front of the Fifth Army. The Canadian Corps was not directly involved in the battle and my dispositions on that date were as follows:

3rd Canadian Division:	(Major General L.J. Lipsett), in the line, Méricourt–Avion sections
4th Canadian Division:	(Major General Sir D. Watson), in the line, Lens–St. Emile sections
1st Canadian Division:	(Major General Sir A.C. Macdonell), in the line, Hill 70 section
2nd Canadian Division:	(Major General Sir H.E. Burstall), resting, Auchel area

At 3:50 pm on the 21st, First Army ordered Canadian Corps to take over the front of the 62nd Division (left division of XIII Corps) in the Acheville sector,

the relief to begin on the night 21st/22nd and to be completed on the night 23rd/24th.

The 2nd Canadian Division was warned immediately for this relief, but at 4:04 pm First Army ordered the Canadian Corps to keep one complete division in army reserve. The warning order to the 2nd Canadian Division was, therefore, cancelled. The 3rd Canadian Division was then ordered to extend its frontage and relieve the 62nd Division in the Acheville–Arleux sector. A little later, a further order arrived from First Army instructing Canadian Corps to be prepared to relieve the 56th Division (right division of XIII Corps), and in accordance with this the 2nd Canadian Division was warned by wire at 7:40 pm. In the evening this order was cancelled.

On the 22nd, at 9:00 pm, I ordered the relief of the 1st Canadian Division, then holding the Hill 70 sector, by the 4th Canadian Division, so as to have a reserve in hand. During the same night, 22nd/23rd, at 11:00 pm, following a telephonic conversation with GHQ, the 1st Canadian Motor Machine Gun Brigade, then in the line on the Vimy sector, was withdrawn and ordered to be prepared to move south to the Fifth Army area. On confirmation of the order by telephone through the regular channels, this unit left Verdrel at 5:30 am on the 23rd to report to the Fifth Army. By midnight all batteries were in action on a thirty-five mile front east of Amiens, having traveled over 100 miles during the day.

> The 1st Canadian Motor Machine Gun Brigade (Lieutenant Colonel W.K. Walker), under orders of the Fifth and later of the Fourth Army, was ordered to fight a rearguard action to delay the advance of the enemy and to fill dangerous gaps on the army fronts. For nineteen days that unit was continuously in action north and south of the Somme, fighting against overwhelming odds. Using to the utmost its great mobility, it fought over 200 square miles of territory (see Sketch Number 4).

> It is difficult to appraise to its correct extent the influence, materiel and morale, that the forty machine guns of that unit had in the events which were then taking place. The losses suffered amounted to about seventy-five per cent of the trench strength of the unit, and to keep it in being throughout that

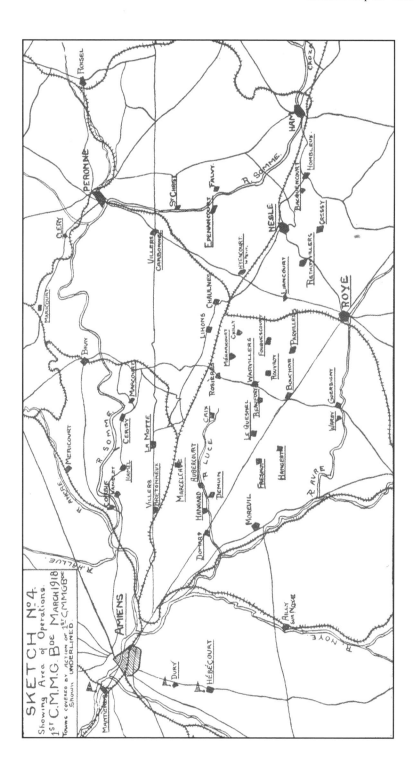

fighting, I authorised its reinforcement by personnel of the infantry branch of the Canadian Machine Gun Corps.

On the 23rd, at 10:50 am, the 2nd Canadian Division was ordered to concentrate at once west of Arras in the Mont St. Eloi area, and having carried this out passed into General Headquarters Reserve. The 1st Canadian Division, in process of relief by the 4th Canadian Division, passed therefore into army reserve in compliance with the First Army order of the 21st, referred to above. The relief was completed on the 24th, and my dispositions were then as follows:

> *In the Line (on a total front of 17,000 yards):*
> 3rd Canadian Division: Acheville–Méricourt–Avion sections
> 4th Canadian Division: Lens–St. Emile–Hill 70 sections
> *In Army Reserve:*
> 1st Canadian Division: Château de la Haie area
> *In General Headquarters Reserve:*
> 2nd Canadian Division: Mont St. Eloi area

On the night of the 25th/26th, at 12:40 am, I was ordered to extend my front to the north, and preparations were made accordingly to relieve the 11th and 46th Divisions with the 1st Canadian Division. The intention was to concentrate an army corps on the southern flank of the First Army for action on the northern flank of the German attack, which was still progressing rapidly. This order was, however, cancelled at 10:20 pm on the 26th, and instead the following dispositions were substituted, with effect from the night 27th/28th:

> A. The 3rd Canadian Division in the line to come under orders of the General Officer Commanding (GOC) XIII Corps at noon, March 27
> B. The 1st Canadian Division to move to the area to be vacated by the 2nd Canadian Division, west of a line Maroeuil–Carency, and to pass into GHQ Reserve
> C. The 4th Canadian Division to be relieved by the 46th Division (I Corps) and pass into GHQ Reserve
> D. Canadian Corps Headquarters to pass into GHQ Reserve

Meanwhile, under instructions from First Army, the 2nd Canadian Division was ordered by telephone at 3:30 pm, 26th, to move as soon as possible to the area Pommier–Bienvillers–Bailleulval, with headquarters at Basseux. On completion of the move, the 2nd Canadian Division would cease to be in General Headquarters Reserve and be transferred to Third Army. Accordingly, during the night of the 26th/27th the 2nd Canadian Division moved by bus and march route to the Basseux area. On the 27th, at 4:05 pm, the 1st Canadian Division was ordered to move to Couturelle area. Both these divisions were transferred from General Headquarters Reserve to Third Army.

> The 1st Canadian Division was moved by buses to Couturelle area, embussing at about midnight, 27th/28th. At dawn, March 28, the enemy struck heavily astride the River Scarpe, and the 1st Canadian Division was ordered at 10:30 am to retain the buses by which they had moved south and to move back to the Arras–Dainville area at once, coming there under orders of the XVII Corps.

> This move was very difficult because some buses had already been sent back to the park, many units were still en route to the Couturelle area, and the mounted units and transport were in column on the road Hauteville–Saulty–Couturelle. The division, however, extricated itself, and on the night of the 28th, under orders of the XVII Corps, placed two battalions in the forward area in support of the 46th Infantry Brigade, 15th Division. At daybreak on the 29th, the 3rd Canadian Infantry Brigade moved to support the 15th Division, and during the night 29th/30th 1st Canadian Infantry Brigade relieved the 46th Infantry Brigade in the Telegraph Hill sector, that brigade front being transferred from the 15th Division to the 1st Canadian Division on March 30.

> The 2nd Canadian Division passed under orders of the VI Corps on March 28, and moved forward in support of the 3rd (British) Division in the Neuville Vitasse sector. On the night of March 29th/30th, it relieved the 3rd (British) Division in

the line, and on the night of March 31st/1st April extended its front southwards by relieving the left battalion of the Guards' Division.

The front held by the 2nd Canadian Division extended from south of the Cojeul River, east of Boisleux-St. Marc, to the southern slopes of Telegraph Hill (where it joined with the 1st Canadian Division), a total length of about 6,000 yards. The 2nd Canadian Division held this front for an uninterrupted period of ninety-two days, during which time it repulsed a series of local attacks and carried out no less than twenty-seven raids, capturing three officers, 101 other ranks, twenty-two machine guns, two trench mortars, and inflicting severe casualties on the enemy. The aggressive attitude adopted by this division at such a critical time and under adverse conditions had a most excellent effect on our troops, and it certainly reduced to the lowest point the fighting value of two German Divisions, namely, the 26th Reserve Division and the 185th Division. The 2nd Canadian Division returned under the orders of the Canadian Corps on July 1.

In compliance with First Army orders, I had handed over command of the 3rd Canadian Division in the line to the XIII Corps at noon, March 27. The 4th Canadian Division was warned for relief by the 46th Division on the night 27th/28th, and would then come into General Headquarters Reserve. The 1st and 2nd Canadian Divisions had been placed under orders of the Third Army. Thus, under the pressure of circumstances, the four Canadian divisions were to be removed from my command, placed in two different armies (Third and First), and under command of three different corps (VI, XVII and XIII Corps). This disposition of the Canadian troops was not satisfactory, and on receipt of the orders above referred to I made strong representation to First Army, and offered suggestions which to my mind would reconcile my claims (from the standpoint of Canadian policy) with the tactical and administrative requirements of the moment.

Battle of Arras

The Germans launched a very heavy attack at dawn on the 28th from Gavrelle to Puisieux, and were successfully repulsed by the 3rd, 15th, 4th, and 56th British Divisions. The attack was renewed in the afternoon, north of the Scarpe, on the front of the 56th Division, but did not there meet with greater success. A certain amount of ground had, however, been captured by the enemy. The troops of the Canadian Corps were not directly engaged in this fighting.

The renewed attack on the 56th Division had considerably lowered its power of resistance. German prisoners captured in the morning were insistent that the attack would be renewed again on the 29th, by storm troops which had been held in reserve for the purpose of capturing the Vimy Ridge by attacking it from the south. It was most urgent that the 56th Division should be supported without delay.

I received instructions from the First Army at 8:15 am, March 28, to the effect that the 4th Canadian Division, then holding the Lens–St. Emile–Hill 70 sector, would be relieved on the night of the 28th/29th by the 46th British Division, I Corps, and would in turn relieve the 56th British Division in the Oppy–Gavrelle sector. On the completion of this relief the Canadian Corps would relieve the XIII Corps, and I would assume command of the 3rd and 4th Canadian Divisions. In the meantime, all the battalions which the 4th Canadian Division could spare were to be sent at once by the quickest way to the support of the 56th Division. The 4th Canadian Division, therefore, immediately organized a composite brigade, under Brigadier General V.W. Odlum, consisting of the three reserve battalions of the 10th, 11th, and 12th Brigades, and the support battalions of the 11th and 12th Brigades. This composite brigade was moved in haste by light railway and lorry to the vicinity of Mont St. Eloi, from whence it marched into reserve positions during daylight on the 28th.

On the night of the 28th/29th the units of the 56th Division which had been most heavily engaged were relieved by these five Canadian battalions, which came under orders of the 3rd Canadian Division. It was not until about 10:00 pm on the night of the 28th/29th that the leading troops of the 46th Division arrived and began to relieve the 4th Canadian Division. In view of the seriousness of the situation, units of the 4th Canadian Division were moved, as the relief progressed, by lorry and light railway to Neuville St. Vaast, and marched quickly into the line to relieve elements of the 56th Division.

Due to the energy shown by the GOC, 4th Canadian Division (Major General Sir D. Watson), and his staff, and to the initiative and discipline of his troops, this difficult three-cornered relief, under the menace of an impending attack, was quickly and smoothly carried out.

On the morning of the 29th, at 8:00 am, the GOC, 4th Canadian Division, handed over command of the Lens–St. Emile–Hill 70 sector to the GOC, 46th Division, I Corps, and the I Corps took over this sector from the Canadian Corps at 8:30 am on the same day.

At 6:45 am on March 30, the relief of the 56th Division by the 4th Canadian Division having been completed, the command of the XIII Corps front passed to the Canadian Corps. This was the first result of my representations regarding the removal of the Canadian troops from the control of the Canadian Corps. The situation of the Canadian divisions at noon, March 30, was as follows (see Sketch Number 5):

Third Army:

Under VI Corps—2nd Canadian Division: Neuville Vitasse sector

Under XVII Corps—1st Canadian Division: Telegraph Hill sector

First Army:

Under Canadian Corps—3rd Canadian Division: Acheville–Méricourt–Avion sector

Under Canadian Corps—4th Canadian Division: Gavrelle–Oppy sector

In furtherance of those of my suggestions which had been accepted, it was arranged that the 1st Canadian Division should relieve the 4th British Division astride the Scarpe on the 7th/8th April, and come under orders of Canadian Corps; the Army boundaries being altered so as to include the sector taken over by the 1st Canadian Division in the First Army front.

In the meantime, on the night 28th/29th, owing to operations astride the River Scarpe, the front line system had been abandoned under orders of the XIII Corps and the troops withdrawn to the Blue Line in front of the Bailleul–Willerval–Chaudière–Hirondelle line, as far north as the Méricourt sector.

This Blue Line was originally sited and constructed as an intermediate position, and consisted in most parts of a single trench none too plentifully supplied with dugouts. This meant that until a support line was dug and made continuous, the

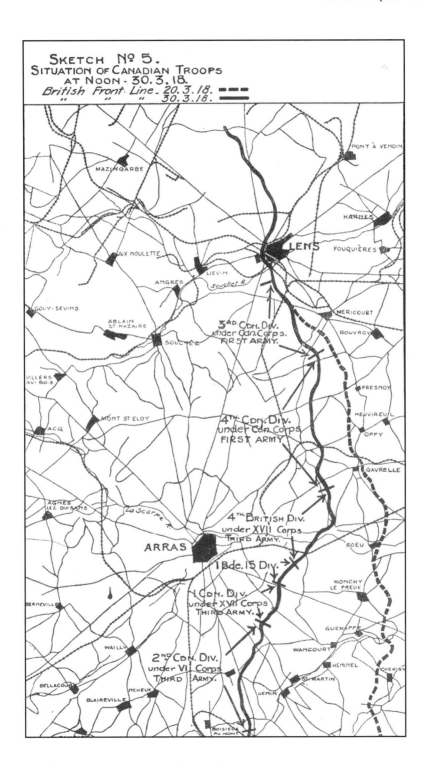

troops had to be kept in strength in the front line, subject to heavy casualties from hostile shelling and to probable annihilation in case of an organized attack.

Any advance beyond the Blue Line on the 4th Canadian Division front would have brought the Germans within assaulting distance of the weakest part of the Vimy Ridge, and the severity of the shelling seemed to indicate that a renewal of their attacks was probable.

I therefore directed that every effort should be made to give more depth to our new front line system by pushing forward a line of outposts and by digging a continuous support line, as well as by constructing reserve lines at certain points of greater tactical importance. Switch lines facing south were also sited and dug or improved. Every available man was mustered for this vital work, and the need of properly organized engineer services was very keenly felt.

To increase the depth of our defences, machine gun detachments were extemporised by borrowing men from the machine gun battalions, who had then completed their organization on an eight-battery basis. Some fifty extra machine guns were secured from ordnance and other sources, and also a number of extra Lewis guns. Personnel from the Canadian Light Horse and the Canadian Corps Cyclist Battalion were organised in Lewis and Hotchkiss gun detachments and sent forward to man the defences in Vimy and Willerval localities, under orders of the 3rd and 4th Canadian Divisions. The machine gun companies of the 5th Canadian Division had arrived in France on March 25, and in view of the extreme urgency of the situation the personnel and armament had been moved by lorries, sent specially by Canadian Corps, from Le Havre to Verdrel, where they were in corps reserve. Their horse transport, having now arrived, these machine gun companies (17th, 18th, and 19th) were moved to the Vimy Ridge and allotted definite positions of defence on March 30.

The relief of the 4th British Division by the 1st Canadian Division was completed at 7:00 pm, April 8, and at that hour I took command of this additional sector astride the River Scarpe. The front held by the Canadian Corps on April 8, 1918, was approximately 16,000 yards in length. It will be remembered that the 2nd Canadian Division under the VI Corps (Third Army) was holding 6,000 yards of front, making a total of 22,000 yards of front held by Canadian troops (See Sketch Number 6).

Battle of the Lys

On April 9 the Germans attacked on the Lys Front between La Bassée and Armentieres. Making rapid progress, they crossed the Lys River on the 10th, and

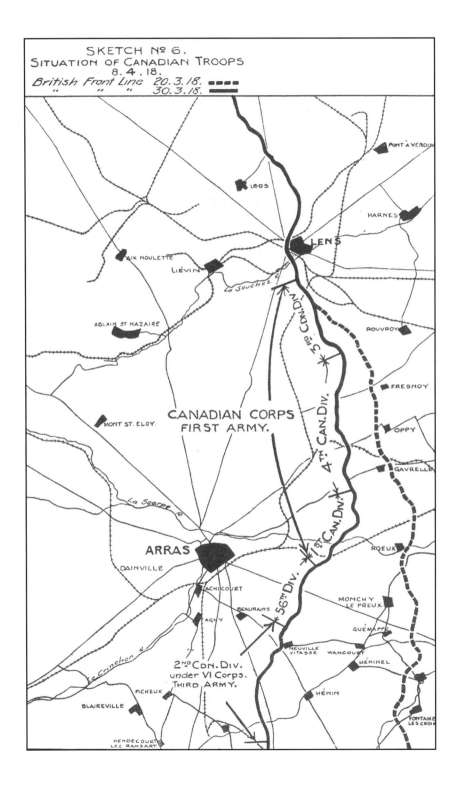

SKETCH Nº 6.
SITUATION OF CANADIAN TROOPS
8.4.18.
British Front Line 20.3.18. ▬▬▬
    "   "   "   30.3.18.

on the following days advanced west of Merville–Bailleul. They were well held at Givenchy by the 55th Division and their attack made no progress southwards. The Canadian Corps was not involved in this fighting, but it now found itself in a deep salient, following with anxiety the development of the Battle of the Lys.

Orders had been issued (9 May 1918) for the 2nd Canadian Division to be relieved from the line on the VI Corps front and to then come into Canadian Corps Reserve in the Château de la Haie area. These orders were now cancelled.

The Battle of the Lys added a new burden to the already sorely tried British Army, and it was imperative that troops should at once be made available to stop the German advance. On the 10th, at 8:40 pm, I received orders from First Army to extend my front by taking over from the I Corps the line held by the 46th Division (Lens–St. Emile–Hill 70 sector), the relief to be commenced on April 11 and to be completed as soon as possible. This relief was completed on the night of the 12th/13th by the 3rd Canadian Division; concurrently with it, the inter-divisional boundaries were readjusted and the artillery redistributed to meet as well as possible the new conditions.

The front held by the three divisions then in the Canadian Corps had a length of approximately 29,000 yards; and of necessity the line was held very thinly and without much depth. To deceive the enemy regarding our dispositions and intentions, we adopted a very aggressive attitude. The artillery constantly harassed the enemy's forward and rear areas and our infantry penetrated his line at many points with strong fighting patrols and bold raiding parties. Gas was also projected on numerous occasions.

This activity on the immediate flank of the Lys salient greatly perturbed the enemy, who gave many indications of nervous uncertainty. The situation was critical, and extensive steps were taken at once to increase the ability of the Canadian Corps to withstand hostile attacks. The success of the German offensives emphasised the need of greater depth for defensive dispositions, which depended very largely on the stopping power of the machine gun. Unfortunately the number of machine guns with a division was inadequate to give the required depth of defence on a front exceeding 4,000 yards in length. Each of my divisions was now holding a front approximately 10,000 yards in length, and the extemporised machine gun detachments formed previously, added to the machine gun companies of the 5th Canadian Division, in my opinion were far from sufficient for the task.

I decided, therefore, to add a third company of four batteries to each battalion of the Canadian Machine Gun Corps, thus bringing up to ninety-six the number of machine guns in each Canadian division. This entailed an increase in personnel of approximately fifty per cent of the strength of each machine gun battalion. These companies were formed provisionally on April 12 by withdrawing fifty men from each infantry battalion. Of these men a portion was sent to the machine gun battalion to be combined with the trained personnel, so that each machine gun crew would include at least four trained gunners. The remainder of the infantry personnel withdrawn as above stated was sent to a special machine gun depot, formed for the purpose, and there underwent an abridged but intensive course of training. Thus an immediate supply of reinforcements was ensured. Twenty three-ton lorries had been borrowed from GHQ to supply a modicum of transport to the new units, and on April 13 some of the new machine gun batteries were already in the line at critical points.

Sufficient troops were not now available to garrison the local defences of Vimy Ridge, or to reinforce parts of the front if the enemy was successful in effecting a deep penetration. Two special brigades were therefore organized as under:

> *The Hughes Brigade*—Commanded by Lieutenant Colonel H.T. Hughes and composed of:
>> 'A' Battalion: 185th, 176th, 250th Tunnelling Companies RE, and 2nd, 4th, and 5th Army Troops Companies CE
>> 'B' Battalion: 1st Canadian Divisional Wing.
>> 'C' Battalion: 4th Canadian Divisional Wing.
>> Approximate strength: officers, 184; other ranks, 4,050.
>
> *McPhail's Brigade*—Commanded by Lieutenant Colonel A. McPhail and composed of:
>> 'D' Battalion: (5th Canadian Division Engineers, pioneer reinforcements).
>> (1st Tunnelling Company CE and 3rd Army Troops Company CE).
>> 'E' Battalion: 2nd Canadian Divisional Wing.
>> 'F' Battalion: 3rd Canadian Divisional Wing.
>> Approximate strength: officers, 148; other ranks, 4,628.

Proper staffs were organized for these brigades and several alternative plans of engagement providing for different contingencies were prepared and practised. In addition to these measures, each division organized its own 'last resort' reserves, consisting of the personnel of the infantry battalions left at transport lines, transport personnel and divisional headquarters. All these units were given a refresher course in musketry and drill and they were detailed to defend definite localities.

Two companies of the 11th Tank Battalion (twenty-four tanks) were placed at the disposal of the Canadian Corps on April 13. These tanks had officers, drivers, and armament, but no other personnel. A sufficient number of trained Lewis gunners were found from the 1st, 3rd, and 4th Canadian Divisional Wings, and the Canadian field artillery supplied the required number of gunners. The tanks were then distributed at the critical points in the Corps area, namely:

> A. Behind the St. Catherine Switch at intervals of about 300 yards, facing south: eighteen tanks
> B. In the gap between the Souchez River and Bois-en-Hache, facing east: three tanks
> C. On the Ridge line behind Angres, facing east: three tanks

It was intended that these tanks should form points of resistance to check any forward flow of hostile forces and so give time to our infantry to re-form in case they should be forced back. In any event the tanks were to remain in action for twelve hours after coming in contact with the enemy and thus gain the time so essential in a crisis.

The 1st Canadian Motor Machine Gun Brigade, now returned from the Amiens battle, was held as a mobile reserve at one hour's notice.

Bridges, railways, roads, and pumping stations were prepared for demolition, to be blown up as a last resort. Every contingency was prepared for down to the minutest detail, and nothing could be more inspiring than to witness the extraordinary spirit displayed by everybody in their untiring labour and ceaseless vigilance. Extended almost to the breaking point, in danger of being-annihilated by overwhelming attacks, the Corps confidently awaited the assault. All ranks of the Corps were unanimous in their ardent resolve to hold to the last every inch of the ground entrusted to their keeping. It was for them a matter of great pride that their front was substantially the only part of the British line which had not budged, and one and all felt that it could not budge so long as they were alive.

Eventually, the 1st, 3rd, and 4th Canadian Divisions were relieved in their sectors by the 15th, 51st, 52nd, 20th, and 24th British Divisions. The relief started on May 1 and was completed on the 7th. As the relief progressed, the Canadian Corps handed over command of the Avion–Lens–St. Emile–Hill 70 sectors to the XVIII Corps and the balance of the front to the XVII Corps.

The length of front held by the Canadian Corps at the various stages of the German offensive has been given previously, but it is here recalled that from April 10 until relieved the Corps held a line exceeding 29,000 yards in length; the 2nd Canadian Division, then with the VI Corps, was holding 6,000 yards of front, making a total length of 35,000 yards of front held by the four Canadian divisions.

The total length of the line held by the British Army between the Oise and the sea was approximately 100 miles, therefore the Canadian troops were holding approximately one-fifth of the total front. Without wishing to draw from this fact any exaggerated conclusion, it is pointed out that although the Canadian Corps did not, during this period, have to repulse any German attacks on its front, it nevertheless played a part worthy of its strength during that period.

Third Period, May 7-July 15

The depth to which the enemy had penetrated in the Somme and the Lys Valleys had created a situation of extreme gravity with regard to the maintenance of communication. It was known that notwithstanding the heavy losses suffered by the Germans they still enjoyed a sufficient superiority of forces to retain the initiative, and a renewal of their attacks on the line between the Oise and the sea was possible. In prevision of these expected attacks, reserves comprising British and French divisions were assembled behind the threatened front.

Tactical Dispositions

On completion of the relief on May 7, with the exception of the 2nd Canadian Division which was still in the line in the Third Army area, the Canadian Corps was placed in the General Headquarters Reserve in the First Army area and disposed as follows:

> Headquarters: Pernes, and later Bryas
> 1st Canadian Division: Le Cauroy area
> 3rd Canadian Division: St. Hilaire area
> 4th Canadian Division: Monchy–Breton area

Under instructions received from First Army, one infantry brigade and one machine gun company from each Canadian division were billeted well forward in support of the Corps in the line as follows:

A.   One infantry brigade: Anzin area support
One machine gun company: XVII Corps
B.   One infantry brigade: Château de la Haie area
One machine gun company: support XVIII Corps

    C.   One infantry brigade: Ham-en-Artois area
           One machine gun company: support XI Corps

These brigades were kept under one hour's notice from 5:00 am to 7:00 am daily and under four hours' notice during the remainder of the day. The remainder of the Canadian Corps was under four hours notice. Reconnaissance of the front which the Corps would have to support in case of an attack was ordered and carried out by staff and regimental officers. The brigades billeted forward were relieved from time to time under divisional arrangements.

On May 23 the 74th British Division, newly arrived in France from Palestine, came under Canadian Corps for administration and training. It was then necessary to rearrange the areas amongst the divisions in the Corps to make room for the 74th Division and to equalise the training facilities. With the exception of these moves, the disposition of the Canadian Corps remained substantially the same until June 25, 1918.

Organization

The reorganization of most branches had been delayed by the considerable efforts of the preceding months, by the shortage of transport and materiel consequent on the great demands made by the reorganization of British units, and by the simultaneous requirements of the American Army, which was, in part, being equipped from British stores. In some cases also the necessary authority had not yet been obtained.

On May 24, 1918, it was decided to proceed with the reorganization of the Canadian Engineers, for which authority had been obtained on March 21, 1918, but which had not been begun earlier for the reasons mentioned above. This reorganization was effected by the expansion of the three field companies then with each division into one engineer brigade, consisting of three engineer battalions and a pontoon bridging and transport unit. The additional personnel required was furnished by the absorption into the new units of the following: 107th, 2nd, 123rd, 124th Canadian pioneer battalions, 1st and 2nd Tunnelling Companies, Canadian Engineers, and the three field companies of the 5th Canadian Division Engineers. Motor transport was included in the establishment, and later the Canadian Engineer Motor Transport Company was formed. The amount of work involved was considerable, nevertheless all the units were substantially completed and made cohesive before the end of July. Adequate staffs able to deal with the larger scope of activity of the new organization were provided for the GOC, Canadian Engineers and for the engineer brigades. Authority was also received and immediately acted upon for the formation of Anti-Aircraft Searchlight Companies, Canadian Engineers. This had been asked for in view of the increase in hostile night bombing, which, in addition to causing casualties, interfered greatly with the resting of the men. The reorganization of the Tramways Company, Canadian Engineers, was also completed.

Application had been made early in the year for authority to form a field survey company to assist in counter-battery work, and in the collection of intelligence; this unit to consist of an artillery flash-spotting section and a section of intelligence observers. The personnel had been selected and trained during the winter. Final approval having now been obtained, this Field Survey Company was definitely organized and placed for the time being under the GOC, Canadian Engineers, for administration, and under the Counter Battery Staff Officer and Intelligence Branch for operations.

The addition of a third company to the battalions of the Canadian Machine Gun Corps was authorised on May 7, 1918, and the organization, which was already well under way, was rapidly completed with the exception of the transport of the 3rd Battalion, Canadian Machine Gun Corps, which did not become available until August. The reorganization of the Motor Branch, Canadian Machine Gun Corps, having been approved on June 3, 1918, two motor machine gun brigades, of forty guns each, were formed by absorbing the Canadian Motor Machine Gun units already existing and the 17th, 18th, and 19th machine gun companies of the 5th Canadian Division. A Canadian Machine Gun Corps Mechanical Transport Company was also formed for the administration and maintenance of the motor transport.

Reinforcements

While the reorganization of the various arms and services was being carried out, the machinery both to receive, train, and despatch reinforcements from England and to deal with returned casualties, was also being revised and improved, (see chart on page 241 for the new organization).

The number of reinforcements maintained was increased so as to meet the increased establishments, and at the same time great attention was paid to the training of those reinforcements by the specially selected officers placed on the staffs of all units of the Canadian Corps Reinforcement Centre. The provision of a staging camp enabled reinforcements to be handled quickly without moving the Canadian Corps Reinforcement Centre, no matter where the Canadian Corps was engaged.

The areas where the reinforcement camp, wings, and schools of the Canadian Corps were established were now congested with troops and within range of shellfire since the advance of the Germans in the Lys Valley. These units not being mobile, and the eventual movements of the Canadian Corps being rather uncertain, all divisional wings, reinforcement camps, and schools were removed from the Corps area and concentrated in the Aubin St. Vaast area, where suitable Camps were constructed by our engineers.

Training

As soon as the Corps was out of the line intensive training in open warfare offensive tactics was begun. General Staff, General Headquarters, were publishing from time to time translations of captured German documents bearing on the latest tactics, and supplemented these by 'Notes on Recent Fighting,' dealing with the lessons of the fighting then in progress, both from the point of view of offence and defence. These documents were carefully studied and, to a large extent, inspired our training.

Detailed instructions were issued by the Canadian Corps at various times practising the methods of employment of artillery, engineers, and machine guns in combination with the tactics of the infantry. The laying down of a definite Corps tactical doctrine was necessary by reason of the different organization, the greater strength, and the particular methods which characterised the Canadian Corps.

It was not possible to forecast the length of time the Canadian Corps would be out of the line, and under these circumstances it was decided that combined training by brigades should be given precedence to familiarise the commanders and staffs with the handling of troops in open warfare, and so give the different arms and services an opportunity of practising co-operation and mutual support.

Concurrently with this tactical training, the closest attention was paid to individual training, particularly to musketry in all its phases.

In the early part of June, in view of the good progress made, I directed that all commanders should now concentrate on the training of smaller units, especially the platoon.

Many tactical schemes were carried out during May, June, and July, each emphasising some definite lesson, more particularly how to overpower resistance in an area defended by machine guns in depth by using covering fire and smoke grenades; how batteries of machine guns should co-operate in assisting infantry to get forward; and how sections of field artillery could best carry out an advance in close support of attacking infantry.

During this period means were devised for making Stokes guns and six inch Newton trench mortars more mobile, and special mountings were designed, manufactured and tested. The calibration of field guns was also carefully carried out, and experiments made on the use of high explosive for barrages.

Preparations were being made in the meanwhile to recapture Merville and part of the Lys salient. This operation, for the purpose of maintaining secrecy, was always referred to as Delta. The preparations for the projected 'Delta' attack exercised a most vivifying influence on the training of the Canadian Corps; it familiarised all arms and services with the difficulties, both administrative and tactical, inherent to a surprise attack intended to penetrate suddenly to a great depth.

Relief of 2nd Canadian Division

The 2nd Canadian Division had been in the line since March 30, and I was most anxious that it should be relieved. I had made representations to this effect from time to time, but the situation was such that no troops were available for this relief. On June 24 it was arranged, however, that the 3rd Canadian Division would be transferred to the Third Army area from General Headquarters Reserve and would relieve the 2nd Canadian Division in the line. On completion of relief, the 2nd Canadian Division would come under the Canadian Corps in General Headquarters Reserve, First Army area.

This relief was carried out and completed on the morning of July 1, at which date the disposition of the Canadian Corps was as follows:

> *In General Headquarters Reserve, First Army Area:*
> Headquarters Canadian Corps: Bryas
> 1st Canadian Division: Monchy–Breton area
> 2nd Canadian Division: Le Cauroy area
> 4th Canadian Division: Auchel area
> 74th British Division: St. Hilaire area

In the Line, under VI Corps, Third Army Area:
3rd Canadian Division: Headquarters, Basseux

Dominion Day

Since the arrival of the Canadians in France the celebration of Dominion Day had always been made the event of the year, but never before had it been so brilliant as on July 1, 1918. The sporting events were keenly contested, and nothing could have been finer than to see the thousands of clean-limbed, healthy, sun-burned young Canadian soldiers who congregated for this occasion. The Duke of Connaught, the Prime Minister of Canada, and a number of other distinguished Canadian visitors, together with a large concourse of British officers from the neighbouring formations, were interested spectators. In addition to the Corps sports, the divisions had arranged various entertainments, and these were greatly appreciated by the men.

Back to the Line

On July 6, the Canadian Corps was warned to be prepared to relieve the XVII Corps in the line. It was released from General Headquarters Reserve on July 10, and the relief was carried out, being completed at 10:00 am, July 15, when I assumed command of the XVII Corps front. Disposition at that time was as follows:

Headquarters Canadian Corps: Duisans (First Army Area)
2nd Canadian Division, in the line: Telegraph Hill section
1st Canadian Division, in the line: Feuchy–Fampoux section
4th Canadian Division, in the line: Gavrelle–Oppy section.
3rd Canadian Division, in the line: Neuville-Vitasse section
(Under VI Corps, Third Army Area)

General Situation

The Germans had not attacked again on the northeast portion of the Western Front, but they had secured considerable success elsewhere, and the general situation was still very threatening (see Sketch Number 7). On May 27 they had struck a very heavy blow between Rheims and Soissons and advanced rapidly on the following days as far south as the Marne, capturing Soissons and Château-Thierry. Again on June 9 they had struck between Soissons and Montdidier and

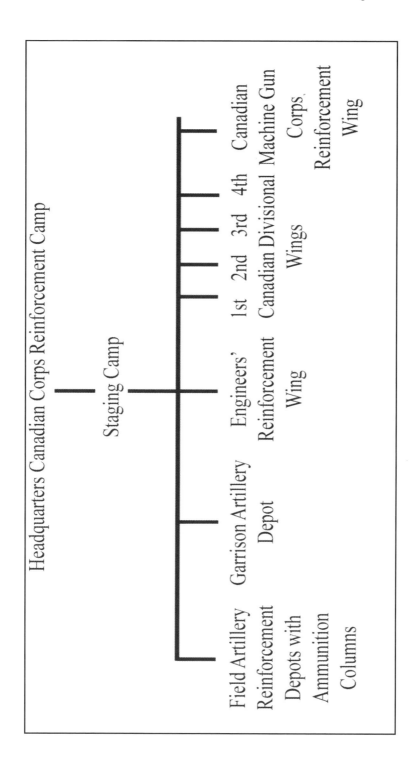

Headquarters Canadian Corps Reinforcement Camp

Staging Camp

Field Artillery Reinforcement Depots with Ammunition Columns

Garrison Artillery Depot

Engineers' Reinforcement Wing

1st 2nd 3rd 4th Canadian Divisional Wings

Canadian Machine Gun Corps Reinforcement Wing

captured the Massif of Lassigny. This attack had met with only partial success and very severe losses had been inflicted on the Germans.

On July 15 two other powerful attacks were launched as part of the same plan; the one east of Rheims in the direction of Châlons, and the other southwest of Rheims in the direction of Epernay. All news received during the day indicated that the Germans were being repulsed east of Rheims with over-whelming losses, and although they had succeeded in crossing the Marne south-west of Rheims, the situation appeared to be well in hand and the Germans were suffering heavily. Everywhere on the Allied Front minor enterprises of ever-increasing magnitude seemed to indicate that the time of passive resistance was definitely past.

Fourth Period, July 15-November 11

The relief of the XVII Corps by the Canadian Corps on July 15, after the Corps' long period of rest and training, with the attendant movement and activity, made the enemy alert and anxious as to our intentions on this front. He was successful in securing identifications at various points of our line, which he penetrated by raiding. As it was desired to keep him fully occupied on our front, the artillery activity was increased and our infantry engaged in vigorous patrolling and raiding. This change of attitude confirmed the enemy in the opinion he had already formed, that an attack on this front was impending. Prisoners belonging to different units which we captured in various parts of our front made repeated statements to that effect, and also disclosed the fact that two additional divisions had been brought into the line.

On the night 18th/19th the Telegraph Hill front held by the 2nd Canadian Division was taken over by the 1st Canadian Division, and the former came into General Headquarters Reserve at twelve hours notice in the Le Cauroy Area. On the same night the 4th Canadian Division extended their line, taking over the left brigade front of the 1st Canadian Division. The reason given for this sudden readjustment was that an attack on the Second Army was impending.

On the afternoon of the 20th, Major General J.H. Davidson, General Staff, Operations, General Headquarters, called at Corps Headquarters and explained that the Commander-in-Chief was considering a scheme submitted by the GOC Fourth Army for freeing the Amiens–Paris railway. He stated that the Commander-in-Chief proposed to use the Canadian Corps in this operation if the scheme was approved. It was the intention to effect a surprise, and therefore absolute secrecy was required.

On the following day, July 21, I attended a conference at Fourth Army Headquarters, where the operations contemplated were discussed. The Fourth Army Commander dwelt upon the importance of secrecy, and said that the only persons outside those at the conference to whom it was permitted to mention the coming operations were the GOC Royal Artillery, Australian and Canadian Corps, the Counter-Battery Staff Officers, Canadian and Australian Corps, the Major General, General Staff (O a), the Brigadier General, General Staff (O a), GHQ, and the GOC Tank Corps.

The officers present at the conference were:

> *From Fourth Army Headquarters*:
>> The Army Commander, General Sir HS Rawlinson
>> Major General, General Staff, Major General A.A. Montgomery
>> GOC, Royal Artillery, Major General C.E.D. Budworth
>> General Staff Officer (GSO) 1 Operations, Lieutenant Colonel R.M. Luckock
>
> *From Canadian Corps Headquarters*:
>> The GOC, Lieutenant General Sir A.W. Currie
>> Brigadier General, General Staff, Brigadier General N.W. Webber
>
> *From Australian Corps Headquarters:*
>> The GOC, Lieutenant General Sir J. Monash
>> Brigadier General, General Staff, Brigadier General T.A. Blarney
>
> *From Tank Corps Headquarters:*
>> GSO 1, Lieutenant Colonel J.F.C. Fuller

The operation as outlined at the conference was of limited scope, and was designed to relieve the pressure on Amiens and free the Amiens–Paris railway line, thus improving the situation at the junction of the French and British Armies. A large number of tanks were to be made available for this operation. The methods for maintaining secrecy and misleading the enemy were discussed. I pointed out that I had been considering a scheme for the capture of Orange Hill, and it was agreed that it would help materially to deceive *everybody* if preparations for this scheme were still continued.

It was decided that the Australian Corps would arrange a series of demonstrations of co-operation between tanks and infantry at their training school near Flixecourt, and that during the following week the Canadian Corps

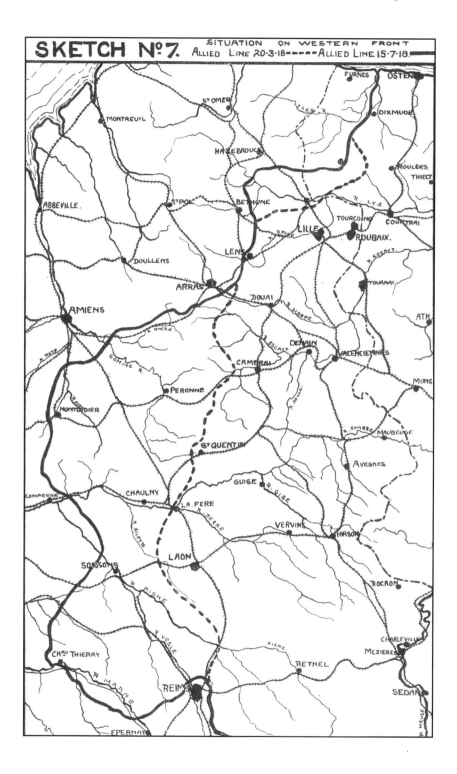

SKETCH Nº 7. SITUATION ON WESTERN FRONT ALLIED LINE 20·3·18━━━━━ALLIED LINE 15·7·18

would send parties of officers each day to watch these demonstrations. The Brigadier General, General Staff, the GOC, Royal Artillery, and the Counter-Battery Staff Officer, would meanwhile be enabled to carry out a reconnaissance of the probable front of attack of the Canadian Corps.

The following day a conference of divisional commanders and members of the Corps staff was held at Canadian Corps Headquarters, where the outline of the scheme for the capture of Orange Hill was explained, and the divisional commanders and heads of branches and services concerned were asked to make all preparations for this attack as quickly as possible. It was stated that tanks would be available for the operation and that it was therefore essential that all concerned should familiarise themselves with the combined tactics of infantry and tanks. I explained that demonstrations had been arranged with the Australians, and that it was my wish that the greatest possible number of officers should witness them.

In the meantime, the enemy was to be harassed on the whole Canadian Corps front by artillery and machine gun fire, and numerous raids were to be carried out to procure positive identifications. Further conferences were held from time to time at the Fourth Army Headquarters, where plans were made for the necessary reliefs and moves, and the question of the maintenance of secrecy further emphasised.

On July 26 the Fourth Army Commander stated that the plans originally put forward, and which had been approved by the Commander-in-Chief, had been modified by Marshal Foch, in that the First French Army would now co-operate with the Fourth British Army and be responsible for the right flank of the attack.

On the 27th the general boundaries and the objectives for the first day were fixed, and movements of the Canadian Corps and tank units were arranged. It was decided notably that units were to leave their areas without knowing their destinations, and that it would be given out freely that the Canadian Corps was moving to the Ypres front, where the Second Army expected a German attack.

With a view to deceiving the enemy, two battalions of the Canadian Corps were to be put in the line in the Kemmel area, and two Canadian casualty clearing stations were to be moved to the Second Army area. Wireless and power buzzer sections were to be despatched to the Kemmel sector, and messages were to be sent worded so as to permit the enemy to decipher the identity of the senders.

Meanwhile the Canadian divisions were busy preparing their scheme of attack on Orange Hill, and numerous tanks were ostentatiously assembled in the vicinity of St. Pol. A readjustment of boundaries between divisions was made during the night July 23rd/24th, when the 1st Canadian Division relieved the left brigade of the 3rd Canadian Division in the Neuville Vitasse sector, which sector came under the Canadian Corps (First Army). The remainder of the front held by the 3rd Canadian Division was taken over by the 59th British Division, and on completion of these reliefs, on July 27, the 3rd Canadian Division returned under Canadian Corps, and was held in General Headquarters Reserve in the Hermaville area.

On July 29 the XVII Corps was ordered by First Army to relieve the Canadian Corps in the line during the night July 31st/August 1st, and August 1st/2nd, reliefs to be completed by daylight on August 2, the Command of the Canadian Corps front to pass to the GOC XVII Corps at 10:00 am, July 30, at which hour all units and formations then in the Canadian Corps area were to come under the command of the XVII Corps. This army order stated plainly that the Canadian Corps would be prepared to move to Second Army, which, as indicated above, was then holding the northern section of the British front.

The 27th Canadian Infantry Battalion and the 4th Canadian Mounted Rifles Battalion respectively, from the 2nd and 3rd Canadian Divisions, were moved by strategical train to Second Army area where they were placed in the line. They did not rejoin their divisions until August 6.

On this day, July 29, the Canadian divisional commanders were personally informed of the operations which were to take place on the Fourth Army front, and they were instructed not to discuss the operations with any of their subordinate commanders.

On July 30 Canadian Corps Headquarters handed over to the XVII Corps at 10:00 am, leaving a liaison officer to keep in touch with the 1st and 4th Canadian Divisions, which were still in the line.

The Canadian Corps Headquarters moved the same day to Molliens–Vidame, and the transfer of the Canadian Corps from First Army area to Fourth Army area began (see Sketch Number 8).

When this move was well under way, and in order to continue to deceive our troops as to their eventual employment, a letter issued by First Army was repeated to all Canadian divisions and communicated by them to their formations and units, stating that the Canadian Corps was being transferred to the Fourth

Army area, where it would be held in General Headquarters Reserve and be prepared in case of attack to:

> 1. Move south at short notice to assist the French on the
> Rheims–Soissons front
> 2. Support either the First French Army or the Fourth
> British Army

This move, beginning on July 30, was completed on August 7th/8th, and was carried out in three main phases as follows:

> 1. Move from the line to embussing or entraining areas
> (west of Arras)
> 2. Move from the embussing and entraining areas to the
> concentration area (south west of Amiens, a distance of
> approximately forty miles)
> 3. Approach march to battle assembly positions

These moves were carried out by strategical train, buses and route marches with the utmost secrecy, the entraining and detraining taking place during the hours of darkness.

The entire move to the concentration area was carried out without a serious hitch. The dismounted personnel had no marching of any great length, and all ranks arrived fresh and in excellent spirits. Owing to the short space of time available to transport troops and to get them into the concentration area, it was necessary for divisions to entrain the infantry first so as to ensure their having a rest before starting on the march of approach. The area of concentration was well wooded, and it was possible to conceal the movements then in progress.

All moves forward of the Corps concentration area towards the battle assembly positions were carried out during the hours of darkness, and no movement of troops in formed bodies was permitted by day east of a north and south line through Molliens–Vidame.

The approach march was especially difficult, the nights were very dark, the country new and most of the roads very narrow. In the case of the 1st Canadian Division especially, the moves were very hard on the transport sections. Owing to the speed necessary to enable the troops to get into position in time, the greater part of the approach march was accomplished in one jump by the use of buses. This necessitated a forced march of upwards of thirty kilometres for all horsed transport before rejoining their units in the concentration area. This was particularly trying for the train companies, who throughout the march had to carry on with their normal supply duties. All these moves had to be carried out during the hours of darkness, a severe handicap, as the nights were very short at this time of the year.

Administrative Arrangements

While the moves of the Canadian divisions were in progress the Administrative branches of the Corps were facing a most difficult problem. The battle area to be taken over had just passed from the French to the Australians, and none of the organizations necessary for British troops existed, part of the scheme to ensure secrecy being that nothing should be done in the area which might arouse the suspicion of the enemy.

The Deputy Adjutant and Quartermaster General of the Canadian Corps (Brigadier General G.J. Farmar) had received no information regarding the actual operation until July 29. The difficulties attending the accumulation of all kinds of ammunition required for the operation in such a short space of time were very great. The nearest army dump from which we could draw ammunition was so far away that lorries could not make more than one trip a day. The advanced refilling points had not been selected, and the dumping of ammunition at these points did not really begin until August 3. There was a great shortage of lorries, a considerable number of the heavy artillery brigades arriving only two or three days before the attack. When the lorries of these brigades became available, there was not sufficient petrol to keep all of them in operation.

In addition, all forward traffic was restricted to two main channels, the Amiens–Roye road and the Amiens–Villers Brettoneux road. The congestion on the latter was increased by reason of its being used in common with the Australian Corps.

There were no dumps of trench ammunition in the area, and, notwithstanding all efforts made by our administrative branches in that direction, the supply of small arms ammunition and bombs was not quite adequate. As a matter of fact, some units, failing to obtain British hand grenades in time, used French grenades gathered at the French dumps.

The lack of adequate preparations to receive the large number of horses resulting from the great concentration of artillery caused endless columns of horses to block the roads in the vicinity of the watering points.

Fortunately, the weather was unfavourable for flying, being cloudy and misty till August 6, and the abnormal traffic on roads resulting from these conditions remained undetected by the Germans. With a view to drowning the noise of the tank engines, large bombing airplanes flew over the area while the tanks moved forward into position from their lying-up places.

All sorts of expedients were resorted to, and in the main the difficulties encountered were overcome, thanks to the energy, discipline, training and untiring efforts of all concerned.

General Situation

The general situation had now undergone very material changes. A sudden stroke at the appropriate time had definitely crippled the plans for further offensive action which the Germans had formed. The Allied counter-offensive of July 18, on the Soissons–Château Thierry front, following the breakdown of the German attacks of July 15 east and west of Rheims, left a large portion of the German Army badly involved in a deep salient, and on July 26, having lost all hope of extricating their troops in any other way, the German High Command ordered a retirement on that part of the front to the line of the Aisne River. This had the immediate local effect of considerably shortening the Allied front and relieving the pressure on Paris.

By this time the Germans had learned that they could not win, and so they began to follow a defensive policy (this is revealed by their retirements on the Avre and the Ancre, where, in an endeavour to obtain better defensive positions, they abandoned positions favourable to the resumption of offensive operations). The magnitude of the German forces engaged on the Rheims–Soissons front, suffering as they were from the miscarriage of their offensive and from the effects of the Allied counter-stroke, was such that it affected adversely the general situation of their reserves, and created a condition favourable to further attacks by our forces elsewhere.

The first step towards the exploitation of these favourable conditions was the enlargement by Marshal Foch of the operations against the salient of the Somme. The operation east of Amiens which, as originally conceived, was of a purely local character, was now given a much larger scope, namely, the reduction of the entire salient created by the successful German offensive on March 21 and the following days. Just as the reduction of the salient of the Marne had been determined primarily by the successful Allied counter-attack of July 18, the reduction of the salient of the Somme was determined primarily by the deep and sudden penetration effected by our attack of August 8.

General Scheme of Attack

The outline of the operations of August 8 had now been definitely fixed and was substantially as follows:

The front of attack was to extend from Moreuil to Ville-sur-Ancre on a front of approximately 20,000 yards. The dispositions of the troops participating in the attack were as follows:

> A. On the right from Moreuil to Thennes (inclusive): the First French Army under orders of Commander-in-Chief, British Army
> B. In the centre from Thennes (exclusive) to the Amiens–Chaulnes railway: the Canadian Corps
> C. On the left from the Amiens-Chaulnes railway to the Somme: the Australian Corps
> D. The left flank of the Australian Corps was covered by the III (British) Corps attacking in the direction of Morlancourt

The object of the attack was to push forward in the direction of the line Roye–Chaulnes with the least possible delay, thrusting the enemy back in the general direction of Ham, and so facilitating the operations of the French on the front between Montdidier and Noyon.

The Canadian Corps Front

The battle front of the Canadian Corps extended from a point about 800 yards south of Hourges to the Amiens–Chaulnes railway. It crossed the River Luce about 800 yards northeast of Hourges, and remaining well west of Hangard passed through the western portion of Hangard Wood. The total length exceeded 8,500 yards in a straight line.

The right boundary was along the road Hourges–Villers-aux-Erables for a distance of about 2,600 yards, then east of Bertin Wood (inclusive), thence along the Amiens–Roye road, inclusive to the Canadian Corps, in liaison with the First French Army.

The left boundary was along the Amiens–Chaulnes railway, inclusive to Canadian Corps, in liaison with the Australian Corps.

The objectives for the first day were:

> I. The Green Line, just east of the line Hamon Wood–
> Courcelles–Marcelcave–Lamotte-en-Santerre
> II. The Red Line, just east of Mézières–White House–
> Camp Vermont Farm–and the high ground east of
> Guillaucourt
> III. The Blue Dotted Line, comprising the outer defences
> of Amiens, which ran east of the line Hangest-en-
> Santerre–Le Quesnel–Caix–Harbonnières

This Blue Dotted Line was not meant to be a final objective, and the cavalry was to exploit beyond it should the opportunity occur. The average depth of penetration necessary to capture the Blue Dotted Line approximated to 14,000 yards.

The Ground

The greater part of our forward area consisted of bare slopes exposed to enemy observation from the high ground south of the River Luce and east of Hourges; the trenches were very rudimentary.

On the right the River Luce and the marshes, varying on that portion of the front from 200 to 300 yards wide, created an obstacle impassable to troops. Here the only practicable access to the jumping-off line was by the bridge and the road from Domart to Hourges, a narrow defile about 200 yards long. This was commanded absolutely from the high ground, immediately to the east, and more particularly from Dodo Wood and Moreuil Wood.

These conditions rendered the assembly of troops prior to the attack very difficult, while the siting of the forward field batteries was not an easy task. Some distance west of the front line a small number of woods, villages, and sunken roads afforded a certain amount of cover from view. Gentelles Wood in particular was used, very extensively for the assembly of tanks as well as troops.

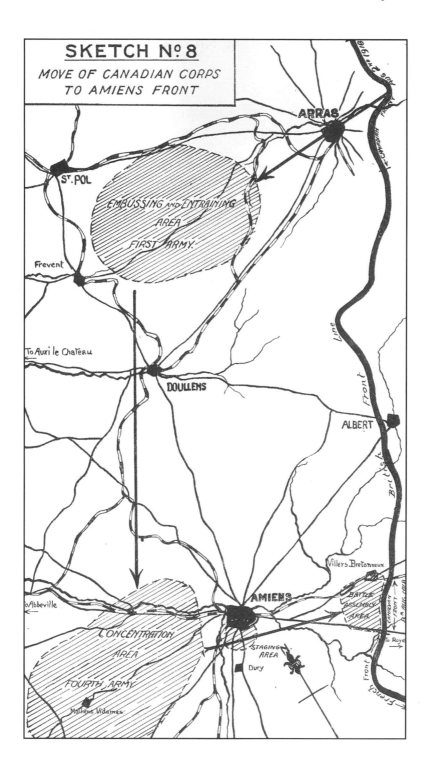

SKETCH Nº 8

MOVE OF CANADIAN CORPS
TO AMIENS FRONT

Opposite our front the ground consisted of a rolling plateau cut diagonally by the deep valley of the River Luce. This river flows almost due west through a strip of wooded marsh land some 300 yards wide, from which the sides of the valley rise steeply. Numerous ravines running generally north and south cut deep into the plateau, the ground between these ravines forming, as it were, tactical features difficult to access and more or less inter-supporting. Woods and copses were scattered over the area, and many compact and well-built villages surrounded by gardens and orchards formed conspicuous landmarks. The remainder was open, unfenced, farmland, partly covered with fields of standing grain. The hostile defences consisted chiefly of unconnected elements of trenches, and a vast number of machine gun posts scattered here and there, forming a fairly loose but very deep pattern.

The Troops

In addition to the four Canadian divisions, the following troops were placed under Canadian Corps for the operation:

5th Squadron, RAF
4th Tank Brigade
3rd Cavalry Division

A mobile force was organized consisting of the 1st and 2nd Canadian Motor Machine Gun Brigades, the Canadian Corps Cyclist Battalion, and a section of six-inch Newton mortars mounted on motor lorries. This force was named the Canadian Independent Force, placed under the command of Brigadier General R. Brutinel, and given the task of co-operating with the cavalry in the neighbourhood of the Amiens–Roye road, covering the right flank of our right division and maintaining liaison with the French.

I was notified that two British divisions were held in army reserve, and could be made available in the event of certain situations developing. The total artillery at my disposal amounted to seventeen brigades of field artillery and nine brigades of heavy artillery, plus four additional batteries of long-range guns.

The enemy troops were believed to consist of twenty-four battalions (less than three divisions) in the forward area and about six battalions in support, the latter belonging to divisions on the French front, but known to be situated within the area we were to attack. It was believed that the enemy had four divisions in reserve immediately available, and that two of these were west of the Hindenburg Line.

The Scheme of Attack

The general scheme of attack was to overrun rapidly the enemy's forward area to a depth of about 3,600 yards under cover of a dense artillery barrage which would begin at zero hour; then without halting to seize the Red Line, relying on the help of tanks to overcome the machine gun defences. At that moment the cavalry was to pass through the infantry and seize the area as far as the Blue Dotted Line, supported on its right flank by the Canadian Independent Force. The cavalry was to be followed as quickly as possible by the 4th Canadian Division, passing through the 3rd Canadian Division on the right, and by reserve brigades of the 1st and 2nd Canadian Divisions in the centre and on the left. Every effort was to be made to exploit success wherever it occurred. Special arrangements had been made to support the attack beyond the Green Line as long as possible with heavy artillery, and sections of field artillery were detailed to advance in close support of the attacking infantry.

The attack had been synchronised with the Australians, who were to jump off at the same hour as the Canadian Corps. The First French Army was to submit the Bois de Moreuil to a forty-five minute bombardment before developing infantry action, but the GSO had agreed that the bombardment should only begin at zero hour. The Canadian Corps being, as it were, the spearhead of the attack, the movements of other formations were to be synchronised with ours.

At 10:00 am on the morning of August 5, I took over command of the battle front, then held by the 4th Australian Division. During the hours of darkness on the 4th, 5th, 6th, and 7th the attacking Canadian troops relieved the Australian troops, with the exception of those holding the outpost line, who remained in position until the night 7th/8th.

Dispositions

The dispositions of the Canadian Corps on the morning of the 8th at zero hour were as follows:

> *On the Right*: the 3rd Canadian Division, in liaison with the French
> *In the Centre*: the 1st Canadian Division
> *On the Left*: the 2nd Canadian Division, in liaison with the Australians

In Reserve—behind the 3rd Canadian Division—the 4th Canadian Division

Each of these divisions had their allotment of tanks. East of the Noye River, the 3rd Cavalry Division. Behind Gentelles Wood, the Canadian Independent Force.

The Battle

At 4:20 am, August 8, the initial assault was delivered on the entire army front of attack, and the First French Army opened their bombardment. The attack made satisfactory progress from the outset on the whole front (see Sketch Number 9). East of Hourges, opposite the 3rd Canadian Division, the high ground which dominated our front and a portion of the French front had been seized quickly by the 9th Canadian Infantry Brigade (Brigadier General E.M. Ormond), and the way was opened for the Canadian Independent Force and the 4th Canadian Division.

The very complete arrangements made by the 3rd Canadian division to keep the bridge open, and to repair the road quickly, allowed the reserves to go forward without delay. The heavy task of the engineers was remarkably well carried out. By the afternoon the Canadian Corps had gained all its objectives, with the exception of a few hundred yards on the right in the vicinity of Le Quesnel, where stiff resistance was offered by unexpected reserves, but this was made good the following morning. The day's operations, in which the four Canadian divisions took part, represented a maximum penetration of the enemy's defences of over eight miles, and included the capture of the following villages: Hangard, Demuin, Beaucourt, Aubercourt, Courcelles, Ignaucourt, Cayeux, Caix, Marcelcave, Wiencourt-l'Equipee, and Guillaucourt. In addition to these, the Canadian Independent Force assisted the French in the capture of Mézières, which was holding up their advance.

The surprise had been complete and overwhelming. The prisoners stated that they had no idea that an attack was impending, and captured documents did not indicate that any of our preparations had been detected. The noise of our tanks going to the final position of assembly had been heard by some men and reported, but no deduction appears to have been made regarding this. An officer stated that the Canadians were believed to be on the Kemmel front.

On the following day, the 9th, the advance was continued with the 3rd, 1st, and 2nd Canadian Divisions in the line, the 4th Canadian Division being held in corps reserve. Substantial progress was made, and by evening the average depth of our advance was about four miles, with a maximum of six miles at some points. The following additional villages were captured: Le Quesnel, Folies, Bouchoir, Beaufort, Warvillers, Rouvroy, Vrely, Meharicourt, and Rosières.

The infantry and tanks of the 3rd Canadian Division and the Canadian Independent Force co-operated with the French in the capture of Arvillers. During the day the enemy's resistance stiffened considerably, and whatever gains were made resulted from heavy infantry fighting against fresh troops, with only a few tanks available for support. This advance had brought our troops into the area of the trenches and defences occupied prior to the Somme operations in 1916. These trenches, while not in a good state of repair, were, nevertheless, protected by a considerable amount of wire, and lent themselves readily to a very stubborn machine gun defence.

The attack was continued on the morning of the 10th, with the 3rd Canadian Division on the right and the 4th Canadian Division on the left, the 1st and 2nd Canadian Divisions being held in corps reserve. After the 3rd Canadian Division had taken the village of Le Quesnoy-en-Santerre, the 32nd Division, which had come under the Canadian Corps on the night 9th/10th, and had been · ordered to relieve the 3rd Canadian Division, passed through it and advanced the line somewhat further through the old British trenches west of Parvillers and Damery. The 4th Canadian Division during the day succeeded, after very hard fighting, in occupying Fouquescourt, Maucourt, Chilly, and Halm.

During the night 10th/11th a strong enemy counter-attack developed against a part of the front of the 4th Canadian Division east of Hallu. This counter-attack was beaten off, but owing to general conditions the line at that point was slightly withdrawn to the railway embankment immediately to the west of Hallu. Subsequent upon this slight withdrawal, and with a. view to reducing the existing salient forward of Chilly, the line was further withdrawn to the eastern outskirts of that village.

On the 11th, at 9:30 am, the 32nd Division launched an attack against Damery, but was not successful. The 4th Canadian Division improved their line by advancing it locally to reduce the Chilly salient, which was still very pronounced. During the night of the 11th/12th the 32nd Division and 4th Canadian Division were relieved by the 3rd and 2nd Canadian Divisions respectively.

It now became increasingly apparent that strong enemy reserves had been sent forward to stem our advance six fresh divisions and a large number of light and heavy batteries had been brought in, and were fighting hard in a strongly entrenched defensive position.

I considered that it was inadvisable to try to progress mainly by infantry fighting, and recommended that the operations should be slackened to give time to organize a set piece attack on a broad front. I further suggested that rather than expose the Canadian Corps to losses without adequate results it should be withdrawn from this front, rested for a few days, and used to make another surprise attack in the direction of Bapaume. Plans to organize a set piece attack to take place on August 15 or 16, and having for its objective the Roye–Liencourt–Omiécourt road, were prepared. This operation was to be carried out in conjunction with the French and the Australian Corps.

The 12th, 13th, and 14th were characterised chiefly by patrol encounters and local trench fighting. The 3rd Canadian Division cleared the network of trenches between Fouquescourt and Parvillers, and advanced the line as far as the northern and western edge of Parvillers and Damery. These two villages were captured in the evening of the 15th, and were held in spite of heavy counter-attacks. Bois de Damery was also taken, and this enabled the French to capture the important position known as Bois-en-Z.

On the nights 15th, 16th, and 16th/17th the 1st Canadian Division relieved the 3rd Canadian Division, the latter being withdrawn to corps reserve. Progress was made during the 16th/17th, the enemy being driven out of Fransart by the 4th Canadian Infantry Brigade (Brigadier General R. Rennie) of the 2nd Canadian Division, and out of La Chavatte by the 1st Canadian Division, our line on the right being advanced in co-operation with the French. The relief of the 2nd Canadian Division by the 4th Canadian Division was carried out on the nights 15th/16th and 16th/17th, the former being withdrawn to corps reserve on the 17th.

The operation, which had been projected for August 16, had been postponed, and it had been decided to transfer the Canadian Corps back to the First Army, the move to begin by strategical trains on the 19th. The 18th was quiet along the front, but on the 19th the 4th Canadian Division carried out a minor operation near Chilly, which greatly improved our line in that neighbourhood. Four hostile counter-attacks to recover the newly won ground were beaten off during the night. On the 19th, the 2nd and 3rd Canadian Divisions started their move to

First Army, and on the night 19th/20th the relief of the 1st Canadian Division by the French commenced. This relief was completed on the 22nd, and the 1st Canadian Division was placed in corps reserve.

On the 22nd I handed over command of the Canadian Corps front, and of the 1st and 4th Canadian Divisions, 2nd Canadian Motor Machine Gun Brigade, the 8th Army Brigade, Canadian Field Artillery, and the Canadian Corps Heavy Artillery, to the GOC, Australian Corps, and my headquarters moved north to Hautecloque, opening there at 10:00 am on the same day.

Between August 8 and 22 the Canadian Corps fought against fifteen German divisions: of these, ten were directly engaged and thoroughly defeated, prisoners being captured from almost every one of their battalions; the five other divisions, fighting astride our flanks, were only partially engaged by us. In the same period the Canadian Corps captured 9,131 prisoners, 190 guns of all calibres, and more than 1,000 machine guns and trench mortars. The greatest depth penetrated approximated to fourteen miles, and an area of over sixty-seven square miles containing twenty-seven towns and villages had been liberated. The casualties suffered by the Canadian Corps in the fourteen days heavy fighting amounted to:

	Officers.	Other Ranks
Killed	126	1,688
Missing	9	436
Wounded	444	8,659
TOTAL:	579	10,783

Considering the number of German divisions engaged, and the results achieved, the casualties were very light.

Following the deep advance effected on August 8 and 9, the French Third Army attacked at 4:20 am on the 10th astride the Paris–Roye road, and advanced rapidly in the general direction of Roye. The French First Army extended the front of attack, and capturing Montdidier pushed on also in the general direction of Roye. On the 20th the front of attack was further extended west of Soissons in the direction of Noyon. The battle was now in full swing on the centre and southern parts of the Somme salient. North of the Somme the British Third Army made some local attacks on the 21st, and on the 24th attacked heavily on a broad front in the direction of Bapaume. On the whole Somme salient the Germans were retiring slowly, fighting a stubborn rearguard action, actively pressed everywhere by the Allied armies (see Sketch Number 9a).

Transfer to First Army Area

The transfer of the Canadian Corps to the First Army area was effected without serious difficulty and in a very short time. As already stated, the 2nd and 3rd Canadian Divisions entrained and embussed in the Boves area on the nights 19th/20th and 20th/21st August respectively. They detrained and debussed on the 20th and 21st in the Bouquemaison area, whence they proceeded by route march to the Etrun and Hermaville areas. Passing under the XVII Corps the 2nd Canadian Division relieved, on the nights 22nd/23rd and 23rd/24th part of the 15th Division in the line in the Neuville Vitasse–Telegraph Hill sector, the GOC 2nd Canadian Division assuming command of that front at 9:30 pm, August 23. Headquarters, Canadian Corps, moved from Hautecloque to Noyelle-Vion on the 23rd, and at noon that day I assumed command of the XVII Corps front, extending from Neuville-Vitasse to Gavrelle, the 15th and 51st (British) divisions coming under my orders.

On the night 23rd/24th the 3rd Canadian Division relieved the balance of the 15th Division in the line from the Arras–Cambrai road to the Scarpe River, immediately on the left of the 2nd Canadian Division; the command of this centre sector passing to the GOC 3rd Canadian Division on August 24 at 10:00 am.

On the 25th the 1st Canadian Division detrained at Tinques, Savy, and Aubigny, returning under the Canadian Corps, and the 4th Canadian Division rejoined the Corps on the 28th, having been relieved in the line on the Amiens front on the 25th by the 34th and 35th French Divisions.

General Situation

In sympathy with the severe reverses suffered on the Marne, and consequent upon the actions now fully developed in the Somme salient, signs were not wanting that the enemy was preparing to evacuate the salient of the Lys. This evacuation began under pressure of the First Army on August 25. All these attacks and their results, direct or indirect, enabled the Allies to recover the ground they had lost in the course of the German offensive operations. The recapture of that ground was, however, of secondary importance as compared to the morale results of these successive victories. The German Armies had been impressed in the course of these operations by the superiority of our generalship and of our organization, and by the great determination of our troops and subordinate commanders. The Hindenburg System, however, was intact, and the enemy Higher Command hoped and believed that behind this powerfully organized area the German Armies might be collected and reorganized (see Sketch Number 10).

Fighting the most determined rearguard action in the Somme salient, they expected that our armies would be tired and depleted by the time they reached the forward area of the Hindenburg System. The Battle of Cambrai, now about to be begun, shattered their hopes. By breaking through the Drocourt–Quéant Line, itself but a part of the Hindenburg System, the Canadian Corps carried the operations forward to ground that had been in the hands of the Germans since 1914. This advance constituted a direct threat on the rear of the German armies north and south of Cambrai. Dominated at all times, paralysed by the swift and bold strokes on vital points of their line and by the relentless pressure applied everywhere, the German Higher Command was unable to take adequate steps to localise and stop our advance. After the Drocourt–Quéant Line was broken, the retreat of the enemy became more accelerated, and our attacks met everywhere with less and less organized and determined resistance. The morale effect of the most bitter and relentless fighting which led to the capture of Cambrai was tremendous. The Germans had at last learned and understood that they were beaten.

ARRAS–CAMBRAI OPERATIONS

The Task

On August 22 I received the details of the operations contemplated on the First Army front. The plan was substantially the following:

The Canadian Corps, on the right of the First Army, was to attack eastwards astride the Arras–Cambrai road, and by forcing its way through the Drocourt–Quéant Line south of the Scarpe to break the hinge of the Hindenburg System and prevent the possibility of the enemy rallying behind this powerfully organized defended area. These operations were to be carried out in conjunction with the operation of the Third Army then in progress. This attack had been fixed for the next Sunday, August 25. It was represented that this gave barely forty-eight hours to concentrate the necessary artillery, part of which was still in the Fourth Army area, and that, furthermore, the Canadian Corps had sentimental objections to attacking on the Sabbath Day. It was then agreed that the attack should take place on Monday the 26th.

On the evening of the 22nd I held a conference of divisional commanders at Corps Headquarters (Hautecloque), and outlined the projected operation and my plans for carrying it out. In addition to a detailed knowledge of the ground, which we had held before, we were particularly benefited by all the reconnaissance and plans made for the capture of Orange Hill during the period of simulated activity at the end of July. The excellence of trench railways, rear communications, and administrative arrangements in the area were also of great value, and enabled the Canadian Corps to undertake to begin, with only three days' notice, the hardest battle in its history.

Reinforcements had come up, and although all units were not up to strength, they were all in fighting condition. The efficiency of the organization peculiar to the Canadian Corps, and the soundness of the tactical doctrine practised, had been proved and confirmed. Flushed with the great victory they had just won, and fortified by the experience acquired, all ranks were ready for the coming task.

The Ground

The ground to be attacked lent itself peculiarly to defence, being composed of a succession of ridges, rivers, and canals, which formed natural lines of defence of very great strength. These natural positions, often mutually supporting, had been abundantly fortified. Their organization was the last word in military engineering, and represented years of intensive and systematic labour. Barbed wire entanglements were formidable, machine gun positions innumerable, and large tunnels had been provided for the protection of the garrison. The four main systems of defence consisted of the following lines:

> I. The old German front system east of Monchy-le-Preux
> II. The Fresnes–Rouvroy Line
> III. The Drocourt–Quéant Line
> IV. The Canal du Nord Line

These, with their subsidiary switches and strong points, as well as the less organized but by no means weak intermediate lines of trenches, made the series of positions to be attacked without doubt one of the strongest defensively on the Western Front.

Broad glacis, studded with machine gun nests, defended the immediate approaches to these lines, and this necessitated in each case heavy fighting to gain a suitable jumping-off line before assaulting the main position. In addition to these systems, and as a preliminary to the attack on the old German system east of Monchy-le-Preux, it was necessary to capture the very well organized British defences which had been lost in the fighting of March, 1918. These defences were intact to a depth of about 5,500 yards, and were dominated by the heights of Monchy-le-Preux, from which the Germans were enjoying superior observation.

Throughout these operations there could not be any element of surprise, other than that afforded by the selection of the actual hour of the assaults. The positions to be attacked formed the pivot of the movements of the German Army to the south, and the security of the armies to the north depended also on these positions being retained. There was consequently little doubt that the enemy was alert, and had made every disposition to repulse the expected attacks. Therefore the plan necessitated provision for very hard and continuous fighting, the main stress being laid on the continuity of the operations.

To carry this out, I decided to do the fighting with two divisions in the line, each on a one-brigade front, thus enabling both divisions to carry on the battle for three successive days; the two other divisions were to be kept in corps reserve, resting and refitting after each relief (the severity of the fighting did not, however, allow this plan to be adhered to, and on many occasions the divisions had to fight with two brigades in the front line). It was understood that British divisions from the army reserve would be made available as soon as additional troops were required.

To maintain the utmost vigour throughout the operation, the divisions were directed to keep their support and reserve brigades close up, ready to push on as soon as the leading troops were expended. As the protection of the left flank of the attack could not at the outset be dissociated from the operations of the Canadian Corps, the 51st (Highland) Division in the Gavrelle sector remained under my orders. The initial attack on the 26th was to be launched by the 2nd Canadian Division on the right and the 3rd Canadian Division on the left. The XVII Corps was on our immediate right, they being the left corps of the Third Army.

On the night of the 24th/25th the 2nd Canadian Division, in conformity with operations carried out by the Third Army on its right flank, advanced the outpost line on the outskirts of Neuville-Vitasse, later capturing the sugar refinery and some elements of trenches south of that village. That same night the 51st (Highland) Division, north of the Scarpe, advanced the outpost line opposite Greenland Hill without meeting much opposition.

The objectives for the attack of 26th were indicated as follows:

> *The 2nd Canadian Division* was to capture Chapel Hill, then work south through the old British support system and join up with the British troops on the right on the northern end of the Wancourt spur, thus encircling the enemy troops in the forward area towards Neuville-Vitasse. They were at the same time to push forward and capture the southern end of Monchy-le-Preux Heights.

> *The 3rd Canadian Division* was to capture Orange Hill, then Monchy-le-Preux. The success of the advance was to be exploited as far east as possible.

> *The 51st (Highland) Division*, north of the Scarpe, was to cover the left flank of the 3rd Canadian Division by advancing towards Mount Pleasant and Roeux.

After mature consideration zero hour which had been orignally set at 4:50am, was changed to 3:00 am in order to take advantage of the restricted visibility produced by moonlight and so to effect a surprise; the attacking troops would thus pass through the enemy's forward machine gun defences by infiltration, and be in position to assault at dawn his line of resistance on the eastern slopes of Orange Hill.

The initial assault was to be supported by seventeen brigades of field and nine brigades of heavy artillery, in addition to the long range guns of the army heavy artillery (throughout the Arras–Cambrai operations the artillery allotted to the Canadian Corps was at all times adequate, varying at times in accordance with the tasks assigned. In the operation against the Drocourt-Quéant Line the attack was supported by twenty brigades of field and twelve brigades of heavy artillery).

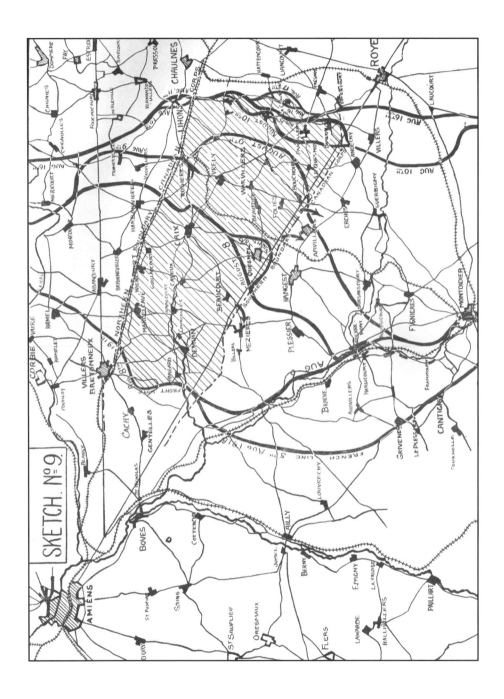

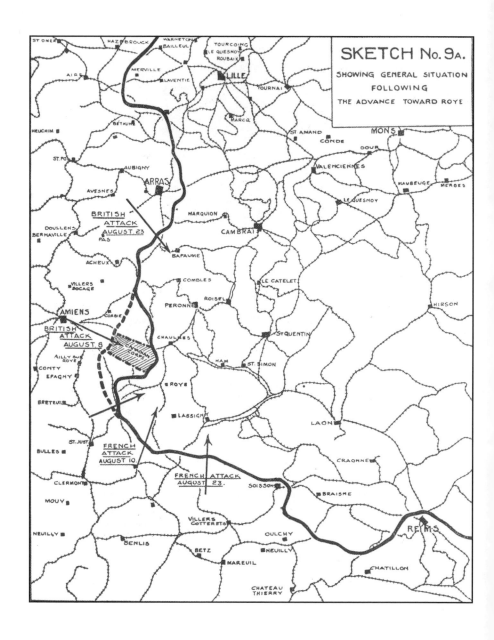

SKETCH No. 9A.

SHOWING GENERAL SITUATION
FOLLOWING
THE ADVANCE TOWARD ROYE

ST OMER
HAZEBROUCK
WARNETON
BAILLEUL
TOURCOING
LE QUESNOY
ROUBAIX
MERVILLE
AIRE
LAVENTIE
LILLE
TOURNAI
MARCQ
BETHUNE
MONS
HEUCHIM
ST AMAND
CONDE
DOUR
ST POL
AUBIGNY
VALENCIENNES
MAUBEUGE
MERBES
AVESNES
ARRAS
LE QUESNOY
BRITISH
ATTACK
AUGUST 23
PAS
MARQUION
DOULLENS
BERNAVILLE
CAMBRAI
BAPAUME
ACHEUX
COMBLES
LE CATELET
VILLERS
BOCAGE
HIRSON
AMIENS
CORBIE
PERONNE
ROISEL
BRITISH
ATTACK
AUGUST 8
CHAULNES
PERONNE
CORRAN
ST QUENTIN
AILLY SUR
ROYE
HAM
ST. SIMON
CONTY
EPAGNY
ROYE
BRETEUIL
ST JUST
LASSIGNY
LAON
FRENCH
ATTACK
AUGUST 10
BULLES
CRAONNE
CLERMONT
SOISSONS
FRENCH ATTACK
AUGUST 23.
BRAISNE
MOUY
VILLERS
COTTERETS
REIMS
NEUILLY
OULCHY
NEUILLY
SENLIS
CHATILLON
BETZ
MAREUIL
CHATEAU
THIERRY

Troops attached to the Corps

The following were attached to the Canadian Corps for the operations:

      5th Squadron, RAF

      3rd Brigade, Tank Corps

As a result of lessons learned during the Amiens operations, it was laid down, as a general principle, that tanks should follow rather than precede the infantry. The 3rd Tank Brigade was asked to supply, if possible, nine tanks to each attacking division each day, and the necessity of exercising the greatest economy in their employment was impressed on divisional commanders.

The Attack: 1st Phase

On August 26, at 3:00 am, the attack was launched under the usual artillery and machine gun barrages. It made good progress, the village of Monchy-le-Preux being entered early in the day, after a very brilliant encircling attack carried out by the 8th Canadian Infantry Brigade (Brigadier General D.C. Draper). The trenches immediately to the east of Monchy-le-Preux were found to be heavily held, and were not cleared until about 11:00 am by the 7th Canadian Infantry Brigade (Brigadier General H. Dyer; see Sketch Number 11).

Guemappe was captured by 4:00 pm and Wancourt Tower and the top of Heninel Ridge were in our hands at 10:40 pm. The defenders of the latter feature fought hard, but eventually succumbed to a determined attack delivered by the 6th Canadian Infantry Brigade (Brigadier General A.H. Bell), under cover of an extemporised barrage fired by the 2nd Canadian Divisional Artillery (Brigadier General H.A. Panet). During the night this brigade captured, in addition, Egret Trench, thus securing a good jumping-off line for the operation of the following day.

The situation along the Arras–Cambrai road was at one time obscure, following a change in the inter-divisional boundary ordered when the attack was in progress. A gap occurred for a few hours, but it was filled as soon as discovered, by the Canadian Independent Force. The enemy fought strenuously and several counter-attacks were repulsed at various stages of the fighting, three German divisions being identified during the day and more than 2,000 prisoners captured, together with a few guns and many machine guns. North of the Scarpe, the 51st (Highland) Division had pushed forward east of the Chemical Works and Gavrelle without meeting serious opposition.

The Canadian Engineers had been actively employed, and all the roads in the forward area were cleared and repaired, thus establishing good communications. The light railways, which up to this date had been delivering an average of 1,800 tons daily, were pushed forward, closely following up the advance.

The attack was renewed at 4:55 am on August 27 by the 2nd and 3rd Canadian Divisions, in the face of increased opposition, under a uniformly good initial barrage. The 2nd Canadian Division pushed doggedly forward through the old German trench system, where very stiff hand-to-hand fighting took place, and crossed the Sensée River, after capturing the villages of Chérisy and Vis-en-Artois.

The 3rd Canadian Division encountered very heavy opposition, but succeeded in capturing Bois-du-Vert, Bois-du-Sart, and reaching the western outskirts of Haucourt, Remy, Boiry-Notre-Dame, and Pelves.

The enemy throughout the day pushed a large number of reinforcements forward, bringing up machine gun units in motor lorries in the face of our accurate field and heavy artillery fire. Hostile field batteries in the open, firing over open sights, showed remarkable tenacity, several remaining in action until the personnel had been destroyed by our machine gun fire.

Our casualties were heavy, especially on the 2nd Canadian Division front, and after discussing the situation with the GOC, 2nd Canadian Division, and taking into consideration the uncertainty of the situation on the right flank of this division, the operations were, after 5:45 pm, restricted to the consolidation of the line then reached east of the Sensée River.

North of the Scarpe, the 51st (Highland) Division had pushed forward and gained a footing on Greenland Hill, but were forced to withdraw slightly by a heavy German counter-attack. During the night August 27th/28th the 8th Division (VIII Corps) took over the northern half of the 51st Division front.

As the enemy was still holding Plouvain and the high ground north of the Scarpe, the 3rd Canadian Division had been compelled to refuse its left flank, and the front now held by this division was increased from about 3,700 yards to about 6,000 yards.

It was intended to continue the battle on the 28th, with the 1st Canadian Division on the right and the 4th (British) Division, then coming under my command, on the left; the latter division, however, was unable to reach the battle position in time. As it was undesirable at this stage to employ a fresh division alongside a division which had already been engaged, the orders issued were cancelled and the battle was continued by the divisions then in the line.

At 9:00 am on the 28th the 3rd Canadian Division resumed the attack, followed at 12:30 pm by the 2nd Canadian Division. The objective for the day was the capture of the Fresnes–Rouvroy Line , the possession of which was vital to the success of our further operations. On the left, the 3rd Canadian Division had pushed forward, captured the Fresnes–Rouvroy Line from the Sensée River to north of Boiry-Notre-Dame, and had secured that village, Jigsaw Wood and entered Pelves. They had, however, been unable to clear the village of Haucourt.

On the front of the 2nd Canadian Division the fighting was most severe. The wire in front of the Fresnes–Rouvroy Line was found to be almost intact, and although at some points the 5th Canadian Infantry Brigade (Brigadier General T.L. Tremblay) had succeeded in penetrating the line, the first objective could not be secured, except one short length on the extreme right. Subjected to heavy machine gun fire from both flanks as well as frontally, the attacking troops had suffered heavy casualties, which they had borne with the utmost fortitude.

At nightfall the general line of the 2nd Canadian Division was little in advance of the line held the night before, although a few small parties of stubborn men were still as far forward as the wire of the Fresnes–Rouvroy Line . Enemy reinforcements were seen dribbling forward all day long.

2nd Phase

During the days succeeding the capture of Monchy-le-Preux the enemy's resistance had been steadily increasing, and it became clear that the Drocourt–Quéant Line would be very stubbornly defended.

On the 28th instructions had been received fixing tentatively September 1 as the date on which the Drocourt–Quéant Line was to be attacked by the Canadian Corps, in conjunction with the XVII Corps. The intention was to capture also the Canal du Nord Line in the same operation. It was therefore essential to secure, before that date, a good jumping-off line roughly parallel to, and approximately 600 yards west of, the Drocourt–Quéant Line. This was indeed a very difficult task, entailing the capture of the Fresnes–Rouvroy Line , of the Vis-en-Artois Switch, and of a number of defended localities of very great strength, notably the Crow's Nest, Upton Wood, and St. Servin's Farm.

The 2nd and 3rd Canadian Divisions were now exhausted, and during the night 28th/29th they were relieved by the 1st Canadian Division on the right, the 4th (British) Division (which had been placed under my orders on the night 26th/27th) on the left, and Brutinel's Brigade (formerly the Canadian Independent Force) on the extreme left flank. The heavy artillery from now on concentrated on the cutting of the broad belts of wire in front of the Drocourt–Quéant Line, and the engineers prepared the bridging materiel required for the crossings of the Sensée River and the Canal du Nord.

During the day (August 29) our line had been considerably improved by minor operations. Brutinel's Brigade had pushed forward on their front and captured Bench Farm and Victoria Copse, north of Boiry-Notre-Dame. The 4th (British) Division, in the face of strong opposition, had advanced their line in the vicinity of Haucourt and Remy. North of the Scarpe the 51st Division had captured the crest of Greenland Hill. The command of the 51st Divisional front now passed to the GOC XXII Corps; and during the night August 29th/30th the 11th Division, which had been transferred to the Canadian Corps from I Corps, relieved Brutinel's Brigade in the line, the command of that division also passing to the GOC XXII Corps on completion of the relief. This shortened the line considerably and relieved me of the anxiety caused by the length and vulnerability of the northern flank.

On the 30th, following the reported capture of Hendecourt by the 57th Division, the 1st Canadian Division attacked the Vis-en-Artois Switch, Upton Wood, and the Fresnes–Rouvroy Line south of the Vis-en-Artois Switch. The attack, a daring manoeuvre organised and carried out by the 1st Canadian Infantry Brigade (Brigadier General W.A. Griesbach), under cover of very ingenious barrages arranged by the Commander Royal Artillery, 1st Canadian Division (Brigadier General H.C. Thacker), was eminently successful, all objectives being captured and the entire garrison either killed or taken prisoner. Heavy counter-attacks by fresh troops were repulsed during the afternoon and following night.

On the 31st the remainder of the Fresnes–Rouvroy Line south of the Arras–Cambrai road, including Ocean Work, was captured by the 2nd Canadian Infantry Brigade (Brigadier General F.O.W. Loomis).

In the meantime the 4th (British) Division had doggedly pushed ahead, crossing the valley of the Sensée River and capturing the villages of Haucourt, Remy, and Eterpigny. This advance was over very difficult, thickly wooded country, and the fighting was very heavy, particularly in the vicinity of St. Servin's Farm, which, after changing hands several times, remained in possession of the enemy until September 2.

On the night August 31–September 1 the 4th Canadian Division came into the line on a one-brigade front between the 1st Canadian Division and 4th (British) Division. The GOC 4th (British) Division having now reported that he considered his division unable successfully to attack the Drocourt–Quéant Line on the front allotted to him, in view of the losses suffered in the preliminary fighting for the jumping-off line, I decided that the 4th Canadian Division would extend their front and take over 1,000 yards additional frontage from the 4th (British) Division. This necessitated a change of plan on the part of the 4th Canadian Division, who a few hours before zero had to place an additional brigade in the line for the initial assault. Accordingly, the 12th Canadian Infantry Brigade (Brigadier General J.H. McBrien) carried out the attack on the right and the 10th Canadian Infantry Brigade (Brigadier General R.J.F. Hayter) on the left divisional front, having first advanced the line to conform with the 1st Canadian Division.

It was necessary to postpone the attack on the Drocourt–Quéant Line until September 2 on account of the additional wire cutting which was still required, and the day of September 1 was employed in minor operations to improve the jumping-off line for the major operation. The important strong point known as the Crow's Nest was captured by the 3rd Canadian Infantry Brigade.

During the afternoon and evening of September 1 the enemy delivered violent counter-attacks, directed against the junction of the 1st and 4th Canadian Divisions. Two fresh divisions and two divisions already in the line were identified in the course of this heavy fighting. Our troops were forced back slightly twice, but the ground was each time regained and finally held. The hand-to-hand fighting for the possession of the crest of the spur at this point really continued until zero hour the next day, the troops attacking the Drocourt–Quéant Line as they moved forward, taking over the fight from the troops then holding the line.

At 5:00 am, September 2, the major operation against the Drocourt–Quéant Line was launched. Preceded by a dense barrage, and assisted by tanks, the infantry pushed forward rapidly, and the Drocourt–Quéant Line (the first objective) and its support line (the second objective) including the village of Dury were captured according to programme. With the capture of the second objective the field artillery barrage was shot out, and the attack further east had to be carried forward without its assistance. The enemy's resistance, free of the demoralising effect of our barrage, stiffened considerably, the open country being swept continually by intense machine gun fire. In addition, the tanks soon became casualties from enemy guns firing point blank, and the advance on the left and centre was held up.

Brutinel's Brigade, reinforced by a regiment of cavalry (10th Royal Hussars) and armoured cars, endeavoured to pass through to capture the Marquion Bridge on the Canal du Nord. Wire, trenches, and sunken roads, however, confined the movements of the force to the Arras–Cambrai road; and this was rendered impassable by machine gun fire and batteries firing over open sights. On the right, however, the 1st Canadian Division pushed forward despite very heavy machine gun and direct artillery fire, and captured the villages of Cagnicourt and Villers-lez-Cagnicourt, the Bois de Bouche and Bois de Loison to the east of Cagnicourt.

> Taking advantage of the breach thus made by the Canadian Divisions, a brigade of the 63rd (Naval) Division, XVII Corps, which had followed the attack behind the right brigade of our right Division, now turned south and advanced in the direction of Quéant.

Further progress made by the 1st Canadian Division in the afternoon resulted in the capture of the heavily wired Buissy Switch line as far south as the outskirts of Buissy; this largely outflanked the enemy still holding out in front of the 4th Canadian Division, and compelled their retirement during the night behind the Canal du Nord.

Although the crossings of the Canal du Nord had not been captured, the result of the day's fighting was most gratifying. The Canadian Corps had pierced the Drocourt–Quéant Line on its whole front of attack, and the exploitation of our success by the XVII Corps on the right had further widened the breach and made possible the capture of a large stretch of territory to the south.

To stem our advance, and hold the Drocourt–Quéant Line, the enemy had concentrated eight fresh divisions directly opposite the Canadian Corps, but the unparalleled striking power of our battalions and the individual bravery of our men had smashed all resistance. The number of unwounded prisoners captured exceeded 5,000, and we had identified every unit of the seven infantry divisions and the one cavalry division engaged. Our infantry had penetrated the enemy's defences to a depth exceeding 6,000 yards.

In prevision of the attack on the Canal du Nord taking place the same day, the engineers had rapidly prepared the bridges and roads, advanced the light railways, and pushed forward the personnel and all materiel necessary for future construction.

During the night of September 2nd/3rd the 4th (British) Division, by a minor operation, captured the village of Etaing without serious opposition.

At dawn our infantry pushed forward strong patrols, and meeting very slight resistance from the enemy contact patrols established a line just west of the canal along the Corps front, freeing the villages of Buissy, Baralle, Saudemont, Rumaucourt, Ecourt St. Quentin, and Lecluse. A certain number of French civilians were liberated during this advance. The enemy had blown up all the bridges on the previous night, and was holding a commanding position on the eastern bank of the canal with a large number of machine guns. His artillery was very active, more especially from the north, and it was impossible to send bodies of troops by daylight over the long and bare slopes bordered by the canal.

Our left flank was now very exposed to artillery fire from the north, and the nature of the ground we were holding, the strength of the obstacle in front of the Corps, and the resolute attitude of the enemy, forbade any attempt to further exploit our success. It was necessary to prepare minutely the details of the operations required to attack successfully the Canal du Nord Line. Accordingly, no further attempts were made at this time.

In the night of September 3rd/4th the 2nd and 3rd Canadian Divisions relieved the 1st and 4th Canadian Divisions respectively, and the 4th (British) Division was relieved by the 1st (British) Division, which had come under the Canadian Corps on September 1 and had been concentrated after that date in the Monchy-le-Preux, Vis-en-Artois, Guemappe area.

3rd Phase

The left flank of the Corps was again very long, and in accordance with the policy adopted the 1st (British) Division was transferred in the line from the Canadian Corps to the XXII Corps. I handed over command of that sector—extending from Palluel (exclusive) to Etaing (inclusive), and facing north—to the GOC XXII Corps at midnight, September 4th/5th. The enemy had flooded the valley of the Sensée River and all the bridges had been destroyed. Our engineers were very actively engaged in an effort to lower these floods and wrest the control from the enemy. On the right flank the XVII Corps was engaged in heavy fighting in and around Moeuvres, and all their attempts to cross the Canal du Nord at that point had been repulsed.

A thorough reconnaissance of our front had shown that the frontal attack of the Canal du Nord Line was impossible, the eastern bank of the canal was strongly wired and was generally much higher than the western bank. The whole of our forward area was under direct observation from Oisy-le-Verger and the high ground on the northern flank, and any movement by day was quickly engaged by hostile artillery. No battery positions within a range sufficient to carry on the preparation of the attack, or to support it, were available, and any attempt to bring guns forward of the general line Villers-lez-Cagnicourt–Buissy was severely punished; the battery positions south and west of this general line were subjected to intense gas shelling every night.

The Canal du Nord was in itself a serious obstacle. It was under construction at the outbreak of the war and had not been completed. Generally speaking, it followed the valley of the River Agache, but not the actual bed of the river. The average width was about 100 feet and it was flooded as far south as the lock, 800 yards southwest of Sains-lez-Marquion, just north of the Corps southern boundary. South of this and to the right of the Corps front the canal was dry, and its bottom was at the natural ground level, the sides of the canal consisting of high earth and brick banks. The attack of the Canal Du Nord could not, therefore, be undertaken singly by the Canadian Corps, but had to be part of a larger scheme. This required considerable time to arrange, and until September 27 no changes developed on the Corps front.

The obstacles which had stopped our advance also made our positions very strong defensively, and advantage was taken of this fact to rest and refit the divisions. As much of the corps artillery as could be spared was withdrawn from the line to rest the men and horses. The line was held very thinly, but active patrolling at nights and sniping were kept up. A complete programme of harassing fire by artillery and machine guns was also put in force nightly. The Corps Heavy Artillery (Brigadier General R.H. Massie) carried out wire cutting, counter-battery shoots, and gas concentrations daily, in preparation for the eventual operations. Light railways, roads, bridges, and water points were constructed right up to the forward area, and the bridging materiel which would be required for the Canal du Nord was accumulated well forward. Ammunition dumps were established at suitable places.

Detailed reconnaissance of the canal and trenches were carried out by aeroplane, and also by daring patrols, and all available documents regarding the canal construction were gathered with a view to preparing the plans for the future attack. On September 13 Major General (then Brigadier General) F.O.W. Loomis took over command of the 3rd Canadian Division from Major General L.J. Lipsett, who went to command the 4th (British) Division; the former was succeeded in command of the 2nd Canadian Infantry Brigade by Brigadier General (then Lieutenant Colonel) R.P. Clark.

The Task

On September 15, I received the details of a large operation to be carried out later in the month by the Third and Fourth Armies, in which the Canadian Corps was to co-operate by crossing the canal, and by capturing Bourlon Wood and the high ground to the northeast of it, to protect the left flank of the attack. The XXII Corps on the left was to take over the front held by the Canadian Corps to a point 1,200 yards north of the Arras–Cambrai road, and the Canadian Corps was to take over part of the front held by the XVII Corps (Third Army) as far as Moeuvres (exclusive), which was to be the Canadian Corps right boundary for the attack.

> By this side-slip to the south the right of the Canadian Corps was to be placed opposite a dry portion of the Canal du Nord on a front of about 2,500 yards. The Germans were then holding in strength a strip of ground on the west side of the canal, and every effort made by the XVII Corps to clear this ground and reach the canal banks had been repulsed.

On September 22 the task of the Corps was enlarged so as to include, in addition to the objectives already mentioned, the capture of the bridges over the Canal-de-l'Escaut, north of Cambrai, and the high ground overlooking the Sensée Valley. The right boundary was not altered. To assist in carrying out the above additional task, the 11th Division and the 7th Tank Battalion were placed under my orders.

The date of this operation was definitely fixed for September 27, 1918, at dawn. It was decided that the 4th and 1st Canadian Divisions would carry out the initial attack, capture the villages of Bourlon and Marquion respectively, and immediately thereafter seize Bourlon Wood and bring the line up to the high ground north of Bourlon Wood and east of Bois-de-Cocret and Dartford Wood. At this stage the 3rd Canadian Division would pass through the right of the 4th Canadian Division and advance from a line east of Bourlon Wood in an easterly direction towards Neuville-St. Remy, in liaison with the XVII Corps. The 11th Division was to come up on the left of the 1st Canadian Division and advance in a northeasterly direction towards Epinoy and Oisy-le-Verger. The 4th Canadian Division on the right centre was to advance towards Blecourt and the 1st Canadian Division on the left centre was to advance in the direction of Abancourt.

This attack was fraught with difficulties. On the Corps battle front of 6,400 yards the Canal du Nord was impassable on the northern 3,800 yards. The Corps had, therefore, to cross the Canal du Nord on a front of 2,600 yards, and to expand later fanwise in a northeasterly direction to a front exceeding 15,000 yards. This intricate manoeuvre called for most skilful leadership on the part of commanders, and the highest state of discipline on the part of the troops.

The assembly of the attacking troops in an extremely congested area known by the enemy to be the only one available was very dangerous, especially in view of the alertness of the enemy. A concentrated bombardment of this area prior to zero, particularly if gas was employed, was a dreaded possibility which could seriously affect the whole of the operation and possibly cause its total failure. To meet such an eventuality careful arrangements were made by the Counter-Battery Staff Officer to bring to bear an especially heavy neutralising fire on hostile batteries at any moment during the crucial period of preparation. These arrangements were to be put into effect, in any case, at zero hour, to neutralise the hostile defensive barrage on the front of attack.

With the exception of the 2nd Canadian Division which was now holding the entire front, and would be in corps reserve at the time of the attack, every resource of the Canadian Corps was to be crowded in that narrow space. The provision of an effective artillery barrage presented considerable difficulty owing to the depth of the attack and its general direction. On the 4th Canadian Division front particularly, the depth to the initial objective was such that the batteries were compelled to move forward into captured ground and continue firing the barrage from these new positions. Provision was made for the advance of a number of batteries with their echelons to the canal line and beyond whilst the attack was in progress. A large number of machine gun batteries were detailed to supply the initial barrage and, later, to advance in support of the infantry. Provisions were also made for engineer units to move forward immediately following the assaulting troops, to effect immediate repair to the roads and crossings of the canal in order to enable the artillery to move up in support of the infantry.

The greatest precautions had been taken to ensure secrecy, and camouflage had been used extensively to prevent detection of the preparations of all kinds that were in progress. Further to conceal our intentions, it was decided that no preliminary fighting to secure a jumping-off line would take place, and that the Germans would be left in possession of their positions west of the canal until the hour of the attack. It was also hoped that, by letting the Germans retain this ground, their defensive barrage would remain well west of the canal instead of being placed on the canal itself, where the banks offered a serious obstacle and reduced very considerably the rate of advance of the assaulting troops.

On our right the XVII Corps was to advance and capture Fontaine-Notre-Dame, in conjunction with the capture of Bourlon Wood by the 4th Canadian Division. On the night September 25th/26th the XXII Corps on the left took over the front as far south as the Arras–Cambrai road and arranged to extend the artillery and machine gun barrage to their front so as to deceive the enemy regarding actual flanks of the attack. The 4th and 1st Canadian Divisions went into the line on their respective battle fronts. The 2nd Canadian Division, on completion of the relief, passed into corps reserve. During the night September 26th/27th all final adjustments and moves were made, and everything was ready before zero hour. This was for everybody a night full of anxiety, but apart from the usual harassing fire and night bombing nothing untoward happened.

The Attack

At 5:20 am, September 27, the attack was successfully launched, and in spite of all obstacles went well from the first. The barrage was uniformly good, and the 3rd and 4th Canadian Divisional Artilleries, commanded respectively by Brigadier General J.S. Stewart and Brigadier General W.B.M. King, were successful in advancing into captured ground, and continued the barrage as planned.

Early in the afternoon the First Phase of the attack was substantially over, and the readjustments of the fronts preparatory to the Second Phase were under way. On the extreme right, however, the XVII Corps had failed to keep pace with our advance, and our right flank, submitted to severe enfilade machine gun fire from

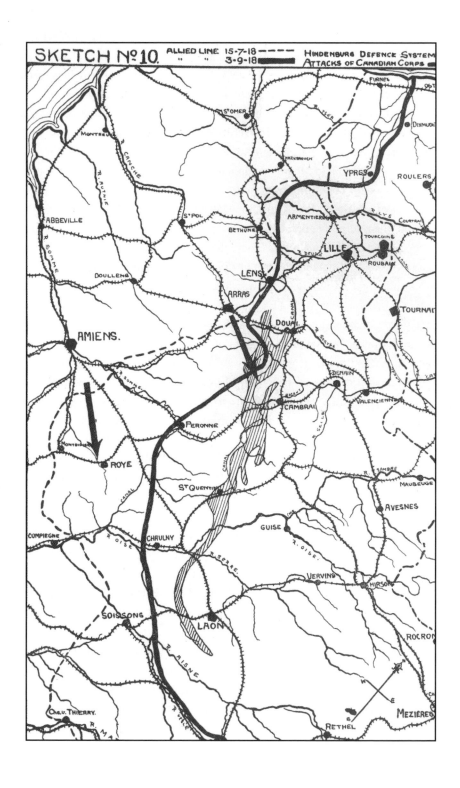

the vicinity of Anneux, had to be refused for a considerable distance to retain touch with the left of the XVII Corps; therefore, the encircling movement which was to have given us Bourlon Wood could not be developed. Fully alive to the gravity of the situation which would be created on the flank of the Third Army by the failure to capture and hold Bourlon Wood, the 4th Canadian Division attacked from the north side of the Wood and captured all the high ground, pushing patrols as far as Fontaine-Notre-Dame.

> It is recalled here that Bourlon Wood, which is 110 metres high, dominates the ground as far south as Flequieres and Havrincourt; and that its loss after very heavy fighting in November, 1917, during the first battle of Cambrai, caused eventually the withdrawal of the Third Army from a large portion of the ground they had won by their surprise attack.

A severe counter-attack launched from the direction of Raillencourt, against the left of the 4th Canadian Division, was repulsed in the afternoon with heavy losses to the enemy.

Owing to the situation on our right flank, already explained, the 3rd Canadian Division could not be engaged this day. The 1st Canadian Division and the 11th (British) Division, however, made substantial gains after the commencement of the Second Phase, the former capturing Haynecourt and crossing the Douai–Cambrai road, and the latter pushing on and taking Epinoy and Oisy-le-Verger by evening.

The attack was continued on the 28th. The 3rd Canadian Division captured Fontaine-Notre-Dame (one of the XVII Corps objectives), and, penetrating the Marcoing Line, reached the western outskirts of St. Olle. The 4th Canadian Division captured Raillencourt and Sailly, and the 11th (British) Division established posts in Aubencheul-au-Bac and occupied the Bois-de-Quesnoy. The 1st Canadian Division, in view of their advance of the previous day which had produced a considerable salient, did not push forward.

Heavy fighting characterised the 29th. The 3rd Canadian Division, the 4th Canadian Division, and the 1st Canadian Division all made progress in the face of severe opposition. The 3rd Canadian Division pushed the line forward to the junction of the Arras and Bapaume road, the western outskirts of Neuville St. Remy and the Douai–Cambrai road. They also cleared the Marquion Line from the Bapaume–Cambrai road southwards towards the Canal de l'Escaut. These trenches were in the XVII Corps area, but it was difficult for our attack to progress leaving on its flank and rear this strongly held position. The 4th Canadian Division captured Sancourt, crossed the Douai–Cambrai railway and entered Blecourt, but later withdrew to the line of the railway in the face of a heavy counter-attack. The necessity for this withdrawal was accentuated by the situation on the left. The 11th Division, in spite of two attempts, had been unable to occupy the high ground northeast of Epinoy. This had interfered materially with the progress of the 1st Canadian Division, and had prevented their holding positions gained early in the day in the neighbourhood of Abancourt Station, the relinquishment of which, in turn, endangered the flank of the 4th Canadian Division.

The operation of the 30th was planned in two phases. In the first, the 3rd and 4th Canadian Divisions were to push forward across the high ground between the Canal de l'Escaut and the Blecourt–Bantigny Ravine, when Brutinel's Brigade was to pass through them and secure bridgeheads at Ramillies and Eswars. The second phase, to take place on the success of the first, provided for the seizing of the high ground overlooking the Sensée River by the 1st Canadian Division and 11th (British) Division. The attack commenced well, and the villages of Tilloy and Blecourt were captured by the 3rd and 4th Canadian Divisions respectively. A heavy counter-attack, however, against the 4th Canadian Division and the left flank of the 3rd Canadian Division, assisted by exceptionally severe enfilade fire from the high ground to the north of the Blecourt–Bantigny Ravine, forced the line on the left back to the eastern outskirts of Sancourt. The second phase of the attack was not carried out, and the net gains for the day were the capture of Tilloy and some progress made on the right of the 3rd Canadian Division from Neuville St. Remy south. Prisoners taken during the day testified to the supreme importance, in the eyes of the enemy, of the positions held by him and the necessity that they be held at all costs.

The tremendous exertions and considerable casualties consequent upon the four days of almost continuous fighting had made heavy inroads on the freshness and efficiency of all arms, and it was questionable whether an immediate decision could be forced in the face of the heavy concentration of troops which our successful and, from the enemy's standpoint, dangerous advance, had drawn against us. On the other hand, it was known that the enemy had suffered severely, and it was quite possible that matters had reached a stage where he no longer considered the retention of this position worth the severe losses both in men and morale consequent upon a continuance of the defence. It was therefore decided that the assault would be continued on October 1, the four divisions in line attacking simultaneously under a heavy barrage, coordinated by the GOC, Royal Artillery. During the night the XXII Corps took over a portion of the front held by the 11th Division, the 56th Division becoming responsible for the defence of the relieved front at 6:00 am, October 1st.

The attack made excellent progress in the early stages, and the troops reached the general line Canal de l'Escaut (east, of Neuville St. Remy)–Morenchies Wood–Cuvillers–Bantigny (all inclusive). The decision of the enemy to resist to the last quickly manifested itself. About 10:00 am heavy counter-attacks developed up the Bantigny Ravine from the direction of Paillencourt. These, supplemented by enfilade fire from the high ground just south of Abancourt, which still remained in the enemy's hands, due to a certain extent to the inability of the 11th Division on the left to make progress, were sufficient to press back our advanced troops. Pockets of the enemy in Blecourt and Bantigny continued to give trouble, and our line was ultimately forced by greatly superior numbers out of Cuvillers, Bantigny, and Blecourt. To continue to throw tired troops against such opposition, without giving them an opportunity to refit and recuperate, was obviously inviting a serious failure, and I accordingly decided to break off the engagement. The five days' fighting had yielded practical gains of a very valuable nature, as well as 7,059 prisoners and 205 guns. We had gone through the last organized system of defences on our front, and our advance constituted a direct threat on the rear of the troops immediately to the north of our left flank, and their withdrawal had now begun.

Although the ground gained on the 1st was not extensive, the effects of the battle and of the previous four days' fighting were far-reaching, and made possible the subsequent advances of October and November, in so far as the divisions engaged against the Canadian Corps drew heavily on the enemy's reserves, which had now been greatly reduced. It is worthy to note that the enemy employed six divisions to reinforce the four divisions already in the line, making a total of ten divisions engaged since September twenty-seven by the Canadian Corps. In addition to their ten divisional artilleries and large number of heavy guns, these German divisions had been reinforced by thirteen Marksmen Machine Gun Companies. In the same period only three additional divisions and one Regiment were employed by the Germans to reinforce the front from

Honnecourt to Cambrai, a front of approximately 18,000 yards in length. This comparison of employment of reserves showed clearly that the enemy was greatly perturbed by the success of our advance, and the serious threat it offered especially to his northern defences.

Throughout this phase very heavy calls had been made on the Corps Artillery (Major General E.W.B. Morrison) and the Canadian Engineers. With the exception of the advances of the 1st Canadian and 11th (British) Divisions in the second stage of the attack of September 27, all operations carried out during the five days took place under cover of artillery barrages. The amount of ammunition fired was exceptionally large, and it was only by the most strenuous efforts on the part of all ranks of the artillery that the supply could be made to keep pace with the expenditure. The success in this respect was to a large extent due to the exertion and skill displayed by the Canadian Engineers (Major General W.B. Lindsay) in every branch of their activities, notably in bridge building and repair of roads. The enemy had set a large number of tank mines and 'booby traps,' and in one sector alone the engineers removed over 200 tank mines, thus greatly facilitating the operation in progress.

4th Phase

The 2nd Canadian Division had been in close support throughout the day, and during the night of October 1st/2nd relieved the 4th Canadian Division and parts of the 3rd and 1st Canadian Divisions in the line from the railway south of Tilloy to Blecourt inclusive. On relief, the 4th Canadian Division came into corps reserve in bivouacs in the Inchy–Quéant area. The relief considerably thinned out the infantry, and in anticipation of possible counter-attacks a large number of machine gun batteries were placed in the line.

October 2 passed without any substantial change in the situation. The enemy's artillery was very active throughout the day, and at 6:15 pm he delivered a determined counter-attack, with a force estimated at about a battalion strong, against the ridge northeast of Tilloy, on the 2nd Canadian Division front. This counter-attack was repulsed with heavy loss to the enemy. During the night October 2nd/3rd the 11th Division extended its frontage to the right as far as Blecourt (inclusive), relieving the remainder of the 1st Canadian Division, who came into corps reserve west of the canal on completion of the relief. The dispositions of the Canadian Corps at noon, October 3, were as follows:

In the line:

> The 3rd Canadian Division on the right on a one-brigade
> front, from the Arras–Cambrai railway to the Cambrai–
> Douai railway south of Tilloy;
> The 2nd Canadian Division in the centre, on a two-
> brigade front, extending to the northern outskirts of
> Blecourt;
> The 11th Division on the left continuing the line to a
> point 1,000 yards south of Aubencheul-au-Bac.

In Corps Reserve:

> The 1st and 4th Canadian Divisions (the latter was
> moved to billets in the Haute Avesnes–Arras area on the
> night of October 7th/8th, to give more opportunity to
> rest and refit).

The period from October 3 to 8 passed without any material changes on the Corps front. An enemy counter-attack was beaten off by the 2nd Canadian Division opposite Bantigny on the morning of October 4, and the 11th Division considerably improved the line on the northern flank by successful minor operations on October 5 and 6. Many patrol encounters took place, in which some prisoners were captured, and our artillery and machine guns kept the enemy under continual harassing fire day and night. In addition, our heavy artillery carried out a daily programme of gas concentrations and counter-battery shoots.

Orders were received on October 3 for the relief of the Corps by the XXII Corps. Concurrently with this relief, and as it progressed, the Canadian Corps was to take over the front of the XXII Corps. Plans for further operations having been formulated to take place on the Third Army front, the Canadian Corps was ordered on October 5 to co-operate by forcing the crossings of the Canal de l'Escaut, north of Cambrai, and the relief contemplated was, therefore, postponed. The Third Army had been successful in crossing the Canal de l'Escaut south of Cambrai between Crevecoeur and Proville. The operation now contemplated had for object the capture of Cambrai by envelopment. This was to be carried out in two phases.

In the first phase the XVII Corps was to capture Awoingt by attacking from the south, the Canadian Corps was to co-operate by an artillery demonstration. In the second phase the Canadian Corps was to cross the Canal de l'Escaut and, advancing rapidly, capture Escaudoeuvres, joining hands with the XVII Corps northeast of Cambrai.

The positions occupied by the 3rd and 2nd Canadian Divisions were not favourable for an attack by day; the 3rd Canadian Division was in front of Cambrai, and house-to-house fighting was out of the question; the 2nd Canadian Division was separated from the canal by glacis-like slopes, devoid of cover, and on which the enemy had good observation from the numerous houses on the east side of the canal as well as from the high ground east of Escaudoeuvres. In addition, Morenchies, Pont d'Aire, Ramillies, and the villages to the north were strongly held by the enemy.

In spite of the difficulties of a night operation it was decided that the 2nd Canadian Division would attack by night, and attempt to seize the bridges before they were blown up by the enemy. The 3rd Canadian Division was to cover the right of the 2nd Canadian Division by capturing the railway embankment, and entering Cambrai as soon as possible to prevent any action of the enemy against the right flank of the 2nd Canadian Division, which, under the best circumstances, was bound to be in the air for some time after the crossing of the canal. Brutinel's Brigade was to cross the canal as soon as possible, and extend the gains of the 2nd Canadian Division by seizing the high ground east of Thun St. Martin. Ten brigades of field artillery were available for the operation.

The Attack

At 4:30 am, October 8, the Third Army attacked, and at the same hour an artillery demonstration was carried out on the Canadian Corps front. The XVII Corps on the right did not reach Awoingt, but in the evening they were ordered to continue their advance on the morning of October 9 to capture this town; concurrently with this advance the Canadian Corps was to secure the crossings of the Canal de l'Escaut.

In spite of the darkness of a rainy night the assembly was completed, and the attack was launched successfully at 1:30 am, October 9. Rapid progress was made, and at 2:25 am the 2nd Canadian Division had captured Ramillies and established posts on the canal there, and patrols were pushing out to the northeast. On the right the infantry, assisted by a party of engineers, rushed the crossings at Pont d'Aire, and, after sharp fighting, captured the bridge intact, with the exception of the western spillway, which had been partially destroyed. Two cork bridges were thrown across, and by 3:35 am our infantry were well established on the eastern side of the canal. The 3rd Canadian Division had cleared the railway, and their patrols were pushing into Cambrai, while the engineers were commencing work on the bridges.

By 8:00 am the 2nd Canadian Division had captured Escaudoeuvres, and had established a line on the high ground immediately to the north and east. Detachments of the 3rd Canadian Division had by this time completely cleared Cambrai of the enemy, and troops of the Third Army could be seen coming up towards it from the south.

Cambrai was to be deliberately set on fire by the enemy. Huge fires were burning in the Square when our patrols went through, and many others broke out in all parts of the city. Piles of inflammable material were found ready for the torch, but the enemy was unable to carry out his intention owing to our unexpected attack and rapid progress. A party of one officer and a few men, which had been left with instructions to set fire to Cambrai, was discovered and dealt with before it could do any further damage. The fires were successfully checked by a large detachment of Canadian Engineers who entered the city with the patrols. A considerable number of road mines, 'booby traps,' etc., were also located and removed.

An air reconnaissance at dawn indicated that the enemy had withdrawn from the area between the Canal de l'Escaut and the Canal de la Sensée, and that all bridges over the latter had been destroyed. Brutinel's Brigade, passing through the infantry of the 2nd Canadian Division, seized the high ground at Croix St. Hubert and pushed cavalry patrols into Thun Lévecque. The 2nd Canadian Division east of the canal progressed towards the north and occupied Thun Lévesque, Thun St. Martin, Blecourt, Cavillers, and Bantigny, and the 11th Division occupied Abancourt and reached the outskirts of Paillencourt. The 3rd Canadian Division was withdrawn at 7:10 pm when the 24th Division (XVII Corps) passed through and joined up with the 2nd Canadian Division, and Cambrai and our positions to the east were taken over or occupied by the XVII Corps. The 3rd Canadian Division was moved on the following day to bivouacs in the Inchy–Quéant area to rest and refit after twelve days of battle.

The attack was continued at 6:00 am, October 10, by the 2nd Canadian and 11th (British) Divisions, and good progress was made. The 2nd Canadian

Division captured Naves, and by nightfall reached a point one and a half miles northeast on the Cambrai–Salzoir road. From there our line ran westwards to the Canal de l'Escaut, exclusive of Iwuy, where we were held up by machine gun fire.

In this attack Brutinel's Brigade operated along the Cambrai-Salzoir road, but finding the Bridge over the Erclin River destroyed could not get their cars further forward.

> This bridge, although on the outpost line under heavy fire, was immediately replaced by the engineers, a covering party being supplied by Brutinel's Brigade.

Machine gun crews from the cars went forward on foot, however, and materially assisted the infantry advancing at this point, and the Corps Cavalry, by a brilliant charge, helped in the capture of the ground east of the Rieux–Iwuy road. On the left, the 11th Division cleared the enemy from the area between the Canal de l'Escaut and the Sensée Canal, captured Paillencourt and Estrun, and reached the outskirts of Hem-Lenglet, which they occupied during the night.

The 49th and 51st Divisions were released from army reserve and transferred to the Canadian Corps on October 10. During the night 10th/11th the former relieved that part of the 2nd Canadian Division east of Iwuy, and the 51st (Highland) Division moved to the Escaudoeuvres area.

At 9:00 am, October 11, the Canadian Corps resumed the attack with the 49th Division on the right and the 2nd Canadian Division on the left. The enemy laid down a heavy artillery barrage and both divisions encountered stiff opposition. After fierce fighting, however, our attack made good progress, the 49th Division gaining the high ground east of Iwuy, and the 2nd Canadian Division capturing Iwuy and the high ground to the north. About 10:30 am the enemy delivered a heavy counter-attack under an artillery barrage and supported by seven tanks, from the direction of Avesnes-le-Sec, against the 49th and 2nd Canadian Divisions. Our line was forced back slightly at first, but six of the tanks were knocked out by our artillery, the assaulting infantry dispersed by our machine gun and rifle fire, and the attack repulsed. Meanwhile, on October 7th/8th, the 1st Canadian Division had relieved the 4th (British) Division (XXII Corps) on the frontage between Palluel and the Scarpe River, and passed under the command of the GOC, XXII Corps.

At 5:00 pm, October 11, I handed over command of the Corps front (less the 11th Divisional sector) to the GOC, XXII Corps, and the 2nd Canadian and the 49th and 51st Divisions were transferred to the XXII Corps. At the same hour I assumed command of the former XXII Corps front, and the 56th and the 1st Canadian Divisions were transferred in the line to the Canadian Corps. During the night of October 11th/12th the 2nd Canadian division was relieved in the line east of the Iwuy–Denain railway by the 51st (Highland) Division, and on completion of the relief I assumed command of the remainder of the 2nd Canadian Divisional front, extending from the Iwuy–Denain railway exclusive, to the Canal de l'Escaut.

The battle of Arras-Cambrai, so fruitful in results, was now closed. Since August 26 the Canadian Corps had advanced twenty-three miles, fighting for every foot of ground and overcoming the most bitter resistance. In that period the Canadian Corps engaged and defeated decisively thirty-one German Divisions, reinforced by numerous Marksmen Machine Gun Companies. These divisions were met in strongly fortified positions and under conditions most favourable to the defence. In this battle 18,585 prisoners were captured by us, together with 371 guns, 1,923 machine guns and many trench mortars. Over 116 square miles of French soil, containing fifty-four towns and villages, and including the city of Cambrai, were liberated. The severity of the fighting and the heroism of our troops may be gathered from the casualties suffered between August 22 and October 11, and which are as follows:

	Officers	Other Ranks
Killed	296	4,071
Missing	18	1,912
Wounded	1,230	23,279
TOTAL:	1,544	29,262

Considering the great number of German divisions engaged and the tremendous artillery and machine gun fire power at their disposal, the comparative lightness of our casualties testified to the excellence of the precautions taken by divisional, brigade, and regimental officers to minimise the loss of life, having ever in mind the performance of their duty and the accomplishment of their heavy task.

General Situation

While the Canadian Corps was tenaciously fighting to break through the hinge of the Hindenburg System of defence, the Third and Fourth British Armies were pushing forward through the devastated areas in the Somme, meeting everywhere strong and determined rearguards. The outer defences of the Hinderburg Line were captured by them on September 18 and 19, and a good position secured for the assault of the main defences.

The storming of the Canal du Nord Line, which brought the Canadian Corps definitely behind the areas organized for defence, was immediately followed by the capture of the main Hindenburg Line on the fronts of the Third and Fourth Armies, and on October 8 and 10 the Canal de l'Escaut was crossed north of Cambrai. Cambrai was seized and the German rearguards pushed back in open country to the Selle River.

The Germans were falling back everywhere; they had now evacuated completely the Lys salient and a portion of the ground east and south of Lens, but they were still holding a line west of Lille–Douai and along the Canal de la Sensée.

The Canadian Corps, although tired and depleted in numbers, began to push forward as soon as it had taken over the new front on the Canal de la Sensée south of Douai. On October 14 the Second Army, in conjunction with the Belgian armies and French detachments, attacked the northern part of the salient and precipitated the German retreat.

OPERATIONS: DOUAI-MONS

The Battle Front

The new front of the Canadian Corps (at 5:00 pm, October 11) extended from Iwuy–Denain railway, north of Iwuy, to the Canal de l'Escaut at Estrun, thence following the southern bank of the Canal de la Sensée to Palluel, thence crossing the Sensée River at Hamel to the Scarpe River east of Vitry. The front was held by the 2nd Canadian Division from the right to the Canal de l'Escaut—the 11th Division from Estrun (inclusive) to Aubencheul-au-Bac (exclusive)—the 56th Division from Aubencheul-au-Bac (inclusive) to Palluel (inclusive), and the 1st Canadian Division from Palluel (exclusive) to the western boundary (see Sketch Number 12).

The fronts of the 11th and 56th Divisions were then stationary, but on the front of the 1st Canadian Division crossings had been forced over the Sensée and Trinquis Rivers that morning, and the enemy was retiring, closely followed by battle patrols of the 1st Canadian Division.

> The 1st Canadian Division had relieved the 4th British Division in the line along the south side of the valleys of the Sensée and Trinquis Rivers, from Palluel exclusive to the Scarpe, during the nights October 5th/6th and 6th/7th, coming under orders of the XXII Corps.

> The front had been a quiet one, the river valleys having been flooded by the enemy to an average width of from 300 to 400 yards, and the bridges destroyed.

> The enemy was expected to withdraw shortly, and this barrage was repeated daily at dawn with the object of harassing the enemy and testing his strength. At 3:00 am, October 10, battle patrols were pushed out by 3rd Canadian Infantry Brigade (Brigadier General G.S. Tuxford) from the bridgehead at Sailly, and after capturing the village they entered the Drocourt–Quéant Line to the northeast. Thirty prisoners and six machine guns were sent back from Sailly at daylight; a strong enemy counter-attack (estimated at two battalions) overran the force at the Drocourt–Quéant Line and recaptured Sailly, driving our line back to the line previously held.

> On October 11, in conjunction with an attack on the left by the 8th, our troops forced their way over the narrow crossings of the Sensée and Trinquis Rivers in the face of considerable machine gun fire and pushed northwards and eastwards, meeting only resistance from isolated machine gun nests. The performance of the first patrols in forcing their way across the narrow causeways, all stoutly defended by machine guns, was a splendid achievement.

By the night of October 11 the 1st Canadian Division, on the left, had reached the line Hamel–Estrées–Noyelles (all inclusive), and at dawn, October 12, pushed forward, clearing Arleux and reaching the west bank of the canal from Palluel to the Scarpe.

On October 12 the line remained stationary between the Canal du Nord and the Canal de l'Escaut. East of the Canal de l'Escaut the 2nd Canadian Division attacked at noon in conjunction with the XXII Corps on the right and captured Hordain. Attempts to push forward to Basseville were, however, stopped by machine gun fire. The restricted area and the inundated condition of the ground prevented further progress on this front until the troops on the right could get forward.

It was apparent from many indications that the enemy was preparing to carry out a withdrawal on a large scale. Prisoners reported the evacuation of civilians and the removal or destruction of all stores, also that roads and railways had been prepared for demolition. These statements were confirmed by our observers, who reported numerous and frequent explosions and fires behind the enemy's lines.

On the Canadian Corps' front, the divisions in the line were confronted by the Canal de la Sensée, and this in its flooded condition was a serious obstacle, the few crossings possible being narrow and easily defended. Orders were issued, however, that a policy of aggressive patrolling should be adopted to detect at the earliest moment any retirement, and that all preparations should be made for an immediate and rapid pursuit. Our patrols were most daring during the next few days, but no weak spot was to be found along the enemy front, our attempts at crossing the canal being stopped by heavy machine gun and rifle fire.

During the night October 12th/13th the 2nd Canadian Division, extended its left to Aubencheul-au-Bac exclusive, relieving the 11th Division in the line, with the 4th Canadian Infantry Brigade (Brigadier General G.E. McCuaig) on the right, and the 6th Canadian Infantry Brigade (Brigadier General A. Ross) on the left. At this stage the GOC 56th Division represented that his troops were too weak and tired to carry out the vigorous pursuit required in case of an enemy withdrawal. The 4th Canadian Division was, therefore, ordered to relieve the 56th Division by the morning of October 16, and in the meantime to place one brigade at the disposal of the GOC 56th Division to be used in following up the enemy. On October 13 the 10th Canadian Infantry Brigade, which had been resting in Arras, was accordingly moved up to Marquion, and came into reserve under the 56th Division.

During the early morning of October 13 the 56th Division crossed the canal and succeeded in establishing a bridgehead at Aubigny-au-Bac, capturing the village with 201 prisoners. At 10:00 pm the following night, however, an enemy counter-attack in strength caused our withdrawal from the village, but the bridgehead was retained. The relief of the 56th Division by the 4th Canadian Division was carried out on the nights October 14th/15th and 15th/16th without incident, and the former moved back to rest in the Arras–Haute Avesnes–Maroeuil area, coming into army reserve. Patrols of the 1st Canadian Division succeeded in crossing the canal near Ferin, on its left brigade front, during the early morning of October 14, but meeting strong resistance, the parties withdrew, taking with them some prisoners and machine guns.

The Advance

Test barrages were carried out on the Corps' front each morning to ascertain the enemy's strength and attitude, and on October 17 the enemy was found extremely quiet and did not retaliate to our artillery fire on the front of the 1st Canadian Division. Patrols were, therefore, sent out on that front and succeeded in crossing the canal in several places, meeting only slight opposition. Stronger patrols followed and made good progress. On the front of the 4th Canadian Division, however, all attempts to cross the canal were still met by machine gun fire. After the 1st Canadian Division had secured crossings, a battalion of the 4th Canadian Division was sent up to take advantage of these crossings and, working down the east side of the canal, cleared the enemy on the 4th Canadian Division front, and enabled the advance to commence there. Further to the right, at Hem Lenglet, the 2nd Canadian Division succeeded in crossing the canal later in the day, and patrols were pushed on in the direction of Wasnes-au-Bac. Only enemy rearguards were encountered during the day, and the opposition was nowhere heavy, although more organized and stubborn on the right opposite the 2nd Canadian Division.

By 6:00 am, October 18, practically all the infantry of the 1st and 4th Canadian Divisions and several battalions of the 2nd Canadian Division were across the canal, and the following towns had been liberated: Ferin, Courchelettes, Goeulzin, Le Racquet, Villers-au-Tertre, Cantin, Roucourt, Brunemont, Aubigny-au-Bac, Féchain, Fressain, Bugnicourt, and Hem Lenglet.

During that day two armoured cars, one squadron of the Canadian Light Horse, and one company of Canadian Corps cyclists from Brutinel's Brigade, were attached to each of the 1st and 4th Canadian Divisions to assist in the pursuit of the enemy. These troops rendered valuable service to the divisions to which they were attached, although the enemy's very complete road destruction prevented the armoured cars from operating to their full extent.

Throughout the advance now begun a great amount of work was thrown upon the engineers, and their resources in men and material were taxed to the utmost. The enemy's demolition had been very well planned and thoroughly carried out, all bridges over the canals and streams being destroyed, every crossroad and road junction rendered impassable by the blowing of large mines, and the railways, light and standard, blown up at frequent intervals. The enemy also considerably impeded our progress by his clever manipulation of the water levels in the canals which he controlled.

Footbridges were first thrown across the canal, and these were quickly followed by heavier types of bridges to carry battalion transport and artillery, and in addition eight heavy traffic bridges, ranging in length from ninety to 160 feet, were at once put under way. On the front of the 1st Canadian Division on the left the enemy drained the canal, and it was found impossible to complete and use the pontoon bridges first commenced.

The engineers in the forward area concentrated their efforts on road repair, craters being quickly filled in, for the most part with material gathered on the spot and found in enemy dumps. In addition, the whole areas were searched immediately after their occupation, many 'booby traps' and delayed action mines being discovered and rendered harmless, and all water supply sources being tested.

It was clear from the wholesale destruction of roads and railways that the reconstruction of communications would be very slow and that it would be difficult to keep our troops supplied. Canadian railway troops were brought up, and, as soon as the enemy had been cleared away from the canal, work was commenced on the repairing of the standard gauge railway forward from Sauchy Lestree. The construction of a railway bridge over the canal at Aubencheul-au-Bac was immediately commenced.

The enemy retirement now extended considerably north of our front, and the VIII Corps on our left began to move forward. During October 18 rapid and fairly easy progress was made, and the following towns and villages were liberated from the enemy: Dechy, Sin-le-Noble, Guesnain, Montigny, Pecquencourt,

Loffre, Lewarde, Erchin, Masny, Ecaillon, Marquette, Wasnes-au-Bac and the western portions of Auberchicourt and Monchecourt.

During the day the advance had carried us into a large industrial area, and well-built towns became more frequent. It also liberated the first of a host of civilians, 2,000 being found in Pecquencourt and a few in Auberchicourt. These people had been left by the retiring enemy without food, and faced as we were by an ever-lengthening line of communication, and with only one bridge yet available for anything but horse transport, the work of the supply services was greatly increased. This additional burden was, however, cheerfully accepted, and the liberated civilians, whose numbers exceeded 70,000 before Valenciennes was reached, as well as our rapidly advancing troops, were at no time without a regular supply of food.

On October 19 the advance was continued on the whole Corps' front, nearly forty towns and villages being wrested from the enemy, including the large town of Denain. The XXII Corps, advancing on our right from the south, gained touch with the 4th Canadian Division just east of Denain on the evening of October 19, pinching out the 2nd Canadian Division, which was then concentrated in the Auberchicourt area, where good billets were available. In spite of bad weather and increased resistance more ground was gained on the 20th, and the villages of Hasnon, Les Faux, Wallers, and Haveluy, with a large population, were freed.

During the day resistance had stiffened all along the line. The ground over which we were advancing was very flat, and there was no tactical advantage to be gained by pushing forward, and a further advance would also increase the difficulties of supply. In addition, on the left, the VIII Corps had not been able to cope with the supply question and had not advanced in conformity with our progress. In view of these considerations, orders were issued that divisions were to maintain touch with the enemy without becoming involved in heavy fighting. For a time on the 20th the 4th Canadian Division was held up just east of Denain by machine gun and artillery fire, and it was not until late in the afternoon that our troops could make progress there.

Continuing the advance on the 21st, a footing was gained in the Foret-de-Vicoigne, and the following villages were captured: Aremberg, Oisy, Herin, Rouvignes, Aubry, Petite Forêt, Anzin, Prouvy, Bellaing, and Wavrechain. As on the previous day, all these villages contained civilians, who subsequently suffered considerably from deliberate hostile shelling. The 1st Canadian Division had now been in the line for two weeks without having an opportunity to rest and

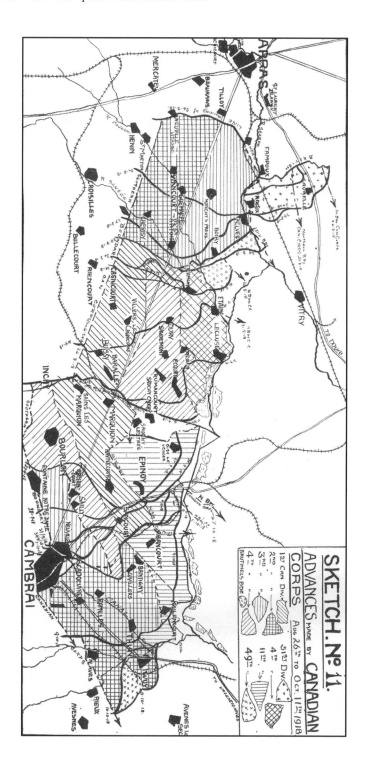

refit since the hard-fought battle of the Canal du Nord, and orders were issued for its relief by the 3rd Canadian Division. At dawn on the 22nd, in order that touch with the enemy be maintained, the 1st Canadian Division pushed forward. Following closely, the 3rd Canadian Division passed through the 1st Canadian Division during the forenoon, on the left brigade front, about 9:00 am, on the line of the St. Amand–Raismes road, and on the right about 12 noon on the line of the St. Amand–Raismes railway, the Forêt de Vicoigne having been cleared of the enemy. On relief, the 1st Canadian Division came into rest billets in the Somain–Pecquencourt–Masny area.

The 3rd and 4th Canadian Divisions pushed on during the 22nd, and by nightfall Trith St. Leger, La Vignoble, La Sentinelle, Waast-le-Haut, Beauvrages, Bruay, and practically the whole of the large forest of Raismes, were in our hands. On the left brigade front of the 4th Canadian Division the Canal de l'Escaut had been reached in places. A very large area northeast of Valenciennes and a smaller area to the southwest had been flooded, and to the west of the city the canal itself provided a serious obstacle. To the southwest, beyond the flooded area, Mont Houy and the Famars Ridge made a natural line of defence.

The XXII Corps on our right had been held up along the Ecaillon River, and the VIII Corps on our left had not been able to make any considerable advance, chiefly owing to supply difficulties, and were still some distance behind us. The divisions continued to push forward in the face of steadily increasing opposition, and by the 25th had reached the canal and the western edge of the inundated area along the whole Corps' front. Our troops had had a very arduous pursuit, and the railhead for supplies and ammunition was still very far to the rear. It was therefore decided that we should make good the west bank of the canal and stand fast until the flanking corps had made progress.

Attempts to cross the canal proved that the enemy was holding in strength a naturally strong position, and it was ordered that no crossing in force would be attempted without reference to Corps Headquarters. The engineers established dumps of materiel well forward on selected sites so that the bridges necessary to cross the canal on the resumption of our advance could be constructed without delay. It had become apparent that, unless the enemy withdrew, Valenciennes could only be taken from the south. The XXII Corps, on the right, had meanwhile succeeded in crossing the Ecaillon River after a hard fight and captured the Famars Ridge. They had, however, been unable to take Mont Houy, which commanded Valenciennes from the south.

On October 27 the First Army Commander outlined the plans for operations to be carried out in conjunction with attacks on a large scale by the Third and Fourth Armies to the south as follows:

The First Army was to capture Valenciennes. The operation to be carried out in three phases as follows:

> A. The capture of Mont Houy and Aulnoy: to be carried out by the XXII Corps on the morning of October 28
> B. The capture of the high ground overlooking Valenciennes from the south: to be carried out by the Canadian Corps on a subsequent date, probably October 30
> C. The capture of the high ground east of Valenciennes: to be carried out after (B) above, probably on November 1

Valenciennes would thus be outflanked from the south. The Canadian Corps would take over, probably on the night of October 28th/29th, the left brigade frontage of the XXII Corps (approximately 2,500 yards) in order to carry out phase (B) and (C) of this operation. The above attacks were to be carried out simultaneously with the attacks of the Third and Fourth Armies. In accordance with the above, instructions were issued to the 3rd Canadian Division to take over the frontage of the left brigade of the 4th Canadian Division. The 4th Canadian Division was, in turn, ordered to relieve the left brigade of the XXII Corps (51st Division), both side-slips to take place on the night of October 28th/29th, subsequent to the capture of Mont Houy by the XXII Corps.

The attack of the 51st Division on Mont Houy on October 28 was not successful. In the first rush the troops succeeded in gaining a foothold on the objective, but were subsequently driven out by repeated counter-attacks. In view of this, the relief of the left brigade of that division by the 4th Canadian Division was postponed. During the night of October 28th/29th, however, the 3rd Canadian Division relieved the left brigade of the 4th Canadian Division.

Capture of Mont Houy and Valenciennes

Orders were received that the Canadian Corps was to carry out all three phases of the operation against Valenciennes in conjunction with attacks of the XXII Corps. Accordingly, the 4th Canadian Division was ordered to relieve the left brigade of the 51st Division during the night of October 29th/30th on the line then held, and to be prepared to carry out the attack on the morning of November 1. In conjunction with the attack the 3rd Canadian Division was ordered to cross the canal and the inundated area on its front, and establish a bridgehead to enable the engineers to reconstruct the bridges leading into the city.

In the short period available elaborate preparations were made for the support of the attack. The position was eminently suitable for the use of enfilade as well as frontal fire, the general direction of the attack on Mont Houy being parallel to our front, and full advantage of this was taken in arranging the artillery and machine gun barrages.

The application of heavy artillery fire was restricted because the enemy had retained many civilians in Valenciennes and the adjoining villages. Strict orders were issued that the city and villages were not to be bombarded, with the exception of a row of houses on the eastern side of the canal which were occupied by a large number of machine guns. To hinder the good observation which the enemy would otherwise have been able to enjoy from the city and villages, very elaborate arrangements were made to place heavy smoke screens along certain areas.

Despite great difficulties of transport, the supplies of ammunition, bridging materiel, etc., moved forward were sufficient, and before dawn on November 1 all preparations were completed. The time for the assault was fixed for 5:15 am, November 1. The plan of attack was as follows:

> The right brigade of the 4th Canadian Division (10th Canadian Infantry Brigade, Brigadier General J.M. Ross), southeast of the canal, was to carry out the attack at zero hour under a co-ordinated barrage in a northerly direction and capture Mont Houy, Aulnoy, and the high ground south of Valenciennes, and then to exploit the success by pushing on to the high ground east of the city.

> Subsequently, the troops northwest of the canal (left brigade: 4th Canadian Division and the 3rd Canadian Division) were to force crossings north of the city and encircle it from that side.

At 5:15 am, November 1, the attack was launched, and from the first went entirely according to plan on the Canadian Corps front. The enemy barrage dropped quickly and was very heavy, but shortly afterwards slackened down under the influence of our efficient counter-battery fire. In the meantime the attacking infantry got well away, advancing under a most excellent barrage, and reached their objective, the line of the Valenciennes–Maubeuge railway, on time right behind the barrage. The fighting during the advance was heavy, especially around the houses along the Famars–Valenciennes road and in Aulnoy. The thoroughness of the preparations made for this small but important battle is better illustrated by the following striking figures:

> Number of enemy dead buried: over 800
> Prisoners captured: over 1,300 *(exceeding the number of assaulting troops).*
> Our casualties (approx): eighty killed and 300 wounded

On the left, the left brigade of the 4th Canadian Division and the 3rd Canadian Division had, in the meantime, succeeded in crossing the canal. Bridgeheads were established north of the city, the station and railway yards were seized, and the engineers commenced the construction of bridges. The enemy did not counter-attack against the Canadian Corps during the day, but continued to hold out strongly in the southern outskirts of Valenciennes and Marly, and in the steel works to the southeast until dark. Two counter-attacks against the XXII Corps front on the right caused some anxiety, but that flank was strengthened and no trouble developed

During the night the 4th Canadian Division took over an additional brigade frontage from the 49th Division (XXII Corps) on the right preparatory to the capture of the high ground east of Marly. Patrols of the 4th Canadian Division pushed forward during the night and ascertained that the enemy was withdrawing. In the early morning our troops had completely cleared Valenciennes and Marly, and patrols had entered St. Saulve.

The advance was continued in the face of stubborn resistance from enemy rearguards throughout November 2 on the whole Corps front, and by nightfall had reached the line Marly–St. Saulve–Bas Amarais–Raucourt Château, all inclusive. On the front of the 3rd Canadian Division the advance was particularly difficult, the country being under water except where railway embankments, slagheaps, and houses stood up out of the flood and afforded excellent cover for enemy machine gunners and riflemen.

Some stiff fighting took place when the advance was continued on November 3, but in spite of this good progress was made, especially on the right on the front of the 11th Canadian Infantry Brigade (Brigadier General V.W. Odlum), where the line was advanced 3,000 yards and the village of Estreux captured. Progress on the left was necessarily slower owing to the flooded nature of the ground.

The front of the 3rd Canadian Division had now become very extended, and on the night of the 3rd/4th a portion of it, from Odomez to Fresnes—about a mile in extent—was handed over to the 52nd Division of the VIII Corps.

On November 4 the line was carried forward about two miles on the front of the 4th Canadian Division. The 3rd Canadian Division was still forcing its way through marsh and water, and made good the Vicq–Thiers railway. On the extreme left of the 3rd Canadian Division a strong point east of the Canal de l'Escaut was captured and the Escaupont–Quievrechain railway bridge was taken. The village of Onnaing and the western part of Rombies fell into our hands during the day.

During the early hours of November 5 the 3rd Canadian Division entered the town of Vicq, following the capture of two points of local tactical importance west of the town. A large portion of the line of the Escaupont–Quievrechain railway was also made good, and the northern part of Quarouble captured during the day. The 4th Canadian Division attacked on November 5, and, clearing Rombies and the southern part of Quarouble, crossed the River Aunelle between Rombies and Marchipont, the enemy fighting very stubbornly to prevent our crossing. By this advance the first troops of the Canadian Corps crossed into Belgian territory, the Aunelle River being the boundary at that point.

The advance was resumed on November 6 and important progress made. The villages of Marchipont, Baisieux, and the southern portion of Quievrechain were taken by the 4th Canadian Division, while the 3rd Canadian Division took the railway station and glassworks at Quievrechain and the northern part of the village, and also captured Crespin further north. The enemy's resistance was very stubborn. The XXII Corps on the right were forced to give up a portion of the ground gained and to withdraw to the west bank of Honelle River at Angre, in the face of severe counter-attacks.

The 2nd Canadian Division relieved the 4th Canadian Division during the night 6th/7th, and the latter was withdrawn to rest in the Anzin–Aubry area, just west of Valenciennes. On our right we were now getting into the heart of the Belgian coal district—a thickly populated area, where the numerous towns and villages, the coal mines, and the commanding slag-heaps complicated the task. The 2nd Canadian Division, on the right, cleared the remainder of Baisieux, captured the sugar refinery northeast of that town, the town of Elouges, and the many small settlements that surrounded it. In conjunction with the 3rd Canadian Division Quievrain was taken, and an advance of about two and a-half miles made. On the left the 3rd Canadian Division, in addition to co-operating with the 2nd Canadian Division in the capture of Quievrain, pushed along the Mons road for about 4,000 yards and took La Croix and Hensies, north of the road. The VIII Corps on our left had still been unable to negotiate the Canal de l'Escaut. In order to better protect our rapidly lengthening left flank the 3rd Canadian Division was ordered to extend its attacks to the north, and, in addition to clearing the country south of the Conde–Mons Canal, to secure the crossings of the canal.

When the advance was continued on the 8th, the 3rd Canadian Division pushed troops to the north, and by noon had secured the villages of Thievencelle and St. Aybert. Later in the day a footbridge was constructed across the Conde–Mons Canal, and under cover of darkness patrols crossed and a bridgehead was established. Further south the 3rd Canadian Division had surprised the enemy in the villages of Montreuil-sur-Haine and Thulin at an early hour, and these towns were quickly captured. Pushing on from here the village of Hamin was taken, and by nightfall our troops were on the western outskirts of Boussu. The 2nd Canadian Division met with strong opposition. Good progress was, however, made, and by midnight the important village of Dour and the smaller villages of Bois-de-Boussu, Petit Hornu, Bois-de-Epinois, and a portion of the Bois-de-L'Eveque were cleared.

Resuming the advance on the 9th, the 2nd Canadian Division captured Warquignies, Champ-des-Sait, Petit Wasmes, Wasmes-Pâturages, La Bouverie, Lugies, Frameries, and Genly with little opposition. The advance made by this division was over four miles through densely populated areas, the twin towns of Wasmes-Pâturages combined having a population of about 30,000. By nightfall the 2nd Canadian Division was clear of the main mining district.

The 3rd Canadian Division had on its left front crossed the River Haine during the night, north of Montreuil-sur-Haine, and later secured a further hold on the north bank of the Conde–Mons Canal near Le Petit Crepin. During the afternoon, further troops were sent across the canal, and the villages of Petit Crepin, Ville Pommeroeul, Hautrage, and Tertre were taken. Further west, the patrols which had crossed the canal on the previous day entered Pommeroeul and Bernissart.

The 3rd Canadian Division had also occupied Boussu, on its right, before daylight on the 9th, and rapid progress eastward was made during the day towards Mons, the villages of Cuesmes, Jemappes, Flenu, Hornu, Wasmes, Quaregnon, Wasmuel, and St. Ghislain all being captured. The rapidity of our advance had evidently surprised and disorganized the enemy, although some opposition was met.

By the morning of November 10, the 52nd Division (VIII Corps) had advanced and relieved that part of the 3rd Canadian Division operating north of the left boundary of the Canadian Corps. The 3rd Canadian Division's advance on the 10th brought our troops to the southwestern outskirts of Mons, while the 2nd Canadian Division had reached the Mons–Givry road, outflanking the city from the south, but owing to the large number of civilians still in the city, it was not possible for us to bombard the town. To the north of the Conde–Mons Canal, a further advance was made and the village and Fosse of Ghlin secured.

During the night November 10th/11th the divisions resumed their advance, and immediately after dark the troops of the 7th Canadian Infantry Brigade (Brigadier General J.A. Clark) commenced to close in. The villages of Nimy and Petit Nimy were quickly captured and an entry into Mons by way of the railway station was effected before midnight. By 6:00 am on November 11 the stubborn machine gun resistance had been broken and the town cleared of the enemy.

The 2nd Canadian Division had, during the night, taken the Bois-le-Haut, a wood crowning a large hill on the southeastern outskirts of Mons, thus securing the right flank of the 3rd Canadian Division. The capture of this high ground forced upon the enemy a further retirement, and our troops, still pressing on, reached and captured St. Symphorien and Barthelemy by 8:00 am.

In the meantime, word had been received through First Army that hostilities would cease at 11:00 am on November 11, the Armistice having been signed in acceptance of our terms. To secure a satisfactory line for the defence of Mons, our line was further advanced, and the Bois d'Havre, Bois du Rapois and the town and villages of Havre, Bon Vouloir, La Bruyere, Maisières, St. Denis, and Obourg were captured before hostilities ceased.

Between October 11 and November 11 the Canadian Corps had advanced to a total depth exceeding ninety-one thousand yards (91,000 yards), through a country in which the enemy had destroyed railways, bridges and roads, and flooded large areas to further impede our progress. To the normal difficulties of moving and supplying a large number of men in a comparatively restricted area were added the necessity of feeding several hundred thousand people, chiefly women and children, left in a starving condition by the enemy. Several deaths by starvation, or through suffering consecutive to privation, were experienced in villages or towns which, being kept under hostile shellfire and defended by machine guns, could not be captured rapidly by our troops.

The fighting was light up to the Canal de L'Escaut, but stiffened perceptibly from there on until the capture of Mons, and added a great deal to the physical exertion caused by such a long advance in adverse weather. The table hereunder shows the average daily advances made by the Canadian Corps in that period:

From	To	Yards
Oct. 1	Oct. 12	4,000
Oct. 12	Oct. 17	7,000
Oct. 17	Oct. 18	5,000
Oct. 18	Oct. 19	12,000
Oct. 19	Oct. 20	2,500
Oct. 20	Oct. 21	5,000
Oct. 21	Oct. 22	6,000
Oct. 22	Oct. 23	3,000
Oct. 23	Oct. 24	1,000
Oct. 24	Nov. 1	3,500[1]
Nov. 1	Nov. 2	3,000
Nov. 2	Nov. 3	2,000
Nov. 3	Nov. 4	3,000
Nov. 4	Nov. 5	1,500
Nov. 5	Nov. 6	4,000
Nov. 6	Nov. 7	4,000
Nov. 7	Nov. 8	3,500
Nov. 8	Nov. 9	11,000
Nov. 9	Nov. 10	1,500
Nov. 10	Nov. 11	9,000
	TOTAL:	*91,500*

1 A note in the original reads, 'Held up in front of Valenciennes till after the capture of Mount Houy'.

When it is recalled that since August 8 the Canadian Corps had fought battles of the first magnitude, having a direct bearing on the general situation, and contributing to an extent difficult to realize to the defeat of the German Armies in the field, this advance under most difficult conditions constitutes a decisive test of the superior energy and power of endurance of our men.

It is befitting that the capture of Mons should close the fighting records of the Canadian troops, in which every battle they fought is a resplendent page of glory.

The Canadian Corps was deeply appreciative of the honour of having been selected amongst the first for the task of establishing and occupying the bridgeheads east of the Rhine. A long march of 170 miles under difficult conditions was ahead of them, but they ungrudgingly looked forward to what had always been their ultimate objective—the occupation of German soil.

Between August 8 and November 11 the following had been captured:

Prisoners	1,537
Guns (Heavy and Field)	623
Machine guns	2,842
Trench Mortars (Heavy and Light)	336

Over 500 square miles of territory and 228 cities, towns and villages had been liberated, including the cities of Cambrai, Denain, Valenciennes and Mons.

From August 8 to October 11 not less than forty-seven German divisions had been engaged and defeated by the Canadian Corps, that is, nearly a quarter of the total German Forces on the Western Front. After October 11 the disorganization of the German Troops on our front was such that it was difficult to determine with exactitude the importance of the elements of many divisions engaged.

In the performance of these mighty achievements all arms of the Corps have bent their purposeful energy, working one for all and all for one. The dash and magnificent bravery of our incomparable infantry have at all times been devotedly seconded with great skill and daring by our machine gunners, while the artillery lent them their powerful and never-failing support. The initiative and resourcefulness displayed by the engineers contributed materially to the depth and rapidity of our advances. The devotion of the medical personnel has been, as always, worthy of every praise. The administrative services, working at all times under very great pressure and adverse conditions, surpassed their usual efficiency. The Chaplain Services, by their continued devotion to the spiritual welfare of the troops and their utter disregard of personal risk, have endeared themselves to the hearts of everyone. The incessant efforts of the YMCA and their initiative in bringing comforts right up to the front line in battle were warmly appreciated by all.

I desire to record here my deep appreciation of the services of Brigadier General N.W. Webber, Brigadier General, General Staff, Canadian Corps, and of the generous efforts and untiring zeal of the general officers, regimental officers, the heads of all arms, services, and branches, and the members of the various staffs.

Fifth Period, November 12–December 31

Upon the cessation of hostilities and in accordance with the terms of the Armistice the leading troops of the Canadian Corps stood fast on the line reached, and examining posts were placed on all roads. Generally speaking, the policy adopted was as follows:

> 1. Our own troops were not to advance east of the line reached, and our aeroplanes were to keep at a distance of not less than one mile behind that line.

> 2. No intercourse or fraternisation with, the enemy was to be allowed, and he was not to be permitted to approach our lines.

In order to maintain the highest state of efficiency throughout the Corps, I ordered commanders to pay the strictest attention to discipline and smartness, and especially the well-being of their men. All troops not on duty were given every opportunity for rest and recreation.

The general outline of the plan for the advance of the British Armies to the Rhine provided that the Second and Fourth British Armies would advance, and that the Canadian Corps would form part of the Second Army. The advance was to commence on November 17 and continue for thirty days. The Second Army would advance on a two-corps front, the Canadian Corps to lead on the right. It was decided that the Corps would march on a front of two divisions, the 1st and 2nd Canadian Divisions leading, and the 3rd and 4th Canadian Divisions following.

At the time of cessation of hostilities the Canadian Corps was disposed as follows:

Corps Headquarters: Valenciennes.
1st Canadian Division: Masny–Montigny–Somain area.
2nd Canadian Division: in the line on the right, south east of Mons
3rd Canadian Division: in the line on the left and in Mons
4th Canadian Division: Valenciennes–Anzin–St. Vaast area

In order to concentrate the Corps as far forward as possible prior to commencing the march to the Rhine, the following moves were carried out prior to the night November 15th/16th:

2nd and 3rd Canadian Divisions:	Closed up in the eastern ends of their respective areas.
1st Canadian Division:	Concentrated in the area Thulin–Boussu–Hornu–Jemappes (west of Mons).
4th Canadian Division:	Concentrated in the area La Bouverie–Paturages–Wasmes (southwest of Mons).
Corps Troops:	Jemappes area.

The instructions for the carrying out of the advance to the Rhine were issued during this period. The conditions generally were as follows:

1. The country through which we were to advance was divided into zones, from each of which the enemy was to withdraw on the day before our entry.

2. The advance was to be carried out under active service conditions, and all military precautions against surprise were to be taken. During the march each column was to be covered by an advanced guard, and on arrival at destinations, outposts were to be established in accordance with 'Field Service Regulations.' Troops were to be billeted in sufficient depth to facilitate supply, but adequate forces would be kept ready on 48 hours notice to overcome any attempted resistance by the enemy should he oppose our advance.

3. The advance would be covered by a cavalry screen, one day's march ahead of the leading infantry.

At 10:00 am, November 16, headquarters of the Canadian Corps moved from Valenciennes to Mons, and on the 16th and 17th, the concentration being completed, the troops of the Corps stood fast, completing the final arrangements for the advance.

On November 18, 1918, the 1st and 2nd Canadian Divisions commenced the march to the Rhine (see Sketch Number 13), the heads of the columns crossing the outpost line at 9:00 am on that day. The 2nd Canadian Division advanced on the right and the 1st Canadian Division on the left, each in three columns. Each column found its own close protection, assisted by Cavalry and Cyclists attached from the Corps Troops. No enemy troops were encountered during the march, and the following line was reached by dusk: Haine St. Pierre–Houdeng–Aimeries–Roeulx–Haute Folie–Soignies–Horrues. The examining posts and outpost line of the 3rd Canadian Division were relieved and withdrawn as soon as the advanced guard of the 1st Canadian Division passed through.

The Corps halted on November 19 and 20, the 4th Canadian Division closing up into the area south and southwest of Mons, vacated by the 2nd Canadian Division, and the Corps Troops concentrating in and around Jemappes.

The 1st and 2nd Canadian Divisions resumed the advance on November 21, the heads of main bodies crossing the outpost line at 9:00 am, and the following line was reached by nightfall: Gosselies–Nivelles–Lillois road. The 3rd and 4th Canadian Divisions and Canadian Corps Troops did not move, as was previously intended, owing to supply difficulties. The Corps stood fast on November 22 and 23, all units resting and smartening up.

For some time past the question of the demobilization of the Canadian Corps had been frequently discussed. Having often conferred on this subject, not only with the general officers and staffs, but also with the men themselves, I had represented from time to time that there was a strong feeling in the Corps that demobilization should be carried out by units.

I now wished, before taking any further step, to ascertain definitely the desires of the Corps. To that end, a conference was held on November 23, 1918, at Mons, at which all-available divisional and brigade commanders, heads of services and branches, were asked to be present.

The following took part in this conference:

Major General A.C. Macdonell, CB, CMG, Commanding 1st Canadian Division.

Major General Sir H.E. Burstall, KCB, Commanding 2nd Canadian Division.

Brigadier General W.A. Griesbach, CMG, DSO, Commanding 1st Canadian Infantry Brigade.

Brigadier General R.P. Clark, DSO, MC, Commanding 2nd Canadian Infantry Brigade.

Brigadier General G.S. Tuxford, CB, CMG, Commanding 3rd Canadian Infantry Brigade.

Brigadier General G.E. McCuaig, CMG, DSO, Commanding 4th Canadian Infantry Brigade.

Brigadier General T.L. Tremblay, CMG, DSO, Commanding 5th Canadian Infantry Brigade.

Brigadier General A. Ross, DSO, Commanding 6th Canadian Infantry Brigade.

Brigadier General J.A. Clark, DSO, Commanding 7th Canadian Infantry Brigade.

Brigadier General D.C. Draper, DSO, Commanding 8th Canadian Infantry Brigade.

Brigadier General D.M. Ormond, DSO, Commanding 9th Canadian Infantry Brigade.

Brigadier General J.M. Ross, DSO, Commanding 10th Canadian Infantry Brigade.

Brigadier General V.W. Odlum, CB, CMG, DSO, Commanding 11th Canadian Infantry Brigade.

Brigadier General J.H. McBrien, CMG, DSO, Commanding 12th Canadian Infantry Brigade.

Colonel A. Macphail, DSO, CRE, 1st Canadian Division.

Lieutenant Colonel S.H. Osier, DSO, CRE, 2nd Canadian Division.

Colonel H.F.H. Hertzberg, DSO, MC, CRE, 3rd Canadian Division.

Colonel H.T. Hughes, CMG, CRE, 4th Canadian Division.

Major General W.B. Lindsay, CMG, DSO, GOCCE

Brigadier General G.J. Farmar, CB, CMG, DA and QMG, Canadian Corps.

Brigadier General R. Brutinel, CMG, DSO, GOC, Canadian Machine Gun Corps.

Lieutenant Colonel The Honourable C.M. Hore-Ruthven, CMG, DSO, GSO 1, 3rd Canadian Division.

Lieutenant Colonel M.C. Festing, DSO, GSO 1, Canadian Corps.

The question of demobilization was fully and freely discussed, every individual present being asked to express his definite opinion on the subject. All present were unanimous in the opinion that from every point of view it was most desirable to demobilise the Corps by units and not by categories. As the outcome of this consultation, a letter was sent to the Minister, Overseas Military Forces of Canada, embodying the sentiments of the Canadian Corps. On November 23 instructions were received that the Canadian Corps would be composed as under for the purposes of the advance to the Rhine:

Corps Headquarters
1st Canadian Division
2nd Canadian Division
Corps Troops

The 3rd and 4th Canadian Divisions, with the 8th Brigade, Canadian Field Artillery, and the 126th Army Brigade, Royal Field Artillery (attached to 3rd and 4th Canadian Divisions), together with the 1st and 3rd Brigades Canadian Garrison Artillery, were transferred to the IV Corps, Fourth Army. These two divisions remained billeted in Belgium for the rest of the year.

The general plans for the advance were amended, it being decided that only the Second Army would cross the Rhine and establish bridgeheads. This amendment was made necessary by the difficulty of bringing forward the necessary supplies owing to the thorough destruction of railways and roads in the battle areas, and the immense amount of work required to effect temporary repairs sufficient to take care of the needs of the army and of the Belgian population.

On November 24 the leading divisions continued the march without incident, reaching the line Velaine–Sombreffe–Mellery, and Corps Headquarters moved to Gosselies at noon.

On November 25 the march was continued, the leading divisions halting on the line Namur–Meux–Grand Leez.

The Corps halted on November 26. The weather, which had continued generally good up to this time, now broke, and the daily rains, coupled with the heavy traffic, greatly damaged the surface of the roads. During the fine weather it had been possible to use side-roads to a great extent for the infantry, reserving the first-class roads for heavy guns and motor transport. All traffic being now compelled to use the first-class roads, the two divisions had to move each in two columns for the march on the 25th.

On the 27th each division again moved forward in two columns. The dirty weather, very muddy roads, and the heavy traffic encountered—accentuated by the overturned lorries left inconveniently by the enemy—made the march that day a real hardship for the men; even the first-class roads were now in a very bad condition.

The general direction of the Corps advance was now changed half right, and the boundaries between divisions were rearranged so that each would have one first-class road as follows:

> *2nd Canadian Division:* Namur–Andenne–Chey–
> Havelange–Maffe–Barvaux–Villers St. Gertrude–Grand
> Menil–Hebronval–Bovigny–Beho.

1st Canadian Division: Lauze–Solieres–Modave–Hamoir–
Werbomont–Basse Bodeux–Grand Halleux–Vielsalm–Petit
Thier.

Commencing with the march of November 28, each division moved in one
column in depth, owing to lack of billeting accommodation in the sparsely
inhabited hills of the Ardennes and Eifel. The three brigade groups of each
division usually moved one day's march apart. By nightfall on November 27 the
leading troops of the 1st and 2nd Canadian Divisions had reached Seilles and
Coutisse respectively, and on the 28th reached Clavier and Mean respectively.

The difficulties of bringing forward supplies had meanwhile become more and
more serious. The railhead was still west of Valenciennes, necessitating a haul of
over 100 miles by road to the leading troops, and mention has already been made
of the congestion of traffic on the roads. As a result, supplies had been reaching
the units later each day, and the safety margin ordinarily maintained, of one day's
rations in hand, had been lost. The climax was reached on November 28, when
the rations for that day were received just as the day's march was commencing
—in fact some of the units of the 1st Canadian Division had already passed the
starting point. As the same situation recurred on the 29th, it was necessary to
cancel the march of the 1st Canadian Division for that day. The rations of the
2nd Canadian Division were, however, received in time, and the leading troops
reached Villers St. Gertrude by nightfall.

By securing extra lorries and utilising the lorries of the Canadian Machine
Gun Corps for supply work the situation was improved sufficiently to permit of
the continuation of the march on November 30, the leading troops of the 1st and
2nd Canadian Divisions reaching Ferrières and Regne by nightfall.

On December 1 the 1st Cavalry Brigade (1st Cavalry Division) came under
my orders, and I assumed command of the cavalry screen on the Canadian
Corps front. The 2nd Canadian Division resumed the march that day, the head
of the leading troops reaching Beho, and Corps Headquarters moved forward to
Vielsalm. The 1st Canadian Division stood fast, owing to the situation as regards
supplies being still acute.

The leading troops of the Canadian Corps crossed the German frontier on
the morning of December 4 at 9:00 am, the 1st Canadian Division at Petit Thier
and the 2nd Canadian Division at Beho, with flags flying and bands playing. No
advance had been carried out on December 2 and 3, but the marching divisions

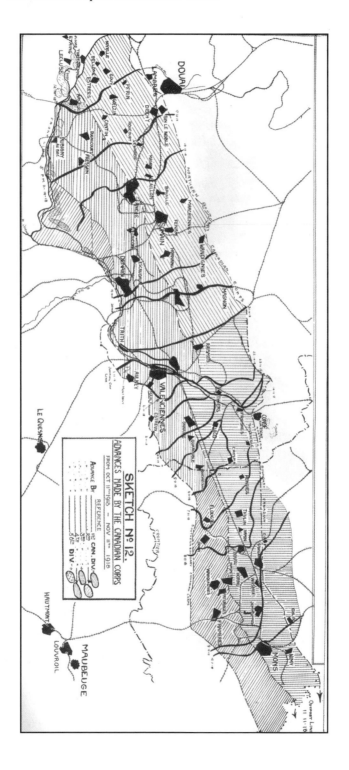

had moved forward and concentrated prior to the subsequent crossing of the frontier. I personally entered Germany, with the divisional commander of the 1st Canadian Division, at the head of the main body at Petit Thier at noon that day.

The completion of the march to the bridgehead at Cologne was carried out during the subsequent eight days, in weather that was generally very bad, without incident or trouble other than that of supplies. By the night of December 10 the 1st Cavalry Brigade had reached the west bank of the Rhine and posted guards at all the crossings, and the 1st and 2nd Canadian Divisions had reached points just west of Cologne and Bonn respectively.

The German people have been well schooled regarding the attitude to be adopted towards conquering troops, and our presence was marked by a quietness approaching indifference on the part of the inhabitants. Whatever apprehensions they may have entertained were quickly set at rest by the exemplary conduct of the men of the Corps.

December 13 was set as the date on which the Allies would cross the Rhine at all points to be occupied, and on the 11th and 12th the leading divisions concentrated as far forward as possible in their respective areas prior to crossing.

On December 12, the 1st Cavalry Brigade crossed the Rhine at Bonn, and reached the line Obercassel–Moholz–Sieburg–Altenrath–Rosrath–Lustheide (exclusive), establishing control posts on that line, and on the following morning the Canadian Corps crossed and took their place, while the cavalry pushed on to take up positions on the perimeter of the bridgehead.

The 1st Canadian Division crossed by the southern bridge at Cologne, the passage being witnessed and the salute taken by General Sir Herbert Plumer, Commanding the Second British Army; and the 2nd Canadian Division crossed by the Bonn Bridge, where I took the salute. The leading troops of the respective divisions crossed at 9:30 am.

The weather was bad, the day being dark, and a steady rain poured down throughout. In spite of this the spectacle was magnificent. The smart, sturdy infantry, with bayonets fixed, marching perfectly, with colours flying and bands playing our national airs, was an impressive sight, which did not fail to bring home to the German population the great potential strength of our army.

On December 14 and 15 the Canadian Corps moved forward and relieved the cavalry screen on the southern half of the perimeter of the Cologne bridgehead, taking over control of the roads and railways leading into the occupied territory, and being disposed in depth for its defence. I moved my headquarters to Bonn, the headquarters of the 1st Canadian Division being at Cologne and those of the 2nd Canadian Division at Bonn.

During the remainder of the year nothing of great moment occurred. The time was employed in preparing the men for the resumption of their duties as citizens. Great stress was laid on the educational work of the Khaki University of Canada and on the professional re-education carried out under arrangements made by GHQ. Each unit found teachers from their own ranks, and lecturers from both Britain and Canada addressed large audiences on varied subjects. A wholesome interest was fostered and maintained in all forms of sport. The greatest possible freedom from duty was allowed all ranks, and everything was done to brighten what all hoped would be their last Christmas spent away from Canada.

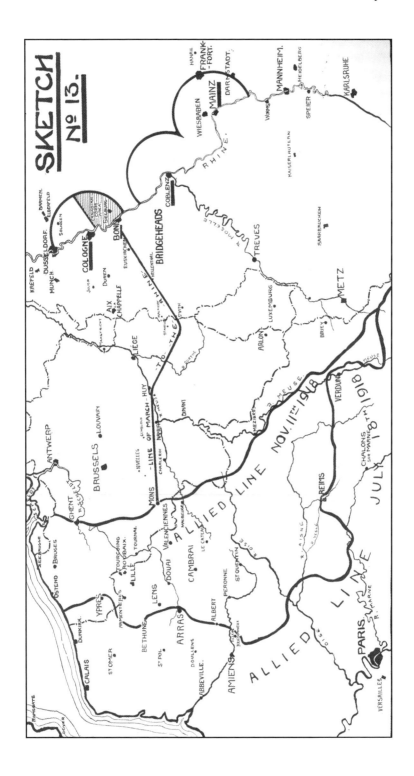

The victorious generals in Bonn, December 1918. Left to right: Currie, unknown, Major General David Watson, Major General Burstall, Field Marshal Sir Douglas Haig, and unknown (PA 4254).

Lieutenant General Sir Arthur Currie on his war-horse, Brock (PA 1574).

General Sir Julian Byng talking to Sir Arthur Currie in February 1918. Their body language indicates a close friendship (PA 2448).

Preparing for Passchendaele, October 1917. Left to right: Prince Arthur of Connaught, Sir Arthur Currie, Brigadier General Victor Odlum, and Major General David Watson (PA 2121).

Canadian stretcher bearers bringing in wounded at the Battle of Amiens (PA 2919).

Tanks passing through a field at the Battle of Amiens, August 1918 (PA 2879).

9 August 1918: Tanks going forward to attack Germans in the woods with infantry to the right. Note the German prisoners in the foreground (PA 3668).

Canadians entering Cambrai in the advance east of Arras on 9 October 1918. Note the smoke in the background (PA 3270).

Sir Arthur Currie and Major General Loomis in the Grand Place of Mons on the afternoon of 11 November 1918 (PA 3524).

Correspondence and Personal Papers

1919 - 1933

Ridge had to be taken. While the victory was an expensive one, I think you would be wrong in calling it a disastrous one...

Ever yours faithfully,

A.W. Currie

Currie to Lieutenant Colonel J.G. Rattray, 19 January 1920[4]

My dear Rattray,

I enjoyed your letter of January 12th and am glad to know that what the department has already done in the matter of reorganization meets with your approval.

The artillery reorganization has been agreed upon and will be published in General Orders in a day or so.

We found the gunners of the Dominion very easy to deal with. They willingly agreed to change their old numbers and adopt the numbers of batteries overseas, with the result that every battery which fought overseas will be perpetuated in a battery in Canada carrying the same number.

The cavalry and infantry present greater difficulties, but we think the scheme we shall shortly adopt will work out very well. Ontario presented the greatest difficulties. I wish some time that we could adopt the same plan with reference to the Permanent Force as we have adopted with reference to the active Militia, but there are many questions involved which do not arise in the reorganization of the non-permanent units—such questions as pensions, etc. One finds it harder to clean house in the permanent staff and permanent Militia than anywhere else. The result will be that I shall be disappointed in not being able to get as much new blood in the permanent staff and Permanent Forces as I at one time hoped. When the active Militia is reorganized, one shall have to watch very carefully the selection of the commanding officers, for if there is any intention in any quarter to make the Militia a political machine, the evidence of that intention will come to the surface in the choice of commanding officers.

I have become fairly well settled down in my work, but find that things cannot be moved with the same speed as in the field. However, one must keep on being patient and persevering. I know what I want, but hope for success.

I saw what Cluny MacPherson said in his speech before the United Farmers. I am very anxious to see Mr. Crerar and find out whether he agrees with some of

4   File 15, vol 5, CP, LAC. Brigadier General John Grant Rattray (1867-1944), commanding officer of the 10th Battalion.

his henchman who were talking about insidious propaganda and the ugly head of militarism, etc.

Some people cannot understand that the militarism of Germany is an entirely different brand to what we hope will characterize the military policy of Canada.

I shall always be pleased to hear from you and hope you will keep me in touch with the local situation.

With all good wishes,

A.W. Currie

Currie to General Percy 'P. de B.' Radcliffe, 2 January 1920[5]

My dear P. de B.,

Thank you very, very much for your letter from Cannes which I was more than glad to receive, and also for the picture which we both think is a splendid likeness.

I am glad you got away for a holiday at last and hope that you and Lady Radcliffe will thoroughly enjoy your stay at the Riviera.

I have just finished a long letter to Lady Byng and hardly feel equal to giving you all the news I endeavoured to outline to her. As you know, I got back to Canada about the middle of August and some three weeks ago took over my duties here in Ottawa. The first six weeks I was home, I spent in Ontario. I visited a great many places and addressed a great many audiences, receiving everywhere the most cordial receptions. We went out to our old home in Victoria early in October and there remained until about the end of November. We had a real good rest there and one's health has been very much benefited as a result. It seemed that as soon as one finished in England, one's health gave out. I suppose we did not realize just now much a rest was necessary. I have lost a good deal of weight, but have not worried very much over that.

We are now busy with the reorganization of the Militia, and I am most anxious for the early return of MacBrien. I can see no reason why he should be kept in England, but Sir Edward Kemp apparently thinks that MacBrien must remain there until the last dog is hung. I am sure the country would get the best value from his service if he were functioning here rather than in Argyll House. He is to be my Chief of the General Staff; Morrison is to he head of the artillery while I had hoped that Lindsay would be head of the engineers. Bill, as one might have expected, applied for a long leave on his return to Canada, and got it. When he reached the farthest distance away it is reported that he collapsed and now physicians advise us that it will take him quite six months to recover. While everyone would be sorry if his health went back on him altogether, still his case does not get that sympathy which in other instances might be expected. Morrison is getting along well with the reorganization of the artillery, and has been greatly helped by McNaughton. Walker has organized our Machine Gun Corps, and has met with much success. The reorganization of the infantry is causing most trouble. Some of us are determined to have the units which fought in France perpetuated while others seem to desire to forget the Corps and to keep the old Militia going as it was. However, I believe a solution satisfactory to all will be arrived at, but whether we shall be able to do very much training in 1920 is not thought very probable. I am greatly in sympathy with the idea of an exchange of officers between the old country forces and the Canadians, and possibly we can work out something on those lines next year. Whether you or Bill Thwaites survive, I hope that you will pay your promised visit to Canada in 1920, and that when you come to Ottawa, you will stay with us.

Lady Currie joins me most cordially in good wishes to Lady Radcliffe and yourself. I cannot tell you how much I have missed being associated with all the good fellows one worked with so long in France.

Yours ever,

A.W. Currie

Currie to Rev. J.R. Paterson, 8 March 1920[6]

Dear Reverend Paterson,

I do not know how I can sufficiently thank you for your letter of March 3rd. There are so many things in connection with the war that I would like to tell the Canadian people because such things would be of intense interest to them. I refer principally to the reasons why certain campaigns were lost, and continued. Yet one hesitates to do so because statements I would have to make would reflect on the conduct of the troops, Allied and otherwise with whom we fought. You can naturally understand one's diffidence; yet, at the same time, it is a pity that the Canadian people must go on with wrong impressions. No better illustration of this can be given than the Battle of Passchendaele, to which you have referred.

6   File 15, vol 5, CP, LAC.

As guardedly as I could, I tried to point out that in the summer of 1917, grave internal disorders had arisen in the French Army. For your private information I will go further and state that when General Gouraud, the one-armed hero of the French Army was asked what in his opinion were the most anxious days of the war, his reply was the days of the mutiny, for it is a fact that many tens of thousands of the French Army, in that year, were in mutiny. You can well appreciate how, under those circumstances, the British Army had to fight in order to keep the Germans from assuming the offensive. I gave the reasons for the choice of the British battlegrounds vis-à-vis the securing of the ports which were the German submarine bases. The Third Battle of Ypres, which began on July 31st, was a most bitterly contested battle; practically every British division was in it, and yet they had been able to penetrate only about six miles being stopped before the Passchendaele Ridge. It is not too much to say that the morale of the British Army, and of the British Government was seriously affected, and it was for the sake of the morale of the French Army, the French Government, and the French people, as well as for the morale of the British Army and the British people, that our Commander-in-Chief did take this Passchendaele Ridge which had withstood all assaults against it. For that reason, he sent the Canadians to that area, something which was a great disappointment to him, because it was his plan to use us in what may be known as 'Byng's Battle of Cambrai,' the battle which promised so well, but which turned out in a disappointing way because he did not have sufficient troops to carry it through. Every Canadian hated to go to Passchendaele. I carried my protest to the extreme limit, to an extent which the Canadian people do not realize, and which I believe would have resulted in my being sent home had I been other than the Canadian Corps Commander. I pointed out what the casualties were bound to be, and asked if a success would justify the sacrifice. I was ordered to go on and make the attack. You know that we were uniformly successful in the four battles fought on October 26th, October 30th, November 6th, and November 10th.

At that time I did not know of the disaffection in the French Army but the Chief many times urged upon me the absolute necessity of taking the risk, promising that some day he would tell us the reason, a promise which he kept when we met in Paris, at the Peace Conference. I know that I have been accused of volunteering the Canadian Corps for this battle. Such a statement is entirely untrue and is only repeated for the sake of doing harm to me. It is in keeping with many, many other statements from which I suffer, and all because I refused to allow the Canadian Corps to be turned into a political machine.

I am sorry that your son will not return to you. One hopes and prays that the sacrifices have not been made in vain. If they have not, much yet remains to be done by all unselfish, patriotic and God-fearing Canadians.

May kind Providence grant you every consolation. Ever yours faithfully,

A.W. Currie

Currie to Lieutenant Colonel J.G. Rattray, 22 April 1920[7]

My dear Rattray,

On my return from Montreal a day or so ago I found awaiting me your letter of April 15th, and note that you have selected as the subject for your address the events from August 1st, 1917, to August 1st, 1918. This gives you a scope for most interesting revelations.

You will remember that in the spring of 1917 there was fought the very successful Battle of Vimy, or as the old army called it Arras. This battle was continued somewhat longer than what Haig originally planned in order that by keeping pressure on the enemy we might help the French who had launched their Battle on the Aisne towards the end of April, 1917. You will remember that General Joffre[8] had been removed from the command of the French Army, and his place taken by General Nivelle[9] who had won great fame in the two battles fought by the French in the last months of 1916. On a day late in October, 1916, and on another day in December, 1916, they had attacked north and east of Verdun and had recovered in those two days all the ground which the Germans had wrested from them in all the months of fighting from February 20th, 1916, to the end of June of the same year. As a result of that terrible fighting around Verdun it is stated that over 500,000 Frenchmen lost their lives, and to get back that ground in two days impressed the French politicians so much that they decided to remove Joffre and place Nivelle in command for Nivelle had assured them that equal success would attend his efforts if plans for making attacks elsewhere were placed in his hands.

---

7   Ibid.

8   General Joseph Joffre (1852-1931) was Chief of the French General Staff from 1911–December 1916.

9   General Robert Nivelle (1856-1924) was Joffre's replacement in 1916. He was sacked after only five months in favour of Henri-Philippe Petain (1856-1951).

I may say that at the end of 1916 after the battle of the Somme Joffre and Haig had made plans for the campaign of 1917. Those plans were much upset in order to give Nivelle a free hand, and the French Government confidently anticipated that great results would follow the big French attack in April, 1917. You know how bitterly they were disappointed. The attack was an absolute failure, no gains being made and most frightful casualties were the only result. It was a very, very bitter blow to the French Government and had a most depressing effect on the French Army and the French people. Nivelle was relieved of his command. There is no doubt that the plans had become known to the Germans, and I have heard some Frenchmen go so far as not to excuse Nivelle from complicity in the loss of his plans.

In order to help the French the British continued their attacks in the vicinity of Arras, attacks which included our fighting at Arleux and Fresnoy. Regarding Arleux and Fresnoy it is a matter of interest that on the dates April 20th and May 3rd when these battles were fought the Canadians were the only units successful of the six British divisions involved. Later on in the year, that is in June, the British Army fought the Battle of Messines which resulted in the flattening out of the Ypres Salient.

Perhaps I ought here to make farther reference to the defeat of Nivelle and its effect upon the French. When General Gouraud, the one arm hero of the French army, was asked what were the most anxious days of the war he replied 'the days of the mutiny' having in mind what is so little known namely, that in the year 1917 more than 200,000 of the French Army were in a state of mutiny. The French people were sick of the war, and the French Government considered final success out of the question. They were willing to ascertain what were the best peace terms which could be procured. Under these conditions there was only one thing for the British Army to do, and that was to fight. They had to fight in order to keep the enemy from attacking the French, and so they prepared for the battle which was fought in August, September, October, and November of 1917, choosing as their battle ground the Ypres Salient. The reasons for the choice of such an area were briefly as follows:

In March, April, May and June of 1917 the submarine menace was at its height, and was causing our Government, our high military and naval authorities the greatest possible concern. It is not too much to say that had the menace continued at the same rate for another three months we would have lost the war. So the battle above referred to was put on having for its objective Ostend,

Zeebrugge, and the other submarine bases on the North Sea. The battle began on July 31st, and was waged with little interruption until the middle of November. When we went to Passchendaele in the middle of October progress that had been made from July 31st did not equal a penetration on all fronts of six miles. Compare that penetration with the penetration of eight miles in a single day on August 8th, 1918, at Amiens. Practically every division in the British Army had been involved, and more than 600,000 casualties had been the result. All efforts stopped before the Passchendaele Ridge and it seemed the latter place was impregnable. The army began to lose heart, and the British Government was very much concerned. It seemed to them worse than the Somme, and you know their cry after the battle at the Somme was 'no more Sommes.' So, at the beginning of August, 1917, we had this condition: the French Army practically useless and certainly unwilling to fight; the French Government anxious to see what the best terms of peace might be; the French people sick of the war; the British Army losing its morale and the British Government also very much concerned. For the sake of restoring that morale in both armies, and for the sake of restoring the morale and the willingness to go on in both governments and in both people, Haig decided that he would take this Passchendaele Ridge which had so successfully resisted all attempts at its capture, and he decided to put into the battle the only troops that he believed were capable of successfully carrying to a conclusion such an operation. That is why the Canadians were brought to Passchendaele.

Let me now go back to what we were doing after August 1st. In preparing for the battle at Ypres the First Army, with whom we were, were asked to make a holding attack opposite their front, that is, to make such an attack as would prevent the enemy thinning out his divisions and moving them to Ypres to reinforce the Ypres battleground. Whenever the First Army were asked to do such a thing they invariably called upon the Canadians and we were asked to do this job. We were then in the line from just west of Lens down south to Arleux for, I may say, although we took Fresnoy on May 3rd it had been lost on May 7th by the British division which relieved us on the night of May 4th–5th.

General Horne who commanded the First Army ordered us to make this holding attack to the south of Lens, advancing our line to the railway which you will see runs into Lens from the south. I went down there and reconnoitred the ground and became convinced that such an attack was not desirable for the following reason. I considered that when we reached the objective we would have a less satisfactory line from a tactical point of view than the one we were then holding. Secondly, I considered the attack as suggested would not have the effect of holding the enemy, that it offered no serious threat to his position and that he would soon see that it did not amount to anything. There are two keys to Lens and I may say our higher authority considered it would have a good morale effect on the French if Lens were to be taken. These two keys to Lens are Hill 70 to the north which was not on our front, and Sallaumines Hill which rises to the southeast of Lens. I suggested that it would be better to make the attack on either one of those tactical positions believing that if we were to fight at all we ought to fight for something worth having, and I suggested to the Army Commander that we make the attack on either one of these tactical features, but I also told him that I believed Hill 70 should be taken before an attack was launched on Sallaumines Hill. The reasons for my conclusions being that were we to take Hill 70 it would enable us to set satisfactory gun positions, thus enabling our artillery to better support an attack on Sallaumines Hill. Also that the observation gained by our holding Hill 70 would enable us to look in behind Sallaumines Hill directly on many of the enemy's principal battery positions. The Army Commander told me that he would have to consult with Sir Douglas regarding my suggestion and Sir Douglas himself visited the Corps to discuss the matter with me personally. He was good enough to say that he liked what I had suggested much better than previous suggestions and fully agreed with the desirability of attacking Hill 70 first, though he warned me that the Boche would never let us have Hill 70. You know the bitter fighting which took place there at the time of the Loos Battle in 1915.

Sir Douglas desired that the attack on Hill 70 should be made within a few days after the first attack at Ypres which was to take place on July 31st. I pointed out to him that we would not be ready, and his reply to me was 'my boy this is your own battle, attack when you are ready and I will hold you responsible.' We waited for the fine weather, and attacked on the morning of August 15th with entire and complete success. During the course of the next eight days the Boche launched against our newly won positions no less than thirty counterattacks. We identified no less than sixty-nine German battalions although we were employing not more than twenty-four. Not only did we succeed in holding the Boche opposite to us but he became so alarmed that he withdrew from the battle line of Ypres two divisions and put them in the line against us at Hill 70.

Sir Douglas Haig's telegram of congratulations to the Canadian Corps read as follows: 'I desire to congratulate you personally on the success with which you have inaugurated your Command of the Canadian Corps. The two divisions employed by you were successful in completely defeating more than four enemy divisions, and you have gained ground of great tactical importance.'

In later fighting at Ypres our intelligence gained information by which they came to the conclusion that the casualties suffered by the enemy in the fight at Hill 70 were more than 30,000. Our gunners have always maintained that they never had such shooting throughout the Great War at the enemy's personnel as they had at the Battle of Hill 70. Our own casualties were less than 8,000. In September we planned an attack on Sallaumines Hill and our divisions practised such an attack over the tapes but I may say that this was known, only to myself, to be camouflage, because it was intended to use the Canadian Corps in the battle afterwards known as 'Byng's Battle of Cambrai.' General Byng had often discussed with me the utilization of tanks in a surprise attack, and I paid many visits to him during the summer months to see trial attacks by tanks, and to further discuss the matter with him.

I may say that it was a very great surprise and disappointment to me, and to the Corps generally, when I was told early in October that the Canadian Corps had to go once more to the Ypres Salient. I have been accused of suggesting that the Corps be sent to take Passchendaele Ridge. My experience in the salient in 1915 and in 1916 were such that I never wanted to see the place again, and as I say it was a most bitter disappointment when the Army Commander told me that the Chief had decided we were for Passchendaele. I remember very well the day he told me, and possibly it was my annoyance and disappointment which gave me the courage to say to him that if we did go north we would not fight under General Gough who was then in command of the operations at Ypres. The Army Commander replied to that statement, 'my God Currie that is a terrible thing to say' and had I been a British corps commander I know I would have been sent home for making such a statement, however, we were sent north, but we did not fight under Gough. The line of the Second Army was extended and we fought in it under Plumer though in the same area as we would have fought had we fought under Gough.

We therefore suffered for all of Gough's lack of preparations and they were indeed countless, though we were spared being forced to comply with Gough's hasty judgments and the decisions of his incompetent staff. This was the same

Gough who was relieved of his command in the spring of the following year after the horrible retirement of the Fifth Army. We went to the north and our troops entered the line on October 22nd, although I had taken over and some of the troops were in the line on October 16th. I told the army authorities that in order to take the ridge we would have to fight in four stages or phases, and I nominated the following dates; October 28th, October 31st, November 6th, and November 10th. I was urged to fight the first battle on October 22nd.

I remember a conference held at my headquarters at Ten Elms just north of Poperinghe at which was General Gough and his staff and General Plumer and his staff. Gough urged Plumer to fight on the 22nd. I most persistently refused to agree to that date on account of lack of preparation, and I remember Gough's annoyance and his angrily asking General Plumer who was in command of the Second Army. General Plumer remained unperturbed and stated 'If Currie would not fight on the 22nd than the Second Army would not fight.' I did though agree to fight the first battle on the 26th, the second on October 30th while the other two dates, November 6th and 10th, remained as originally outlined. We were successful in all our battles and the Commander-in-Chief in his despatch dealing with the operations of 1917 states that the Canadians at Passchendaele were, for the third time during 1917, successful in taking all their objectives in accordance with their allotted plan. On our flanks the same measure of success did not attend the attack. On the north the troops who attacked with us on each day were unable to gain a single inch of ground, and although we won the ridge we made it a more pronounced salient.

The casualties at Passchendaele in the month from October 16th to November 18th were just under 17,000 a far different figure from the 25,000, 50,000 and 65,000 sometimes mentioned in Canada. I believe history will say that for the great recovery the casualties were high when compared with other battles fought by us, but history will also say that the Canadians never won a battle fraught with greater results morally, for I fully believe that had we failed at Passchendaele, as everybody else had failed who tried, there might well have been peace negotiations in the winter of 1917–18.

It had a most marvellous effect in restoring the morale of the French. They immediately awarded me a *Croix de Guerre* with palms and did what they did not do for any other general in the war, namely asked me to go to Paris to receive this decoration. I went and on November 23rd attended a banquet given in my honour by the French Government at the Hotel Meurice in Paris. Monsieur Hantaux the

French Minister of the Interior proposed to my health, and in his speech stated that he hoped some time I would take the title Duke of Passchendaele. The actual presentation was made by the Minister of War.

You know the conditions as regards mud, water, etc., under which the battle was fought. It would take too long to describe the lack of preparations we found existing in the area, and the very low morale of the extra artillery allotted to us for the battle.

I think I have here given you enough, Rattray, to add somewhat to the interest of your talk. The events of 1918 are very well set forth in my despatch a copy of which I am mailing to you. I will get Willis to look into the matter of maps and slides and see what can be done to help you out. Most cordially reciprocating your good wishes,

I am ever yours faithfully,

A.W. Currie

After the war Currie frequently received letters from ex-service men who were struggling to readjust to civilian life. He took the time to respond to almost every letter at length.

Currie to F. Nicholls, 28 April 1920[10]

Dear Nicholls,

I wish to acknowledge your letter of the 17th instant. I am sorry you have found it so hard to start in business again and I most sincerely sympathize with your desire for a loan to aid in that re-establishment. You case appears to be one of those which the Government of Canada might, with every justification, assist, and I have constantly urged them to adopt the policy which would enable them to grant assistance to deserving cases like your own. Apparently they will not adopt such a policy at least they have not yet done so, although a committee of the House is now considering the question again, and nobody knows what their recommendations are likely to be.

Your case and similar cases appeal to me very much. You gave up your business to fight for your country, and I think you are entitled to help in getting that business going again. You do not ask for a gift of money, but you most reasonably ask for a loan. I can do no more than urge upon the Government

10 File 14, vol 5, CP, LAC.

the adoption of a policy which will cover your case and cases like your own, of course, they will not make an exception in favour of one man.

Let us hope that the committee which is now sitting will bring in recommendations which will cover cases like your own, and that Parliament will approve. I am sorry to have to give you an answer which does not give you much assurance that anything will be done.

Yours faithfully,

A.W. Currie

Principal of McGill University,

April 1920–November 1933

Currie was unhappy in Ottawa—personally and in his work. He had been unable to effect the changes he wanted in the Canadian military and was appalled at the lack of funds. He also disliked the politics inherent in the position. In the spring of 1920, he and Lucy were ready for a change. When Currie was offered the position of Principal of McGill University in April, the couple leapt at the chance to escape Ottawa.[1]

Currie to General Percy 'P de B' Radcliffe, 6 July 1920[2]

My dear P. de B.,

...I shall not attempt to give you all the Canadian news which would interest you. In the first place there is a very pronounced feeling amongst the people of Canada that it is an inopportune time to spend very much money on the Militia. They profess to believe that the last war ended all wars despite the positive evidence to the contrary. They say that we have some 400,000 trained soldiers in Canada so why should we make provision for the training of any more. In these days governments, as you know, do not lead the people they simply try to guess what the people want and govern their policy and action accordingly. Consequently in our department we are very much hampered in what we consider necessary by the refusal of the Government to provide for the necessary finances. Although the statute provides for a Permanent Force of 10,000 our Government has agreed with labour that it shall not be more than 5,000. Owing to the lack of proper accommodation for our Permanent Force it is now very much less than 5,000. We have tried our best to make what we have into a well-balanced force,

---

1   Dancocks, 202-7; Hyatt, 126-36; Urquhart, 282-8.
2   File 15, vol 5, CP, LAC.

but yet I cannot get the Government to provide for such a necessary organization as a signal corps either camouflaged or otherwise. The reorganization of the non-permanent Militia has gone on very well. We have succeeded in perpetuating in the Militia every unit which fought overseas as such, but in doing so we have had to encounter and overcome considerable opposition for there are many men who apparently think, if judged by their actions, that the war was fought in Canada rather than in France. Then to, one has found it hard to clean out the Permanent Force as the operation should be done because in the past many of our permanent officers owed their appointments and their promotion to political pull. The same influences are at work to keep these officers in the force, whereas one is trying hard to make it a force which commands the respect not only of the general public but particularly of the Militia so many members of which know by experience what to expect and demand in a thoroughly qualified officer. However, I believe much good work has been accomplished and that good results will follow.

You probably would know personally the vast majority of the officers at Militia Headquarters here, and at the headquarters at the different districts. The appointment I hold is Inspector General and Military Counsellor. Really I have become a GOC in all but name with the result that I would be tied too much to headquarters. If the department brings its troubles to me, and had I been remaining in the service, I would have found it necessary to appoint another officer to do more of the inspecting. However, as you know I am going and the organization will be changed. I believe that Burstall will be Inspector General without a seat on the council. MacBrien will be Chief of Staff and first military member of the council; Elmsley[3] is likely to be Adjutant General with Ashton[4] as QMG, and Morrison as Master General Ordnance. Lindsay has left the service for good. On several occasions since returning to Canada he has been very ill nor is he any too well now. Andy McNaughton, formerly GOC, Heavy Artillery, is Director of Training and Staff Duties. I have found him a most invaluable helper and he will be even more so after he has taken the staff college course at Camberley where he is going next year. I am also sending over to the course Constantine, Hertzberg, and Cook who was a major in the RCR.

---

3   Brigadier General James Harold Elmsley (born 1878) was commanding officer of 8th Brigade (June 1916-May 1918) and later commanded the Canadian expedition to Vladivostok.

4   Lieutenant General Ernest Charles Ashton (1873-1957) was the Adjutant General (Canada) from January 1918 to August 1920. He later became the Chief of the General Staff (1935-38) and was Inspector General of Canada's Military Forces (1939-41).

I suppose you have wondered at my going as Principal of McGill University. I was pressed very hard to accept the appointment and did so with great diffidence realising my lack of academic qualifications. I believe though that the opportunities for useful service to Canada and to Canadians are greater at McGill than in my present position. Furthermore, the financial reward is very much greater. I hope, therefore, to welcome Lady Radcliffe and yourself in Montreal some day rather than in Ottawa.

My wife is very much pleased at the prospect of going to Montreal. It is the largest city in Canada and the most important. It has been exceedingly kind to us and we like very much the people who live there.

Please remember me kindly to General Byng, to Tim Harrington, to Lyndon Bell and to any of my friends in the War Office. I should be glad indeed to have a letter from you if ever so short.

With all best wishes to Lady Radcliffe and yourself, I am, dear P. de B.,

A.W. Currie

Currie to Brigadier General Victor Odlum, 10 March 1921[5]

My dear Odlum,

...I was sorry that during my trip to Vancouver last fall we did not get together for an old fashioned chat. I remained in the hotel throughout my last afternoon there fully expecting that you would return. While there I heard a rumour, which was more or less confirmed by press comments, that you were going to run for the Liberal Party in the City of Vancouver. I fully expected this would happen and was disappointed in one way when you did not contest the seat. In another way I was not sorry because your action disclosed to me that you were not moving hurriedly in any plans that you have for the future and that you were restraining your impetuosity.

If you ever come east I hope that you will find time to spend a day or two with me in Montreal. There are many things about which I would like to talk with you.

Personally I am very happy here. I cannot tell you how glad I was to get away from Ottawa, to get away from a government position. I always felt when I was there that many people regarded my position as a reward for overseas services. I did not like to be so placed, and I get a certain amount of satisfaction from the

5   File 14, vol 5, CP, LAC.

fact that any honour which is coming to me does not place me in any debt to the Canadian Government. I have received from them not even a formal vote of thanks, and Ottawa is perhaps the only city where anything like a formal welcome was attempted, which did not give me a printed address or a memorandum of the same.

I like Montreal very much, and next to living on the coast, would prefer to live here than in any other city of the Dominion. I like the men whom one meets oftenest here. I like the teaching staff of the university, who are a very interesting and self-sacrificing body of men. The association with the student life is fascinating and I know of no position in Canada which offers better opportunities for useful service to the common welfare.

I am going to England this summer to attend a conference of the Universities of the Empire, this will give me an opportunity of renewing my friendship with so many good fellows whom I met during the war. I shall take the opportunity of revisiting the battlefields and in this connection I remember that today is the anniversary of the 'Battle of Neuve Chapelle.' You were in the line on that day and I remember your battalion suffered the loss of Major...of the Kootenays, whose name I cannot at the moment recall.

Regarding the Governor-Generalship, I hope you agree with me that Lord Byng would be the most acceptable appointment. From what I can hear he has a very good chance of getting the position. I think it wise though that propaganda on his behalf should be unceasing. The Canadian press has been very kind about the matter, but it would be just as well if they would keep on saying fine things about him. In this connection will you please give me your opinion as to the advisability of sending the Prince of Wales to Canada as Governor General; he is young and unmarried. I believe that if his father lives and reigns for a good many years yet that we may expect to have the Prince as Governor General. I know the matter has been debated in England and some people there would like to know what some of us in Canada think about it.

Now I think I have worried you enough. Please remember me kindly to any of my old friends and to Mrs. Odlum, and with all good wishes to yourself.

   I am ever yours faithfully,

   A.W. Currie

Currie to General J.H. MacBrien, 23 September 1921[6]

My dear MacB.,

Since my return from England I have been wanting to write to you and tell you something of my impressions received during the visit.

I saw quite a number of our old friends—Haig, Lawrence, Currie-Burch and Travers, Clark, Radcliffe, Farmar, Webber, Ross, Hayter, Gavin and others. I also had to lunch one day, McNaughton,[7] Constantine, Cook and Hertzberg. They all seem to be getting on well, something which the teachers at the staff college confirm. Farmar tells me that next year he is going on half-pay, while Weber is leaving the service and going into business.

I went across to France and spent three days on the battlefields. Certainly much has been done to remove the traces of war's devastation, but it will be many, many years before the country resembles its former appearance. As far as removing the wire is concerned and the filling in of the trenches and shell-holes, that work has been practically completed. There are a few sections in the Vimy area and in the Ypres area where practically nothing has been done to level the ground. In many places the old German pillboxes still remain and are being used by the inhabitants as places of residence and as granaries. Attempts have been made to blow up these pill boxes but apparently they have been made to stay.

All the battlefields are in crop. The plains around Ypres were covered with grain stacks, while at Vimy cattle were peacefully grazing.

The Belgians seem to have done more rebuilding than the French. This is particularly noticeable in the farms, but perhaps that is because the Belgians lived in isolated farms, whereas the French live in villages. Everywhere east of Ypres new redbrick farmhouses are springing up. Quite a number of temporary buildings have been put up in Ypres. I suppose there are half a dozen hotels there, quite flimsy affairs, in the construction of which iron has largely entered. Not much building of a permanent character has been done at Lens, Bapaume, or Albert, but at Loos, I suppose there are thirty or forty miners' new houses. Some of the mines near Lens are already working. You will remember that at

6   File 34, vol 11, CP, LAC.
7   General Andrew George Latta McNaughton (1887-1966) was an innovative artillery officer during the Great War, Chief of the General Staff (1929-35), and head of the National Research Council (1935-9). In the Second World War he served as the commanding officer of 1st Division (1939-40), 1st Canadian Corps (1940-2), and First Canadian Army (1942-3). He was appointed Minister of Defence in 1944 and served as Canada's Ambassador to the United Nations (1948-9) and on the Joint International Commission (1950-8). See, John Swettenham, *McNaughton* (Toronto: Ryerson Press, 1968-1969).

one time it was thought nothing could be done with them for at least six years after war ceased.

I went down the main road from La Bassée to Lens, which runs across Hill 70. Just about where the Hythe Tunnel was an enterprising Frenchman has constructed an *estaminet*, one of the chief attractions of which is to view this subterranean passage which old Mac was so keen on putting through. I suppose 500 years from now it will form an interesting attraction.

I saw quite a number of cemeteries, some of which were completed. The completed ones are very fine. You know the layout of them as well as I do. On the headstones of Canadians there is a particularly fine impression of a maple leaf. I know that complaint has been made that the lettering has been poorly done and that already names are becoming hardly discernible, owing to weather effects. Personally, I saw no evidence of such and I would conclude that such a report savoured of exaggeration. I gathered from Goodland that there is a strong probability that he will be the officer who shall remain permanently in charge of that work. I knew Goodland in British Columbia before the war, where he was an officer in the New West Minister Regiment; which was affiliated with the Munsters. He was in England at the time war broke out and, joining up immediately, was sent to the Munsters with whom he served throughout, finally winning his way to the command of one of their regular battalions. He is a very good fellow indeed...

Speaking of cemeteries reminds me of a suggestion I want to make to you. I believe the old wooden crosses are being returned to Canada. I never approved of that policy but that doesn't matter now. There are a few crosses though, that units and divisions put up, such as the 1st Division monument at Vimy, the 28th Battalion at Posieres and the 1st Pioneers cross on the road near Courcelette, and many others which you will remember. These are made of wood and in a few years must tumble down, owing to the rotting of the wood. I do not think it would cost very much to replace them in stone, something which, I believe, the Graves Commission would readily undertake. The cost would be trifling. There would be no cost of the land, because the owners will no doubt leave the wooden crosses up as long as they will stand. I would be in favour of replacing these unit crosses by permanent stone crosses. I wish you would think about that.

I also noticed particularly the sites for the battlefields memorials. The one at St. Julien seems all right and the one at Great Farm has a very good location, but I think you should purchase a little additional ground there, not very much, probably about seventy-five yards square. If you do not, somebody will come along and put an *estaminet*, or some such objectionable building, on the ground to the west of your memorial, that is between it and Ypres. I hope I make clear what I mean. The site is on a knoll, but it should take in enough of the knoll so that no building is erected on the lower slope that would shut out the memorial. The one at Hill 61 and 62 is a splendid site and the road leading in to it was practically completed. I shall have something more to say about this road later on. Those at Vimy, Cambrai, near Dury and the Somme are all right. I did not see the one at Amiens battlefield and am led to believe that the site is not the best that could be chosen, inasmuch as it is situated rather in a depression and from a distance of half a mile or a mile would not be noticeable. I think, in general terms, that is an objection. The site should be in a place where the monument could be seen from quite a distance.

I saw General Hughes in London who told me that he did not think he was returning to France. I gathered that he was rather tired of the job, and if that is the case, I would consider it only a waste of money to keep him on. I think he has not had very much to keep him busy in France and that others there could now carry on the work very well. I know that possibly this is a matter for our Battlefields Memorial Commission to decide, but I suppose the Militia Department is paying him his allowance. You will, of course, understand, MacB, that what I am writing to you is confidential. Hughes has as an assistant to himself Major Pope. They were chosen because they are engineers and, I should consider, qualified to supervise any engineering work necessary. Yet I am told that when it came to making a road from the Ypres–Hooge road to Hill 61 and 62 near Mount Sorrel, a Belgian engineer was engaged and did supervise the work. If that was the case, and I am assured it was, there is 'something rotten in the State of Denmark.' What is the good of paying two engineers if an outsider is called in when there is any engineering work to be done?

To a casual observer like myself it also seemed as if Colonel Gagnon could not possibly have enough to do to keep himself warm. I daresay two hours work a month would be all that Gagnon would be called upon to perform. To me it is wrong and I know it is calling forth a considerable amount of adverse criticism that the Battlefields Commission should keep employed in France as paymaster to a few men a full colonel. He may have other work to do of which I know nothing, but in these days of rigid economy it seems to me that our Battlefields Memorial Commission might very well cut down the number of men it has in France. You would remember Ross, who commanded a Brigade in the 4th Division. He always struck me as a capable, painstaking and efficient officer and, I think, might do what is necessary to be done if Major Pope were left to assist him. I think that Hughes would like to be relieved and I know that Gagnon ought to be.

I must bring this letter to a close as it is already too long.

I hear the most splendid reports concerning the reception of Bungo[8] and I am very, very pleased in consequence. I hope that when you come to Montreal you will make time to come and see me.

With all good wishes, I am yours ever,

A.W. Currie

Currie to Brigadier General Victor Odlum, 14 January 1922[9]

My dear Odlum,

...I was sorry Odlum when I learned that you had not been successful in the election in South Vancouver. Reports we had here were that you stood a very good chance for election. Ryan, as you know, called to see me when he was in Montreal. He gave me the factor contributing to your defeat. We discussed very thoroughly the matter which caused him to visit the Premier at Ottawa. I did what I could, and Ryan felt quite encouraged when he left Ottawa for the Coast, but apparently his confidence was not justified, because I note that the premier has apparently appointed his namesake the Hon. Dr. King, to the position of Minister of Public Works. I suppose it was considered that the claims of those who had been into political life for many years were superior to others who had not yet been a member of any house. I know Dr. King and he is a very decent fellow, and is a very good surgeon, but I have never heard even his most intimate friends claim that he had any superior qualifications, either as a statesman or as a politician, and I do not believe that the Prime Minister in appointing King Minister of Public Works has added very much to the strength of the Liberal Party throughout Canada.

Apparently the Liberal Party pursues the same policy as the other party, namely, that it gives its cabinet positions to those who politically regard themselves as worthy of reward.

8   Sir Julian Byng.
9   File 14, Vol 5, CP, LAC.

I am afraid Odlum that there is not very much to choose between parties when it comes down to the matter of getting the cleanest, most upright, most fearless and most broad visioned men to fill the important posts. I find no fault with the Prime Minister for endeavouring to give Manitoba, Saskatchewan and Alberta representation in the new cabinet. I am sorry that he did not succeed, but I would rather see him fail than compromise on principles. He and the Liberal Party have a great task before them, and also have a great chance as a party. If they do not try to create false issues as Meighen did when he sought re-election, and if they have any success in the solution of the main problems such as the railway question, the immigration question and the development of national unity in Canada they ought to stand a very good chance of increasing their strength in the country when they make the next appeal.

I see that King has announced that he intends to unite the Militia Department, the Naval Department, Air Service Department, and the Canadian Mounted Police Department under one minister. This is in line with the recommendation I made when I was Inspector General and to which I called King's attention after his election. I believe such an amalgamation could easily be brought about and that it will best serve Canada's purpose and that a good deal of unnecessary expense can be avoided...

Yours faithfully,

A.W. Currie

Currie to Major General A.C. Macdonell, 19 April 1922[10]

My dear Mac,

...Yesterday I had a visit from Skipper Hughes regarding the Vimy memorial. He wants me to write a letter stating that I would be in favour of placing the large memorial on Vimy. I have no particular objection to doing this and many arguments can be advanced supporting such a decision. There is just one objection to it and I do not know how hard such an objection should be pressed. If they place the large memorial at Vimy it will confirm for all time the impression which exists in the mind of the majority of the people of Canada that Vimy was the greatest battle fought by the Canadians in France. In my mind that is very far from being a fact. We fought other battles where the morale and material results were greater and more far reaching than Vimy's victory. There were other

10   File 33, vol 11, CP, LAC.

victories also that reflected to a greater degree the training and efficiency of the Corps. Vimy was a set piece for which we had trained and rehearsed for weeks. It did not call for the same degree of resource and initiative that were displayed in any of the three great battles of the last hundred days—Amiens, Arras, Cambrai.

However, Hughes tells me that the committee think now that Vimy would be a better site than Mount Sorrel, and when we remember that the Canadians fought in France for a greater period of time than in Belgium and that our greatest losses were sustained in France, I suppose that it is more fitting for the monument to go in France rather than in Belgium. If placed in France it might as well go at Vimy as anywhere else.

With all good wishes, I am, ever yours faithfully,

A.W. Currie

Currie to General Percy 'P de B' Radcliffe, 13 October 1922[11]

My dear Percy,

It seems a long while since I heard from you, but from time to time we have visitors in Canada who know you and are able to let me know something of your movements. I think the last I heard of you was that you and Lady Radcliffe had gone to Egypt, where you hoped the change might benefit her health.

I was also told that you were seriously contemplating an entrance into political life and I wondered what was the influence that could lead you to come to such a conclusion, nothing but an appreciation that it was your duty to do so would, I feel, induce you to take such a step.

Naturally all we in Canada have been very much interested in the Turkish situation and our interest has been somewhat personal because our old friend Tim Harrington has been so prominent.[12] He seems to have done very well indeed and I have no doubt he has. He is shrewd, capable, straightforward and always on the job, and I cannot think of anyone among our senior officers who would do much better than Tim. While not thoroughly familiar with the purposes of our policy in that part of the world, one cannot help feeling that British prestige has fallen when the despised Turk ignores our ultimatum and sends others, which we, apparently, obey. I quite realize how war-weary the old country is and how willing her people are to do much and sacrifice much in order to avoid war.

11   File 39, vol 13, CP, LAC.
12   The Chanak Crisis of September 1922.

France seems to have let us down very badly. Kemal,[13] like everyone else, must have early realized that there was no unanimity of opinion amongst the Allies or amongst the dominions of the British Empire, and of that lack of unanimity he took full advantage...

I am glad to tell you that everything is going very well at the university and I am liking Montreal more and more all the time. I hope sometime to have the great pleasure of welcoming you and Lady Radcliffe to our city and to Canada. Lady Currie sends her kindest wishes to you both and I also want to be most kindly remembered to Lady Radcliffe, and of course, P. de B., for yourself I always wish every good fortune.

Ever yours faithfully,

A.W. Currie

Currie to Lieutenant Colonel D. Tamblyn, 8 March 1923[14]

My dear Colonel,

Apparently I have no photo of my horse which shows the animal by himself. I am sending along two to you and regret that I must force myself into the picture.

The horse, as you will remember, was a very tall animal, strong shouldered, good carriage, red bay in colour. He was really not an officer's charger but a large hackney. I always called him 'Brock' short for 'Brocklebank,' but, as a matter of fact, that was not his registered name. The horse was sent to Valcartier from the stable of E.J. Howe of Vancouver. I remember at horse shows at the coast I had often seen him driven tandem and in these shows he was quite a consistent winner. I think probably the best thing for me to do would be to write to Mr. Howe and ask him to give me the history of the horse.

I can only say that he stood the rigours of the campaign in the most splendid fashion. I do not know of his being ill at any time. No horse stood the trip across the Atlantic or from England to France (and you know how rough that trip was) any better and few as well. He was a horse with a mind of his own, but we usually got on very well together. The only peculiarity that I remember was that if we disagreed while I was riding him he undertook to rough-ride me for the

13 Mustafa Kemal Atatürk (1881-1938) was a successful Ottoman military leader during the Great War and Turkey's first modern president.

14 File 43, vol 14, CP, LAC. Lieutenant Colonel David Sobey Tamblyn (1880-1943) was Assistant Director of Veterinary Services from 1916. Tamblyn compiled information on famous Canadian war horses which is now held at LAC.

next five minutes or so, but he didn't sulk long. I rode him at all the principal parades which I attended—the reviews by the King in England and France, the Field Marshal's reviews and also when we crossed into Germany when I rode at the head of the 3rd Battalion and also when we crossed the Bonn Bridge. I have a picture which shows myself and staff seated on our horses at the east end of the Bonn Bridge when the first troops went across. If you would like a copy I will get it for you.

I brought the horse back to Canada, where he now finds a home on my brother's farm in western Ontario. I visit my old home about three times a year and am always glad to know that he recognizes me. He immediately comes up to me, smells around my pockets for apples or some other sweet and kisses me very frequently.

With all good wishes, I am yours faithfully,

A.W. Currie

Currie to Brigadier General Victor Odlum, 12 July 1924[15]

My dear Odlum,

You will not, I hope, think me casual or indifferent because I have not before this answered your letter of last May.

I must, in the first place congratulate you on your election to the local legislature of British Columbia. It must have been exceedingly gratifying to you, as it was to all your old friends, to learn that you polled such a splendid vote in Vancouver. You will have an opportunity, which I know you will seize, of doing whatever one man can do to raise the tone of political life in British Columbia, something which I suppose is as necessary there as it is in the eastern sections of our country about which I happen to know more at the present time.

I often wonder, Odlum, why it is that so many men seem to lose their sense of right and fair dealing just as soon as they enter political life. It would appear that they are satisfied to act in such a sphere in a way which would be fatal if practised in ordinary business life. Is it the spirit of the age, with its premium on the power which wealth gives or is it the lack of morale teaching in our educational system? In the examinations held for entrance to this university every year we detect all too many cases of deception. Even in the university examinations the same low standard of honour appears. We also find low standards in our athletic

15   File 37, vol 12, CP, LAC.

competitions. Men are satisfied to win in any way whatever, until the true spirit of amateurism is in danger of being entirely lost. This is a matter about which I have many talks in private with students, graduates, and athletic leaders and you would be surprised to know the justification which is attempted of reprehensible practices. For instance, many students can see no harm in their accepting financial reward in exchange for their ability to play football and hockey. They ask me what is wrong in their exchanging that ability for an education which is something that will enable them to make more out of their lives. That argument is a subtle one and apparently very satisfying to a goodly number. I pointed out to them that in a financial sense he owes the university far more than what he paid in fees, because it is a fact that a student's fees cover between thirty and forty per cent of the cost of his education. I pointed out that they should be proud to represent their alma mater in intercollegiate contests and that the privilege of playing on the university team gives them an opportunity to serve their university, which they ought gladly to accept.

Furthermore, I contend that when men holding such views enter political life, where they have an opportunity to serve their country which they ought gladly to accept and regard as an honour, they will doubtless be willing to exchange that opportunity to better their own financial position. It is because of such opportunists in university life that I value highly the privilege of being associated with an institution like McGill. Every year we send out $500 or more to young men and women who ought, by virtue of their education, to be leaders in their respective communities and if they have the right ideals their influence ought to be very great and extensive.

Recently a great deal of pressure has been brought to bear upon me to enter political life, but I have steadfastly refused to accept the bait and will continue so to act. For it seems to me that the influence one can exert from such a position as this added to the influence one might have in such an organization as you outline, ought to prove as powerful as any position in political life and certainly much more pleasant...

Give my best and kindest regards to Mrs. Odlum and any of my old friends there. With best wishes and most cordial congratulations,

I am yours faithfully,

A.W. Currie

On 31 March 1925 the Montreal Gazette printed a story about the twenty-five Canadians who had been executed during the Great War. It pointed out that in comparison no Australians had been executed. Currie regarded the story as another personal attack on his character and he believed that it would fuel the long-standing rumours that he had wasted Canadian lives.[16]

Currie to Montreal *Gazette*, 1 April 1925[17]

It is most unfortunate that any such figures as those given in the cable should have been asked for and it is hard to see what conceivable good anyone can derive from the information conveyed. It seems, moreover, a little hard to explain why such a question should have been asked or answered in the British House of Commons without reference to Canada. The matter is one which concerns Canada alone.

The subject of military executions was always painful, was never discussed except when necessary, and it is lamentable to have it re-awakened. There is, however, another aspect of the matter. The answer given by the Secretary of State makes a most unfair comparison between Canadians and Australians. The governments of the dominions never gave up their authority over their own troops, but so far as discipline was concerned this authority was delegated more or less completely to the Commander-in-Chief of the British Armies in France. This principle was definitely stated in an agreement made between the War Office and the Minister of Overseas Military Forces of Canada in 1918. Australia delegated authority on this point less completely than did Canada. For one thing, no court martial on an Australian soldier could take place without one or more Australian officers being on the court. In the same way it was generally known that no death sentences on Australian soldiers were ever to be approved. While this fact was, so far as I know, never published in orders and was a matter solely between the British Government and the Commander-in-Chief and his Adjutant General, the situation was perfectly well known and realised.

I do not wish to make any reflections on the conduct of the Australians, but the fact that none were executed while twenty-five Canadians were proves nothing whatever.

16 Dancocks, 231.
17 File 31, vol 10, CP, LAC. It is unclear whether this statement was made in the form of an interview with the *Gazette* or whether it was written by Currie as an unprinted letter to the editor.

If the facts of the case are as reported in this morning's Gazette, I consider the British Government has committed another stupid blunder and struck a dangerous blow at Imperial friendship.

The implications of the article profoundly bothered Currie and as in 1919 he wanted the Canadian Government to defend his reputation. As before, the Government was content to allow the allegations against Currie to stand, lest any public outcry be associated with the politicians in power.

Cable from Currie to Prime Minister Mackenzie King, 31 March or 1 April 1925[18]

Consider this statement most regrettable and none which should never have been made. Matter is no concern whatever of British House of Commons. Canada delegated to Commander-in-Chief full authority regarding discipline. Australia required one or more Australian officers on all courts martial of Australian soldiers and it was common knowledge that, presumably at request of Australian Government, death sentences on Australian soldiers were never approved. A most unfair comparison is therefore established between Canadians and Australians.

Cable from Prime Minister Mackenzie King to Currie, 2 April 1925[19]

I brought representations of your telegram received yesterday to attention my colleagues all whom in entire accord with your point of view should any question be asked in our house you may rely on matter being dealt with satisfactorily unless question is asked we think inadvisable to invite further public attention.

Currie to Field Marshall Douglas Haig, 27 April 1925[20]

Dear Lord Haig,

I thank you for your letter of March 30th, in which you refer to your forthcoming visit to Canada, to the pleasure it will give you to meet again the Canadians who

---

18   *Ibid.* William Lyon Mackenzie King (1874-1950) was the Liberal Prime Minister of Canada (1921-26, 1926-30, 1935-48). King admired Currie and kept in contact with the former Corps Commander until Currie's death in 1933. See, Robert MacGregor Dawson, *Mackenzie King: A Political Biography* (Toronto: UTP, 1958-1976) and J.L. Granatstein, *Canada's War: the Politics of the MacKenzie King Government, 1939-1945* (Toronto: Oxford University Press, 1975).

19   *Ibid.*

20   File 29, vol 9, CP, LAC.

served with you in the Great War, and to the hopes you have that one result of your visit will be the union of all ex-service men's societies in Canada.

May I assure you, Sir, that a warm welcome awaits you in Canada not only from those of us who were proud to serve under your leadership but from the great mass of Canadians who do not forget that you are the general who led the British armies to victory over the greatest peril which ever menaced the Empire. I am glad that the British Empire Service League is holding its biennial conference in Canada. It will serve to give emphasis to the fact that British soldiers, no matter what part of the Empire is their home, are one in their service and in their loyalty to the Empire.

It would be a wonderful thing if all ex-service men were joined in one organization and such an organization could not fail to be a most potent influence not only for the welfare of ex-service men but for the welfare of our Empire. Unfortunately in Canada we have some half-dozen soldiers' organizations—the Great War Veterans, the Army and Navy Veterans Association, Grand Army of United Veterans, the Canadian Legion, and others. I suppose the Great War Veterans Association is the strongest one of all, but the membership of all of these organizations would not be twenty per cent of the ex-service men in Canada. That is, eighty per cent do not belong to any organization and, in my opinion, the union of the various ex-service men's societies now in Canada would not by any means be completely representative of the ex-soldiers in Canada.

You have honoured me by asking me to give a message from you to the various ex-service men's societies in Canada asking them to unite. With every diffidence and deference I submit that such an appeal would have far more effect if coming direct from yourself. I think that you should know that for some years past the different organizations above mentioned have let it be known that they were making efforts to link up in one large organization, but apparently no success has ever attended their efforts. The Army and Navy Veterans would be very glad to unite all the ex-service men of Canada in one organization provided they joined the Army and Navy Veterans, and the other organizations act very much in the same way. Each of these organizations have their paid officials and if all were joined together very probably some of these officials would have no duties to perform. The negotiations so far have been carried on largely by the officials and perhaps that is the reason so little progress has been made. I am a member of the Great War Veterans Association and the Army and Navy Veterans, but have never attended, nor have I been invited to attend, any of their annual conferences.

In my opinion the great majority of the soldiers in Canada will not unite under the auspices of any of these organizations, nor do I believe they would enter an organization formed by union of these. I may, of course, be wrong.

The Army and Navy Veterans Association is an old organization, is a respectable one and has always pursued a sane policy and does a certain amount of good. The Grand Army of United Veterans were formed to extract from our government a $2,000 bonus for each returned soldier. At one time it had quite a large membership, but it was led by a blackguard named Flynn who, while he reigned as the head, did great mischief inflaming men's minds against the government and against the officers. Flynn has been deported, but the organization still exists. The Great War Veterans Association has undoubtedly done the greatest work for the ex-service men's cause, that is, that kind of work which consists in getting satisfactory pensions and hospital treatment. This organization began in 1917 and unknown to itself was a political organization. I have most positive evidence that some of the wary politicians in Canada feared the political power of the ex-soldiers when the war was over and so they encouraged the formation of the Great War Veterans Association. The political fathers of the association injected a poison into the minds of the members and there began to appear immediately the men returned to Canada a most hostile attitude on their part towards all officers. This hostility most mightily surprised me when I returned in 1919, for there was no evidence whatever of such a feeling in France, although the propaganda was being spread there. This agitation was political, but yet it prevailed to such an extent that in the great majority of GWVA organization's officers were told frankly that they were not wanted.

The result has been that very few officers belong to any ex-service men's organization, although the feeling is now vastly different from what it was, but the ex-service men's organizations do not enjoy in the minds of the great mass of ex-soldiers and in the minds of the public generally anything like the esteem they should. On the return from over-seas every man who thought he had a grievance, who thought he had some back pay or extra pay coming to him, who thought the country was obligated to keep him forever, joined these organizations. The better men paid no attention to them and went quietly to work. So it has appeared to the public that the main policy of ex-service men's organizations was to get something to which they were not entitled. I believe that much of what they sought to get constituted a fair and just claim and it is regrettable that great pressure had to be brought to bear upon the government to do justice in the matter of treatment and pensions. Even now, in my estimation, the conditions attached to the awarding of pensions are altogether too rigid.

I am writing thus fully to you to try to make you understand two things: (1) that in my opinion, you cannot bring about a union of existing ex-service men's organizations; and (2) even if such a union were consummated, more than eighty per cent of ex-service men would be un-represented. I believe, Sir, that the most you can hope to accomplish is to plant a seed which at not too distant a time will germinate and grow into an organization which will be thoroughly representative of those who were your comrades in the Great War.

I regret more than I can say that I shall not be in Canada during the time of your visit. When I was first told of it and that you were coming in September, I arranged my vacation in order to be here at that date. When it was next changed and I was told you were coming in August, I altered my plans accordingly, but now the final announcement is that you are coming in June and I cannot change my plans again. I am sailing for England on June 5th and therefore shall not be here when you arrive. I greatly regret this but can give you the assurance of a very warm welcome.

Believe me, dear Lord Haig, ever yours faithfully,

A.W. Currie

In the mid 1920s the war of reputations was beginning to heat up anew as the first volumes of the British Official History began to appear in print. When the British treatment of the Second Battle of Ypres was circulated for review in 1926, Currie was convinced that the British Official Historian, Brigadier James Edmonds,[21] was intentionally diminishing the contribution of Canadians. As the former Corps Commander, he believed that it was his duty to right the situation.

---

21 Brigadier General James Edmonds (1861-1956) was an engineer in the Great War and the Official Historian. On the writing of the official history see, Andrew Green, *Writing the Great War: Sir James Edmonds and the Official Histories, 1915-1948* (London: F. Cass, 2003).

Currie to Lieutenant Colonel H.D.G. Crerar, 20 April 1926[22]

My dear Crerar,

Thank you very much for your letter of April 2nd and for the clipping from the *Times*. I had read the substance of it before in a despatch from the old country which appeared in our local papers.

I think there was much good sense in your remarks and I hope something will result from your speaking so plainly to the authorities at home. Perhaps I am wrong, but I sometimes get the impression that there are a goodly number of people in the old country who are anxious to maintain the status which existed before the war; that is, they wish the mother country to be sitting at the top, and on the tier below the dominions, little farther down the colonies, and so on with the other dependencies and protectorates. I am not fully convinced that it is the unanimous desire of many in the old country to admit us to equal standing in all affairs.

I think the spirit to which I am referring exists in the Army to as large an extent as anywhere else. I have just finished reading the official account of the first three days of the Battle of Ypres. I understand it has been somewhat revised, but even yet it is a most unfair and ungenerous document. If this is to be a sample of what we may expect in official histories, Canada and the other Dominions will be most bitterly disappointed. It looks as if the official history will determine that after all, while the Canadians may have been very fair fighters, they really were not quite the same class as what we used to call the Imperials. This applies more particularly to the officers. Of course, many of us were merely militia officers before the war and, apparently, history is to set forth that fact with all it implies. I notice you advocate that Canadian officers might look forward to being given positions on the unitary staff at Washington. You won't live long enough, Crerar, to see that an accomplished fact. With reference to the Ypres description, Duguid is coming down to see me tomorrow.

I am sorry but I am not going across this summer. Those trips to the old country cost too much money. I should like very much to have played you again on the Wentworth course and I should also like to see some of the cricket matches.[23]

I saw Alston at the Tiny Dinner and also Basil Brooke. It was a very fine affair and, I believe, quite the best dinner we have had. No doubt full accounts of it

---

22 File 21, vol 7, CP, LAC. Henry Duncan Graham Crerar (1888-1965) was an artillery officer in the Great War and commanded First Canadian Army in Northwest Europe (1944-45). See, Paul D. Dickson, *A Thoroughly Canadian General: A Biography of HDG Crerar* (Toronto: UTP, 2007).

23 Crerar was serving in the War Office in London.

have reached you before this. I cannot see how it can be carried on, because a Vimy Dinner without Byng would not be complete at all. There are always, of course, many officers to whom other battles loom larger than Vimy.

Please remember me very kindly to Mrs. Crerar and to the Browns, and to many of my old military friends.

With all good wishes, I am yours faithfully,

A.W. Currie

Currie to General J.H. MacBrien, c. 1926 [Undated][24]

My dear MacBrien,

I have read carefully and critically the draft of Chapters VII, VIII, IX and X of the British Official History which purports to be the story of Ypres, 1915, during the days of April 22nd, 23rd, 24th and 25th. I have also read very carefully the comments which Colonel Duguid, the Director of the Canadian Historical Section, has been called upon to make, and the pity is that it requires forty pages of foolscap to set forth the corrections which he feels must be made. While some of his comments are suggestions that the matter be arranged in a different way, the majority of them are positive corrections of misstatements the historian has made, corrections which must be made if this work is to be regarded as a serious history.

In his very excellent *History of the Medical Services of the Canadian Forces* Sir Andrew Macphail[25] says this:

> History is something more than record and something less than praise; it demands selection and judgment, judging events as if they were far in the past and men as if they were already dead; it implies censure as a warning, lest those who read may be misled. History is for the guidance of that posterity which follows and finds itself involved in historical circumstances which always recur in identical form; for history is the master to which all must go—history with its pensive and melancholy face.

---

24 File 22, vol 8, CP, LAC.
25 Sir Andrew Macphail (1864-1938) was a Canadian physician, author, and public figure. He served in the Canadian Army Medical Corps in the Great War and wrote the official medical history of the war. See Andrew Macphail, *Official History of the Canadian Forces in the Great War: Medical Services* (Ottawa: Department of National Defence, 1925).

I thoroughly agree with Sir Andrew that history is something more than record; that it requires selection and judgment. The historian must take a detached view of the events of which he writes. What he puts down must be accurate in every particular; it must be fair; it must be unbiased; it must not seek to put up one and pull down another, yet it must not hesitate to give full appreciation and even praise when such has been earned. Neither must it hesitate to set forth all the vital facts without reserve, but these should be displayed so that unfair, unjustifiable, or ungenerous criticism is not evoked in the mind of the reader. I am quite sure that the feelings of any Canadian, on reading these chapters, particularly those who survived Ypres, 1915, and served in the Canadian Corps throughout the war, will be feelings of disappointment, resentment, and even despair. Because there is a particular reason why this particular history must be written with particular care.

The war of 1914–1918 was the greatest threat ever delivered against the integrity of the British Empire; at the beginning and throughout it called for the most magnificent gesture in British history. Even before war was declared this Dominion gave the assurance to the mother country that in every eventuality she could count on whole-hearted support, an assurance amply and increasingly fulfilled, as the days went on.

The men of the First Canadian Contingent left the shores of Canada with no very definite opinion as to the cause of the war, its probable length or its results. They knew only that the mother country was in danger and they felt that their place was by her side. Nothing else mattered so long as they could help. They were not in England long before much criticism was heard and some doubts expressed as to their being of very much practical use. In the mind of every one of them was the determination that at the earliest opportunity ample proof would be given to friends and critics alike, of the fact that they were troops to be counted upon with confidence. Let me say at once that after the battle of Ypres they thought that generally they had succeeded, and I recall with pardonable pride that throughout the war the reputation and tradition of British arms did not suffer at their hands.

In reporting the part they played at Ypres, Sir John French[26] said:

> The Canadians had many casualties, but their gallantry and determination undoubtedly saved the situation. Their conduct has been magnificent throughout...In spite of the dangers to which they were exposed the Canadians held their ground with a magnificent display of tenacity and courage; and it is not too much to say that the bearing and conduct of these splendid troops averted a disaster which might have been attended with the most serious consequences.

I also recall a conversation I had early in May, 1915, with General Smith-Dorrien.[27] He told me that when he first heard of the gas attack and retirement of the French colonial troops he threw up his hands and foresaw the greatest disaster that ever overtook the British Army. He said that if every man in the salient had tried to get out that night he would not have blamed them, and when he pictured all the men, guns and transport crossing the few bridges over the canal, with a victorious enemy thundering at their heels, he shuddered. Then, he said, he got a message that the Canadians were holding on. At first he refused to believe it and sent his own staff officer to verify the report. He said that every message was better than the one before. He also referred to their action as 'magnificent.' You will search in vain in this historian's account for any indication, however remote, that the Canadians 'saved the situation,' or that their 'bearing and conduct averted a disaster,' and none of their actions are described as 'magnificent'

...The historian's account as set forth is unfair and inaccurate and must inevitably lead to serious Imperial consequences. I, for one, have sufficient faith in the fair-mindedness and integrity of British officers to see that justice is done, because I will never forget my intimate and wholly pleasurable association with them during all the long years that the war lasted. Many of my warmest friends are officers in the British Army and I recall with much pride and pleasure my association with them. No one will testify more gladly than myself to their worth as men and comrades.

---

26   Sir John D.P. French (1852-1925) was the Commander-in-Chief of the BEF from the outbreak of war until December 1915 when he was relieved of command. There are many books on French. See, for example, George H. Cassar, *The Tragedy of Sir John French* (Newark: University of Delaware, 1985).
27   General Horace Smith-Dorrien (1858-1930) was the commander of II Corps and later Second Army.

I understand that this is a second draft and that it was only after some pressure that the historian was induced to submit this second draft for Canadian comment. I can only say that it would have been nothing short of a calamity in inter-Imperial relations had the history been allowed to go to press in its present form...

Yours faithfully,

A.W. Currie

Currie to Fred Richardson, 16 September 1926[28]

My dear Fred,

...Well, the elections are over here and to me are somewhat of a surprise, although at no time did I have any opinion that the Meighen Party would be returned to power. The result is satisfactory in one respect for now Mr. King will have sufficient majority to keep on without the support of any group. Stability in government counts for a good deal.

There are several facts about the situation today which should cause all serious minded Canadians to think. In the first place, we have a solid French Canadian vote. In every French Canadian constituency in Quebec they supported the Liberal Party, and it would seem that they have appropriated that party as their own. The Liberals gained in Nova Scotia in those counties where the French Canadian population forms a considerable percentage. In Eastern Ontario, into which the French Canadians are penetrating, the Liberals also gained, while in Manitoba, where there is a large French Canadian element, the Conservatives have no representation at all. It is not a question of tariff or anything else other than the determination on the part of the French Canadians to stick together and to dominate wherever they can. I can see very great dangers in such a situation, because I cannot appreciate how you are ever going to develop a strong Canadian citizenship when you have the French Canadians on one side and the Anglo Saxons on the other. I might delate much on this aspect of the case, but I have said enough to indicate what my fears are.

Another serious situation today is that Canada is divided into two populations, one rural and the other urban. The cities are all Conservative and the country districts are Liberal. One or two cities like Ottawa and Quebec are Liberal, but that is owing to the predominance of French Canadians. Now this is a very unhappy state of affairs when you have country people on one side and city people on the other. It does not make for harmony or for prosperity. What we need is to bring these two populations together rather than to emphasise their division.

There is also the question of Roman Catholics versus the Orangemen, but I do not lay outstanding stress on that. So you see Fred instead of us becoming a more united whole our divisions have become more marked, and for this state of affairs I blame the Conservative Party. Any fool could have realized that French Canadians would not support Meighen, but the Conservative Party insisted on having him as their leader. Tuesday's election may be the very best thing that ever happened to them if they learn that one lesson that they must get a new leader before they can hope to win a fight. Meighen has been before the country three times in the last six years and has failed on every occasion.

There is another thing which the Conservative Party preaches which the people of Canada will not have, and that is the gospel of high protection. We are all protectionists to the extent that we believe our industries should be protected where necessary, but this gospel of high protection is unwise, unnecessary and unmoral. I know manufacturing establishments whose profits last year were enormous and yet their representatives appeared before the Tariff Commission asking for higher protection. That sort of thing cannot and will not be tolerated.

Now as to the Liberal Party, I have no use for Mackenzie King. He is no more to be trusted than you say is Stevens because he is in my opinion, unpatriotic, selfish and insincere. There is one consolation and that is that Canada is showing evidence of returning to prosperity, and although our politicians have tried to bedevil our country apparently they cannot destroy our progress even though they retard it. We need a strong immigration policy, but this is something which Mackenzie King never had.

With all kind personal wishes, I am ever yours faithfully,

A.W. Currie

Field Marshal Sir Douglas Haig died on 29 January 1928. The Canadian Minister of Defence, James Ralston, wrote to Currie asking him to reflect on Haig's tenure as Commander-in-Chief.

Currie to Colonel J.L. Ralston, 9 February 1928[29]

My dear Colonel,

...I suppose two of the things a successful leader must have are the confidence and respect of those whom he commands. Haig's army was so large that it was impossible for him as Chief to come into any sort of personal contact with the great bulk of the men he commanded. Add to that his natural shyness and reserve and one can readily understand that not many men ever saw him. With the officers, particularly those holding higher rank, he came into more intimate contact and I can say that he held their confidence and their respect to an unusual degree. I met him many times and although he never had much to say, he always impressed one greatly. Leaving to one side his manner, his bearing, his appearance—all of which fitted so well with his high rank—one felt that here you were dealing with a thoroughly honest, decent, manly man. You will remember the gruff way in which some generals left their instructions. Haig was never like that. He told you what his plans were, the part he wanted you to play, and he listened with every respect to what you had to say. He trusted you so thoroughly to help him that you [were] more than usually anxious to carry out his wishes.

Let me tell you of the Hill 70 incident. In July 1917 the Army Commander instructed me to carry out an advance from our line at Avion to the Lens–Mericourt railway. This was to be a holding attack and of sufficient threat to the enemy to induce him not to send divisions north, where the great attack at Ypres was to be made. I remember lying all one morning on the east end of the Bois–Hirondelle spur and coming to the conclusion that while we could make the advance quite easily, it was an unwise thing to do, because it would leave us in a worse position than before. It would pull our guns more out on the plain and would alter our general defensive system, and would not be a sufficient threat to the enemy to deceive him in any particular [way]. I went to see the Army Commander—General Horne—and told him what my objections were. He asked me what I had to suggest and I said that if we were going to fight at all, let us fight for something worth having. I named Hill 70 on the north of Lens or Sallaumines Hill on the east. He asked which one I thought should be done first and I said Hill 70. He said he would have to see the Chief and a few days later Haig came up to see me. He asked me to explain fully what was in my mind and then commented that he liked the suggestion for Hill 70 very much better than

29 File 39, vol 13, CP, LAC.

the Lens–Mericourt objective, but he warned me that the Boche would not let us have Hill 70. He most warmly approved the plan and then I asked him when he would like it done. He told me that the big attack in the north was to be made on July 31st and he would like this attack on Hill 70 about the 4th of August. We were not then on the Hill 70 front and I assured him that it would be impossible for us to make the attack on the date suggested. Now here is where Haig was very different from some generals I met. Instead of saying that it had to be done on the 4th, he put his hand on my shoulder and said something like this: 'My boy, this is your own attack. I leave it to you to carry it out when you are ready. You know what I want and I trust you to help me in every way you can.' As a matter of fact, owing to wretched weather, the attack was not made until August 15th. You know something of the hard fighting. Not only did we hold the Germans on our front, but he brought down two divisions from the big battle at Ypres. We used twenty-four battalions and identified sixty-nine German battalions in the prisoners we took in the eight days fighting. The Chief was immensely pleased and always regarded Hill 70 as one of the finest minor operations of the war—a fact which Andy McNaughton tells me the German files confirm. When the committee on battle honours met after the war they first determined not to include Hill 70. I wrote to the Chief and he personally appeared before the committee for the express purpose of insisting that a battle honour be given for that engagement. I daresay it is probably the only honour which the Canadians share with no one.

I always sympathized with Haig because I knew of his troubles with the British Cabinet and with the Allies. The Canadian Corps always liked and respected him and I know the regard was mutual. I remember (and this is confidential) saying to Byng after the battle of Vimy that the Chief seemed very pleased. Byng replied that he should be, and when I ventured to ask why, he said 'when the Canadians consolidated Vimy Ridge they consolidated Douglas Haig's position at the same time.'

I hope, Ralston, I have given you something that will be of use.

Yours faithfully,

A.W. Currie

While Haig was given a state funeral and buried as hero, Currie was still battling for his reputation. On 13 June 1927, as a plaque dedicated to the memory of the liberation of Mons in was being dedicated in France, the Port Hope Evening Guide published an editorial repeating Hughes' old allegations.[30]

'Mons,' Port Hope *Evening Guide*, 13 June 1927[31]

Cable dispatches this morning give details of the unveiling of a bronze plaque at the Hotel de Ville (the City Hall) at Mons, commemorative of the capture of the city by the Canadians on November 11th, 1918. This is an event which might very properly be allowed to pass into oblivion, very much regretted rather than glorified.

There was much waste of human life during the war, enormous loss of lives which should not have taken place. But it is doubtful whether in any case there was a more deliberate and useless waste of human life than in the so-called capture of Mons.

It was the last day; and the last hour, and almost the last minute, when to glorify the Canadian Headquarters staff the Commander-in-Chief conceived the mad idea that it would be fine thing to say that the Canadians had fired the last shot in the Great War, and had captured the last German entrenchment before the bugles sounded eleven o'clock, when the Armistice which had been signed by both sides would begin officially.

Canadian Headquarters sounded the advance upon the retreating Germans, unsuspecting that any mad proposal for further and unnecessary fighting was even contemplated. The men were sent on in front to charge the enemy. Headquarters, with conspicuous bravery, brought up the rear. The fighting may have been more severe than was expected. Certain it is the Germans did not take the attack lying down.

Of course the town was taken just at the last minute before the official moment of the Armistice arrived. But the penalty that was paid in useless waste of human life was appalling. There are hearts in Port Hope stricken with sorrow and mourning through this worse than drunken spree by Canadian Headquarters. Veterans who had passed through the whole four years of war lie buried in Belgian cemeteries as the result of the 'glories of Mons.'

Headquarters staff assembled in the centre of the town as the eleven o'clock signal sounded that the official armistice was effective from that hour. Along the

30 See Dancocks, 237-55; Hyatt, 139-43; Urquart, 317-321. The most detailed description of the trial is Sharpe. On its broader implications see Vance, 163-97 and Cook, *Cleo's Warriors*, 56-62.
31 W.T.R. Preston, 'Mons,' *Evening Guide* (Port Hope, Ontario), 13 June 1927, 1.

route that they had carefully and with safety made their way to the centre of the town, passing the dead and dying and the wounded, victims of their madness. It was common talk among the soldiers that while the staff were congratulating themselves upon the great victory and enjoying the pride upon having 'fired the last shot in the Great War,' a sergeant advanced and whispered to one of the staff that unless they withdrew immediately to a place of safety, they would not be allowed to leave the place alive, as the guns of the indignant Canadian soldiers were already trained on them. In less time than it takes to tell the story, headquarters got into motors and were fleeing for their lives.

It does not seem to be remembered that even Ottawa, neither by government nor Parliament, gave Sir Arthur Currie any official vote of thanks, or any special grant as an evidence of the esteem or appreciation for his services. And this is the only case of the kind in connection with any of the high commanding officers of the war. He was allowed to return to Canada unnoticed by officials of the Government of Parliament and permitted to sink into comparative obscurity in a civilian position as President of McGill University. The official desire to glorify Mons, therefore, deserves more than a passing or silent notice. Canadian valour won Mons, but it was by such a shocking useless waste of human life that it is an eternal disgrace to the headquarters that directed operations.

The front-page polemic, written by Liberal Party organizer William T.R. Preston, gave Currie the opportunity to clear his name. Previous comments by Hughes had been made in the House of Commons and had therefore been protected from legal action. The Evening Guide was not. After months of deliberation, and despite the advice of friends and colleagues, Currie decided to sue for libel. As Corps Commander he expected the Government to protect his name, but he had been sorely disappointed. Now Currie the private citizen was determined to secure his reputation once and for all.[32]

Currie to General Ross Hayter, 22 March 1928[33]

My dear General,

I have only time for a word, but thank you very much for your letter of the 6th of March.

---

32 See note 37.
33 File 64, vol 18, CP, LAC.

The charge is one that has been repeated freely for the last ten years, but this is the first time it has appeared in print. Briefly it accuses me of ordering an attack on Mons after I knew the Armistice was coming into effect, that there was an appalling loss of life, and that I did it for my own glorification. I cannot yet find an incident of any of the units engaged suffering the loss of a single life on the 11th.[34] I shall have plenty of evidence from officers and men to this effect. The trouble is that they are going to try and widen the case to embrace almost all the incidents of the war. Garnet [Hughes] is here and I am sure he is busy. Can you by any means look up the files and let me know when he was in the police court, having been arrested for driving a car when drunk.

If the judge keeps the trial within decent limits there is nothing to do, but if the defence are permitted to wander it may be nasty. However I feel that this lie had better be nailed now and not be allowed to go undisputed. I shall write you again and a much longer letter.

With every good wish, yours faithfully,

A.W. Currie

Currie to Brigadier General Robert P. Clark, 30 March 1928[35]

My dear Bob,

...I appreciate very much, Bob, your own telegram and the others that have come from Vancouver with reference to this libel suit of mine. I do not mind admitting to you that it is giving me a great deal of worry. There can be only one issue if the case is kept within the four walls of the article of which I complain, but the defendants are trying to bring in every kind of irrelevant matter. I sometimes think this article about Mons was simply an excuse. They knew I was very tender on that spot and so they goaded me into taking an action and now they are going to try to bring in everything that they can which can injure whatever reputation I have got...

I saw Harold McDonald several times in the last few days and he wanted to know if there was anything he could do, saying that he was charged to offer the help of all the fellows in Vancouver. In the same conversation he told me that he had seen Garnet Hughes in Toronto and that Garnet seemed to be engaged on some mysterious mission. I think I can guess what Garnet's main activity is at

---

34 Only one soldier was killed on 11 November 1918, George Lawrence Price of the 28th Battalion. He did not die in the capture of the city itself.

35 File 64, vol 18, CP, LAC.

the present time. The threat he made to me in London when I refused to take him as GOC 1st Division is being carried out at the present time.[36]

Of course, I know there are those who say that I should have taken no notice, but this charge has been made for ten years now and only appeared boldly in print last June. I felt I could not let it go by as it was so scandalously untrue. It reflected not only upon me, but upon every officer and non-commissioned officer who had anything to do with the leading of troops in the closing days of the war. If I had taken no notice of this charge it would only have been followed by others and my life would have been made a misery. I am sure of that, and if I can't win this I can't win anything.

There are those who say that I should have ordered 'cease firing' on November 9th or when I knew the German plenipotentiaries had gone to Foch. This must be the contention of all those who support the Port Hope charges, and yet these are probably the very people who said that we should have gone on to Berlin to dictate the terms of peace from there. Just think of the horrible suggestion they are making—that the Canadian Corps, with all its fine record and the great help it had given towards winning the war, was to lie down and quit on the 9th, thus disobeying our orders, repudiating the instructions of the Commander-in-Chief not to relax the pressure, and being false to every principle of war as to the decisive battle enunciated by Marshal Foch, who was supreme in command. Furthermore, we would have remained fast and allowed the British to go forward on our right and on our left. It would have been a most cowardly thing to have done, and had I suggested doing so I would probably have been replaced in command of the Corps by someone who would carry out orders. The whole suggestion is contemptible, and yet they talk of bringing hundreds of witnesses to support them. The Corps doesn't quite appreciate how its honour is being attacked. However, if the truth is to prevail there should be no doubt about the issue, and although many are sorry it is being tried by a jury largely composed of farmers,[37] I am willing to trust in their good sense.

I cannot tell you. Bob, how profoundly pleased I am that you are doing so well in business. No one will begrudge you every possible success and I hope it will increase day by day.

36 Currie's biographer Hugh Urquhart suggests that on 15 June 1917 Garnet Hughes shouted 'I will get you before I am finished with you' after Currie refused his promotion to the command of 1st Division. Urquhart's source for the quote is unclear. See Urquhart, 163-5.
37 Farmers, it will be remembered, did not generally support conscription or the Union Government in the 1917 election. Currie was probably worried that his support for conscription and his association with the Borden government would come back to haunt him.

With all my good wishes, I am yours faithfully,

A.W. Currie

The trial began in Cobourg, Ontario on 16 April 1928. For the next two weeks
former generals, lieutenant colonels, officers, and enlisted men paraded across
the witness stand, including Currie himself. In the end, Preston and the Evening
Guide were found to have committed libel. Currie was awarded $500.00 in
damage—one per cent of the amount he had claimed in his suit—but in his eyes
the trial was a success and he was pleased with the outcome. However the stress
of the trial had taken a toll on the health of the aging Corps Commander.[38]

Currie to Brigadier General R. Brutinel, 14 June 1928[39]

My dear General,

For weeks, even months, I have been wanting to write to you and acknowledge
your kindness in wiring me as you did in the early spring. Since then the Cobourg
battle, or, as they call it here, the 'Third Battle of Mons' has been fought and
won. It was just as nasty a fight as the meanest of men could make it, but after all
it was worth while. The result has brought the returned men of Canada together
in a way they have not been for ten years. They looked upon it as their fight as
much as mine and so it was. I could have had thousands of witnesses at Cobourg
if I had wanted them. The verdict has been unanimously endorsed by the people
of Canada who look upon it as a victory for Canadian decency and Canadian
justice.

However, I do not intend to say very much to you about it in this letter,
because I have been urged by my medical advisers to forget all about it as soon as
possible and that I am trying to do. I am almost ashamed to have to acknowledge
that the worries incident to the trial bowled me over completely and that for over
a month I have been under the doctor's care and have just returned to my home
from the hospital. They insist that I adhere to a very rigid diet and also that I take
a complete rest, and so I am sailing on June 28th for the other side. That means
I shall arrive in London on July 5th or 6th, and I hope that shortly after I shall
have the pleasure of seeing you again. I want to spend the summer as quietly
as possible and I thought that after a couple of weeks in London I would try to

38 See note 37.
39 File 64, vol 18, CP, LAC.

find some place on the Brittany or Normandy coast where I could get plenty of sunshine, some bathing, a bit of golf and a complete change of environment.

I have a good story to tell you of how we worked into the evidence Marshal Foch's order to the armies to keep up the pressure. Do not let me forget to tell you when I see you again.

With my very kindest wishes, I am, yours ever,

A.W. Currie

Despite the victory at Cobourg, Currie remained concerned about the legacy and memory of the Canadian Corps and public perceptions of the war effort and its leaders.

Currie to H. Clendining, 13 November 1929[40]

Dear Mr. Clendining,

...I have from time to time spoken to those in charge of the erection of the memorial at Vimy Ridge with a view to finding out when the work would be completed and when a possible unveiling or dedication might take place. My answers so far have been altogether indefinite. I do not expect that there will be any unveiling until the year 1931, when, I agree with you, there should be some proper representation of the Canadian Corps. It is true it is a national war memorial and the government of our country should be suitably represented, but I do not think government representation should constitute the main body, as they did when the monument in honour of those Americans who served in the Canadian Corps was unveiled at Washington, D.C. two years ago. If we are not watchful the Corps will receive scant recognition, as it appears to be the spirit of the time to minimize what it did.

I know the matter of the unveiling and a pilgrimage will be considered at the convention of the Canadian Legion which takes place at Regina in two weeks' time. Let us wait until we see what action is taken there.

With all good wishes, I am yours faithfully,

A.W. Currie

40 File 21, vol 7, CP, LAC.

Currie to W. Edgar, 14 January 1930[41]

Dear Mr. Edgar,

I have given further consideration to your request that I make a statement regarding certain allegations concerning Canadians in Robert Graves' *Goodbye to All That*.

I am still of the opinion that I should not give an interview, and therefore do not wish to be quoted in any way in the *[Toronto] Star* concerning this matter.

I read *Goodbye to All That* two months ago and the thought never struck me to rush into print to comment on some report which Graves said he heard. Last night I read certain of the passages again. He states in his book that he heard of these acts of violence committed by the Canadians in revenge for the Canadian found crucified; but in his book he also says that there was a report that a German was crucified, and that neither of these stories was to be believed.

Anyone who knows anything about life among soldiers would pay no attention to the yarn about putting Mills bombs with the pins withdrawn in prisoners' pockets. If any Canadian soldiers told Graves a yarn like that, they were simply pulling his leg, as all soldiers are prone to do. In my opinion, the reputation of the Canadian soldier stands too high for me to rush into print to defend them, not from charges, but from certain insinuations made in a novel. No doubt a bit of controversy now would provide spice for the readers of the *Star* and help to sell Graves' book. But there is another factor which ought to be considered. We are all anxious to promote peaceful relations among nations. We have had enough of war, and I do not think any betterment of our relations with our late enemies is likely to accrue if we begin talking about their having crucified some of our men and our denying that we ever bayoneted prisoners or blew them up with Mills bombs. The thing is not only silly: it is dangerous. I am not going to make any comment about it.

As I said to you last night, there never was any foundation for the story that a Canadian soldier had been crucified.

I am ever yours faithfully,

A.W. Currie

As the Canadian economy faltered in the early 1930s, Currie became increasingly worried not only about the memory of the war but also the plight

41   Edgar was a reporter for the *Toronto Star*. File 23, vol 8, CP, LAC.

of veterans and their families. In the last years of his life he spent much of his time lobbying for veteran's rights. He became more involved in veteran's organizations and more vocal in his criticism of government policy. In March 1930 he appeared in Ottawa as a witness before the House of Commons Special Committee on Pensions and Returned Soldier's Problems.[42]

Arthur Currie's Statement before the House of Commons Special Committee on Pensions and Returned Soldiers' Problems, 27 March 1930[43]

Mr. Chairman and Gentleman I should like, in the first place, to express my appreciation for the opportunity of appearing on behalf of the returned soldiers and all veteran organizations, and as a citizen of Canada, before this Parliamentary Committee. At the same time, I should like to acknowledge gratefully the kind consideration that has been given by previous parliamentary committees to all matters referred to them affecting the interests and welfare of the veterans of the Great War. I, for one, regret, and I know that you do, that more than eleven years after the close of the war there still remains the necessity for further consideration of these problems; and as to the urgent necessity for further consideration, to my mind there can be no doubt.   It arises from a belief which, I am sure, is worthy of notice, that the intentions of the people of this country with reference to their fellow citizens who served in the Great War, are not being fulfilled as they should be. I cannot impress upon you too emphatically that that feeling does prevail. I know that all of you are conscious of it, because I am sure that every member of the House has had it impressed upon him, personally, many times. It exists in veterans' organizations, and many private citizens have told me the same. Only last evening a private citizen in Toronto told me that yesterday afternoon he had eleven men appear before him in the justice of whose pleas he felt there was reason.

My excuse for asking to be heard before you is this, that I am profoundly interested, as I know you are, in the welfare of all those with whom I was so intimately associated in the days of the Great War. I claim to know these men well, because it was my good fortune to serve in the front line areas, the battle areas, from the time the First Canadian Division went to France until the Armistice

---

42   Dancocks, 261-5.
43   Government of Canada, 'Minutes of the House of Commons Special Committee on Pensions and Returned Soldiers' Problems, 27 March 1930,' *Journals of the House of Commons*, 1930, 1-6.

came on November 11th, 1918. During that time it was my responsibility, among other things, to know the men of the Canadian Corps, to realize their strength as well as their weaknesses, to know how they lived, to observe their daily life and their conduct under all circumstances and under all conditions. It was my privilege to know how they bore themselves in battle, to know their pride in themselves and their pride in their country, to know their faith in each other and their faith in the people of Canada, and to know, also, their will to stay on the job until it could be brought to a successful conclusion.

I also understood their longing to get home again. It is an association, gentlemen, in which I have the greatest pride and about which I cherish the most precious memories.

I want to say, also, that I do not appear this morning as the representative, solely, of the Canadians who served at the front. I have a very full appreciation of the manner in which the efforts of the Canadian soldiers were supported by the people at home. We were all members of one organization, working for the success of one cause, some serving in one place and some in another. As we were not divided then, we should not be divided now. I am one of those who believe that the returned soldiers are as patriotic, as truly interested in the welfare of this country, as greatly concerned about the problems of this country, as any other group or class in it; and I am sure I speak for every one of them when I say that they do not wish to add unnecessarily to the burden of taxation under which this country labours, I know there are many men who, as they served Canada in the testing days of the war, unselfishly will continue to serve Canada with the same spirit. I feel, too, that it is the desire of my countrymen to deal with the claims of returned soldiers in a just, fair, equitable, and even generous manner. That was the intention in the days of the war. I believe it is our intention now. The returned soldiers asked no more than that; and so we are both agreed—Canadian citizens and returned men. It only remains to set up such machinery as will bring about that end, and I hold that that machinery should be so fashioned, so regulated and so governed, that both intentions will be fulfilled. That machinery should be as much the instrument of one as of the other. I hold that that machinery has a responsibility to both, and does not hold a brief for only one party. There is no difference in the intentions, therefore, of this country and the returned soldier. There should be no difference arising over the manner in which those intentions are fulfilled.

I should add that I do not appear before you as an expert witness. I am not an expert in the pensions law of this country nor of any other country, nor do I claim to be qualified to draft a legal document. But I do know that it is now altogether impossible to comply with the provisions of the Pension Act which require proof on the part of the claimant that his present disability is directly attributable to war service. It may be equally impossible to prove that the disability is not attributable to the war; and the fact that the Pensions Board feel that they cannot accept such a responsibility only serves to bring home all the more impressively the inability of the men at all times to prove their claims. It is my belief that if the Pensions Board regarded its obligation as belonging to the man as well as to the country, the onus of proof might be shared.

Further, I wish to emphasize the fact that I am not here to plead for those who at the front were technically known as 'malingerers,' a term applied to the relatively few who by one subtle method or another tried, to evade their tasks or to secure immunity from performance of duty or obtain special concessions which were undeserved. I do not think that anybody in the Canadian Corps was more severe on the 'skrim-shanker' than I was, and I would be just as severe to-day with any man who would attempt to claim pension to which he was not entitled. We are sometimes told that 'malingerers' or 'skrim-shankers' still ply their trade. Perhaps they do, but I am convinced that their number is relatively so few that they need scarcely be considered in this discussion. A man's record before the war, during the war and since the war, his honest efforts in the affairs of life—all these help to classify him, and, when of obvious merit, should remove him from the undeserved application of any obnoxious term. I feel there are men who are considered as merely malingerers who are not entitled to have such a term applied to them at all. I speak only for the deserving, whose whole record, as well as their medical history sheet, should be carefully considered.

There is one thing which I wish to make perfectly clear. I am not here for the purpose of destructive criticism. We are confronted with a problem, and my sole purpose is to give what assistance I can in the satisfactory solution of that problem.

There is widespread dissatisfaction throughout the country in regard to the operation of our military pensions system. Your task is to ascertain the causes of this dissatisfaction and to devise means for removing them. As my contribution to that task, I wish to lay before you calmly, reasonably, but clearly and emphatically, the elements of the problem as I see it.

From time immemorial it has been the custom of British Governments to grant pensions to those who have suffered disabilities in the service of their country in time of war. If men are killed, pensions are paid to dependents. If men are disabled, pensions are paid according to the degree of disablement. That makes the Pension Act a contractual thing; it, is a contract into which the government of this country intentionally entered. Our men knew this when they enlisted, and I believe that knowledge helped to keep up their morale through all the turmoil and dangers of war. They were encouraged to enlist; thank Heaven they did not need much encouragement, but they enlisted in the knowledge that while they were absent the matter of separation allowance and other institutions that were set up to look after them would operate to protect their dependents. They knew, also, that if they fell in the field of battle a pension would be paid to their dependents. They knew that if they suffered disability, pension would be paid to them. As they had faith in themselves, they had faith in their country; they believed it would deal with them fairly and justly, they had confidence in the honesty of its purpose and in the fulfillment of all the promises it made. There is no doubt that in the days of enlistment emphasis was laid upon what Canada would do in the matter of pensions and that a man was influenced in voluntary enlistment by the assurance given him that he and his dependents would be taken care of.

In the matter of pensions and hospitalization, vocational training and gratuities, Canada has done well. No fault can be found with the scale of pensions. That is higher than in any other country of which I know. Now, in order that Canada's intentions and promises might be kept, the Pension Act was passed and the Pensions Board established to administer and interpret the Act—and, more than that, I contend that it should be an instrument to help the returned soldier in seeing that the promises of his country are carried out as his country intended they should be carried out. I repeat that the Pensions Board is a court of law and equity; it does not hold a brief for one side only, and it has a responsibility to both. If a man has difficulty in submitting his claim as it should be submitted, it is the obligation of the Pensions Board to tell him what he should do. There is no use saying that he has to get more evidence; he must know wherein his evidence is short, and he must be helped to get that evidence. The Pensions Board should make it their business to see that evidence comes before them in a manner in which they can deal intelligently with it, so that they may carry out the wishes of the people of this country.

In any business organization and in any institution there comes a time when the machinery set up for certain purposes must be examined and renewed, strengthened and brought up to date, in order that it may continue to function satisfactorily. There are those who hold the view that the machinery we have set up is not functioning as satisfactorily as it might. The country is asking why. It expects you and me to determine, if we can, the cause of any dissatisfaction that exists, to see if it is justified, and to eliminate it, if possible. One dissatisfaction, I think, arises from the fact—and it is a fact that we cannot get over—that the Pension Act is a legal document, that it is drawn with all the phraseology of a legal document, and that men applying for pensions do not always understand this, nor do they know the precedents which the machinery for administering and interpreting the Pension Act has in the course of time set up. In the administration of this Act for ten or more years, many precedents, certainly, are established. The man applying for pension does not know about that, and that is another reason why I think the Pensions Board should regard its duty in a somewhat different way than it docs at the present time. I, frankly, admit that many men apply for pensions who are not entitled to pensions, either legally or morally. But it seems to me that when a man's application is refused it would help very greatly if he were told by the board why it is refused. I hold that the extra time and labour involved in order to give these explanations would be more than counterbalanced by the satisfaction that would ensue, for it certainly does no good to have a large body of people feeling that national promises have not been kept and that they have not received fair play. I may be told that the Pensions Board or the Appeal Board has not the time to do these things or that it is loaded with other and more pressing work. Very good, what we must have, then, is a survey and a review of the machinery. It may be that that machinery is called upon to bear a burden which it cannot reasonably be asked to bear.

Furthermore, the Act has from time to time been revised and amended. It is difficult for the ordinary layman to be familiar with all these revisions. Yet he must be, if he is to comply with all the terms when he seeks anything under the act.

In my understanding of the obligations of the Pensions Board, it exists to serve the man as well as the country, and it should have at its disposal an organization to help him present his claim in the form in which the Board can most intelligently deal with it. I realize the difficulty of getting away from formal legal phraseology. I only mention this to point out the difficulties claimants are under.

The consolidated Pension Act is a great improvement and possibly it answers the purpose fairly well. Dissatisfaction arises from other causes.

The first is the degree of disability. A man may be awarded a ten per cent disability when he feels and others feel with him that he should have more. I do not think you can overcome this dissatisfaction by any clause in the Act. The dissatisfaction arises from the interpretation. A man makes a claim. It may well be that the claim is imperfect and incomplete; that it does not comply with the requirements; that it does not conform to the precedents already laid down by the Pensions Board. The man is merely told that more evidence is necessary—I cannot too strongly impress upon you the fact that many times it is physically impossible to furnish the additional evidence in the form and of the nature which apparently is required. It seems to me the man should have more technical assistance in the preparation of his claim. More trouble should be taken to tell him why it is not complete, to make him feel that his claim, if refused, has at least received careful and sympathetic consideration. In this connection I feel that the right of appeal should be given in every case. I shall be told that there is a man to prepare his case the official soldiers' adviser. I am not convinced that these advisers are as effective as they should be. It is my opinion that this work would be more effectively done if the resources of the Canadian Legion were utilized.

Then, of course, in the second place, great dissatisfaction comes from what we so often hear about—the attributability of the disability to war service. This is something about which differences of opinion are bound to arise. You can't remove them by legislation. If you attempt to define 'attributability' you restrict its application. It can only be left to the interpretation of fair-minded and sympathetic men of good judgment and honest purpose.

You can gather from what I have said that the difficulty does not arise so much in the terms of the Act as in the imperfect functioning of the machinery which has been set up to administer the Act. It may not be the fault of that machinery, but again I insist, that the time has arrived when the machinery must be surveyed, examined, renewed and brought up to date.

I have referred to this question, onus of proof; the Pensions Board says it cannot assume the responsibility. Well, I can quite see their difficulty. I doubt if they should he asked to do so, but remember it is frightfully hard, it is impossible sometimes, for the man to prove his claim. You can put all the meritorious clauses in the Act that you like, it will all depend on the interpretation you put on it and the character of the machinery you set up for these things. I am not going to deal with many specific cases but I have one case which will illustrate what I mean. Here is a man who enlisted in a western province in September, 1915. He was thirty-seven years of age, big, strong, and in perfect physical condition. He went to France, where he served in the signal corps. Now, gentlemen, you who know anything about it—and I know the great majority of you do—think what a man does in the signal service. Day and night, rain or shine, he must, get out and keep the lines repaired. It is not a case of eight or ten hours a day, it is a case of twenty-four hours a day, and for days on end, always working in the battle area. His shelter at the best of times is nothing more than a thin sheet of corrugated iron or an old piece of tarpaulin; it may be nothing more than a shell hole in the broken and poisoned earth. Yet, that man must be out all the time in all kinds of weather, wet to the skin, cold, lousy. If he does occupy a rude dugout the chances are he has rats for companions. He is always in the battle area, shelled and bombed. Do you mean to tell me that those conditions will not affect adversely a man's health? Is it any wonder this man got a touch of rheumatism? This man was a corporal who won a military medal, so he was not a bad sort of fellow. That he suffered from rheumatic pains in his hack and sciatica while on service is the sworn statement of his officers and companions, but he was so keen he kept on at work when his commanding officer said he should be in hospital. That was not a strange or unusual thing. I know men who would not go sick, they might go to the horse lines and remain there; skrim-shankers were not common. Why, gentlemen, I remember sending a commanding officer away. There was a battle coming on and I did not tell him the truth about it. What happened? I sent him away because his health was breaking. A battle had begun, the man in command of his battalion was killed. His brigadier telephoned asking me to get him back. I wired to the Base where he was, to get, him back, and received a wire that he was already with his battalion. You could not keep these men away. They were not trying to go back in order to try and build up claims for pensions. He grew so bad that in 1918 he was returned to England to serve as an instructor, and continued in that way until the end of the war, and in 1919 took his discharge. The sheltered life at Seaford made him feel he was all right. I will say this, gentlemen, that the medical examinations when the men left the service were very cursory examinations. I remember very well the man that came to me. He said. 'You are all right.' I said. 'Yes.' Yet the history sheet is thus stressed, that it must be true, nothing else can be true but it.

Soon after his return to this country this man suffered pains and extreme nervousness. He became so bad that on the advice of his doctor he went to California. He had already spent all his money and made application for pension through the efforts of the American Legion. He was suffering from sciatica, and was granted a pension dating from October 1924 at $11 a month, with an allowance of $6.25 for his wife and child. In order to get treatment he had to travel a great distance, and the pension was too small, but it was all he had to live on so in despair he appealed for more generous treatment. They sent him to a home and his case was diagnosed as spinal arthritis, and no permanent cure could be effected. The result was pitiful, his pension was cut off altogether, and the explanation given by the board was that they did not recognize spinal arthritis as a pensionable disability. He had exhausted all his money and was left to starve in a strange country, where he was saved by his wife's efforts to earn money. She keeps a little chicken ranch, and he drags himself around on his hands and knees to feed the chickens. He often falls into convulsive fits. Do you mean to tell me that that is the intention of the people of this country? This man finally got to Mayo brothers, and his case was diagnosed as sciatica which never could be cured. The same diagnosis had been made in many other cases, but there was no difference, the reply was that if it was sciatica it was not caused by war service. Gentlemen, you know the life of the signaller, but he was told by the Pensions Board that he would have to produce evidence that his disability was due to war service. This man I refer to had his pitiful pension first cut off because arthritis, which was the diagnosis of Mayo brothers and other doctors, was not pensionable. That is all I have to say about that. There is a case in point. I know there is not a living man in this country who would say that that man received fair treatment...

Currie to Major General A.C. Macdonell, 25 June 1930[44]

[No salutation],

I have your letter about that disgusting book *Generals Die in Bed*. I have not read it through but I have read sufficient [parts] of it to come to the conclusion that a more scurrilous thing was never published. I only read half of it, and that

44 File 33, vol 11, CP, LAC.

last night, after receiving your letter. Some time ago the *Toronto Globe* asked me to review the book, but I refused. I would not pay this skunk the compliment of reviewing his book or of making any reference whatever to it.

The reputation and prestige of your old division stands too high for you to rush into print now in their defence, and thereby call attention to Harrison's book, and so help his sales. That's all he wrote it for—to make money and he knew that there are a number of people who prefer to read the mean, scandalous things. It appeals to the worst appetite that can be found. His book is a mass of filth, lies and appeals to everything base and mean and nasty. The very title is a mean one, appealing to that feeling which, happily, in growing less each day—that officers were not worthy of the respect of privates. He talks about nothing but immorality, lice, and other not only disgusting but untrue things. On more than one occasion he describes a meal. It is always a piece of dirty, grey, army bread, a raw onion, a bit of cheese, and unsweetened tea. Of course, that is damnably untrue. I knew we had raw onions for soup, but I never knew of their being served out as a ration. I think, on the whole, our fellows fared very well. I have often tasted their meals, and they were good, a fact to which the excellent physical condition of the men attested. This man says that they never had their clothes off. That's a lie. There were times, of course, when baths were impossible, but you know the trouble we went to, to arrange for baths and the establishment of de-lousing plants.

You may think it worth while to deny what this man has written, but he has defeated himself. I don't think a second edition of the book will ever be issued, and it will very soon be forgotten. Harrison would like nothing better than that you or I would accept his challenge. That would give his book publicity and help to sell it. Angry and disgusted as we may be, we most certainly must not do that. The book is badly named, has a weak style, no worthwhile matter, is full of vile and misrepresentation, and cannot have any lasting influence.

When Remarque wrote *All Quiet on the Western Front* he started something which he at that time I am sure did not anticipate. His was the first book written in plain, blunt language, and dealing with many things of which we do not speak. This man Harrison is a cheap imitator. I don't think there is a line in his book that is worth remembrance...

Yours ever,

A.W. Currie

Currie to Lieutenant Colonel H.M. Urquhart, 8 October 1931[45]

[No salutation],

I know that before this I should have answered your much appreciated letter of September 3rd, which I did not see until some time after the middle of the month when I returned to the university after spending a fortnight at my old home.

I took the [manuscript][46] with me and read every word of it, and much of it I read aloud to my sister. I enjoyed every page of it, bringing back so vividly to my mind, as it did, many memories which will never fade away. With almost every name you mention I was familiar—certainly with the names of all the officers, while who can forget the events recorded. I like your style of writing, and your own personality showed in every line. One can see at once that it was written by a man extremely conscientious and painstaking, a man whose sole desire was to be fair and just in every comment and at the same time to give his readers a vivid impression of the character of the men portrayed and of the scenes depicted.

The only part which seemed to me was not 'you' was the epilogue.

Your comments on the screeds that came out from the GHQ, and on the instructions for training are very pertinent. Some of your stories of the pipers are simply splendid, while you have not failed to appreciate the value of touches of humour. I think it would be unfair, untrue, and unjust if you had not portrayed Cy Peck as the soul of the battalion. I will never forget Byng coming to me when we were in the Bruay Area early in 1917 and telling me that I must get rid of Peck; that he was not a disciplinarian, and that he (Byng) feared Peck's influence in the battalion. What poor judges men are: I more than once accused Byng of being a poor judge of men, but his invariable reply was, 'Well, I chose you.' But he was a poor judge of men, as I could I think, prove if I were to mention names. Certainly he was vastly mistaken in Peck...

Your mention of the different incidents where our paths crossed touches on very tender memories. They are like old family treasures that we put away and don't expose to curious guests in company where they would not be understood. We held fast to those old cherished memories, which sustain and comfort us when things go wrong...

Give my love to your sister and with my very kindest wishes to you both,

45 File 43, vol 14, CP, LAC.
46 Urquhart's *History of the 16th Battalion* (1932).

I am, dear Sandy, ever yours faithfully,

A.W. Currie

In the last years of his life, Currie grew pessimistic about the peace he had helped to win in 1918. He saw a resurgent Germany and an emerging Japan as ominous threats on the horizon and he came to dread the prospect of another Great War.[47]

Currie to Major General A.C. Macdonell, 11 December 1932[48]

[No salutation],

The kind thoughts expressed on your Christmas card warm my heart. First, let me say that your good wishes are most cordially reciprocated, and I hope that the coming year brings all the joys possible to you and your good wife.

Like yourself, I think that there is much about the days gone by that one recalls with satisfaction, even with pride. I know it can't be done, but if one could strip war of all its cruelty and sorrow it would be worth while: there is so much in it that makes one more proud of his brother man than he has occasion to be in his peace time efforts. It is the high spot in our lives, and the greatest encouragement to us in these days to go on and do what we can for the benefit of our country and its people, because of the sacrifices that were made over there.

I scarcely blame you for getting some idea that I am becoming a pacifist. Believe me when I say that I am not. I do not want to see the world at war again, because of all the misery and trouble that has followed, in the train of the last war. You and I and millions of others thought that we were fighting the 'last war to end war.' That has not seen the result, and many of these altruistic notions we had have been rudely shattered. Nevertheless, if it were necessary for our country to go to war again, I would not oppose it, and if I had to go I would fight just as ruthlessly as we did in France, and I would do everything I could to help make the Canadian army just as powerful a fighting machine as it was in days of yore. You can't call that pacificism.

I am in favour of disarmament, but I am not fool enough to advocate that we alone disarm. If everyone disarms, or disarms to the same measure and does it honestly, then I am in favour of that kind of disarmament—but some of the things that are going on today, frankly, disgust me.

47 Dancocks, 278-9.
48 File 33, vol 11, CP, LAC.

Take this Manchurian trouble. I believe that Manchuria would be better administered under the Japanese than under the Chinese, but that, to my mind, does not alter the fact that Japan, without warning, made war upon the Chinese in Manchuria, thus violating the Hague Convention. Secondly, they certainly have not preserved the territorial integrity of China, thus violating the Washington Pact of 1922. Thirdly, they have used war as an instrument of national policy (because I contend [they] are at war with the Chinese in Manchuria) and have thus violated the Kellogg–Briand Pact. Furthermore, they have violated the spirit of the League of Nations—but I do not know that that matters, because that body is rather a spineless institution. Japan excuses herself by saying that she was not at war with China. I suppose she did not shell Shanghai and Canton, but she did bomb and shell towns in Manchuria without the slightest excuse. The trouble is that people are so indifferent to facts that they believe the Japanese.

Again, the Japanese say that they have only done what they did in Manchuria to save the Chinese from themselves. For similar reason, we might, with equal propriety, seize Chicago! They also say that seizing Manchuria is necessary to Japan's existence. I think that excuse could be given with equal propriety in every war that has been fought in the world. It is the acceptance by the nations of such damn twaddle as this that provokes me to say some of these things which apparently led you to think that I have become a pacifist. I am not, Mac. I am trying to be honest.

You will probably note with some surprise that Japan said goodbye to her representatives to the Disarmament Conference by announcing to the world that these representatives are given instructions to demand that Japan be allowed to have a higher proportion of naval strength than she now enjoys. A fine temper in which to approach a Disarmament Conference.

Well, I have said enough. With all good wishes, dear Mac, I am yours ever,
A.W. Currie

Currie to General Percy 'P de B' Radcliffe, 8 March 1933[49]

[No salutation],

...Your being in Edinburgh reminds me of the death of Lieutenant Colonel George Gibson, of whom I was very fond, and whom you may remember. He died suddenly in a tram last July or August. I wonder if you ever met him in

49 File 39, vol 13, CP, LAC.

Edinburgh? He lived in Vancouver a few years before the war, and was a member of the Militia there... In 1925, when I made my last trip over the battlefields of France and Belgium, he came with me, and Brutinel obliged by letting us have his chauffeur and Cadillac touring car. We had a wonderful visit together.

By the way, Brutinel was here about three weeks or a month ago. He spent the first evening with us, and although we chatted far into the night he said nothing about his own affairs. He came back again in a week or so, but had left before I could get in touch with him. I think his second visit only lasted about ten or twelve hours. He has had some ups and downs, I know, but he is possessed of the stuff that cannot be permanently downed. I have always been very fond of him, and of course had the highest respect for his military qualities.

Of your old friends, Loomis is by no means well. His heart has gone back on him completely. He sees nobody, never goes to public functions, while his business is not at all good. I feel very sorry for him, and I never see him at all unless I go to his home unannounced.

Old Mac lives at Kingston, retired, of course, and in constant attendance on Lady Macdonell, whose memory has completely gone, and who is very childish indeed. Mac is a model of devotion and seldom leaves her side.

...Andy McNaughton is still Chief of the General Staff at Ottawa, has been a brilliant success in that position and is more and more becoming the trusted adviser of the Government. The Governor General and his staff have, I know, the very highest regard for him personally and for his ability.

MacBrien, you may know, is Chief Commissioner of the North West Mounted Police, which at the present time has charge of police arrangements in Nova Scotia, New Brunswick, Prince Edward Island, Manitoba, Saskatchewan and Alberta, a control I expect to see extended shortly to include British Columbia...

I had Bungo with me for four days last May, who had just completed a month's tour of Canada, where he was everywhere most joyfully welcomed. We are all delighted that at last he has received the Field Marshal's baton. I hear that he is wonderfully bucked up since.

All of us are well at home. Marjorie was married last June and is living in Montreal, while my boy is a student at the university here. My wife is wonderfully well, and wishes to be most cordially remembered to you. Personally, I am in better health than I have been for the last four or five years. Everyone in Canada is feeling the pinch. What a great searching of heart there must be among our neighbours south of the line.

A.W. Currie

In the spring of 1933 the death of an old comrade brought Currie and Garnet Hughes back into contact a final time.

Currie to Major General Garnet Hughes, 29 June 1933[50]

Dear Garnet,

The sad news of old Bill's[51] death came as a shock to me. I had no idea that he had returned to the east. Last I heard of him was in a card from California in which he claimed to have experienced the earthquake. Previously, I had a letter written from the train when he was on his way west to visit his mother, whose health was giving great anxiety. But apparently his mother recovered. She always has been a remarkable woman and I think Bill was extremely fond of her.

His health, of course, has for many years been precarious. He stayed here with me a few years ago when on his way from London to BC, and while here was very abstemious. He told me that he had a rotten heart, high blood pressure, diseased kidneys, a bad tummy, bad knees and weak feet. You knew, of course, how he suffered from his old injury. To me, his condition as related by himself pointed to an early break up, and I ventured to warn him he must take the very best of care of himself, and particularly to cut out the benos [sic]. Nevertheless, when he landed in Vancouver on that occasion to which I refer, he wrote me himself and said that he went on a bender that lasted the best part of a week, after which he went to the hospital. Nobody knew quite as well as old Bill how to work the hospital racket.

He had many excellent qualities, and I suppose his greatest contribution during the war was his plan for the re-organization of the Canadian Engineers, a decided factor in the efficiency of the Corps and one which had a lasting influence on the future organization of the engineers of the British division. No one can take from him the credit for that. Bill had a flair for organization and he also had the faculty of surrounding himself with men who were able and willing to carry out his plans. I never knew a man who knew as much about front line defence, who saw so little of them. He always worked most harmoniously with the general staff. I always had some difficulty in keeping him in the field. I remember when I went to the 1st Division, Alderson was not at all in favour of Lindsay becoming Chief

50 File 29, vol 9, CP, LAC.
51 General William B. Lindsay.

Engineer of that division. And then again, when Charlie Armstrong met with his railway accident, it was only at my strong solicitation and pressure that Lindsay was made Chief Engineer of the Canadian Corps. He was laid up during most of the Battle of Passchendaele and the medical authorities wished to evacuate him. Again, in July 1918 when we knew of the plans for the Big Push which resulted in the Hundred Days' Campaign, his evacuation was strongly urged by the same authorities. But I succeeded in keeping him.

I have known him particularly well since he came to Victoria in 1908 or thereabouts, although I knew him as a small, chubby boy in Strathroy. You of course have known him particularly intimately from your days at the RMC. After the war, when I was Inspector General at Ottawa, I urged him to become Chief Military Engineer for Canada, but at that time he was enthusiastically following his idea of extracting oil from the tar sands of Alberta, a process on which he and his associates spent a considerable sum.

Had he stayed in the Militia service he soon would have been sent to a district, and had he watched his health he might well be holding some such position today.

In later years he often wrote to me concerning his efforts to develop certain gas producing lands in Ontario and I wonder how that turned out?

I learned of his death from Tommy Lawson, who said that he had been playing bridge with him at the Hunt Club the night before his death; I suppose he passed away in his sleep, a comparatively young man, of great capacity in many ways, and one whose death will be universally regretted.

I am very sorry that it will be absolutely impossible for me to be in Toronto to attend his funeral.

Ever yours faithfully,

A.W. Currie

Currie to J.W. McConell, 28 October 1933[52]

Dear Jack,

...Professor Zimmern, Professor of international relations at Oxford, an English Jew, but of distinctly German extraction, has given some five or six lectures under the auspices of the National Council of Education. He was accompanied by his wife, who spoke quite as often; she is a Frenchwoman and both are

---

52 File 33, vol 11, CP, LAC. John Wilson McConnell (1877-1963) was a prominent Montreal businessman and a Governor of McGill University (1927-57).

very definitely anti-Hitler. Both are convinced that Hither is definitely preparing for war and that France is the only one that has sized up the German attitude correctly.

You will be interested to know that Brutinel came into town this afternoon... As you know, Brutinel is very well posted on these matters and has very definite opinions. He also thinks that Hitler is preparing for war but that he will not be able to fight for another year or so. Of course we all know that Germany has been getting ready for war. In one of the English illustrated papers the other day I saw photographs of people in Germany drilling with gas masks. The European countries are very generally supplying their people with gas masks and instructing them in their use. Evidently they appreciate that gas will be very extensively used in the next war.

The great German chemical industry is working twenty-four hours a day. What are they turning out? Surely it is gas to be used in the next war. One of their factories the I.C. Farbenindustrie has some 800 different kinds of gas I am told. You will recall the premature explosion that occurred in the other big German gas or chemical factory a year or so ago, when every single living thing in the path of the gas was killed.

It will not be only the soldiers who will be killed in the next war, but the civilian population as well. And Montreal itself will not be immune. German Zeppelins have definitely proven that they can go all around the world in safety, while Lindbergh has just completed a northern and a shorter route which can be used by aeroplanes without a great deal of risk. We in Canada apparently are quite willing to supply the Germans with death dealing weapons. I cannot help but notice in a dispatch from Ottawa four or five days ago that Mr. Berg, representing the I.C. Farbenindustrie had gone to Sudbury, accompanied by Billy Bishop, VC to make a contract for very large amounts of Canadian nickel, some 3,000 tons. It was given out that this could not be used for war purposes, because the transaction had been so openly announced. But the fact remains that Mr. Berg is the representative of the great German chemical trust, and that overnight they can turn their factories from peace to war materiel. I for one refuse to believe anything else but that the nickel which he is buying now from our Canadian mines is to be used for war purposes.

So that the next few years may bring us realisation of the fact that we have contributed to the death of our own sons and our own civilians for we have a world monopoly on nickel. I am quite sure that in the next Great War it will be absolutely impossible to keep any section of the nations of the world out.

We are all well at home and the younger people are very busy attending deb [sic] dances; I think there are five next week. We all hope that your operation will be completely successful and that you will never again suffer as you have in the past.

With our love to Lil and you, I am,

A.W. Currie

PS Ask Lil to be sure and get for you a copy of the October number of *The Living Age* published at 253 Broadway New York. Read the first article 'Science and Economics' and also read the two articles 'The Man Behind Hitler' and 'Germany Moves toward War.'

Sir Arthur Currie suffered a stroke on 5 November 1933. He was treated by Wilder Penfield and Colin Russel but there was little that could be done. In hospital Currie developed respiratory problems and although he fought the infection, he contracted pneumonia. Three days later, on Thursday 30 November 1933, the former Corps Commander died at the Royal Victoria Hospital in Montreal. Currie was 57.[53]

His funeral brought national recognition. The CBC carried the proceedings live and the former Corps Commander was buried with full military honours in Mount Royal Cemetery. His grave is marked with a Cross of Sacrifice, an official symbol usually reserved for Commonwealth War Graves Cemeteries in France and Belgium. Only Douglas Haig received a similar honour.[54]

Before his passing Currie completed his Armistice address for the annual Veteran's Dinner in Toronto. It was read aloud on the night of 11 November 1933 in his absence.

Address prepared by Sir Arthur Currie and on Account of his Illness Read for him by Lieutenant Colonel Allan A. Magee, 11 November 1933[55]

I deeply appreciate, as always, the privilege of meeting again tonight so many members of the old corps and of saying a few words to so many of my

---

53   Dancocks, 279-80; Urquhart, 354-7.
54   Dancocks, 280-5.
55   File 19801226-287, 58A 1 62.2, ACP, CWM.

comrades of other days. The circumstances of our lives and places keep us for the most part far away from each other, but tonight, and always on Armistice night, whether we are gathered in assembly as we are here, or listening by radio to Armistice programmes, perhaps far distant, or alone and un-companioned, we who were once members of the Canadian Corps are bound by the ties of a common remembrance. I know that to all who lived through the war years, and more particularly to those who saw active service, today has been a day of sacred memories, different perhaps in detail to each one of us, but yet all based on similar experiences and similar emotions.

With the lapse of years, Armistice Day becomes naturally less demonstrative. The ranks of those who saw service grow yearly smaller, as we pay our toll to time. And in future the day will grow less weighted with meaning to the generation born in the years between. As our country looks back to it from a widening distance of years, its memories will perhaps remain vivid only in the minds of the veterans, to whom its importance was then so colossal. But whatever changes may come, and however slight may be the recognition of future generations, I hope that Armistice Day may never cease to be impressive. I hope that the two-minute interval of solemn silence will always be more than a formal, statutory gesture, that it will always mean a reverent pause, in which we gladly remember, with tender and grateful thoughts, those who nobly died for our country's ideals. I hope that the graves of the unknown soldiers, and our National Chambers of Remembrance, will have their eternal tributes on this day, and that our country, in the years to come, and the generations that know not war, will not forget.

Tonight, we who came home, move back in memory fifteen years to the hour when our army halted where it stood, when the firing died suddenly away on the Western Front, when the few last straggling shots echoed down the mightiest battle-line the world had ever seen, and were swallowed up in utter silence. Tonight, we cannot recall the frantic cheering and the frenzied rejoicings of the folks at home, as they gave expression to their sense of relief when they realized that the long nightmare of the years was ended. We recall rather the silence of exhausted effort and of daring hope; we recall that still moment when after four years of a strange life, in which death was ever present, the fighting men were suddenly conscious of the fact that the strain was over and that they had now to adjust themselves to the new world of promised peace and justice and content, which they had been led to believe they were, after all, about to enter. But, like all other silences, there was a puzzled question in it by those fighting men. Was all the agony they had gone through for four years really to achieve its end? Were the hopes which had sustained them, and had sustained their folks back home, through their unparalleled sacrifices, actually to be realized at last? There was a pause without an answer. It was the most impressive and portentous pause in history.

Today the pause—the silence—was reverently repeated. But after fifteen years of the promised new world we were told we fought to create, the puzzled question it tacitly conveyed is still unanswered. The lurid lights of the battle front we knew have been long extinguished by our hands, the mutter of the guns and the crackle of the musketry have long receded down the years. Yet the war and its aftermath are still with us, more terrible even than fifteen years ago. Its effects have not been fully mastered, its issues have not been settled—that is the simple truth, the confession which today brings its shame. Our soldiers, living and dead, performed their part with unquestioned heroism and devotion in those battle days. But in the years since then, the fifteen years misnamed years of peace, the peoples of the world have not so well performed their tasks of understanding the vast forces that were then released, of controlling them and of making good the victory. It is not, therefore, surprising that the men who fought are sometimes, with reluctance, but with the compulsion of obvious circumstances, of the opinion that their sacrifice and that of their comrades who fell was all in vain.

We remember tonight, and it is well that our country should remember, the high resolves of that time fifteen years ago. There was unspeakable sorrow for the great army of youth that had gone so early to its death. We were told that the world would henceforth be safe for youth. But what of youth today, and the opportunity for youth in our modern world? Where, ask the men who fought, is that new world of justice and good will they suffered so keenly to create? Has the world, has our country, in the fifteen years since the Armistice, kept its promised faith with the unreturning [sic] dead? Has the great sacrifice really turned to glory, the glory of a better time? Has the world done anything more in these fifteen years than give lip-service to the ideals for which our fallen comrades gave their lives? The answer to these questions is found in the actual conditions of the hour. And these conditions are such that Armistice Day should smite the conscience of the world.

I need not dwell tonight on these conditions, with all their horrible and terrifying possibilities. They are known, and some of them deeply felt, by everyone in this room and by everyone listening elsewhere to my voice. We are told in cabled dispatches this week that the international situation in Europe today is practically what it was in 1913 on the eve of the late war. And the rest of the world, like Europe, is haunted by the fear of war, a stalking fear, which for the past nine or ten months has dominated the press and private conversation. There is no sense of security in the minds of European countries today. We are told that all that happened before 1914 is now being repeated; that behind the scenes secret agreements for a new balance of power are being made; that war propaganda is at work again, with the old subtle appeals to what is called national honour, national prestige, or national patriotism; that sooner or later another war will wreck our civilization, and we will stand helpless amid the ruins. The outlook for humanity is not hopeful, if we take seriously to heart these persistent and disturbing aspects of the world's condition today. And all this is but fifteen years after the signing of an Armistice we thought was to end war—when we said 'never again,' when the whole world said 'never again,' as a pledge made by the living to the dead. That pledge is now but a faint echo, for old hates are reviving, old fears have come back, and on this fifteenth anniversary of a peace which was to silence battle fronts forever, peace is not a fact, but still a dream.

Apart from the threat of war, with its growing cloud, other conditions in our world are equally disturbing. Bitterness and hate, selfishness and greed, are still entrenched in our social and economic and political life. National finances are disorganized throughout the world, taxes are overwhelming, agriculture and business are everywhere prostrated, and unemployment is more widespread than at any time in history. Our world is a world of suffering, of uncertainty, of demon doubts and fears. Our world is not yet done with the necessity for heroism and sacrifice. Returned men are called upon today as never before to aid every movement to establish a just and lasting peace throughout the world, to lighten the burden of armaments, to usher in a new era of good-will and fraternity among the peoples of the earth, to help solve the new and changing problems of these later years, to rehabilitate the social and economic life of our country, and to compose the hates and prejudices and deep animosities which smoulder and threaten in our land and in other lands. We need, as never before, the healing qualities of devotion and fidelity and self-sacrifice and goodwill and comradeship and friendliness, so that suspicion may be vanquished and justice and mutual trust may he permanently enthroned. All this desire is in harmony with the real spirit of Armistice Day—the day dedicated to sacrifice and loyal remembrance of others.

It is sometimes suggested—and not, I think, frankly, without some justification—that in the fifteen years of reconstruction or re-destruction that have gone since the Armistice was signed, returned men everywhere have not themselves done all they should have done or could have done to establish that better time to which they looked forward when the war ended; that they have not applied to conditions around them the qualities and the principles of life that carried them through to victory along the battle-line. It may be that we have not been sufficiently aggressive, that having done our bit in other fields, we have too far withdrawn in silence or inaction from subsequent events, and have not imposed or inculcated our ideals and the results of our experiences upon our peacetime guides and leaders. This criticism of veterans of the war is heard today in every country that had a part in the conflict. If it has truth, behind the truth are, in my judgment, some potent reasons.

Men returned from the front in a spirit of weariness, but in a spirit of hope, looking forward with confidence, after years of trench life to the peace they had been promised. They soon found that their new world was still a world of struggle, a world of bargain and of battle. They found that they had escaped from one ugly world and one disaster, only to plunge into another. They had to struggle and fight for what they felt and knew was a simple right—some slight form of rehabilitation, and, what was more discouraging, for adequate help for their wounded and incapacitated comrades, and for adequate protection for the dependents of their comrades who had given their lives for their country. I can say without evasion or hesitation that the great mass of returned men in Canada never had the thought that because they fought for their country they were entitled to preferred treatment by their country, in comparison with other citizens. They never, as a rule, contended that because they wore the uniform of our Corps they had therefore a right-of-way to exceptional benefits. There were perhaps some exceptions, as there are always exceptions in every way of life, but these exceptions are infinitesimal compared with the mass of our men. But on one right all are united—the right of the wounded and the broken, the right of the dependents of the dead for adequate provision and care.

I am not going to recall the struggles of these fifteen years. There were disappointments. There was even bitterness. There was cynicism. The result is not surprising—that many returned men withdrew from the struggle, in despair, with the feeling that their participation in the making of the new world was not desired. There were disappointments because of administration of soldiers' affairs, disappointments because of inadequate machinery, and indifference. The struggle still goes on. We read in the press of every Province today of the disappointment of different branches of the Legion because of the most recent changes in pensions administration and the readjustments of methods. But the voice of the veterans, even on their own affairs, is unheard, or at least unattended.

One of our defects or weaknesses in the past has been, doubtless, a lack of unity. We have not had the same cohesion, the same unanimity that was ours in the old Corps. Naturally, geographical conditions keep us apart as groups of men; but geographical distances may be conquered by a spirit, the spirit of service that should bind us into one great and useful force...

I am not a pessimist when I think of the future. And I am sure that the returned men who are listening to me tonight are not pessimists, however cynical some of them may be with respect to certain phases of our national life. We have seen dark nights together. And we have also seen the dawn of new and specious days. I know that as in the battle hours we will again take the morning into our hearts. In our deliberate and final thought, as returned men, we have faith that these moments of discouragement are fleeting, and perhaps misleading; that those whose memories we especially cherish did not make their sacrifices in vain, and that in the end the stern determination of millions of men and women, who are minted with no spirit of unworthy pacifism, will prevail over those whose views would tend to perpetuate the horrors of war, even though some of these latter may be seated in the high places of national executive and legislative power.

Armistice Day is primarily a commemoration of the dead. But a commemoration of the dead should be likewise an appeal to the living not to deplore the past, but to awaken our sense of responsibility to make our world less deplorable. The disappointment—even the bitterness—of many who came back may be traced to the monstrous paradox that only because of the nobility of individual sacrifice does war in any way ennoble civilization. We saw at first hand the sacrifice of much that was best in our country. But the weariness and the disillusion- ment from which we could not escape are no longer fitting to a new generation charged with the tasks of peace. We know from experience the stupidity of war, and the stupidity of those who made or caused wars. Does our responsibility end with condemning the follies of the stupid or the vicious twenty years ago? What can we do as veterans to make the world less deplorable? Are we bestirring ourselves in this night of hysteria which may end in war? Ours is a man-made world, and in it are we doing all we can do to prevent a catastrophe which we will later deplore? Are we fighting to the last, as we fought fifteen years ago, for the vitality and the continuity of civilized standards in public and private affairs, in national and international life? Are we fighting so that the next generation of youth will not condemn our stupidity as we condemned in the trenches the stupidity of our elders in 1914 and the era immediately before it? On those nights and days of suffering and death, when we saw our comrades fall in the fire of savages fed by the so-called gods of civilization, we endured and 'carried on,' in the firm hope that out of the embers and the broken human dust would rise a new order, in which war and greed and injustice would have no place. That hope will yet be realized, despite discouragements, even in a world which has to make its way out of sickness and despair, if we but keep our shield and our faith, and if we insist on leadership in all affairs that is not leadership for apathy. If another war comes, the responsibility will not be upon the militarists, but on ourselves, because of our inertia. We are to blame if we allow others, interested only in greed, to take the reins from our hands and drive us into another abyss.

The truest commemoration of our honoured dead will be in the vigorous enlistment of our own lives and capacities in the struggle between unselfishness and greed, honesty and corruption, justice and injustice, and in the serious application to our national problems of those qualities which distinguished our Corps in the war days, and enabled us always to advance and conquer.

Armistice Day reminds our country of the steadfastness of our fighting troops. It should also be a reminder to every citizen that he still has a duty to discharge, if the war is to be fully won and its high objectives permanently secured. It should call us to a realization that we still have to complete the unfinished task of our dead comrades who speak to us tonight with a voiceless eloquence—the task of replacing the present system of suspicion and fear and conflict with the enduring fabric of confidence in humane law and order.

And so, in conclusion, we drop the rose of remembrance on the supreme devotion of our sacred dead. We linger, like our country, in our tribute of reverent memory of our glorious youth who gave their lives to defend our liberty: 'Sleep well, heroic souls, in silence sleep, Lapped in the circling arms of kindly death!

No ill can vex your slumbers, no foul breath of slander, hate, derision, mar the deep Repose that holds you close.'

And on this Armistice night, as we recall the nobility of your sacrifice, we turn away from trenches and wounds and death and we re-dedicate our lives with hope to the still unfinished work which you so gallantly advanced and for which you died.

Select Bibliography

Lieutenant General Sir Arthur Currie

Barrett, Roger R. 'General Sir Arthur William Currie: A Common Genius for war,' *Army Doctrine and Training Bulletin* 2, 3 (1999): 53-57.

Borys, David A. *The Education of a Corps Commander: Arthur Currie's Leadership from 1915-17*. MA Thesis, University of Alberta, 2006.

Brode, Patrick. 'A Soldier with Plenty of "Go,"' *Military History* 4, 7 (1991): 10-20.

Brown, Ian Malcom, *Lieutenant General Sir Arthur Currie and the Canadian Corps, 1917-1918: The Evolution of a Style of Command and Attack*. MA Thesis, University of Calgary, 1991.

Brown, R. Craig and Morton, Desmond. 'The Embarrassing Apotheosis of a "Great Canadian": Sir Arthur Currie's Personal Crisis in 1917,' *Canadian Historical Review* LX, I (1979): 41-64.

Cook, Tim. 'The Madman and the Butcher: Sir Sam Hughes, Sir Arthur Currie, and the War of Reputations,' *Canadian Historical Review* 85, 4 (2004): 693-719.

Dancocks, Daniel. *Sir Arthur Currie: A Biography*. Toronto: Methuen, 1985.

Demill, Robert Scott. *The 1928 Cobourg Libel Trial of Sir Arthur Currie and the Port Hope Evening Guide: The Rehabilitation of the Reputation of a Corps Commander*. MA Thesis, University of Ottawa, 1989.

England, Robert. 'A Victoria Real Estate Man: The Enigma of Sir Arthur Currie,' *Queen's Quarterly* 65, 2 (1958): 208-221.

Entin, Martin A, *et al*. 'The Principal and the Dean,' *Canadian Bulletin of Medical History* 20, 1 (2003): 151-70.

Harris, Stephen. 'The Canadian General Staff and the Higher Organization of Defence, 1919-1939,' *War and Society* 3, 1 (1985): 83-98.

Hyatt, A.M.J. 'Corps Commander: Arthur Currie,' in Marc Milner (ed). *Canadian Military History: Selected Readings,* Toronto: Copp Clark Pitman, 1993.

—. 'The King-Byng Episode: A Footnote to History,' *Dalhousie Review* 43, 4 (1963): 469-473.

—. 'Sir Arthur Currie,' *Canada* 2, 3 (1975): 4-15.

—. 'Sir Arthur Currie and Conscription: A Soldier's View,' *Canadian Historical Review* 50, 3 (1969): 285-296.

—. 'Sir Arthur Currie and the Politicians: A Case Study of Civil-Military Relations in the First World War,' in A. Preston & P. Dennis (eds). *Swords and Covenants*. Totowa: Croom Helm, 1976.

—. 'The Military Leadership of Sir Arthur Currie,' in Bernd Horn & Stephen Harris (eds). *Warrior Chiefs: Perspectives on Senior Canadian Military Leaders*. Toronto: Dundurn Press, 2001.

—. *General Sir Arthur Currie: A Military Biography*. Toronto: University of Toronto Press, 1987.

Jackson, Geoffrey. *Hill 70 and Lens, the Forgotten Battles: The Canadian Corps in the Summer of 1917*. MSS, University of Calgary, 2007.

Sharpe, R.J. *The Last Day, The Last Hour: The Currie Libel Trial*. Toronto: The Osgoode Society, 1988.

Travers, T.H.E. 'Currie and 1st Division at Second Ypres, April 1915: Controversy, Criticism, and Official History,' *Canadian Military History* 5, 2 (1996): 7-15.

Urquhart, Hugh M. *Arthur Currie: The Biography of a Great Canadian*. Toronto: J.M. Dent, 1950.

Wilson, Barbara. 'The Road to the Cobourg Court Room: New Material from the Archives of the Canadian War Museum on the Sir Arthur Currie–Sir Sam Hughes Dispute, 1918-19,' *Canadian Military History* 10, 3 (2001): 67-73.

Canada and the First World War

Borden, Robert Laird. *Robert Laird Borden: His Memoirs*. Toronto: Macmillan, 1938.

Brennan, Pat. 'Byng's and Currie's Commanders: A Still Untold Story of the Canadian Corps,' *Canadian Military History* 11, 2 (2002): 5-16.

Brown, Robert Craig. *Robert Laird Borden: A Biography, 2 volumes*. Toronto: MacMillan, 1975-80.

Brown, Robert Craig and Cook, Ramsay. *Canada, 1896-1921: A Nation Transformed*. Toronto: McClelland and Stewart, 1974.

Cook, Tim. 'Documenting War and Forging Reputations: Sir Max Aitken and the Canadian War Records Office in the First World War,' *War in History* 10, 2 (2003): 157-87.

—. 'The Blind Leading the Blind: The Battle of the St. Eloi Craters,' *Canadian Military History* 5, 2 (1996): 24-36.

—. *At the Sharp End: Canadians Fighting the Great, 1914-1916.* Toronto: Viking Canada, 2007.

—. *Clio's Warriors: Canadians and the Writing of the World Wars.* Vancouver: University of British Columbia Press, 2006.

—. *No Place to Run: The Canadian Corps and Gas Warfare in the First World War.* Vancouver: University of British Columbia Press, 1999.

—. *Shock Troops: Canadians Fighting the Great War, 1914-1918.* Toronto: Viking Canada, 2008.

Dancocks, Daniel. *Spearhead to Victory: Canada and the Great War.* Edmonton: Hertig Publishers, 1987.

Duguid, A.F. *Official History of the Canadian Forces in the Great War 1914-1919: Vol. 1, Aug.1914–Sept.1915.* Ottawa: Department of National Defence, 1938.

Granatstein, J.L. and Hitsman, J.M. *Broken Promises: A History of Conscription in Canada.* Toronto: Oxford University Press, 1977.

Granatstein, J.L. and Morton, Desmond. *Marching to Armageddon: Canadians and the Great War, 1914-1919.* Toronto: Lester & Orpen Dennys, 1989.

Haycock, Ronald. *Sam Hughes: The Public Career of a Controversial Canadian, 1885-1916.* Waterloo: Wilfrid Laurier University Press, 1986.

Hayes, Geoffrey, Iarocci, Andrew and Bechthold, Michael (eds), *Vimy Ridge: A Canadian Reassessment.* Waterloo: Wilfrid Laurier University Press, 2007.

Humphries, Mark and Maker, John. 'The First Use of Poison Gas at Ypres, 1915: A Translation from the German Official History' *Canadian Military History* 16, 3 (2007): 57-73.

Humphries, Mark. 'The Horror at Home: The Canadian Military and the Great Influenza Pandemic of 1918,' *Journal of the Canadian Historical Association* 16 (2006): 231-65.

Iarocci, Andrew. *Shoestring Soldiers: The 1st Canadian Division at War, 1914-1915.* Toronto: University of Toronto Press, 2008.

Keshen, Jeff. *Propaganda and Censorship During Canada's Great War.* Edmonton: University of Alberta Press, 1996.

Leppard, T. '"The Dashing Subaltern": Sir Richard Turner in Retrospect,' *Canadian Military History* 6, 2 (1997): 21-28

Mackenzie, David (ed). *Canada and the First World War: Essay's in Honour of Robert Craig Brown* Toronto: University of Toronto Press, 2005.

McCulloch, I. '"Batty Mac": Portrait of a Brigade Commander of the Great War, 1915-1917,' *Canadian Military History* 7, 4 (1998): 11-28.

Morton, Desmond. '"Kicking and Complaining": Demobilisation Riots in the Canadian Expeditionary Force, 1918-19,' *Canadian Historical Review* 61, 3 (1980): 334-360.

—. *A Peculiar Kind of Politics: Canada's Overseas Ministry in the First World War*. Toronto: University of Toronto Press, 1982.

—. *Fight or Pay: Soldier's Families in the Great War*. Vancouver: University of British Columbia Press, 2004.

—. *When Your Number's Up: The Canadian Soldier in the First World War*. Toronto: Random House, 1993.

Morton, Desmond and Wright, Glenn. *Winning the Second Battle: Canadian Veterans and the Return to Civilian Life, 1915-1930*. Toronto: University of Toronto Press, 1987.

Moss, Mark. *Manliness and Militarism: Educating Young Boys in Ontario for War*. Toronto: Oxford University Press, 2001.

Nicholson, G.W.L. *The Canadian Expeditionary Force, 1914-1919*. Ottawa: Queen's Printer, 1964.

Pulsifer, Cameron. 'Canada's First Armoured Unit: Raymond Brutinel and the Canadian Motor Machine Gun Brigades of the First World War,' *Canadian Military History*, 10, 1 (2001): 44-57.

Rawling, Bill. *Surviving Trench Warfare: Technology and the Canadian Corps, 1914-1918*. Toronto: University of Toronto Press, 1992.

Schreiber, Shane. *Shock Army of the British Empire: The Canadian Corps in the Last 100 Days of the Great War*. London: Praeger, 1997.

Swettenham, John. *To Seize the Victory: The Canadian Corps in World War I*. Toronto: Ryerson Press, 1965.

Vance, Jonathan. *Death So Noble: Memory, Meaning and the First World War*. Vancouver: University of British Columbia Press, 1997.

Index